THE

SPIRIT OF

TRAGEDY

HERBERT J. MULLER

ALFRED A KNOPF
NEW YORK
1956

PN 1892
M 95

L. C. catalog card number: 56–5795

© *Herbert J. Muller, 1956*

THIS IS A BORZOI BOOK,
PUBLISHED BY ALFRED A. KNOPF, INC.

FIRST EDITION

TO JACOB HECHLER

PREFACE

Although this book is concerned with the literary form known as tragedy, I have been careful to entitle it *The Spirit of Tragedy*. I am interested here primarily in the vision of life reflected in tragedy, its historical connections, its philosophical issues, its implications for our living as well as our literary purposes. Accordingly I have not attempted to present a complete literary history of tragedy. In the literature of the past I have considered only the major writers, with but incidental reference to the many lesser ones who properly fill out chapters in histories of drama; in modern literature I have concentrated on a selected few who represent what seem to me the major tendencies and major issues. In both I have naturally considered matters of form and technique, the measure of artistic success, but chiefly in relation to the distinctive tragic effect rather than to dramatic art in general. Throughout I have taken the old-fashioned view that literature is not a self-contained, self-sufficient art form, but a comment on life.

Hence my approach raises an immediate issue. The so-called "new critics" have made sophisticated readers very wary of any talk about the logical or social "content" of literature. They assert that we should study literature as literature, the work of art in itself, and concentrate on the form or "*achieved content*," the qualities that make it *literature* and distinguish it from experience or life, as from philosophy and science. They rightly complain of the inveterate tendency to neglect its distinctively literary values, and to judge it primarily by its literal truth, its moral or philosophical soundness, its usefulness for political purposes—in effect, its correspondence with the critic's opinions about God, or the good life, or what this country needs. And tragedy, they might add, has inspired more solemn nonsense than any other literary form. Criticis natu-

viii   *Preface*

rally strain for deep notes and high notes as they dwell on its
universals or their version of the eternal truths about Man,
Fate, and God. Criticism becomes what Unamuno saw in much
philosophy, an "art of spiritual pimping."

Nevertheless I believe that the student of tragedy should
take such risks, if only because the great tragic poets took
them. They were always dealing with the first and last questions about man's fate, and while they were naturally concerned with their craft as poets and playwrights, they appear
to have been as deeply concerned about the questions themselves. Evidently none believed that the chastity of art was
the supreme consideration; all took for granted that art existed
for life's sake. In particular, the supremely artistic Greeks—
the inventors of the art form of tragedy—would have been bewildered by the doctrine that it should be considered exclu-
sively as an art form. Their tragedies were performed exclu-
sively at their annual civic festivals, which were religious and
patriotic festivals, the great occasions of their communal life.
Like them, at any rate, I am assuming that what makes literature important is not only what distinguishes it from other
major interests, but what links it with these interests in the
service of the communal life. The new critics themselves imply
such connections in their favorite terms for the distinctive
essence of poetry—"tension," "complexity," "irony," "ambiguity," "paradox." These qualities are not in fact distinctive of
poetry; they may appear in any thoughtful prose. And in
tragedy, where they are most conspicuous, they most clearly
denote a complex vision of life, not a mere effect of poetic language, and may therefore survive the most prosaic translation.
They help to define its "achieved content," which is an
achieved comment on life.

More specifically, this book grew out of a question that I
believe takes us to the heart of tragedy, and that cannot be
answered on purely literary grounds. Throughout the ages men
have known tragedy in their earthly existence; they have always lamented that life is hard, that man's fate is to toil, to

suffer, and to die. All civilized societies have produced literature, and most have produced drama. Yet men have very
rarely written what we call tragedy. By general consent, there
have been only four important periods, all of them brief: the
ancient Greek, confined to Athens of the fifth century B.C.; the
Elizabethan, in the generation of Shakespeare; the French
classical, in the generation of Corneille and Racine; and the
modern, inaugurated by Ibsen. At that, there is some dispute
about the genuineness of French classical tragedy, and much
more about modern tragedy. Furthermore, these periods have
all been confined to the Western world; none of the great
Eastern civilizations produced tragedy. The question, then, is
why the experience that all men know has so seldom found
its appropriate expression in literature, and only in one quarter
of the globe. This question involves the distinctive values of
Western civilization, its essential differences from all other
civilizations, and finally the basic issues forced by its crisis
today.

It is accordingly a large subject. It is also a highly controversial one, a kind considered un-American nowadays. But it is
forced upon us, I believe, by any serious consideration of the
nature and the uses of tragedy.

ACKNOWLEDGMENTS

I am indebted to recent translators for brief illustrative quotations from classical and Continental texts, and wish to record my obligations to the following: W. H. D. Rouse, *The Iliad* by Homer (Nelson and Sons, Ltd.); Mrs. Henri Frankfort, translations of Babylonian texts appearing in *Before Philosophy* (Penguin Books); Richmond Lattimore, *Oresteia* by Æschylus (University of Chicago Press); Edith Hamilton, *Prometheus Bound* by Æschylus (W. W. Norton & Company); W. B. Yeats, *King Œdipus* by Sophocles (The Macmillan Company); Robert Fitzgerald, *Œdipus at Colonus* by Sophocles (Harcourt, Brace and Company); E. F. Watling, *Electra and Other Plays* by Sophocles (Penguin Books); Dudley Fitts and Robert Fitzgerald, *Antigone* by Sophocles (Harcourt, Brace and Company); Richmond Lattimore, *The Trojan Women* by Euripides (The Dryden Press); David Grene, *Hippolytus* by Euripides (University of Chicago Press); Gilbert Murray, *The Bacchæ* by Euripides (Longmans, Green and Co.); Paul Landis, *Athaliah* by Racine (The Modern Library); Stephen Spender and Goronwy Rees, *Danton's Death* by G. Büchner (Faber & Faber); Elisaveta Fen, *Three Plays* by Chekhov (Penguin Books); and Stuart Gilbert, *No Exit* and *The Flies* by Sartre (Alfred A. Knopf, Inc.).

I also wish to express my gratitude to my students in a seminar on Tragedy at Indiana University, with whom I thought through this subject; to my friends Welsey B. Carroll, Herbert L. Creek, B. A. G. Fuller, and Joshua C. Taylor, who read portions of the manuscript; and in particular to Emerson G. Sutcliffe, who read the entire manuscript with a sharp critical eye, and helped to tone down my pedagogical tendencies.

CONTENTS

CHAPTER I   THE NATURE OF TRAGEDY

1. The Problem of Definition   *3*
2. The Philosophical Implications   *14*

CHAPTER II   THE BEGINNINGS OF TRAGEDY

1. The Ritual Origins   *25*
2. The Homeric Poems   *37*

CHAPTER III   GREEK TRAGEDY

1. The Cultural Background   *48*
2. Æschylus, the Pioneer   *61*
3. Sophocles   *78*
4. Euripides, the Rebel   *103*
5. Epilogue: The Decline to Seneca   *125*

CHAPTER IV   ELIZABETHAN TRAGEDY

1. The Medieval and Renaissance Background   *137*
2. The Beginnings: Marlowe   *149*
3. Shakespeare   *165*
4. The Decline to the Restoration   *195*

CHAPTER V   NEO-CLASSICAL TRAGEDY

1. The Age of Louis XIV   *207*
2. The "Great and Good" Corneille   *216*
3. The "Tender" Racine   *224*
4. The Age of the Enlightenment   *238*

xiv *Contents*

CHAPTER VI   MODERN TRAGEDY

1. The Peculiar Issues   *244*
2. Romantic Tragedy: Wagner   *251*
3. Bourgeois Tragedy: Ibsen   *260*
4. Naturalistic Tragedy: Strindberg and Hauptmann   *274*
5. The Realism of Chekhov   *283*
6. Poetic Drama: T. S. Eliot   *293*
7. Existentialist Tragedy: Sartre   *302*
8. Tragedy in America: O'Neill   *311*

CHAPTER VII   CONCLUSION

1. Some Contrasts with the Ancient East   *320*
2. The Value of Tragedy   *331*

Index   *follows page* *335*

THE SPIRIT OF TRAGEDY

CHAPTER I

THE
NATURE OF TRAGEDY

1. THE PROBLEM OF DEFINITION

According to my dictionary, tragedy is "a dramatic composition of serious or somber character, with an unhappy ending." Add that this ending is usually death, and the popular conception is complete. It is too simple a conception, of course. It is the complement of the naïve assumption that when a Hollywood beauty gets her man her success is a happy ending; whereas any mature person knows that this is actually a beginning, most likely of another mess. The tragic vision of life is the antithesis of the popular vision, or lack of vision, in its comprehension of complexity, incongruity, and paradox. But for this reason we need to keep an eye on the elementary facts of life and literature, begin with the simplicities that are at the heart of paradox and that sophisticates are always apt to overlook. Shakespeare too conceived tragedy as a tale of suffering ending in death, in effect a great many deaths. Other Elizabethans virtually massacred their casts, and were as shameless in expressing their feelings about death; they were forever indulging trite sentiments that would disgrace a contemporary poet. For that matter, all the Greek tragic poets also rang the changes on the platitudes about mortality. The ultimate source of tragedy, historically and psychologically, is indeed the simple fact that man must die.

Then we may add that death is not really a simple matter, nor necessarily tragic. Our subject grows complex as we keep an eye on everyday life. The death of an infant, of a love-sick adolescent, of a psychopath, of a drunken motorist, of a desperado in the electric chair, of a poor clerk after a prolonged illness, of a fretful housewife who has been trying to keep up with the Joneses—these are all sad stories, but hardly suitable themes for tragedy, at least as it was conceived in the past.

Some we might call merely "pathetic," making a distinction not always easy to define. Others might remind us of Shaw's comment on Ibsen's Hedda Gabler, who killed herself in the last act: he objected that the "real" tragedy is that the Hedda Gablers don't kill themselves—they go on living, and poisoning the life around them. And more momentous happenings raise more difficult questions. Hitler died in the ruins of Berlin with a whole world crashing about him—a Wagnerian finale; but was his death tragic? All but his followers rejoiced. On the other hand, was the death of Christ on the Cross a tragedy? Certainly his followers should not regard death as an unhappy ending, or even an ending at all; it is the beginning of life immortal, a reunion with their heavenly Father. The common failure of Christians to rejoice at this glorious prospect recalls the philosophical attitude of Roman pagans, who could remark that the one advantage man had over the immortal gods was that he could die, or sleep forever, whereas the gods had to *live* forever.

The Greeks were of many minds on this as on all other subjects. Most of their extant tragedies, however, do not end in death. Many even do not have unhappy endings. Since everybody agrees that the Greeks invented this literary form, presumably they should have something to say about it. We might well begin at the historical beginning, then, and consider what they did say.

Although Plato referred to an "ancient quarrel between philosophy and poetry," the earliest critical work we have intact is his own. In the *Republic* he dealt with tragic poetry at some length; and he had nothing good to say about it except that it was "charming." Like all poetry, it was a mere imitation of life in the natural world, which was in turn a world of mere appearances, a pale, imperfect copy of the "real" world of eternal Ideas; so it was "thrice removed" from the truth. On ethical grounds tragic poetry was as ruinous to the good life, for it appealed to the passions, the "inferior part of the soul." It encouraged men to weep and make a fuss over their troubles instead of keeping their emotions under control; it imitated not only excessive emotions but positively bad emotions, like fear of death. Hence it spread such false, unwholesome ideas as that the gods are not always perfectly just, and that good men may be wretched while bad men prosper. Plato concluded that poets should be tolerated only on condition that they compose simply hymns to the gods and praises of famous men. In his *Laws* he explicitly prescribed: "The poet shall compose nothing contrary to the ideas of the lawful, or just, or beautiful, or good, which are allowed in the state." As for tragedy, "a state would be mad" to give it free license.

At first glance, this is a remarkably shallow piece of criticism. It seems worth citing only as a classical example of the attitudes that have been ruinous to the understanding of literature, in particular the assumption that literature should, above all, be edifying. In the name of truth Plato attacked poets for telling disagreeable truths, and demanded that they tell pretty lies; in other words, he provided the basic logic for the Hollywood Production Code. But since the complex questions raised by tragedy include neglected simplicities, I should first stress that Plato's argument is neither strange nor wholly unreasonable. In its essentials it is still the argument of the Roman Catholic Church, as of Soviet Russia; it is implicit in the thought of the many critics of un-American literary activities; and for all who cherish literature it forces a fundamental issue. Plato concluded his discussion in the *Republic* with a fair enough challenge: "Let them show that poetry is not only pleasant but useful to States and to human life."

Until this century, lovers of literature usually defended tragedy on Plato's own grounds. Sidney declared that it "maketh Kings fear to be Tyrants" and, like all true poetry, wins the mind from wickedness by exalting virtue and punishing vice. Samuel Johnson substantially agreed with John Dennis that tragedy ought to be "a very solemn Lecture, inculcating a particular Providence, and showing it plainly protecting the good, and chastizing the bad," else it would be "a scandalous and pernicious libel upon the government of the world." Shelley deplored such crude didacticism but turned the tables on the author of the *Laws* by calling poets "the unacknowledged legislators of the world," the ultimate source of all truth and goodness. Today, however, the revulsion against the whole moralistic tradition has led many critics to evade Plato's challenge. For some, a concern with the social utility of literature amounts to treason. W. H. Auden went still further when he met the common charge that Yeats was an obscurantist and political reactionary; he attacked "the fallacious belief that art ever makes anything happen," asserting that "if not a poem had been written . . . the history of man would be materially unchanged." As an Irishman, Yeats himself might not have welcomed this notion that he was harmless because quite ineffectual. Plato at least did poetry the honor of assuming that it was a real force and made a real difference in man's life—a belief that until recently both its enemies and its lovers always took for granted.

So I think we must believe, if we are to take literature at all seriously. Those today who are most concerned about preserving its esthetic purity are usually the most appalled by the vulgarity of democratic culture, the constant debauching of popular taste; and if bad art has the bad influence they imply, great art should have some influence. But this brings us back to Plato's challenge. What, after all, is the use of tragedy?

The most famous answer was given by Aristotle, who apparently had Plato in mind. In his *Poetics* he too described poetry as imitation, but as an imitation of ideal forms or underlying realities, not mere appearances, and so in effect a creative act. It is "a more philosophical and a higher thing than history: for poetry tends to express the universal, history the particular." As for tragedy, Aristotle distinguished it from comedy in that it represents men as better than they are. Likewise he met Plato's objection that it merely stirs up the passions by declaring that it effects a catharsis, or purging of emotion. He thus implied that it helps to achieve Plato's own purpose of keeping emotion under control. But while agreeing that poetry has a social function, he paid it the highest compliment—for a philosopher—by treating it as an autonomous activity, not merely an inferior form of philosophy or a servant of the State. The "standard of correctness," he observed, is not the same in poetry as in philosophy or politics; the poet may represent strict impossibilities if they are "poetically right" and are made poetically convincing. He assumed that art has its own end and means to this end, its own logic and laws.

Specifically, Aristotle defined tragedy as "an imitation of an action that is serious, complete, and of a certain magnitude; in language embellished with each kind of artistic ornament, the several kinds being found in separate parts of the play; in the form of action, not of narrative; through pity and fear effecting the purgation of these emotions." His initial clause is manifestly not very specific; scholars are still debating just what he meant by "action," and what constitutes "completeness." The final clause, however, is of more immediate importance, for it defines the distinctive tragic effect. Hence Aristotle deduced that unhappy endings are the "right" endings for tragedy; pity and fear are most fully excited by a change in fortune from good to bad. By the same logic he arrived at his celebrated doctrine of the "tragic flaw." The downfall of a virtuous man would merely shock us, as would the success of a bad man; the downfall of a villain would satisfy the moral sense but inspire neither pity nor fear. Ideally, therefore, the tragic hero should be a man essentially but not pre-eminently good, whose misfortune is brought about by some "error or frailty."

By this tragic flaw Aristotle did not imply the narrow moralistic interpretation that later critics were happy to give it; the word he used could mean merely a mistake, not necessarily a sin. For the rest, it is hard to do full justice to the penetration of his analysis, which makes his pioneering work, after more than two thousand years, still the most impressive work ever written on tragedy. That unity of plot does not consist in the unity of the hero, that episodic plots are the weakest, that characters should say not what the poet wants but what the plot requires, that arbitrary denouements may be theatrically effective but are artistically inferior, that spectacular means of creating a sense of the terrible are alien to the purpose of tragedy—such observations, which are now commonplaces, may have been fresh insights that have become commonplaces because of Aristotle.

Unhappily, his achievement was all too impressive for later critics. The Renaissance made a gospel of the *Poetics*; in the eighteenth century Lessing could still assert that it was "as infallible as the *Elements* of Euclid." In this reverential spirit critics derived from it the formal rules with which neo-classical drama was saddled, notably the Unities of action, time, and place—the "Weird Sisters" of dramatic criticism. And though Aristotle cannot be blamed for all these rules (he himself insisted only on unity of action), he at least encouraged such formalism by his habits as a systematic analyst and pigeon-holer.

Thus he discussed one by one the six "parts" that tragedy must have—namely, Plot, Character, Diction, Thought, Song, and Spectacle. "Parts" is an unfortunate term, suggesting the kind of inorganic separability that is also implict in Aristotle's mention of language "embellished" by artistic "ornament"; and as he considered each part separately, he tended to make his distinctions too sharp and invidious. Plot, he asserted, is "the soul of a tragedy," more important than Character. If by Plot he meant something like the complete action, it would include Character, but in so far as they can be separated this is a questionable ranking—at least to one who knows Shakespeare, or recalls the "well-made" play of the nineteenth century. As Aristotle went on to classify and rank plots in turn, he took a narrow view of them that led him into an apparent contradiction. The hero, he noted, might (1) perpetrate the deed of horror in full consciousness, or, better, (2) might perpetrate it through ignorance and then discover his fatal error, or, best of all, (3) might learn the truth just in time to avert the fatal deed. Earlier Aristotle had said that unhappy endings are the best for tragedy.

One reason, perhaps, why he overlooked this contradiction is that he failed to consider the final import of tragedy.[1] Aristotle's concentration on a formal esthetic analysis is so surprising that we may forget his rather strange neglect of the philosophical and religious implications of tragedy. Since he asserted that poetry was more philosophical than history, and tragedy the highest form of poetry, he might have been expected to dwell on these implications. As it is, of the six essential parts he has least to say about Thought. When he discusses Recognitions and Reversals of Intention he is in effect dealing with irony, which especially in Sophocles—his favorite dramatist—springs from a tragic vision; but he considers them only as effective plot devices. When he remarks that the poet's function is to relate not what has happened but what may happen, "what is possible according to the law of probability or necessity," he does not go into the nature of this law. One explanation of such casualness is that he himself had little tragic sense of life; there is no sign of pity or terror in the *Poetics*. Another explanation is that he was touching on the commonplaces of Greek thought, the kind of idea that "goes without saying." Thus his simple remark that character in tragedy must above all be "good" may make us wonder, as we recall Euripides' Medea and Shakespeare's Macbeth; and we may be more troubled when he adds that "even a woman may be good," or a slave—"though the woman may be said to be an inferior being, and the slave quite worthless."

We have arrived at a truism that all critics recognize, but not all remember. Aristotle was an ancient Greek. He was addressing fellow Greeks, not Mankind; he was analyzing Greek tragedy, the only kind he knew of. He had a relatively

[1] It should be remembered, too, that we do not have the whole of the original *Poetics*, and that scholars cannot agree on whether it was written by the master himself. It may be a summary of his lectures compiled by a pupil. In any case, it reads like a body of notes for lectures rather than a fully developed treatise, and is obviously incomplete.

simple problem, since he was unaware of all the different possibilities of art, thought, and life that we have to worry about.
We can fully appreciate his contribution only if we keep in
mind that he did not say the last word about tragedy, or for us
always a clear word. Some of his observations—as on Song, the
Chorus, and the proper meters as taught by "Nature"—are
manifestly inapplicable to later tragedies. The obvious question remains: to what extent may his analysis be considered
permanently, universally valid?

Now I assume that we should follow Aristotle's example and
derive our conception of the actual or ideal essence of tragedy
by an empirical analysis. There is no eternal Idea of Tragedy
existing independently of the works of men, but only a host of
works that men have called tragedies. Neither is there any such
thing as a "typical" tragedy—not even a typical Greek tragedy.
Granted that Aristotle's judgment was in general remarkably
sound, we are at once brought up against the fact that most
Greek drama did not meet his specifications. He derived his
ideal largely from the practice of Sophocles, in particular
Œdipus Rex. He was critical of the different practice of Euripides, even though calling him the "most tragic" of the poets.
He drew almost no examples from Æschylus, whose trilogies
often had happy endings and so failed to meet his basic requirement of a reversal from good to bad fortune. On this requirement later writers have generally agreed with Aristotle,
but it is about the only thing they have agreed on. Shakespeare, Racine, and Ibsen differ as widely from one another as
from Sophocles. As for modern literature, it is a jungle growth
of isms that cut across all the traditional genres. The tragic
spirit now finds expression in the novel as well as the drama.
Both forms include many serious works that are neither pure
tragedy nor pure comedy, and cannot be adequately described
as tragi-comedy either.

In the face of this diversity, critics have tended to set up
hard-and-fast criteria that rule out many works called tragedies
in histories of literature. I. A. Richards, who found in Shake-

speare the quintessence of tragedy, referred to Greek drama
as "pseudo-tragedy," whereas Yeats managed to exclude even
Shakespeare, labeling his plays "tragi-comedies." Such defiance of common usage may make for precision, if we can
remember that words mean what the critic says they mean.
But usually it makes for narrowness and fastidiousness, the
doctrinaire attitudes that produce a "trained incapacity" for
the understanding of literature. Failing to find what he is looking for, the critic may fail to see what is there—to understand
what the writer has tried to do, or to consider why he did so.
(One who is for any reason troubled by a work has only these
alternatives, that something is wrong with the author or something is wrong with himself; and the author is unlikely to get
an even chance.) It is better to begin, at least, with a broad,
tentative conception, out of respect for all the great writers
who believed they were writing tragedies. Although we must
seek to define what they have in common—what enables us to
talk about tragedy—we should first try to do justice to all their
different means and ends. Then, instead of arguing over what
tragedy "really" is, we may state why we believe that some
kinds are superior to others, or what it is at its best.

Such an effort calls for a historical approach; and here we
encounter further hazards. While the historical research over
the last century is a most impressive achievement, the study of
literature has perhaps suffered more than it has gained from
this research. In our universities literary history is commonly
confused with literary criticism, or substituted for literary
appreciation. Then literature comes to be considered primarily
as a product of history, not of creative individuals. The work of
art is reduced to a social document, an exhibit of something or
other about its age. As George Boas wrote, "To see a 'century'
in a cathedral or the revolt of the masses in a play is believed
to be a more valuable experience than to see something else
in them." And even to see the artist's intention is not enough.
We naturally try to see it, and to do so must know something
about the tradition he worked in, the expectations of his audi-

ence, the climate of opinion of his age; but if or when we know all this we still do not have the total meaning of his work. Whatever *Hamlet* meant to Shakespeare and his audience, it came to mean something rather different to eighteenth-century readers, to the Romantic poets, to the Victorians, and to us today. Our final concern is its import for us; though by the same token we should not assume that our judgment is the final judgment.

These very cautions, however, spring from a historical sense, and lead us back to the necessity for a historical approach. One must stick to the text of a literary work, we are now told, but the text itself forces a consideration of its historic context. We know how often our ancestors misread the classics they revered by reading them in the light of their own literary conventions and preconceptions. In any case, educated readers today cannot possibly read the plays of Sophocles and Shakespeare as if they were written yesterday, by anonymous poets, for nobody in particular. If they could, they might enjoy a fresh experience, though a somewhat bewildering one; but as it is, they are likely to forget how much historical knowledge they bring to bear in their reading. And the more closely they read Greek tragedy, the more deeply indebted they are to the scholarship that has illumined its ritual origins, its mythical and symbolical content, its structure, its stagecraft, its audience, its role in the communal life of Athens.

Granted the important distinction between literary history and literary criticism, and the common neglect of the literary work as a work of art, it is hard to get a clear idea of the work "in itself" that is allegedly our sole concern. Even a statue, which as a physical object has an independent existence, has no such existence as a work of art; its meaning or beauty depends upon an observer, and varies with different observers in different societies. A poem—words printed on paper, or sounds uttered by a speaker—is a much mistier thing. While it has some kind of objective reality that controls or limits the reader's experience and makes it akin to other artifacts, it remains an intangible affair, existing primarily in the minds of those who know its language.[2] The language of a poem is a continuous reference to things outside itself. Its meaning is never intact, self-contained, self-explanatory. Hence a sensitive reader like Cleanth Brooks, who is most insistent on the necessity of staying inside the poem, is usually carried further afield than most readers just because he finds poetry more profoundly suggestive. In analyzing even a simple lyric by Herrick, "Corinna's Going a-Maying," Brooks reads it as a conflict between the Christian world view and the pagan.

The reader of tragedy is bound to get involved in as momentous issues. He may salve his conscience by employing R. P. Blackmur's concept of "theoretic form," which means vision of life but takes the curse off it by retaining the sacred word "form." If he prefers, he may say that this vision is inside the work. But there is no escaping the outward reference. The author has gone out of his way to deal with the most tragic aspects of man's life, press the ultimate issues of life and death. Whatever we think of his implicit comment on them, we cannot help thinking of it if we are at all moved by his work. Nor can we fully understand and appreciate his artistry, the

[2] The most resolute effort I know of to define the "real" poem was made by René Wellek, in *Theory of Literature*. He scrutinized all the diverse theories about just what and where the poem is: the printed words or the uttered sounds; the conscious intention of the author; the whole experience of the author while composing it, including his unconscious intentions; the experience of the reader, or of "the right kind of reader"; the sum total of the experiences of all its readers; or the common element in all these experiences. Wellek found all these conceptions relevant but either inadequate or impossible to fill out. The "real poem," he concluded, "must be conceived as a structure of norms, realized only partially in the actual experience of its many readers." It has a "special ontological status," for it is "neither real (like a statue) nor mental (like the experience of light or pain) nor ideal (like a triangle)" but is "a system of norms of ideal concepts which are inter-subjective." To me this definition is still not clear. It gets more complicated when Wellek adds that the structure of norms is "dynamic," growing and changing, and so will always remain "in some sense" imperfectly known. But since he is a leading advocate of the analysis of literary works "themselves" or "as such," his idea of dynamic structures is comforting, for it implies that literary works have a history and cannot be fully understood outside of history.

formal organization of his work, unless we consider his peculiar purposes in deliberately writing so harrowing a work. Then we are led to realize how strictly peculiar they are—how rarely men have written tragedy.

Hence we are led back to the initial question: what is tragedy? In a historical view, the clue to its essence is not form but content and purpose. Ultimately, it is the tragic spirit, the tragic sense of life. I now propose to begin over again, at the philosophical beginning.

2. THE PHILOSOPHICAL IMPLICATIONS

Broadly speaking, as one must speak if he is to respect traditional usage, any fiction that deals with terrible and pitiable events, or in other words the "tragic" aspects of human experience, may be called a tragedy. More specifically, and therefore more tentatively, tragedy might be defined as a fiction inspired by a serious concern with the problem of man's fate. Taken literally, word by word, this definition implies more and excludes more than may at first appear. Thus "serious" excludes melodrama, or sensational works that exploit bloody doings chiefly for the sake of thrills. "Concern" and "problem" imply a measure of uncertainty or mystery, the strictly problematical; they exclude popular notions about poetic justice, which usually turns out to be neither poetic nor just. Next, it is the problem of "man": not of an adolescent, of an abnormal individual, of a particular type merely as a type, or of a social class, but of man in a universal aspect, as man-kind. Above all, tragedy is centered on the problem of his "fate": not merely his failures in love, business, or war, nor his sufferings from political or social injustice, but his relations to his total environment, his position in the universe, the ultimate meaning of his life.

Comedy may help to clarify the nature of tragedy. As a humorous play with a cheerful ending, it is apparently the opposite of tragedy; yet they have an underlying kinship. It is suggested by their simultaneous development from a common source in Greece, and by the fact that all the greater tragic dramatists have written comedy too (in Greece, satyr plays). Both dwell on the incongruities in the nature and life of man, which are the subject of either tragic or comic irony. Both recognize a lawfulness in human experience, but also recognize an apparently spontaneous, fortuitous, capricious factor.[3] Both are concerned with human pretension and folly: "Oh Lord, what fools these mortals be!"

But in comedy the Lord has nothing to do with it; whereas tragedy in the past has typically been in some sense, as Macneile Dixon said, "an affair with the gods." Comedy is concerned with man's quirks and foibles, manners and customs, as a social animal. At its most serious it is concerned with his folly, not his mortality; his nature, not his fate. And in spite of its literal improbabilities or extravagances, it finally confirms the normal expectation. To borrow Albert Cook's antinomies, tragedy deals with the wonderful, the extreme, the heroic individual; comedy with the probable, the mean, the social norm. Even satire, which appears to attack the conventional norm, is a confirmation of a "truer" norm, usually an older, more conservative one. Hence the happy ending of comedy is reassuring in a profounder sense. The comic individual has been put in his place, enabling us to enjoy our social superiority to him; the social order has been firmly restored, after a threat that was not really serious. Men are fools, but they are at home in a world they can depend on.

Much closer to tragedy is epic, which has often reflected

[3] In an unpublished essay "Is Reality Really Comic?" Professor B. A. G. Fuller has proposed half seriously, half playfully, that this lawless, incongruous, philosophically undignified factor might be not merely a surface appearance but a "real" characteristic of Reality. It was recognized by the ancients as Chance, by medieval men as Fortune; it has some scientific status as the Indeterminacy Principle recognized in modern physics, the mutations in biology, the irrational in Freudian psychology. Professor Fuller goes on to speculate that God, like man, may be capable of capricious or absent-minded behavior, and have a sense of humor. He might be amused as well as distressed by his unpredictable impulses, or by the strange doings of the intractable material he has to work with— the tricks the universe plays on him. If this behavior seems unbecoming a divine being, we might still wish that he too had the "saving grace" of humor—as Homer's immortals did.

a tragic sense of life. Epic, however, is at once ampler and more limited. It is ampler in that it expresses the whole living faith of its time, which includes beliefs about the destiny of man and how he should face it; it is more limited in that it is more temporal and national, celebrating the ideals of a particular age or group. Tragedy reflects the beliefs of its time, of course, but it is more directly concerned with the relatively timeless, universal problems of life and death—the tragic story of Man, again, rather than the heroic story of certain great men.

Such distinctions are made clearer by adding the well-known clause of Aristotle, that tragedy is designed to excite the emotions of pity and fear. This has become a controversial clause. Some critics are now wary of all reference to emotional effects—what they call the "affective fallacy," the confusion between what a work of art *is* and what it *does*. They wish to study the work objectively, pointing out that reference to our emotions is vague and subjective, and always likely to get sentimental. As one of them wrote, "We might as well study the properties of wine by getting drunk." Nevertheless we cannot rule out such references. We cannot fully understand what a work of art is unless we consider what it does to us. I doubt that we can even know all the properties of wine until we have got drunk on it, or at least exhilarated. Among other things, it is a drink specifically designed to exhilarate us; and if this feeling is vague and subjective, it is not unreal, unimportant, or incommunicable. As for tragedy, the writer is unmistakably trying to move us, and does so in ways that may be specified and broadly agreed upon. Almost all readers have agreed that it does arouse the emotions of pity and fear. To my mind a better word than "fear" is "awe," which includes something of wonder and reverence, but in any case these emotions arise naturally from tragedy as I have defined it: a work seriously concerned with man's fate, and concerned because his fate is to some extent an awful problem.

Now all this applies most clearly to the "high tragedy" of

the past. Modern tragedy raises further questions, which I shall take up in due time. For my immediate purposes I remark merely as illustration the question raised by a common type of modern tragedy, that of social and political injustice. This theme naturally tends to limit the implications of the drama, and often it inspires "impure" art, works leaving chiefly the impression that something ought to be done about it. Even so, no humane man can simply deplore such tendencies. My point at this stage is only that a writer treating this timely theme will not achieve the full tragic effect unless he brings out its timeless implications, or in other words unless he has what I consider the tragic sense of life: a sense that the injustice is not merely the fault of a particular society, but the age-old story of man's inhumanity to man; that we can never do everything about it that we might like to do, or ought to do; that at best there will always remain suffering beyond remedy, bringing us back to the painful mystery of man's being in a mysterious universe.

Such meanings—the final implications of tragedy—are much more controversial. Readers who are deeply moved by tragedy are always apt to find in it a confirmation of their own deepest convictions, or doubts. Philosophers have offered radically different theories of tragedy, each in accordance with his own philosophy; while a Hegel finds in it a proof of eternal justice in a rational universe, a Schopenhauer finds proof of eternal strife in a thoroughly evil, irrational universe. Here again any definite theory is likely to do an injustice to one or more of the great tragic poets, since they manifestly had different visions of life. But from the mere existence of tragedy—and also from its rarity—may be drawn several general conclusions, which are most clearly illustrated by what are commonly regarded as the greatest tragedies, in particular those of Sophocles and Shakespeare.

First, the tragic spirit is more or less pessimistic. It does not necessarily reject belief in Providence or a moral order; pious critics can manage to extract from most tragedies the lesson

that God is just. Yet there would be no tragedy if this simple
lesson were perfectly clear. However it ends, tragedy begins
as a challenge to the universe and goes deeper than the conventional religious spirit. Its characteristic irony itself implies
that the ways of Providence are paradoxical, mysterious, possibly inept. In their realism, the tragic poets recognize some
kind of order in the universe, and of logic in man's fate, but
they suggest that this order is not simply beneficent. While
they show how men bring about their own downfall, they often
show too that their suffering is not wholly deserved, that it is
disproportionate to the wrongdoing, that it can result from
good as well as bad intentions, that the innocent may suffer
too—in short, that man's fate is really tragic. And if flights of
angels sing Hamlet to his rest, Shakespeare's play would
scarcely be improved by an epilogue representing these angels
and their song. "In this harsh world," the dying Hamlet begs
Horatio, "draw thy breath in pain, to tell my story." One who
pictures him with wings has already forgotten his story, if he
ever got it at all.

From this it follows that the tragic spirit is essentially humanistic. Although again it need not deny the interests and
claims of God, it is centered on the interests and claims of
man. It would not arise if men were convinced that their whole
duty was to love and serve God. It is in this respect, paradoxi-
cally, a proud spirit. Thus the hero of Greek tragedy is usually
a proud man who suffers because of his pride; yet he is a hero,
and what makes him a hero is just this pride. As Aristotle said,
pride is "the crown of the virtues," for it makes men aspire to
great things, seek the highest good they render the gods—
honor. The humble man, he added, "seems to have something
bad about him from the fact that he does not think himself
worthy of good things." The tragic poets were more likely to
stress the dangers of pride and the wisdom of humility and
resignation, but even so they did not write in a spirit of glad
humility or preach the holiness of renunciation. No saint has

written tragedy. And pessimism itself is proud, for it implies that man deserves a better fate.

Hence it also follows that the tragic spirit is not cynical. If man is merely a base, selfish creature, and his idealism a mere pretense, there is no real problem in his fate and no reason to pity him. He simply gets what is coming to him. While tragedy is a challenge, none of its masters have questioned the reality of good and evil; they question chiefly the justice of the powers that be, in the name of good and evil. The ordinary reader has some excuse for his tendency to mistake irony and skepticism for cynicism, since an ironical view of man's fate may shade into an ironical view of his aspirations or pretensions, and finally into a disbelief in his values. Yet no attitude—not even the theological insistence on rewards in heaven —is more fatal to the tragic effect than is cynicism.

For all these reasons, the tragic spirit is an affirmation of positive values. The greater tragedies of the past do not end in sheer terror, horror, or despair. In the terms suggested by Kenneth Burke, the basic rhythm of the tragic action is Purpose, Passion, Perception. The hero's purpose is defeated, his passion is harrowing, but through his final perception he comes to terms with his fate—or if he doesn't, the spectator does. There may be such clear compensations for his tragic fate as purification through suffering, the defeat of evil, the restoration of social order. Always there is some human good to place in the scale against the evil, even though the balance is seldom as even or stable as many critics like to make it. The tragic perception may be a clearer awareness that we at once know and do not know and cannot know the whole meaning of the tragic fate; in any event, we somehow accept this fate. There remains the *pleasure* that mature readers get from tragedy. It is a very complex subject but a plain fact of experience, and finally the most significant fact about tragedy.

On this subject Aristotle does not carry us far. It is sufficiently remarkable that he recognized that there is a "true tragic pleasure," that it is good for us, and that a source of its value is the purgation of pity and fear. Modern psychologists still subscribe to his theory of catharsis. But Aristotle has little to say on just how tragedy purges us, or why we ought to be purged of pity, or above all, why the purging is pleasurable. His medical term reminds us that a purge is ordinarily a disagreeable process and at best affords a feeling of relief when it is over. Readers of tragedy will testify that they enjoy the whole experience, that the pleasure seems to come from fully realizing the emotion rather than getting rid of it, and that at the end they feel not relief but a positive exaltation. Hence modern variants on the theory of catharsis still fail to account for this rich experience. It is said, for example, that tragedy infects us with a mild case of the disease in order to build up our resistance to the terrors of real life—as if vaccination were exhilarating. Other critics imply that the tragic poet chiefly veils the dreadful realities, which, like Medusa, would turn us to stone if we looked on them directly; whereas the peculiar thing about tragedy is not its veils—which may indeed be found in all art—but its harrowing realism, or stress upon the dreadful realities. One step more and we reach the popular notion that the pleasure of tragedy comes from self-congratulation, the awareness that our own condition is not so bad after all; whereas such afterthoughts signify that we are no longer under the spell of the drama—the live pleasure is over.

As a complex experience, this pleasure cannot be reduced to a single cause and will vary with the reader. Nevertheless we may agree on certain common elements. One is the mere recognition of truthfulness—that life *is* like this, not as Hollywood would have it. As Aristotle observed, man has an instinct for imitation and naturally takes pleasure in it; so we might expect mature men to be dissatisfied with shallow, crude, or shoddy imitations. Like all literature worthy of the name, tragedy enriches our experience by deepening, widening, refining, and intensifying our consciousness of the possibilities of life. In esthetic terms, it gives the pleasure that men naturally get from the appreciation of artistry: what a simple man may call a beautiful expression of emotion, as in sad songs, or what a contemporary analyst may describe as the formal satisfaction of an expectation fulfilled, a pattern completed, a chord resolved, a curve rounded out. For such reasons a happy ending to a tragic story will jar even though it is plausible on realistic grounds. Realism does not demand that the heroine of *A Farewell to Arms* die in childbirth—ordinarily women do not; but the whole pattern of Hemingway's novel prepares for her death, and requires it.

Such satisfactions, however, may be got as well from formal imitations of joyous actions, since life includes rich possibilities of joy. There is still the question of the pleasure peculiar to tragedy: the paradox that an imitation of the most painful kind of experience is made not only tolerable but uplifting, and to many gives a deeper pleasure than comedy, even the supreme pleasure of literature. And here artistic form gives a further clue, in its suggestion of a mastery of the terrible experience. The final impression left by Greek tragedy, André Malraux remarked, is "not man's defeat but the poet's triumph, his victory over destiny through his art." Historically, it was a sign that man had met death on its own grounds, asserted his own spirit. In terms of the tragic rhythm, the hero not only proves equal to the "perception" of his fate, but is a better man for this perception. Finally he is superior to his fate. The major element in the tragic pleasure, it seems to me—the common element in the diverse visions of life expressed in the great tragedies—is a reverence for the human spirit. Man retains his dignity in failure and death, whether or not he is to enjoy a life to come. Because of this dignity, all is not vanity.

Hence the lift given by tragedy is not the conventional moral uplift, nor does it rise from the vindication of any particular ethical code or religious doctrine. The tragic hero may be a noble figure, like Œdipus or Hamlet, whose grandeur is most apparent in his ruin or death. He may also be a morally evil figure, like Medea or Macbeth, who reveals the terrible

possibilities of the human spirit. In either case he has a greatness beyond good and evil, a dark splendor that overshadows
the more fortunate, sensible, or decent men around him. If he
thinks foolishly, he feels and acts greatly; he is heroic in his
capacity for committing himself to a tragic choice, and then
accepting its full consequences. His pitiable or awful fate is
less significant than the mere fact of his existence. He is a
living proof of the mysterious, incalculable power of the human spirit that enables man to defy natural law or the will of
his almighty Creator, to commit himself to biologically absurd
or rationally inexplicable behavior. He is the supreme demonstration that

> The mind is its own place, and in itself
> Can make a Heaven of Hell, a Hell of Heaven.

He is forever doomed, by whatever divinity or blind chance
has shaped his ends; and he remains free in his thought and
feeling, choosing his ends.

This kind of language is likely to sound hollow these days.
It is foreign to the style of our more sophisticated poetry and
criticism; it is hardly appropriate for much modern tragedy,
whose hero is not at all heroic. Yet we cannot avoid exalted
language if we are to do full justice to the paradoxes of tragedy. There would be no paradox except for the dignity and
power of the human spirit, which remains mysterious on either
scientific or religious grounds. Say that man is a product of
evolution, by natural selection, and it is still not clear just how
nature produced or why it selected a creature capable of
such biologically unnatural behavior as self-punishment, self-
destruction, and martyrdom. Say that man was specially created by God, and it is never clear why a deity reputed to be
self-sufficient and all-good should have designed so refractory
a creature, a source of sorrow to himself, to his fellows, and
even—we have it on the highest authority—to his author. Or
forget the enigma of his origins and take him as he somehow
is: the one animal with a power of conscious choice, capable

of aspiring to truth, beauty, goodness, and holiness, and by
the same token prone to ugly error and evil, capable of a folly
and brutality unknown to the brute world; the one animal who
can say he is the measure of all things, and remain the prey of
all things, always a mystery to himself; and the one animal who
knows that he must die. Then say that his heroic spirit is a
mere whistling in the dark; yet the fact remains that he does
whistle, and sometimes even overcomes his fear of the dark.

Tragedy has embraced these extremes of good and evil,
man's life at its limits. In the literary terms of Coleridge, it is
the clearest illustration of the "synthetic and magical power"
of imagination, with its "balance or reconciliation of opposite
or discordant qualities . . . a more than usual state of emotion, with more than usual order; judgment ever awake and
steady self-possession with enthusiasm and feeling profound or
vehement." In the psychological terms of I. A. Richards, it is
"perhaps the most general, all-accepting, all-ordering experience known," achieving the stablest equilibrium of conflicting
impulses because it brings into play more of our personality
and is less liable to disruption by impulses excluded. In the
philosophical, essentially religious terms of Bertrand Russell,
it is the proudest, most triumphant of the arts, the loftiest mon-
ument to "a free man's worship": it "builds its shining citadel
in the very centre of the enemy's country, on the very summit
of his highest mountain; from its impregnable watchtowers,
his camps and arsenals, his columns and forts, are all revealed;
within its walls the free life continues, while the legions of
Death and Pain and Despair, and all the servile captains of
tyrant Fate, afford the burghers of that dauntless city new
spectacles of beauty." Or in my own prosaic words, tragedy
"goes through the worst, and by going all the way through it
earns an honorable peace, which is more secure because it is
peace without victory."

Since the exaltation of tragedy may carry us too far from
the actualities of everyday life, let us restate its essential faith
in colloquial terms. As the Boy Scout says, "It doesn't matter

whether you win or lose, it's how you play the game." It does matter a great deal, of course, especially to the Boy Scout grown up as a college grad; but after the booing has died away and the bets have been paid, even he may know the satisfaction of a losing game well played, against heavy odds. More vulgar, and more genuine, is the legendary saying of the American sergeant of World War I as he led his men into battle: "Come on, you sons of bitches, d'you want to live forever?" It is the vulgarity that gives dignity to this expression of the human spirit, by precluding the imputation of cheap heroics. We are reminded that the sons are not born Galahads but ordinary men who do want to live forever, and have no passion whatever for dying for any cause. Yet they are still capable of rising above both fear and common sense, and of meeting their destiny in something like the spirit of the tragic heroes.

CHAPTER II

THE BEGINNINGS
OF TRAGEDY

1. THE RITUAL ORIGINS

In comparing the tragedies of Hamlet and Orestes, Gilbert Murray noted that their themes were strangely alike, and also strange to us today—"Yet there is that within us which leaps at the sight of them, a cry of the blood which tells us we have known them always." Beneath the surface of these highly conscious, finely wrought dramas there is, it seems, "an undercurrent of desires and fears and passions, long slumbering yet eternally familiar, which have for thousands of years lain near the root of our most intimate emotions and been wrought into the fabric of our most magical dreams." Although Murray went on to say that he dared not surmise how far back into the ages this undercurrent might carry, he had already followed it back some centuries before the emergence of Greek drama.

Aristotle informs us that tragedy grew out of the Dithyramb, sung in honor of the god Dionysus. Murray and other English scholars developed the thesis, by now widely accepted, that the rites of Dionysus in turn grew out of the prehistoric ritual of the Year-Dæmon, who annually died and was reborn. Other scholars have demonstrated that this ritual pattern was common throughout the Near East, and that it is at least six thousand years old. Its object was to assure fertility, the growth of new life in the spring. Although the pattern took many forms, involving many different deities, it was everywhere centered on a god, or a king acting for the god, who was annually killed and resurrected. It was this idea that carried through the centuries, and that is still woven into the fabric of our "most magical dreams."

The original idea was pure magic. Lacking any conception of natural laws or natural causes, man believed that he could

bend nature to his purposes only by *mimesis,* a ritual enactment of the desired event. The obvious reason why men clung
to the idea for thousands of years is that magic usually works:
every year, almost without fail, the crops grew again. As obvious, however, is the universal truth symbolized by the ritual.
The story of the dying, resurrected god is the story of the Sun
and the Moon, of the Day and the Year, of all life on earth.
It embodies the basic rhythm of nature, the cycle of birth,
death, and birth again. Hence no metaphor in man's art and
thought has been more fertile. The annual triumph of life
over death may be interpreted as the triumph of light over
darkness, of order over chaos, of good over evil. Likewise it
supports man's stubborn refusal to accept the plain evidence
of his senses, that death is the end for him. A ritual developed
to assure the physical survival of the community became a
means of spiritual survival for the individual; the dying god
finally gave birth to the mystery religions that promised salvation both in this life and in a life to come. At their loftiest,
these religions proclaimed what appears to be the most vital
message of the religious spirit: "Ye must be born again!"—and
first you must die to this world. Or in the words of Jesus,
"Whosoever will save his life, shall lose it."

Myth, scholars now believe, was originally not an imaginative effort to explain the universe but a product of the magical
ritual, "the thing uttered" corresponding to the thing done. In
time, however, Myth became a more or less ideal interpretation
of the ritual, and finally embarked on an independent career
(though scholars are prone to forget this in the excitement of
the hunt for ancient ritual elements). One outgrowth that is
especially pertinent for the student of tragedy is the myth of
the hero.

Lord Raglan found striking similarities in the traditional
heroes of widely separated cultures, from Heracles, Theseus,
Romulus, and Moses to Siegfried, King Arthur, and Robin
Hood. The common elements in their stories involve chiefly
their birth, their accession to kingship or leadership, and their

death. The circumstances of the hero's birth are highly un-
usual and almost always involve an attempt on his life, generally by his father or maternal grandfather; he comes into his
kingdom by winning a victory over the old king, or some giant
or dragon; and he dies mysteriously, generally without burial,
though he has one or more holy sepulchers. Among other recurrent details noted by Lord Raglan is that the infant hero is
spirited away and raised by foster parents in a far country,
that on reaching manhood he travels to his future kingdom,
that after winning the kingship he loses favor with the gods
and/or his subjects, and that he is then driven away, to die
his mysterious death in some strange place. (One conspicuous
difference between the mythical hero and most historic ones
is that on ascending the throne he does not embark on a career
of conquest or enjoy a glorious reign; until his final misfortune overtakes him, his reign is ordinarily a blank.) Œdipus
Rex was just such a hero. He assumed the role that both the
mythical heroes and the dying gods commonly assumed—
an agent of purification. In other words, he was a ritual scapegoat.

The deep, lasting influence of this whole ritual-mythical
pattern is most apparent in Christianity. Judaism had fiercely
rejected the pattern. Traces of it survive in some of the Psalms,
such as those that begin "The Lord is become king," but by
the time of the prophets the Hebrews had completely severed
Jehovah's connections with other gods. They were not so
presumptuous as to believe that their Lord could suffer or
would sacrifice himself for mere men; he was undying, invincible, absolutely unique, and absolutely transcendent. Christianity gave up the effort to maintain so pure, so lofty a spirituality, in effect recognizing that an unsuffering God is likely to
be insufferable for ordinary men. In this sense too, Jesus came
"not to destroy, but to fulfil"—to consummate the ancient ritual
of the dying god.

If the synoptic gospels suggest that his own conception of his
mission was rather different, his early followers interpreted it

in the terms long familiar to the Gentiles. With St. Paul the basis of Christian faith became the Resurrection, which had always been the climax of the ritual drama. "If Christ be not risen," he declared, "then is our preaching vain, and your faith is also vain." Paul likewise bequeathed the cardinal doctrine of the Redemption, a sublime version of the old idea of the ritual scapegoat: the Christ had deliberately suffered and died to atone for the sins of all mankind. The life of Jesus, as recorded in the gospels, included most of the familiar elements in the life of the traditional hero, whom he resembled in his humanity—he died only once. The passion plays that developed in the Middle Ages, and are still performed, are the most striking examples of the ancient ritual drama. In this aspect, the chief novelty of Christianity was that it claimed a monopoly on the pattern, rejecting as false all other dying gods, and asserting that salvation could be achieved only through its own rituals.

A curious but highly suggestive version of the scapegoat theme is the "Paradox of the Fortunate Fall," an idea that Professor Lovejoy traced through Christian history, and that Herbert Weisinger has since made out as the core of tragedy, following it all the way back to the ritual pattern of the Near East. When Adam in Milton's *Paradise Lost* is granted a vision of the future, he marvels at the glorious good that will result from his sin—the coming of Christ:

> Full of doubt I stand,
> Whether I should repent me now of sin
> By me done or occasioned, or rejoice
> Much more that much more good thereof shall spring. . . .

Except for his sin, man would not have known the supreme good of Christ. Accordingly, as Lovejoy observes, "The Fall could never be sufficiently condemned and lamented; and likewise, when all its consequences were considered, it could never be sufficiently rejoiced over." This paradox, which is most rapturously expressed in the *Exultet* of Catholic liturgy, has been stated explicitly by eminent theologians, including St. Ambrose, St. Augustine, and Pope Gregory the Great.

The idea is a dangerous one. It leads to such logical conclusions as the apothegm of St. Ambrose: "Sin is more fruitful than innocence." It also raises awkward questions, implying that God himself not only willed the Fall but "*needed* a fallen race," in order to display the plenitude of his power and goodness. Hence theologians have seldom dwelt on the paradox. Yet it is typical of the sublime mysteries, or the logical contradictions, on which religion thrives. It remains at the heart of Christ's mission, and of the proper response to his sacrifice: man must forever lament the Crucifixion—and forever rejoice at its consequences. T. S. Eliot restated it in the sermon preached by his Thomas à Becket in *Murder in the Cathedral*: "It is only in these our Christian mysteries that we can rejoice and mourn at once for the same reason." That actually men were mourning and rejoicing for the same reason long before Christianity, in similar mysteries, might comfort all but the orthodox.

Meanwhile, psychologists have also had much to say about these ancient themes. They represent what Jung calls archetypes or primordial images, and regards as innate in the "collective unconscious," somehow inherited in the structure of the brain. Among his disciples, Maude Bodkin in particular has analyzed the archetypal patterns in tragic poetry, following the lead of Gilbert Murray. Freud, on the other hand, saw behind this whole pattern the Œdipus complex, stemming from the murder of the primeval father. Resentful of the despotic authority of the father, the sons had killed him, and thereafter they and their sons were to be forever haunted by the memory of the crime. The father became the King, the Hero, the God, finally the Only God. The omnipotent God recovered all the grandeur of the primeval father, whose authority had also been unlimited, and he thereby inspired an intenser devotion; but by the same token he stirred a deeper hostility, which had to be repressed and which led to a deeper feeling of guilt. In *Totem and Taboo* Freud described the hero of Greek tragedy as a scapegoat for the primeval crime. "He had to suffer because he was the primal father, the hero of that primordial tragedy . . . and the tragic guilt is the guilt which he had to take upon himself in order to free the chorus of theirs." Hence the Chorus habitually warns him against his pride, tries to restrain him, yet sympathizes with him and laments his fate.

In *Moses and Monotheism,* written at the end of his life, Freud still treated the primeval crime as an actual historic event, and the beginning of all art, religion, and ethics. So it is time to pause and acknowledge that we are dealing with some dubious speculation. That a historic murder would have such momentous, universal consequences is about as hard to believe as the literal story of the Fall of man in the Garden of Eden. It is hard, too, to follow Jung into the misty regions of a racial unconscious, where he finds the deepest sources of spiritual health and truth. Often it seems that one must become as a little child to enter the heaven of Jung; and one may be deterred by the memory of the Hitler-Child. In any case, the human race is still perverse or irrational enough to defy these accounts of its mind. The Œdipus complex is not in fact a universal phenomenon; anthropologists have found no trace of it in some primitive societies. Neither is the theme of the dying, resurrected god a universal theme. It was apparently unknown to the civilizations of America, and the Far Eastern societies made little of the idea, if or when they caught it. It is doubtful whether there is that within a Hindu or a Confucianist which leaps at the sight of Hamlet and Orestes. It is certain only that we are dealing with a theme deeply embedded in our own heritage.

Likewise there is still considerable question whether this ancient ritual pattern was actually the source of tragedy. Conservative scholars (such as Pickard-Cambridge) point out that we have very little positive knowledge of ancient Greek rituals, and virtually none of the early stages of tragedy that supposedly incorporated these rituals. They add that we know of no tragedy in which any god dies and is resurrected. At least it seems clear that the pattern has been radically transformed. I do not believe myself that this approach takes us to the heart of tragedy.

Nevertheless it does throw considerable light on the subject. There remain broad similarities between Greek drama and the ritual dramas, similarities that look more like actual historic connections the more we learn about the religion of the Near East, Minoan Crete, and prehistoric Greece. Similarly the theories of Freud and Jung help to explain why we respond so deeply to dramas that offhand seem foreign to our own experience. We are speculating, on the basis of strictly insufficient and uncertain evidence; but so we must on many matters of vital concern, and on this one it seems to me easy enough to make the necessary discounts.

Thus few historical scholars, if any, accept the Œdipus complex as the key to early history. The cycle of the seasons would appear to be a clearer and quite sufficient explanation of the god who is killed and replaced or resurrected. Yet Freud's theory at least illumines a deep, common source of tension in art and religion. In exercising his authority, the father is likely to inspire both respect and resentment, love and fear. The father of the community—the king, the god—as naturally inspires ambivalent attitudes. Melville once remarked that in their hearts men really hate God; and at least they find it hard simply or wholeheartedly to love a Being whom they are always told they must fear, and who is notoriously given to wrath. Such ambivalence is of the essence of tragedy and its historic connections with religion. Similarly we need not believe that Jung's primordial patterns are universal or innate to recognize their prevalence and persistence. The extensive diffusion of culture, together with the common experience of men everywhere—the uniformities of birth, growth, toil, pain, and death—is sufficient to account for them.

And so with the ritual origins of drama. The prehistoric

rituals always contained the seeds of drama because as magical pre-doings or re-doings, executed with intense earnestness,
they were intensely dramatic. The whole world-view behind
them was dramatic: a sunrise or a spring was not a lawful
event due to natural causes, but a triumph of light over darkness, or of life over death. And always the rites were quite literally a matter of life and death for the whole community.
While the mimetic magic implied a harmony between man
and nature, since man's doing somehow brought about nature's
doings, helped the god to be reborn, it also acknowledged the
"otherness" of nature, the mysterious powers that are often
hostile to man and might make the crops fail. The triumph of
the god or the god-king, and the consequent survival of the
community, was not easy or certain. If the participants in the
annual festivals presumably counted on it, they also knew
that it was temporary—he would have to suffer and die again
the next year; so they evidently knew a real anguish at his suffering and death, a real ecstasy at his resurrection.

In this perspective Aristotle's definition of tragedy becomes
more meaningful: an imitation of a complete action, designed
to purge the emotions of pity and fear. Although just what he
meant by a "complete" action is still not clear, the idea may go
back to the cycle of life and death and life again. At least
Greek tragedy resembled the ritual dramas in the communal
purposes it served. It was not merely a form of entertainment,
a literary performance, or a mode of individual self-expression:
it was an annual ritual performed at a national, religious festival and concerned with the most vital civic issues—in a real
sense, with the spiritual survival of the community. In particular, Aristotle's remarkable theory of catharsis may have been
an elementary observation of fact. Although the spectators at
the Greek dramatic festivals were no doubt less emotional than
the participants in the ritual dramas, what evidence we have
suggests that they were by no means so restrained as modern
playgoers, or as their classical reputation for poise would lead
one to expect. A speaker in a Platonic dialogue tells how a mere

reciter of Homeric poems made his audience weep and look wild; Herodotus informs us that the Athenians were so affected by *The Capture of Miletus*, a tragedy by Phrynichus, that "the whole theater burst into tears"; and we hear that the chorus of Furies introduced by Æschylus caused women to have miscarriages.

Catharsis is the apparent reason why Dionysus, the god who induced orgy, frenzy, and ecstasy, disconcerted his enemies by also inducing an uncanny calm and peace of mind. It is significant that Dionysus—not Athena—presided over the annual dramatic festivals in Athens, and with his priest attended the performance of every tragedy. He was a mysterious, quite unclassical god who was never admitted into the heavenly family on Mount Olympus. We do not know just how or when he entered Greece, or how he acquired all his strange connections—with goats, bulls, snakes, trees, and ships as well as wine, women, and song. But his essential nature is clear enough. He was not merely a god of wine—the "jolly Bacchus" that the obtuse Romans later made of him. He was a mystery god. Whereas Apollo taught the Greeks the wisdom of sobriety, "Know thyself" and "Nothing to excess," Dionysus offered them the at once more spiritual and more primitive states of *ekstasis* ("standing outside oneself") and *enthusiasmos* ("possession by the god"). His worshippers could become one with him because he was both human and divine, and himself at one with the life of nature. As Plutarch observed, he represented "the whole wet element" in nature—wine, blood, semen, sap, and all the life-giving juices. Although he naturally inspired many conflicting legends, his life story mainly parallels the story of the mythical hero, from a miraculous birth to a mysterious death. It is ironical, and fitting, that the tomb of this ever living, dying god was at Delphi, the sanctuary of Apollo himself. In *The Bacchæ* Euripides reveals how inextricably the worship of Dionysus was mingled with other ancient, orgiastic religions, in particular the worship of Cybele and her dying son Attis.

The Bacchæ is among the major exhibits for Gilbert Murray's theory of the ritual pattern underlying the form of Greek tragedy—the prehistoric pattern of the Year-Dæmon. (The Greek *dæmon* was merely a spirit—not necessarily the evil spirit that it became in Hebrew and Christian usage.) An *Agon* or contest, of the Year against its enemy; a *Pathos*, of the death of the Year; a Messenger to announce this death; a *Threnos* or lamentation over the death; an *Anagorisis* or discovery of the slain Dæmon, followed by his Resurrection or some glorious Epiphany, altogether constituting a *Theophany* —this, according to Murray, is the basic ritual form. Again conservative scholars object that no extant Greek tragedy strictly follows this form, and more particularly that in none is a hero or god resurrected. Murray has to work hard to find "faded" epiphanies or theophanies, and at that he virtually gives up on Sophocles. But in a broader view of the Dionysiac festival as a whole, the basic similarities again become plainer.

The dominant mood of this spring festival was unmistakably joyous, all Athens making holiday. The festival opened with a splendid procession that took the god from his temple to the theater, by a roundabout route that prolonged the spectacle and the festivities. The next day or so was devoted to dithyrambs, sung and danced by choruses of fifty citizens, in honor of Dionysus. On the last three days the dramas were performed, again with choruses composed of citizens. The tragedies might therefore correspond to the enactment of the suffering and death of the god in the rituals. The rejoicing that accompanied his rebirth, with its assurance of fertility, would then be expressed in the lively, often obscene satyr play that invariably followed the tragedies, and in the lusty comedies. The tragedies themselves might have happy endings, as the trilogies of Æschylus usually did, in keeping with the triumphant endings of the old rituals. At best they were a means not merely of catharsis but of spiritual regeneration. They left a sense of order, not of chaos; they constituted a mode of acceptance, not an invitation to despair. Like the rituals of the dying god, they represented death in order to promote life.

Altogether, the continuities or the correspondences seem plain enough to warrant Murray's conclusion:

> An outer shape dominated by tough and undying tradition, an inner life fiery with sincerity and spiritual freedom; the vessels of a very ancient religion overfilled and broken by the new wine of reasoning and rebellious humanity, and still, in their rejection, shedding abroad the old aroma, as of eternal and mysterious things: these are the fundamental paradoxes presented to us by Greek Tragedy.

Later we shall find something like them in Elizabethan tragedy, and even in some modern tragedy.

Yet in Murray's own terms I should say that most important is not the ritual form of Greek tragedy but the inner life, the spiritual freedom, "the new wine of reasoning and rebellious humanity." The constant danger of the historical approach is the genetic fallacy, the confusion of origins with essences. Thus Herbert Weisinger and others have described the ritual pattern as the "central core" or the "heart" of tragedy; whereas historically it is at most the beginning of tragedy, and no more clearly its essence than the cave man is the essence of the civilized man, or black magic the essence of Christianity. While it is always interesting and enlightening to learn where any human institution begins, our main concern is what it becomes, where and how it ends.

The rituals remained a form of magic. Frazer observed that "the aim of these elementary dramas, which contain in germ the tragedy and comedy of civilized nations, was the acquisition of superhuman power for the public good." The significant fact about Greek tragedy is the most obvious one, that it was *not* a magical rite, did *not* aim at the acquisition of superhuman power. It was consciously composed by poets, for spectators rather than participants, who had no idea that they might thereby literally assure the survival of Athens, or themselves be ritually purified, reborn, or resurrected. If the poets were aware of a heritage from the ritual dramas, they profoundly altered the meaning of these dramas to suit their own purposes. They asked questions about the nature of man and the cosmos; they read into the mysteries an intellectual mystery, a criticism rather than a mere celebration of life; they introduced a conscious irony that was alien to the spirit of the old rites, or any religious rites; they often implied that there is no clear pattern in man's life, except that tragedy is his normal lot. Performing under the eye of Dionysus, they never invoked his aid, or sought to be possessed by him, or held out any hopes whatever of immortality. Their most explicit and insistent message was that man must always "think mortal thoughts," never act as if he were akin to the immortal gods; to forget his lowly human station was the fatal sin of *hubris*. Greek tragedy promoted life by promoting wisdom. Like the old rituals, it was an earnest play for high stakes, the public good; but its triumph was won on much harder terms, by human rather than superhuman means.

That a basic ritual pattern existed all over the Near East and the Mediterranean area, for some thousands of years, remains a striking and significant discovery. But then another historical fact becomes still more striking and significant—the fact that *only* the Greeks developed tragedy. On the face of it, the clue to its distinctive essence is not its ancient form but its unique content, its new spirit. And this clue leads straight to Homer. As Plato said, Homer was "the first of the tragic writers." At the time when tragedy developed, the Homeric epics were being consolidated, recited at national festivals, and recognized as the Bible of Greece. Æschylus declared that his plays were "slices from the great banquet of Homer"; Sophocles became known as his closest disciple. Homer was acquainted with the "frenzied Dionysus," who was "a joy to mortals," and he must have known of the Year-Dæmons too; but he turned his back on all of them. In effect, he wrote a declaration of spiritual independence that enabled the Greeks to develop tragedy.

2. THE HOMERIC POEMS

In view of the famous "Homeric question," the first thing that must be said about Homer is that we know nothing whatever about the man and his life, and cannot even be certain that there was such a man. Scholars are still debating whether the *Iliad* and the *Odyssey* were written by one poet, or by two, or by many, of whom a "Homer" merely added the finishing touches to the patchwork. They disagree as widely about when he or they lived, their conjectures ranging from the tenth to the seventh century B.C. I am not qualified to express an authoritative opinion on this question, which fortunately makes no difference for my purposes. The Greeks themselves never doubted the existence of their great poet.[1] It is certain that both epics were traditional poems: Homer was not an isolated, eccentric, or revolutionary genius, but a representative poet, speaking out of a developed tradition, to an audience familiar with his materials and his manner. It is as certain that he remained the leading authority for the Greeks, even after they took to strange gods and different conceptions of the good life. "All men's thoughts have been shaped by Homer from the beginning," wrote Xenophanes, who deplored his thoughts about the gods. When Plato attacked him, he likewise testified to his reputation as "the educator of Hellas."

Hence we may dismiss the romantic conception of Homer

---

[1] Those who are inclined to agree with the Greeks (as I am) might comment that by the kind of scholarly arguments used on Homer one could prove conclusively that there never was a Shakespeare, since plays so full of inconsistencies could only be a patchwork by many hands; or that there must have been two Shakespeares, since it is unthinkable that the same man could have written *A Comedy of Errors* and *King Lear*; or that the alleged Shakespeare must have lived more than a century before his supposed Elizabethan Age, since he never once mentions printing, which dates from 1454. For the sake of convenience, at any rate, I propose to speak of Homer instead of "Homer."

as a simple, happy pagan, or in Schiller's words, a "child of nature." The children of nature were still devoted to the Year-Dæmons. Granted that the Heroic Age he pictured was relatively simple and rude, it was far from primitive. The epic form itself, as W. P. Ker points out, represents a considerable advance toward intellectual and imaginative freedom, signifying that a people has come to a conscious realization and command of its living ideals. Homer is pre-eminent for this freedom and this command. And his sovereign spirit is more remarkable because he won his values from an unflinching tragic sense of life.

There is no mistaking the pessimism of the *Iliad*, the first of the epics. While celebrating the Heroic Age of Greece, it is from beginning to end shot through with a somber sense of the commonplaces of mortality: "the generations of men are like the leaves of the forest," and no man can escape his fate, "neither coward nor brave man." Achilles, the greatest of the heroes, sums up the tragic moral: "This is the way the gods have spun their threads for poor mortals! Our life is all sorrow, but they are untroubled themselves." Zeus, he goes on to say, has two jars of gifts, one of good and one of evil things; and the father of the immortal gods mixes his gifts with a royal unconcern for fitness or justice. And if Zeus too is subject to Moira, an impersonal Necessity, this makes the fate of man no less cruel, for the Necessity is as mysterious as inexorable. Homer had outgrown the primitive belief, still popular in the higher religions, that good behavior is rewarded by material prosperity, and that natural calamities are due to human wrongdoings. Likewise he offered no easy consolations, no hopes of a heavenly afterlife. Hero and commoner alike go to Hades, a shadowy underworld without light or leaf or song, fit only for ghosts, which to a heroic spirit was dreadful even though it was not yet equipped with hellfire or the Christian machinery of eternal torture. When Odysseus visits Hades and attempts to console Achilles by the thought that even there he is a mighty prince, Achilles answers that he would rather be the serf of a poor man on earth than the king of all these dead. The best that can be said is that Zeus himself is at times moved to pity, once remarking that "there is no more unhappy thing than man, of all creatures that breathe and move on earth."

More often, however, the father of the blessed gods rejoiced at the spectacle of the strife among men; and chiefly he was concerned about his own Olympian affairs. Certainly he never dreamed of dying for men, who were no creatures of his—he had not made this world. Neither did he acknowledge his indebtedness to Homer. As Herodotus said, Homer was the first to name the Olympian gods and put them in their place, giving them their forms and their offices. He did handsomely by them, not only giving them glorious forms but enabling them to live like lords, "dwell at ease" forever. Although they performed some services in return for the constant attentions they demanded of men, they had no real responsibility for the life of nature or of man. And in their ease they insisted on the absolute separation of mortal and immortal. Their worshippers could never be one with them, in this life or the next. There is no word in the *Iliad* for "god-fearing" or for "love of God." According to the *Magna Moralia*, "It would be eccentric for anyone to claim that he loved Zeus."

Yet the upshot of the *Iliad* is not despair, or even gloom. There is also no mistaking the sunniness of Homer, the astonishing freedom from anxiety. He is always calm, unhurried, and unharried, accepting life as he finds it, and finding more to delight in than to brood over. As the ancients noted, he praised almost everything: all the good things that man could see, feel, know, and do—and finally, alas, must do without, forever; but even so his funeral will be followed by feasts and games for the living. Hence he did not draw the familiar religious conclusions of fatalism, resignation, or renunciation. His heroes often talk like fatalists, attributing both their failures and their successes to the gods, but they rarely act like fatalists. Their talk is a conventional piety, like that of ordinary Americans who give thanks to God for victories that they really believe they have won themselves; or at best it is a sensible recognition that man is at the mercy of greater powers, and that when he "finds heart" he draws on mysterious sources of power. Their action is a triumphant assertion of their own power—and in their passion for glory they demand every ounce of credit for their heroic deeds. When they know they are doomed, as both Achilles and Hector knew, they will still defy death by asserting their "unconquerable soul," and by their death will make legend and song. They appear to agree with Homer that mortality is necessary if only to make poetry immortal. And most of all Homer praises this heroic spirit. As all readers recognize, he shows more respect for his heroes than he does for the blessed gods.

Now, it is hardly necessary to point out the limitations of these heroes, whose main goals in life are fame and plunder ("the oldest labor-saving device"), or the more serious limitations of the Olympian gods, who at their worst are about as irresponsible a set of heavenly playboys and beauty queens as religious history has to offer. The Greeks themselves came to be embarrassed by their great educator. To explain away Homer's strange stories about the gods, they tried vainly to make him an allegorical poet; lacking a historical sense, they could not see him as a spokesman of a different society. But since lovers of Homer are still prone to rhapsodize as if he were a universal, timeless spirit, it is worth remarking that he was a courtly poet, addressing an aristocratic audience, celebrating aristocratic values—what Nietzsche was to call the "master morality."

This explains his feudal conception of the Olympian gods. The blessed gods were not so free from trouble after all, since they were ruled by their often despotic overlord, Zeus; like the Greek chieftains, they quarrelled among themselves and connived against their leader. In their relations with men they displayed the favoritism common to feudal lords. They could be magnanimous and were generally expected to deal justly with those who served them, but they could also be deceitful, tyrannical, and cruel, to the dismay but not the surprise of their worshippers. Because they had the lawful power, heroes and gods alike were not held to high, impersonal standards of right and wrong; their will was law. Hesiod was the first Greek to preach the idea of divine justice, and the apparent reason why he took to it was the need of compensation. As a peasant, he was keenly aware of human injustice; life for him was much harder than it was for Homer. Homer displayed no concern over the tragic lot of common men.

Nevertheless such limitations finally make all the more astonishing the reasonableness, clear-sightedness, and mellowness of Homer. Taken even at its face value, his heroic ideal is admirable enough. The passion for glory and fame that animates his heroes may be called naïve, selfish, vainglorious, and certainly it is irrational—fame will do them no good in the grave. Still, we all know this desire. It is not clearly more selfish than the hope of eternal reward in heaven, it at least manifests the power of the human spirit, and it asserts that what finally counts is not the length but the quality of a life. Thus Achilles is told by his goddess mother that he is marked for certain death if he stays to fight at Troy, whereas if he goes home he will live happily ever after, in wealth and ease; and he chooses to fight and die at Troy. (One might remark that the long, happy, inglorious life he spurns is precisely the life that young America aspires to.) But Achilles by no means represents Homer's ideal. He is fit only for war—and Homer makes plain the horror and futility of this "lamentable war." He provides Achilles with a tutor, Phœnix, to teach him the art of speech and warn him, vainly, against the stubbornness and violence of his temper. Other heroes show a proper respect for the civilized ideals that receive more stress in the *Odyssey*. Most important, Homer himself is superior to the world of the *Iliad*. He is gentler, wiser, and more cultivated than his heroes; more serene, impartial, and truly Olympian in spirit than his gods.

He is too humane and serene, indeed, for some sophisticated

contemporaries to understand. W. H. Auden has pronounced this verdict: ← *Here is an ad hominem attack against Auden as "unsophisticated!"*

> The world of Homer is unbearably sad because it never transcends the immediate moment; one is happy, one is unhappy, one wins, one loses, finally one dies. That is all. Joy and suffering are simply what one feels at the moment; they have no meaning beyond that; they pass away as they came; they point in no direction; they change nothing. It is a tragic world but a world without guilt for its tragic flaw is not a flaw in human nature, still less a flaw in an individual character, but a flaw in the nature of existence.

Actually, the flaws in Homer's characters are plain, at least to those who can recognize evil even though it is not attributed to Original Sin. The very theme of the *Iliad* is the tragic consequences of "the wrath of Achilles," the woe he brings upon both Greeks and Trojans, and upon himself. On the other hand, Homer does stress a tragic flaw in the nature of existence— an irremediable flaw; but for this very reason the emotion does transcend the immediate moment. It points to the whole mystery of the human condition; and if it changes nothing, neither does the emotion of Hamlet, or Auden, or the rest of us. Even so, the world of Homer is not "unbearably sad." It evidently is to Auden, and may be to others who feel an imperious need for a divine redeemer. But it was not so to Homer himself, or to the generations of Greeks who made him their Bible.

Here we see the real reason Herbert disagrees w/ Auden He despises him for being a Christian

Homer's acceptance of life on these hard terms may now seem more paradoxical because his vision included no hint of the paradox of the Fortunate Fall, or of the hero as ritual scapegoat, or of the paradox of humility itself—the supremely proud hope of salvation through a dying god. Having come to realize the value of human personality, he knew that if in nature death is annually followed by new life, the individual dies only once, for good. Nevertheless he encouraged the Greeks to create their greatest work of art, Man himself. Only

Half of Herbert's opinions in this book exist because he hates God & takes every chance he gets to accuse anyone who would dare suggest God's existence as stupid & superstitious.

in this light may one appreciate the real value of his Olympians. By creating the gods in man's own image, he helped the Greeks to realize their humanity, without which there can be no true spirituality. The very limitations of the gods were an advantage for such purposes. In their easygoing ways and their demand for only ceremonial attentions, they left men free to cultivate the Hellenic ideal of *arete,* or all-around "excellence." Having relatively little to do with the life of nature, which was taken care of by the hard-working fertility dæmons, they became primarily civic gods, patrons of culture. Then they too could be educated, as they were by Æschylus.

At their worst, the Olympians were atavistic, recalling the bad old days when they had made barbarous demands upon men, including human sacrifice. But the traces of such beliefs that survive in the legends narrated by Homer only emphasize how far he has moved from the world of black magic, primeval ignorance and primeval fear, which in time lay not far behind him. Just how he and his fellow Greeks had managed to emancipate themselves from this age-old heritage we do not know. Neither can we be sure to what extent he literally believed in the myths he told. What matters is that he *possessed* the myths—he was no longer possessed by them.

Hence we may better appreciate the achievement of Homer (or the flock of little Homers) by considering the Babylonian Epic of Gilgamesh, the supreme literary achievement of the Mesopotamian peoples. Originating in Sumeria, this was the product of a much longer tradition than the *Iliad,* and as a heroic epic with a somber action it offers a fair comparison. It is the more pertinent because its main theme is the problem of mortality. Like the Greeks, the Mesopotamian peoples had only vague notions about an afterlife, and no belief in a heavenly one.

The epic gets under way as the great hero Gilgamesh sets out from his kingdom with his friend Enkidu, on a career of fabulous adventure. While girding his loins to dispose of one terrible monster, he rebukes Enkidu for momentarily losing his courage. Mere man is but wind, he says in the spirit of a Homeric hero, but man should not be so foolish or cowardly as to fear death: it is inevitable, and besides, he may cheat it by winning undying fame. But when Enkidu later dies, the appalling reality of death is brought home to Gilgamesh; and he finds it intolerable. Thereafter his one aim is to escape it. He wanders to the ends of the world on a hopeless quest of eternal life, having more marvelous adventures but everywhere hearing only the same sad wisdom: the gods have decreed that death is the lot of man, so let him fill his belly and make merry, dance and make music, wear fresh clothes, delight in his wife and child—"These things alone are the concern of men." Finally Gilgamesh learns of a magical means of rejuvenation, a plant that grows at the bottom of the sea. Diving to the bottom, he comes up with the plant and sets out for home, happy at last. But on the way, which is long and hot, he pauses for a swim in a pool, leaving the plant on the banks; and a snake crawls up and carries it off. Because they eat of this plant, snakes do not die, merely sloughing off their old skins. We leave Gilgamesh weeping bitterly:

> For whose sake, Urshanabi, have I strained my muscles:
> For whose sake has my heart's blood been spent?
> I brought no blessing on myself—
> I did the serpent underground good service.

Now here is an obvious irony, and something like the tragic spirit. From the beginning, however, the Epic of Gilgamesh differs from the *Iliad* in that its action takes place in an incredible world of supernatural marvels. The hero proves his greatness by slaying monsters; to the end his adventures are those of a fairy-tale hero. The world of the *Iliad* is free from monsters, and from most of the paraphernalia of primitive magic. Although Homer's story is set in the great old days when heroes could hurl stones "such as two men could not lift as men are now," his heroes prove their greatness in human conflict, in a real world. And although they have to contend with the gods as well, essentially they experience the actual terrors and horrors of life on earth. There is remarkably little nonsense in Homer.

But the most important difference appears in the ending of the Epic of Gilgamesh. It is an arbitrary, trivial ending, as unsatisfying philosophically as artistically. It evades the whole tragic issue by implying that mortality is due not to an unalterable necessity of man's being, but to a mere miscarriage of magic. The poet who gave final form to the epic, after the centuries of thought and imagination that had gone into it, still lacked a real command of his subject. It appears that neither he nor his audience had yet won freedom from extravagance and confusion, found a dignified way of life, realized an ideal to which they could give noble expression. By contrast, Homer had a deeper tragic sense, and in his realism gives a more poignant impression of the actual sorrows of man's life; but he also had a much clearer, loftier ideal of excellence, by which man may triumph over them. His heroes are both more human and more god-like than Gilgamesh. So the *Iliad* ends with the heart-rending lamentations of the Trojans over Hector, not with the final victory of the Greeks; but it ends on a high plane where there are no snakes, no jeers, no mere petty tricks of fate, and where one leaves with the feeling not that poor Hector died but that magnificent Hector had lived.

This is Herbert's purely subjective feeling.

A still more pertinent comparison is with the dramatic Book of Job in the Old Testament, the epic of Israel. This is a more mature and profound work than the Epic of Gilgamesh, and more important for us because it represents a major current in Western tradition. It takes us to the heart of the issues raised by tragedy.

The author of Job faced squarely the tragic problem of evil. When Job's property and family are destroyed, and he himself is afflicted with boils from head to toe, he rejects the conventional explanation of his friends, that his calamity is due to his sins. He says flatly that he is not conscious of having sinned; God "multiplies my wounds without cause." Therefore

"I will speak in the anguish of my spirit," "I desire to reason with God," "I will maintain my ways before him." Such anguish of spirit appears elsewhere in the Old Testament, as in some of the Psalms, passages in the prophets, and the Book of Ecclesiastes. It sprang from the national tragedy, the destruction of the kingdom, which made it seem that the chosen people had been chosen to suffer much more than the idolatrous peoples around them. And we must remember that the problem of evil was still harder for the ancient Hebrews because their Jehovah did not promise them personal immortality as a consolation for their earthly sufferings. Later on some of them would pick up the idea of heaven from the idolaters, but all their forefathers could look forward to after death was Sheol, a shadowy underworld much like the Greek Hades. To their way of thinking, it was presumptuous for mere men to consider themselves fit to join their Almighty Lord. Heaven was only for Jehovah.

Yet precisely for this reason the ancient Hebrews did not develop the tragic sense of life as Homer and the Greeks knew it. Jehovah was all in all; man's whole duty was to serve and obey him, without question, without assertion of any rights of his own. As Eli said, "It is the Lord; let him do what seemeth him good." Hence a later writer added a conclusion to the Book of Job, in which the Lord answers Job's questions. The Voice out of the Whirlwind tells Job of the wonders of his creation and asks in turn, Has *he* ever created a universe? Where was *he* when the Lord did create it? Or let him merely consider the behemoth and the leviathan, and then reflect on his littleness. In other words, the Lord does not really answer Job's questions at all. Like Zeus, he only boasts of his power, though there had never been any question of this; he ignores the issue of justice. But Job declares himself satisfied. He had uttered that which he did not understand, "Wherefore I abhor myself, and repent in dust and ashes." Then somebody added the Hollywood happy ending in which Job is given twice as much property as he had had before, and a second set of children, thereby proving that virtue is always rewarded—and missing the whole point of the original book. — *Uhm, again, bad Biblical scholarship which doesn't have anything to do w/ the thosis of this book.*

The great prophets of Israel knew better than this, of course; they did not preach such cheap, easy morals. Still, their spirit was that of Job at the end. It was therefore profoundly different from the spirit of Homer. While his heroes never doubted the power of the gods or the propriety of rendering homage to them, and also knew that "man is born unto trouble, as the sparks fly upward," they never denied the plain facts of their experience by pretending that the gods were always just. Neither did they conclude from the trouble they were born unto that their whole duty was to serve the authors of their trouble. They never took to wearing sackcloth and ashes, or to simply abhorring themselves. They went about their human business, maintaining their own ways. Later Greeks would undergo plenty of tragic experience as they lived in this spirit; and eventually they would lose heart. But first they rose to the great age of Athens. Athenians in particular revered the great educator who had made Hellas conscious of its difference from all other nations.

— Not so. There was extensive religious ritual in this era and as far as abhorring themselves; what about such sacrifices as a man cutting off his genitals for the festival of Dionysus? Sounds a lot worse than ripping your clothes

CHAPTER III

GREEK
TRAGEDY

1. THE CULTURAL BACKGROUND

According to Aristotle, the Greeks disagreed over who had originated their drama, the Dorians claiming credit for the form in which the Athenians were to distinguish themselves. Modern scholars have found much more to disagree about. They have given a dozen different explanations, for instance, of how tragedy got its curious name, which means "goat-song": from a chorus of goat-like satyrs, or a chorus dancing for a goat as a prize, or a chorus dancing around a goat as a sacrifice, etc. But with the help of Aristotle, scholars have by now established clearly enough the main outlines of the development of Greek tragedy. There was at first a purely choral performance, whether or not it went back to the ritual drama of a Year-Dæmon. From the chorus emerged a leader, who at length became an actor with a definite role; the creation of this role was traditionally credited to Thespis. Thespis won the first prize (a goat) when the Athenian tyrant Pisistratus established the festival of Dionysus, in 534 B.C., and made a contest in tragedy its chief feature. Upon the reorganization of the festival in 501, competitors were required to present three tragedies and a satyr play. Then Æschylus introduced a second actor, diminishing the importance of the Chorus in favor of dialogue. Sophocles made a further advance toward drama as we know it by adding a third actor, as well as scene-painting.

The obvious implications of this development, however, continue to elude some authorities in the classics. A Great Book, we hear, is one that is just as true and pertinent today as on the day it was written. So it seems necessary to say bluntly that there is no such thing as this Great Book. All the world's masterpieces reflect some purely temporal, local interests and beliefs, ideas that for us may be neither true nor pertinent. All require of the reader some historical imagination and sympathy. As for the Greek tragic poets, they wrote not for the ages but for a fifth-century Athenian audience, under peculiar, fortuitous conditions not of their own making. Simply to do justice to their masterly creations, we must first take into account these conditions.

The most conspicuous element of Greek tragedy, the Chorus, was not a conscious invention of the Greek artistic genius. The Chorus was simply there from the beginning, whenever or wherever the beginning is placed, and it always had to be there, even though its presence might be something of a nuisance. At their best the poets made of it a superb dramatic instrument. With the accompaniment of music and dance, it made possible grand operatic effects that we can scarcely appreciate in reading and never reproduce exactly, since Greek music and choreography have been lost. Beyond such effects, the poets made various uses of the Chorus, to relieve, amplify, intensify, or complicate their drama—and to mislead simple readers, who habitually look to it for the "moral" of the tragedy. At the same time, it naturally tended to limit the kind of drama that could be represented. Although the poets knew of no rules about the unities of time and place, they usually observed these unities if only because a chorus of townspeople could not readily be moved about; no single tragedy has a wide-ranging action or a protracted development in time. Likewise the typical scene is a public place, such as the front of a palace or a temple; a chorus would be out of place in a private chamber and cannot take part in intimate drama. It was not simply a passion for the universal that made Greek tragedy a symbolic drama, enacted on a symbolic stage.

Indirectly, the choral origins of the drama influenced it by shaping the Greek theater. This was a huge outdoor theater, built around a circular dancing-place called the "orchestra," and designed to accommodate the bulk of the town's citizenry. In such theaters the grand style was natural, as was the broad style in comedy; actors could not convey nuances of thought or feeling by subtle changes in expression or modulations in tone. They wore masks that identified them to the spectators in the farthest rows. The masks in turn strengthened the original tendency of the playwrights to portray types rather than individuals, elemental rather than complex or mixed emotions. The actors also wore formal costumes, including headdresses and high-soled buskins, which enabled them to maintain a dignified appearance and not be dwarfed by the distances; and this costume helps to explain why no violent action is represented in Greek tragedy, murders or suicides almost always taking place offstage. The many gory battle scenes in the *Iliad*, as well as the routine exhibit of the mutilated corpses in the tragedies, suggest that it was not merely a refined artistic sense that prohibited such action on the stage. Actors so elaborately arrayed could not easily manage a graceful fall, much less a physical combat.

All this formality helped to keep Greek tragedy on an ideal plane, and has therefore been sufficiently admired. The difficulties it raises have generally been slighted. While it was directly due to the religious origins of tragedy, it also reflects the conservatism that led the Greeks to stick for centuries to the simple form of the temple. Classicists declare that once they had hit upon the ideal form in any genre, they rightly adhered to it; yet in drama the formalism involved unreasoned conventions that may strike us as mechanical, and at least are not clearly the product of an unerring artistic sense. We may weary of the stock Messenger who regularly narrates the catastrophe. We may be jarred by the *stichomythia,* or line-for-line questions and answers, that recur in the most dramatic situations. We may wonder why to the end the dramatists restricted themselves to three actors, even when they had relatively large casts and sometimes were plainly embarrassed by the restriction.[1] On the other hand, the formality of Greek

---

[1] Each actor assumed various roles; the convention required only that there be no more than three speaking parts in any given scene, apart

tragedy may obscure its actual variety—the continuous innovation long before Euripides took the stage. Admirers of the classical ideal of propriety have seldom done justice to the bold originality of Æschylus and Sophocles.

Similarly with the themes of Greek tragedy. In keeping with its choral origins and its performance at a religious festival, its subject matter was characteristically taken from the traditional myths and legends. As a communal possession, these gave the dramatist more advantages than modern playgoers may realize. He was incidentally relieved of some of the tedious business of exposition and could swiftly achieve ironic effects, since from the outset the audience knew the outcome.[2] Not having to invent new plots, he could concentrate on the more stimulating challenge of giving new meanings to old stories that already had a vital meaning for his audience. (Hence Goethe remarked in his old age that if he were to begin his life as an artist over again, he would never deal with a new story.) Above all, he had the advantage of esthetic distance and perspective. It is always said that the Greek

from the Chorus. Its arbitrariness is illustrated by *Œdipus at Colonus*, the last of the extant tragedies. Ismene enters the play with some fanfare because she has long been separated from her father and sister, but she is presently forced to make an exit, ostensibly to perform some rite, actually to make way for Theseus. When she returns she remains mute during a dramatic scene between her father, brother, and sister; the only reason for her unnatural silence is that she would be a fourth actor. (At the end of the play she speaks up again.) Theseus comes and goes for similar reasons. A further awkwardness is that his part had to be played by all three actors at different times. It may be that the dramatists continued to observe this convention for a purely practical reason—a limited supply of trained actors.

[2] Aristotle has caused some trouble by his casual remark that even the known stories were known only to a few. Perhaps this was true by his own time; though if so, the level of Athenian culture must have been considerably lower than it is reputed to have been. But it is hard to believe that the audience in the classical period was unacquainted with stories that the playwrights were constantly retelling. Comic writers lamented that they alone had to invent everything. "The writer of tragedy is a lucky fellow!" we read in a fragment of Antiphanes. "The audience always know the plot as soon as his play begins. All the poet has to do is to give a jog to their memories. He just says 'Œdipus'; they know all the rest." Sophocles obviously counted on their foreknowledge, for the famous irony of his *Œdipus Rex* depends on it.

tragic poets dealt directly with the permanent, universal problems of man's life instead of the immediate social problems, the confusions and distractions of their own time.

Yet the old stories had a rather different meaning then than they have for the contemporary critics who rhapsodize over the imaginative, symbolic, ideal value of Myth. For the Greeks they were not poetry but history, the records of national heroes; Agamemnon and Œdipus were actual kings who had ruled Greek cities. While Greek drama remains essentially different from the naturalistic, sociological drama of modern times, it was more realistic than the conventional accounts of it suggest. The poets incidentally felt free to introduce a homely realism in their minor characters, or even a measure of humor—for example, the simple guard in *Antigone* who laments that he has to be the one to bear the bad news to the king. Apart from a few tragedies in which they did treat of contemporary events, such as *The Persians* of Æschylus and *The Capture of Miletus* of Phrynicus, they sometimes referred to such events, often went out of their way to glorify Athens, and as often celebrated its political ideals. They were not actually aloof from the life of their times, concerned only with the eternal verities. Their very advantage over the playwrights of all other ages is that they were discharging a major public function, on a major public occasion. In reinterpreting the old stories, to make them "more philosophical than history," they drew upon contemporary philosophy. They found no magic in the myth per se—no timeless truth implicit in it. Æschylus and Euripides in particular *gave* the old stories radically new meanings, adapted to the vital concerns of their fellow Athenians. The traditional myths and legends were only the conventional means for expressing their own thought about the political, moral, and religious issues of fifth-century Athens.

Hence they raise a question about the development of tragedy that Aristotle did not take up, for understandable reasons. He merely outlined its internal development as an art form. He ignored the more provocative question of the underlying

social causes, the reasons why it developed as it did and then
ceased to develop—and why only in Greece, or indeed only
in Athens.[3] Even had Aristotle anticipated our historical interest in matters that he took for granted, he had only an inside
view of Greek culture, and could not see around it. Nor can
we give a positive, complete answer to such questions, despite
the advantage of our far more extensive historical knowledge.
The various factors that seem pertinent—economic, political,
religious, intellectual—cannot be reduced to an "ultimate"
cause, or even to single relations of cause and effect, action and
reaction. We have to deal with a complex of forces, a continuous interaction in which any major development, such as
political democracy, is both cause and effect of other major
developments. Nevertheless so strikingly unique a creation as
Greek tragedy calls for some effort at explanation. It was pre-
eminently a communal affair, once more, not a literary pastime
for an elite. We cannot understand it rightly or fully unless we
see it in relation to Greek culture as a whole, the social conditions it reflected and the social purposes it served. And we
can at least make out apparent relationships, some significant
conditions of cultural achievement. If we cannot wholly "explain" such achievement, we can hope to illumine it.

Assuming, then, that the ritual dramas were the main source
of the form of Greek tragedy, and the Homeric epics of its
content, several centuries elapsed before they coalesced in
this new genre different from both. During these centuries
important changes had come over Greek life. In general, the
Greeks had made a brilliant success. They had developed an
extensive trade and industry that enabled them to spread all
over the Mediterranean world, from western Europe to the

[3] Tragedy was not strictly confined to Athens, to be sure. Æschylus
himself produced tragedies in Sicilian cities, which had developed a
drama of their own, and the known tragedians included non-Athenians,
such as Ion of Chios. But Athens was the acknowledged center, and gave
birth to all the acknowledged masters. Although drama then spread over
the entire Greek world and remained popular for centuries, every city of
any account having its theater, none made any important contribution
to the art of tragedy or produced any writer of first rank.

Black Sea. At the opening of the fifth century the mainland Greeks had successfully met the most dangerous threat to their independence, throwing back the forces of the mighty Persian Empire at Marathon, and then again at Salamis and Platea. They were a people on the march, on all fronts. It is significant that they developed tragedy when at the peak of their vitality.

With this surge, the structure of Greek society had been radically altered. While the Homeric epics pictured an earlier age of kingship, they reflected a feudal aristocratic society. Homer gives hardly a hint of the ambitions of the rising merchant class, or of unrest among the common people; he successfully repressed whatever interest he might have had in the commoners. As the cities throve, however, political power had largely passed from his landed nobility to a wealthy middle class, which in turn had to meet increasing demands from the poorer classes. The "tyrants" arose, usually in the name of the popular cause; the tyrannies in effect served as a transition to democracy. Although the democracies might revert to oligarchy or tyranny, and generally were dominated by the wealthy, Greeks everywhere now regarded themselves as free men. They were citizens with recognized rights, subject to law but not subservient to arbitrary authority. The characteristic *polis*, or republican city-state, was essentially a free, "open" society.

Now, we must be wary of the attractive hypothesis that democracy was the primary cause of the creation of tragedy. Later literary history indicates that it is not even a necessary condition. Yet in Greece it was clearly an important factor. Pisistratus, who supported the popular cult of Dionysus and established the annual festival with its contest in tragedy, made it a folk festival; he was apparently seeking to weaken the hold of the conservative aristocracy on the religious and communal life of Athens. The poets proceeded to write to and for the entire citizenry. Like the Parthenon, drama was in effect the creation of the city, not a class. Or if, more strictly, it was the creation of great poets, these were manifestly stimulated by the free, full life Athens offered its citizens, and repeatedly expressed their pride in their city, their devotion to its ideals of justice and freedom. It is suggestive that the brilliant Ionian cities that had led the intellectual development of Hellas failed to produce any noteworthy tragic drama. They were less jealous of their freedom, more disposed to submit to the rule of tyrants or of the Persians.

Meanwhile Ionia had made its important contribution. Among the astonishing manifestations of the new kind of open society developed by the Greeks was the birth of philosophy in Miletus. Thales and his followers sought to explain the world in wholly natural, rational terms instead of supernatural, mythical ones. If their metaphysics still has a mythical air, the important thing was not the answers they gave—it was the questions they asked. It was the critical, inquiring spirit, which led to the birth of science too. For the first time in recorded history, thought had become free. *← Well, they killed socrates and most men didn't have freedom so who did?*

which *iosph* The early philosophers were not hostile to religion, at least openly. They simply left the gods out of their cosmological speculations. They thereby implied, however, a disbelief in the traditional mythology, and this became explicit in such thinkers as Xenophanes and Heraclitus. While Homer's Olympians remained the national gods, Greek religion was undergoing profound changes that also prepared the way for tragic drama. The cults of Dionysus and other mystery gods became increasingly popular. Thinkers were wrestling with the problem of evil, seeking to rationalize and moralize the gods; the inevitable difficulties of this humane enterprise bred a deal of skepticism. Less agreeable for the lovers of Greece are the signs of an increasing anxiety and dread—feelings from which Homer is almost entirely free.

Thus the gulf between the Olympian gods and man grew wider. The gods became more jealous, apt to punish as *hubris* any eminent achievement of man. Herodotus, among others, repeatedly observed that they destroyed famous men merely because of their fame, as if they begrudged man any glory of his own; and although he managed to remain cheerful, the Ionian poets often expressed bitterness and despair at the futility of man's purposes. Even as Zeus was made over into an agent of justice he became less humane, dispensing a pitiless justice without regard for the motives of the transgressors. Like Jehovah, he punished their children too, unto the third or fourth generation. This idea might be attributed to realism, since children do in fact suffer for the sins of the father, but it may also signify an irrational sense of guilt, engender a religion of fear. Other signs of anxiety include the appalling story of Œdipus: in Homer's version he does not become an outcast when his unconscious guilt is discovered, but continues to reign and at his death is buried with royal honors. Among ordinary people, E. R. Dodds points out, the rise of the professional *cathartai* testified to the widespread, tragic need of catharsis in the literal sense—a ritual purification, of *miasma* or irrational pollution.

The extent of this change may easily be exaggerated. No doubt the common people had always known such dreads, which the aristocratic Homer ignored just as he ignored the popular Dionysus; with the rise of democracy they rose to the surface. By now most scholars accept the thesis of Erwin Rohde that Homer's Olympianism was a temporary break in the continuity of Greek religion. In any event, the apparent anxiety of the classical period, which betrays some deep feeling of insecurity, is a reminder that Greek history in these centuries was by no means a simple success story. The growing freedom in action and thought naturally produced growing tensions. With the expansion of the Greek world came wars between the ambitious city-states, and violent class struggle within them. The democracy that resulted from this struggle did not put an end to it, but often brought more disorder. The increasing individualism meant increasing self-consciousness, conflict with ancient institutions, strife between individuals. The rise of philosophy meant more speculation in the further sense of a risky venture, a gamble with faith. It brought more clarity into thought, and more confusion; it introduced logic, and sharpened contradiction; it produced a new kind of conviction, and testified to a basic uncertainty. Altogether, the achievement of the Greeks was a much clearer, finer, fuller consciousness, of the world without and the world within. They paid the full costs of consciousness.

Tragedy, then, may be regarded as the product of both the growing freedom and the growing tension. In this view Athens was its natural birthplace. Rising to importance in the sixth century, Athens won Homeric glory by leading the resistance to the Persian Empire, and thereupon entered its period of extraordinary brilliance. On both the political and the intellectual fronts it became the leader in the Greek adventure in freedom. It was the most democratic of the greater cities, and a champion of the democratic cause. It was the acknowledged cultural center—in the words of Pericles, the "school of Hellas." At the same time, Athens experienced all the strains of the adventure in freedom, which may also be called *hubris*. It was still torn by class war, and suffered from the individualism it encouraged. Its imperial policy encroached on the freedom of other Greek cities and made it feared and hated. In the glorious Age of Pericles it became embroiled in the Peloponnesian War. And with the disastrous end of the war, Greek tragedy came to an end. Its history not only parallels but mirrors the rise and fall of Athens.

It mirrors obliquely, however—and it is always much more than a mere reflection. As we try to see the tragic poets in relation to their age we are immediately faced with the confusions of this great classical age of Greece: an age of ferment that was given to unclassical turbulence, and did everything to excess. We are faced with three great poets whose purposes were alike conditioned by the interests and expectations of their audience, but three poets manifestly unlike, who had quite different things to say to their fellow Athenians. As we turn to the authorities we discover that they disagree radically on the purposes of these poets. Ultimately we are faced with a problem still more difficult than they usually suggest—the problem of how to read and judge a Greek tragedy.

As I have said, we are bound to read it as a *Greek* tragedy, a product of a distant age, and also bound to lose more or less of the intended tragic effect unless we know something about the age. "Intention" has become another horrid word in literary criticism, to be sure, implying the "intentional fallacy." Strictly we have no way of knowing what went on in the artist's mind, and no need of asking, or even taking his own word for it, if his work speaks clearly for itself. Yet whenever we are puzzled—as we often are, and it would seem ought to be much more often—we naturally ask what the artist was trying to do. And here the complications begin. To understand his purposes fully we must see him in relation to his age, but we must also realize why we are often misled in this effort, in spite or even because of all our impressive historical research; why at best we can never hope to have certain or complete success; and why, even if we could, we would still not have done complete justice to the work or to ourselves.

Let us consider, for example, the word "piety," which constantly recurs in discussion of Greek tragedy. Æschylus and Sophocles are celebrated for their piety, Euripides for his impiety. We can readily understand how Euripides got his reputation. We may be troubled, however, by the report that Æschylus was also charged with impiety, on the grounds of having revealed the secret of the mysteries of Demeter, and that the audience in the theater might have killed him had he not clung to the altar of Dionysus. Just what did piety mean to a fifth-century Athenian?

It is not easy to say. The plainest thing about Greek piety is that it involved attitudes and beliefs strange or incomprehensible to a pious Christian. It did not require "faith" in our sense, much less a love of the gods. It did require ritual attentions, a show of respect. At the same time, it permitted what seems like gross irreverence. The stanchly conservative Aristophanes, who attacked Euripides and Socrates for corrupting the youth, could have Dionysus beaten up in a comedy performed in his own theater, to the applause of his own worshippers. And the immense popularity of Dionysus points to a further complication. As a dying god, he was essentially different in nature from the Olympian gods of Homer; yet the Greeks respected both Dionysus and the Olympians. We must wonder, then, just what they literally believed about these logically incompatible gods, or how seriously they took their beliefs—and we do not really know. Some scholars say that by the time of Euripides ordinary Athenians were obviously skeptical; but presently these Athenians voted to put Socrates to death for his impiety.

In any case, the tragic poets cannot be pinned down to the conventional thought of the age, whatever that was. They plainly differed in their thought, and in an age of intellectual ferment we should naturally expect them to be in advance of popular belief. As naturally, we should look to their plays to find out what they did believe. But here we run into another difficulty, aside from the disagreements among their interpreters. While we hear a great deal about the high religious seriousness of Greek tragedy, we cannot take its religious meanings so seriously as its authors did—cannot, indeed, actually share all their thought and feeling about the gods. With our historical knowledge we can now better understand these gods, the mongrel origins and subsequent intermarriages that explain their multiple personalities and often ungodly behavior; but we cannot know them intimately. They must always look stranger to us than they did to poets for whom they were somehow living personalities, single and whole. The effort to read sympathetically may make us only more uncertain what attitude we are expected to adopt toward them—toward the Apollo of *Eumenides*, for instance, or the Athena of *Ajax*.

Nor is the difficulty here merely a matter of moral judgment, or the considerations of "truth," which some critics would exclude from literary criticism anyway. The dramatic, esthetic values of Greek tragedy do not come through to us intact either, even apart from the loss in translation. Critics are forever praising its clarity and symmetry, and above all its severe economy: every line has its function, not a scene can be cut. Nevertheless many lines have for us a diminished or doubtful value; the frequent passages about mythological geography and genealogy are now chiefly of historical interest. Entire scenes that were evidently crucial for the Greeks may seem anti-climactic to us. Worse, we may be uncertain of the main theme or point of the play; or if we do feel certain, we still have to reckon with the commentators who have found quite different themes. There are surprisingly few Greek tragedies about which there is anything like a general agreement upon the dramatist's purpose—the unifying principle that presumably gives the drama the clarity, symmetry, and economy that everybody praises.

Lastly, we cannot conclude that the ideal reader would suspend all his own interests and beliefs and consider the drama solely in its own terms, view it as the Greeks did. If we could actually do this, we might piously succeed in confining the significance of the drama, reducing its value, and betraying our own vital concerns. We should sacrifice our advantage in the many generations that help to create a masterpiece, by interpretations that may distort it but often illumine or enrich it, whether or not they coincide with what the poet intended or what his age saw. In the final judgment, it is never enough to understand the artistic conventions and expectations of an age. To give an obvious example, we can readily explain the crude horrors in Elizabethan tragedy by the tastes of its audience; yet we still regard them as crude, and deplore them. Greek tragedy was much more disciplined, by a much finer taste; so we should be more hesitant about finding fault with it. Nevertheless we may still question Greek thought and taste, and at least must recognize that they are not always to our taste. Our judgments should be sympathetic and humane, in the awareness that there are no absolute, fixed standards on which men can agree, and that we too are creatures of our time and place.

We should also be honest, loyal to our actual experience in art, and should admit our right to our own living concerns.

On this basis we can still find plenty of enduring interest and value in Greek tragedy. I have been somewhat exaggerating, of course, the difficulties in reading it. The trained reader manages to read it as both ancient and living work; it remains meaningful however it is interpreted; and we may find as wide disagreement upon the basic meanings and purposes of some modern poets. But the fact remains that we are not dealing with an art of perfect clarity and classic simplicity. I have exaggerated the difficulties at the outset in the hope of finally doing more justice to both the Greek poets and ourselves.

2. ÆSCHYLUS, THE PIONEER

The art of Æschylus may be misjudged because of the familiar curve in the history of art. The great styles appear to swing through a cycle of growth, fulfillment, decay, and exhaustion or death. Convention therefore has it that the art of the early phases is fresh and vigorous but relatively crude and immature, like the Greek Archaic or the Romanesque; the art of the later phases is naturally "decadent," like the Hellenistic or the Baroque. Accordingly the drama of Æschylus is often described as primitive or archaic. His genius is patronized by citing the remark of Sophocles, that he did the right thing without knowing why. And even the obvious grandeur of Æschylus has contributed to this idea of his art. The conventional picture of him represents him as a high-minded Athenian of the old school, as statuesque as his characters. He was a patriot and soldier, devoted to the heroic ideal that he had exemplified on the battlefield of Marathon; he was above all a deeply religious man, the most Hebraic of the poets. It might seem unbecoming such a man to write plays—and indeed some of his admirers declare that he was not really a playwright, but a religious poet and prophet. When they stoop to consider his dramatic art they stress its austerity and elevation, his own refusal to stoop to his audience, or to the passing show of things.

If in this view Æschylus looks more like a monolith than a man, his contemporaries apparently took much the same view. Upon his death they honored him almost as a god; other tragic poets used to offer sacrifices at his tomb. Already he was a classic. And, unhappily, he soon met the fate of classics today, in being admired much more than he was read. Aristophanes indicates that ordinary Greeks considered him a master of the grand style, and therefore old-fashioned, high-flown, and long-winded. Within a century he was played hardly at all. Aristotle barely mentioned him, saying nothing about his characteristic form, the trilogy, or his magnificent use of the Chorus. He was entombed for good. And so it may be an act of piety to begin by forgetting for a while the real grandeur of the man and his work, and trying to take an easy look at a life-sized Athenian of the early fifth century who did, after all, compete for a prize by writing plays, including satyr plays, and who in his day was popular enough to win the prize thirteen times.

His success is not surprising. Poet and prophet, Æschylus was also an actor, a director, a choreographer, a designer of masks and costumes—an all-around man of the theater, who evidently did know what he was doing in it. Thomas Mann said that the artist is never an absolutely serious man because "effects and enjoyment are his stock-in-trade." Effects need not entail a sacrifice of integrity; but in any case Æschylus was never so austere as to scorn them.

In *The Suppliants* he offered the spectacle of a chorus of fifty maidens in exotic costumes, who at the climax fly in panic from another chorus of fifty black slaves. In *The Persians* he summoned the first known ghost to appear in a Western theater. In *Seven Against Thebes* he created an exceptionally vivid, realistic picture of a besieged city, with a chorus of terrified women rushing to altars, screaming, apparently to the accompaniment of offstage sounds of battle. In *Prometheus Bound* he opened his play by having a gigantic figure nailed to a cliff, and later provided the daring contrast of a comic character: the pompous Ocean, a busybody and time-server who comes riding in on a four-footed bird, pleased at the thought of offering advice to Prometheus, and who, when his advice is rejected, rides off still happier in the thought that he will not have to risk getting into trouble with the awful Zeus. And *Eumenides*, the last play of Æschylus, was his most spectacular. His Chorus of Furies was a frightening innovation— dreadful creatures swirling in black robes, with bloody faces and snaky locks. Then the Furies made amends by contributing to the gorgeous, stirring spectacle at the end. The goddess Athena has persuaded them to give up their hate and make their home in her city; she now calls upon the women of Athens to join the processional, in crimson robes; and all file out, carrying blazing torches, singing a hymn to the glory of Athens. We may safely assume that Æschylus composed this scene in genuine exaltation of spirit, not as a means of currying popular favor and winning the prize. We might nevertheless be reminded of "God Bless America."

More likely we would not be. One reason why Æschylus seems to many readers remote in his grandeur is that he was so close to the life of his own times. *Eumenides* cannot possibly have for us the same impact that it had for his fellow Athenians; for if we can imagine how thrilled they were by this glorification of their city, the mere effort to do so indicates that we are not so thrilled ourselves. But the main point remains that Æschylus was a bold pioneer. At his grandest he was an enterprising, resourceful playwright who not only knew what he was doing but learned to do new things, and did some things better than Sophocles and Euripides.

What he made of the Chorus, for example, may be appreciated by contrasting his early play *The Suppliants* with *Agamemnon*. In the former the Chorus is still the main actor; it contributes splendid but relatively obvious effects that doubtless owed much to ancient tradition. In *Agamemnon* a chorus of unspectacular old men is a magnificent orchestral instrument, deepening, amplifying, and intensifying the drama as

no chorus in Sophocles or Euripides does. In expressing their
forebodings, the old men establish the dark, haunted atmosphere of the play, build up the background of violence from
which the tragedy is to come. In expressing their hopes that
"good win out in the end," they sound the note of irony that
recurs until the preordained end, of an action from which no
good can come. In expressing their faith that the gods are just
and that wisdom comes only through suffering, they act as
spokesmen for Æschylus, telling the spectator what he should
think. In expressing their simple pity or terror as the dreadful
action unfolds, they speak as eloquently for the spectator, of
what meanwhile he really feels. They convey all this more
subtly as well as more resonantly than a reader can gather
from the best translation.[4] And at the same time the Chorus
constitutes a real actor in the drama, not a mere commentator
on it, and is handled realistically. As the Elders of Argos, these
men are naturally concerned about the fate of their king, and
can speak with the wisdom of age; but they are also very human old men, with the frailty of age. While they pity the unhappy Cassandra, they refuse to believe her plain statement
that Agamemnon is to die, if only because they are afraid to
believe it. When he is murdered they break up into a confused, distracted group that does nothing because each one
suggests a different thing to do.

Æschylus made his major technical contribution to the development of Greek tragedy by adding a second actor. We
may get an insight into this development from *The Suppliants*,
in which he made little use of the second actor, and which
accordingly gives some idea of what a one-actor play might
have been like. There is little possibility of dramatic action
in such a play. The most apparent tragic possibility is a solitary hero on the spot, alone with his fate; here the Chorus puts
the King of Argos in an impossible situation, where he must

[4] Professor Kitto points out that the changing rhythms of the choral
odes in the original give some suggestion of the choreographic effects
designed by Æschylus. A slow iambic measure, for instance, always ac-
companies the idea of punishment of *hubris*, serving as a leitmotiv.

make his choice in the realization that "there is no issue free from disaster." Through the addition of another actor, the hero may be placed in a variety of situations, offered more choices, set off or tested by other characters—as was Prometheus. And in the *Oresteia* (the trilogy composed of *Agamemnon, The Libation Bearers,* and *Eumenides*) Æschylus made some use of the third actor whom Sophocles had introduced by this time, and who made possible still more variety, conflict, and drama as we know it.

Yet Æschylus did not carry this development so far as he might have. We are now faced with the "archaic" aspect of his drama, the reasons why he soon seemed old-fashioned to the Greeks themselves. He failed to exploit some of the most obvious possibilities opened up by his second actor—for example, a conflict between two major characters. Although such a conflict occurs in *Seven Against Thebes,* where the brothers Eteocles and Polyneices are fighting over their native city, he never introduces Polyneices, neglecting the opportunity for a climactic scene between the brothers. Likewise Zeus, the antagonist of Prometheus, never appears in *Prometheus Bound.* Here the drama takes place within the mind of Prometheus, which remains essentially unchanged; the other characters help to expose his mind but scarcely affect his situation. And in this aspect the *Oresteia* chiefly illustrates the surprisingly rich possibilities of the two-actor play, which Æschylus hitherto had seemingly been unaware of or indifferent to. Although a third actor is often present, he seldom says anything and has little effect on the two characters who are carrying the scene. There is none of the ironic byplay or dramatic interplay that Sophocles achieved through him.

Although this limited technique may be attributed to austerity, the brasher commentators have suggested a natural and perhaps more illuminating explanation. It took time to learn how to make use of a second actor, keep a play moving by dialogue, and more time to learn to manage the more varied, complicated situations created by the presence of a third actor. So considered, the often admired "dramatic silences" of Æschylus may take on an added significance. Some are clearly dramatic—for instance, the long silence of Cassandra in *Agamemnon*—and seemingly were deliberate. In Aristophanes' *The Frogs*, Euripides explains that Æschylus did this kind of thing "to lead you on and keep you in suspense" while his play was getting over. Other silences are undramatic or even awkward, and suggest that Æschylus simply did not know what to do with the extra actor. Thus Pylades, the traditional companion of Orestes, is present during most of *The Libation Bearers* but speaks only once, when Orestes suddenly asks and instantly accepts his advice. With important characters the economy of Æschylus could be as arbitrary. Electra, a major character in the first half of *The Libation Bearers*, disappears in the middle and is never heard of again. Orestes in turn fades into the background of *Eumenides* when the gods come on to settle his fate, and does not participate in the grand finale. In general, it may be fairer to Æschylus to regard him as a pathfinder in a difficult new art form, not as a born playwright whose Greek artistic sense was equal to every problem.

Nevertheless the path he chose was for him a natural one. Ultimately, his choice appears to have been due not so much to technical incompetence, or unawareness of other possibilities, as to his vision of life. What he saw most clearly in man's life was the will of the gods. It worked logically, through the violent deeds or misdeeds of men, but always irresistibly; the outcome of the drama was fated and inescapable. Although Æschylus could create great characters, such as Clytemnestra, he was typically not much interested in the study of character, the workings of mind, the conflicts within or between characters, or any other such complications, with their possibilities of uncertainty and surprise; so he had no real use for a third actor. His vision was best realized by the solitary hero—the King of Argos, Eteocles, Prometheus, Orestes—isolated by his destiny. Similarly Æschylus had little interest in plot, as it is ordinarily conceived. His interest was in a doom—what necessarily happened, not so much in just how it happened, still less in any possibility that it might have happened otherwise. The movement in his plays is the fulfillment of the fate indicated at the outset; the growing intensity or suspense is the deepening sense of this inexorable fate.

Æschylean drama accordingly poses a problem for those concerned with dramatic form. E. F. Watling calls it essentially narrative rather than drama, and declares that his introduction of the second actor was not actually a significant advance from the epic, which also had dialogue. Richmond Lattimore describes it more handsomely as "lyric tragedy," an effort to transcend the limitations of drama even before these limitations had become established, as the *Oresteia*, with its immense background, did transcend them on a scale never achieved before or since. All critics, I assume, will grant the monumental, epic quality of Æschylean drama. Almost all will grant its intensity, the excitement it can stir in spite of its slow movement. Call it narrative, lyrical, or epical, it will seem much more obviously dramatic when performed. (An Italian company I once saw managed to make a rousing melodrama of *Agamemnon* by playing it as if it were a Verdi opera.) But dispute on this matter is unprofitable. The drama of Æschylus is unique; it did not become a model in his own time, and has not since. The future belonged to the different kind of drama developed by Sophocles and Euripides.

For my purposes, the chief issues are raised by his vision of life. The most important contribution of Æschylus to Greek tragedy finally amounts to the old-fashioned idea of high seriousness. He was concerned with great ideas, and he established the tradition that made drama the vehicle for such ideas. All we know of the early dithyrambs indicates that their authors had much more modest purposes. So did the Ionian lyric poets, who had become polished professionals addressing a limited audience, entertaining the courts of their patrons. Æschylus linked tragedy with the older tradition of the Homeric epic. In the words of Werner Jaeger, he restored to poetry its "noble function as a guide and inspiration of life." Or since contemporary critics are likely to bridle at such terms, we may translate them into the more fashionable terms of the uses of Myth. The Ionian poets had used the traditional myths chiefly for decorative purposes, much like the vase-painters. Æschylus now used them to express his deepest thought and loftiest imagining, filling the old forms with a rich new content.

But it is a somewhat troublesome content. While the apparent fatalism of Æschylus is in the Homeric tradition, his world is in some respects more sinister than Homer's. He had a stronger conviction of Necessity—the sense of a ruling order that led Whitehead to trace to Greek tragedy the basic scientific assumption of an order of nature. ("The laws of physics are the decrees of fate.") Offhand, man seems more impotent in his world, or at least more conscious of his impotence; the gods are more implacable, punishing not only evildoers but their descendants. Such fatalism may blight the tragic spirit, in particular the essential belief in the dignity and the freedom of man. The drama of Æschylus unquestionably stirs more terror than pity. He has been cited as a prime example of the anxiety and dread to which many Greeks fell prey. He has been charged with reviving the ancient dæmons, leading the Greeks away from the clear daylight of Homer back into the dark, irrational world from which Homer had miraculously freed them.

The answer to this charge is easy: Æschylus was trying to lead the Greeks through and out of the ancient evil. But not so easy is a question raised by this laudable effort. Unlike Homer, he finally insists on the justice of the gods. The Chorus in *Agamemnon* repeatedly affirms what the whole action demonstrates, that tragedy is due to man's own evil deeds; it adds that no evil will come to the righteous and just man. Here is the religious prophet in Æschylus, the reason why he is called the most Hebraic of the Greek poets. And here is a spirit that seems alien to the tragic spirit. It may represent a loftier religious faith than Homer's, but in this faith he usually gave his trilogies happy endings. A sublime expression of it is the ending of the *Oresteia*, with its complete reconciliation of the contending powers, in an ideal of perfect justice and a vision of everlasting order and peace—and, one might add, at the furthest remove from tragedy. So all but the most devout may wonder. Is this ending wholly right and convincing? Is Æschylus strictly a *tragic* poet?

At least *Eumenides* is a tragedy only in the broadest sense of a "serious action." While the more conventional of his admirers dwell on the loftiness of his religious sense rather than the depth of his tragic sense, others usually beg this issue. Thus Kitto defends *Eumenides* by asserting that its chief interest is "moral and intellectual rather than tragic." Just so: the interest is no longer tragic. Or J. A. K. Thomson, who calls the *Oresteia* perhaps the greatest of all expressions of tragic irony, excuses the complete absence of irony at the end by saying that it would obviously be out of place here. So it would—given the absence of tragic intention. Still, one might expect a master of tragic irony to qualify his happy ending by some suggestion that the Furies were not wholly tamed, and never would be; to sing God bless Athens but God help her too, since she had much more to learn, through more suffering. Actually, Æschylus lacked the ironic temper, with its measure of skepticism and reserve. Because of his conviction of an inexorable Necessity he could make effective use of dramatic irony, as he does when Agamemnon proudly treads a royal purple carpet to his palace, and his death; but this illustrates only the familiar idea that pride goeth before a fall, and is not a profoundly "tragic" irony. Æschylus was too exalted to dwell on the ineradicable sources of such irony.

For me, at least, *Eumenides* is weakened by the absence of ironic undertones. On "moral and intellectual" grounds its ending is noble, and a little naïve. On esthetic grounds, the tragic issue is resolved too abruptly and too completely. "I think you will have your way with me," the Furies tell Athena. "My hate is going"—and a moment later it is gone, for good. One who has gone through the terrible drama of *Agamemnon* has reason to be unconvinced.

Yet the fact remains that Æschylus wrote *Agamemnon*. By this drama he earned his triumphant ending, as Beethoven earned the Hymn to Joy that concludes his Ninth Symphony. The traditional admiration of his loftiness has tended to obscure the soundest reasons for regarding him as a great tragic poet—the qualities that make him more akin to Homer and Sophocles than to the Hebrew prophets.

In the first place, this Athenian of the old school was not a pious conservative. As a religious thinker Æschylus was bold, independent, even heretical. "Far from others I hold my mind," declares the Chorus in *Agamemnon* when it affirms its belief that evil sprang solely from men, not the gods. The articles of conventional Greek piety included no such belief. Still bolder is a related theory of religious evolution. In *Prometheus Bound* Zeus is presented as a tyrant, ruling without law, harsh "like upstarts always," and like them jealous of his power, indifferent to the miseries of poor mortals. Although the rest of the trilogy is lost, fragments indicate that the conclusion was a reconciliation vindicating the prophecy of Prometheus: after thousands of years Zeus would finally learn to be just and merciful. In the *Oresteia* this theme is explicit. The Furies represent the old-time religion, rooted in fear, preaching the harsh morality of an eye for an eye and a tooth for a tooth; "gloomy children of the night," they protest bitterly against the new-fangled ideas of the young gods. The triumphant Athena represents the civilized ideals of these new gods, "divinities that face the sun." This concept may not be wholly satisfying either to theologians or to simple worshippers, since it declares that the gods had once been pretty bad, and suggests that they may have still more to learn; they are limited, not perfect gods. But at least Æschylus appears to have realized the historic truths that old gods are never actually killed, that new religious ideas always supplement rather than supersede the old, and that the religious life of man is a continuous quest. In the *Oresteia* his own quest had arrived at the conception of Zeus, the supreme god, who sends his son and daughter to announce to man a loftier ideal of justice.

Or possibly he is not Zeus. *Prometheus Bound* mentions the tradition that Zeus was eventually to be overthrown, just as he had overthrown the older Titans, and the Chorus in *Agamemnon* suggests that he may be only a symbol of the new God that Æschylus has conceived or is trying to conceive:

> Zeus: whatever he may be, if this name
> pleases him in invocation,
> thus I call upon him.

We can never be certain just how Æschylus conceived his gods. We can be certain only that he thought and felt rather differently from us, and that if our own ideas are vague and various, he entertained some that are alien to almost all of us. Among the blessings that Prometheus brought to men he stresses the arts of divination, from the flight of birds to the fire omens. In *Eumenides* we may be disturbed by Apollo, the patron of Orestes, who in his arguments with the Furies indulges in quibbles, falls into plain inconsistencies, and chiefly exchanges insults and threats. Among his curious arguments is the assertion that the father alone is a real parent—the mother is only a "nurse of the newly planted seed." Possibly Æschylus intended him as a kind of transitional figure, since it is Athena who settles the issue; yet he speaks as "the revealer of Zeus" and has been described as the representative of "Enlightened Religious Conscience." His position in the new order is hardly clear. And though Athena here is the symbol of reasonableness, her stated reason for taking the side of Orestes is neither justice nor compassion but partiality: she says that she is always for the male side, since she herself had had no mother. We may understand the force this argument had for Athenian males;

but as we hope to understand the religious thought of Æschylus we had better realize that we are not dealing with transcendent, timeless, purely spiritual concepts.[5]

For the student of tragedy, however, the important thing is that the faith of Æschylus is never simple or easy. It sprang from a deep sense of the terror of human destiny, which his drama still incorporates. He surpasses both Sophocles and Euripides in the creation of tragic atmosphere. While he stresses the idea that men learn by suffering, he shows that they learn *only* by suffering—and their travail has been prolonged because the gods too had to learn. If the *Oresteia* concludes with a vision of civility, justice, and peace, the rest of his plays all testify that this is a vision, a hard-won hope for the future rather than a sublime certitude. Meanwhile man had to endure a painful lot under gods who had not yet learned their lesson, or from whom "grace comes somehow violent." In the words of Cassandra, as she goes to her death through no fault of her own,

> Alas, poor men, their destiny. When all goes well
> a shadow will overthrow it. If it be unkind
> one stroke of a wet sponge wipes all the picture out;
> and that is far the most unhappy thing of all.

Nor does Æschylus explain why life should be so. He never pretended to the kind of intimacy with deity that prophets usually claim.

The tragic quality of his vision has been obscured by the traditional obsession with the Aristotelian principle of the tragic flaw. The invariable theme of Æschylus, commentators still say, is the punishment of *hubris*. This is plainly the theme of *The Persians*. It may also be found in *Seven Against Thebes*, which offers the pious no other comfort: as the conclusion of a trilogy, this tragedy indicates that an Æschylean cycle did

[5] Students of Greek religion must regret the loss of a number of plays in which Æschylus dealt with Dionysiac themes, which were evidently among his favorites. One wonders how he pictured Dionysus, the dying god.

not invariably end in reconciliation. But the Aristotelian formula does not fit the rest of the plays. In *The Suppliants* the
King is faced with a tragic choice that is not of his making;
the apparent reason why there is "no issue free from disaster"
is a flaw in the whole scheme of things. As for *Prometheus
Bound*, it seems incredible that Shelley had to tell scholars
that the sympathies of Æschylus were with Prometheus, the
"high-souled child of Justice" and friend of man, rather than
with Zeus, who from first to last is represented as a brutal tyrant. None could condone the behavior of Zeus except readers
brought up in the belief that a God of love sentences his
enemies to an eternity of torture in hell. Although Prometheus
is no doubt too proud and defiant, and had to learn wisdom before the reconciliation that seemingly concluded the trilogy,
all the characters and scenes in this play are designed to display the grandeur of his unconquerable spirit, and to substanti-
ate his final utterance: "Behold me, I am wronged." He is the
clearest example of another major contribution of Æschylus
to tragedy—the type of the great tragic hero.

In the *Oresteia* the issues are more complex. Here Æschylus
is most plainly the moralist and prophet, most explicitly
preaching the justice of Zeus; yet right and wrong are not
plain or simple. Richmond Lattimore has pointed out the
thematic imagery that dominates and binds the first two plays:
the net, the web, the snare, the toils, the yoke—"necessity's
yoke." The most frequent image is the fatal net, in which
guilty and innocent alike may be entangled. Agamemnon himself is caught by no mere tragic flaw—he is nothing but *hubris*,
without shade or margin; it is a limitation of the tragedy that
he elicits no pity. (Perhaps Æschylus counted on his audience
to endow him with his legendary heroic qualities.) Cassandra,
on the other hand, is a wholly innocent victim, the most pathetic in Æschylus. And though Clytemnestra is unquestionably guilty of adultery and murder, she too is caught in the
tragic web of destiny, avenging the sacrifice of her daughter
Iphigenia, acting for the gods in punishing the king who had

destroyed the temples of Troy and defiled its women and children. She has some right when she tells the Chorus: "It is not I that have slain Agamemnon." Orestes has much more right when he tells her in turn: "It is not I that will kill you." Apollo has commanded him, on penalty of torment and death, to kill the murderers of his father. If there is little conflict in his mind—too little, a modern reader might say—he is doomed to torment, whatever he does. *Eumenides* may be considered a gigantic *deus ex machina* to right the wrong that was not his own doing.

As an apparent scapegoat, Orestes points to another archaic aspect of Æschylus. His tragedy was the closest in spirit to the ancient ritual dramas that seem to underlie Greek tragedy. Its ritualism appears incidentally in such strange scenes as the great litany when Orestes, Electra, and the Chorus invoke the spirit of the dead Agamemnon, but it appears more significantly in the very form of the trilogy. Although there is no evidence to support the hypothesis of Gilbert Murray that this form might originally have represented the birth, death, and resurrection of the god, it at least lends itself to a similar sequence, a kind of Hegelian pattern of thesis, antithesis, and synthesis. It makes possible a "complete action" on a vast scale, with an ample treatment of both the conflict and the resolution, the suffering and the regeneration. In this view the Promethean trilogy is a stupendous version of the suffering god, Christlike in his role if not in his spirit. The *Oresteia* is the *Divine Comedy* of Greece.

Yet the echoes of the ancient rituals finally accentuate the new meanings Æschylus gave these dramas, make more striking the distance he had gone in the evolution from ritual to rationality, and in the literary evolution from the divine to the heroic to the tragic-human. In his imaginative and spiritual freedom he was the son of Homer. He offered no magical salvation, of course, and no hope of immortal life. Neither did he offer Dionysian ecstasy, communion with the god. Like Homer, he assumed an impassable gulf between man and the immor-

tals. And he took his stand with man. At his most exalted,
Æschylus was not a God-intoxicated prophet, dedicated to
the love and service of God. What he exalted was the heroic
spirit, the civilized ideal, the Athenian state—the achievements
of man.

An explicit statement of his humanism is the theory of progress outlined in *Prometheus Bound*. Once upon a time, he says
through his hero, men were fools, living in caves, seeing and
knowing nothing. Then Prometheus had given them not only
fire and minerals but all the goods of civilization: mind, the
power to think; number, "that most excellent device," and
language; memory, "the mother of all arts"; the gift of healing;
and finally hope, that they might "cease to live with death in
sight." A more ironical poet might have noted the tragic contradiction, adding that these blessings are also the source of
the peculiar woes of man, who has been in trouble ever since
he began playing with fire. What concerns us at this point,
however, is the pæan to civilization, which Æschylus represents as the gift of a god who loved man. And if it was a god
who gave man these blessings, it was Æschylus who created
this god. The historic Prometheus was a primitive fire-god, descended from phallic dæmons, who in Athens served as a
patron of certain trades. Hesiod elevated his social status, but
represented him essentially as a cunning god who angered
Zeus by playing a trick on him, getting him to choose the
worst parts of the animals sacrificed to him while men got the
best. Æschylus created Prometheus in his own image, giving
him his passion for justice and his heroic willingness to dare
and endure all, making him for all time the symbol of the
rebel against tyranny.

The deep concern of Æschylus with the problem of justice
was ultimately more political than religious. George Thomson's
interpretation of him as a great democrat, whose art was inspired by the triumph of Athenian democracy over its internal
and external enemies, seems too narrow and forced, in the
usual manner of Marxist interpretations; but it unquestion-

ably points toward a major purpose of his art. He dramatized his new ideas about the gods in the public interest, writing as a patriotic citizen rather than a religious prophet. At this time, to be sure, Athenians did not sharply distinguish the political from the ethical and the religious; art and religion were united in the service of the *polis*. But if Æschylus himself made no such distinctions he prepared the way for them. In his free reinterpretation of the myths, and his challenge of traditional beliefs, he in effect secularized the myths, bending them to the purposes of the State more than to those of the gods. He began the process that with Euripides and the New Comedy ended in the separation of drama and religion. In his own last work, his political concerns became most prominent.

The final issue of *Eumenides* is not the nature of the gods, much less the laws about matricide, but the welfare of Athens. Significantly, Athena sets up a *human* jury to decide the issue between Apollo and the Furies, instead of referring it to Zeus. This jury represents the law court of the Areopagus, one of the most cherished of Athenian institutions. Athena herself, who finally casts the deciding vote, represents the ideals that Athenians had come to realize. Athens, she tells the Furies, is "the place of the just," accustomed to hearing both sides, devoted above all to rule by law. "No anarchy, no rule of a single master"—of a tyrant, such as Ægisthus had been, and Athens had known in the past. Now each citizen must stand upright, "take his ballot in his hand, think of his oath, and make his judgment." On behalf of Æschylus, Athena adds some advice for the future: her citizens must be watchful, guard against the corruption of money-making, and not "cast fear utterly" from their city. She sets them an example of reasonableness by her toleration of the Furies, or the mind of the past, even while proclaiming higher standards of justice, and in particular by her dependence on the "sacred" art of persuasion instead of force. Once persuaded to give up their hatred, the Furies add their prayer: "Civil War . . . shall not thunder in our city."

To repeat, all this is scarcely tragic—except in historical

retrospect. The Athenians did not heed the advice of Æschylus. Within a generation they were to plunge into the tragic folly of the Peloponnesian War, which at that they might well have won except for bitter internal strife; the final disaster was signaled by class war and followed by tyranny again. In this retrospect, however, the prayer of Æschylus looks nobler and less naïve. It was a prayer, and it reveals his awareness of the dangers that beset Athens from within. Implicit in it is the thought of Meredith:

> In Tragic life, God wot,
> No villain need be. Passions spin the plot.
> We are betrayed by what is false within.

Meanwhile his prayer, like his loftier conceptions of civic and divine justice, sprang from the main inspiration of his work as a whole. This was the secular achievement of Athens: the humane, civilized, democratic ideals it had come to conceive without benefit of clergy or revelations from on high. It was Æschylus who educated Zeus, not Zeus who inspired Æschylus.

In short, the "most Hebraic" of the Athenian poets was still more Athenian. The possibility that his *Prometheus Bound* inspired the Book of Job makes sharper the fundamental difference between them. Prometheus is an out-and-out rebel against arbitrary authority who asserts a principle of justice by human standards; the indicated ending of his drama is a reconciliation with a Zeus who accepts this principle. The ending of Job is an unconditional surrender to a thundering Voice that says nothing of justice. If the great prophets of Israel did in fact educate Jehovah, they never thought of him as perfectible, or of themselves as anything but his servants. The spirit of Æschylus was prouder, and worldlier. The last word about this exalted religious poet and prophet might well be that which Greek tradition has it he wrote for himself. On his epitaph he spoke only of his valor at the battle of Marathon.

3. SOPHOCLES

The traditional view of Sophocles is again one to induce an
awed hush, and some suspicion. The ancients called him "the
most god-fearing of mankind," and the most serene and blessed
in his life. For later ages he became the classical example of
sophrosyne, the virtue of self-restraint. He is also considered
the supreme artist of Greek tragedy, representing the apex of
its development. "When a critic can improve a play of Sophocles," writes Kitto, "he may be sure that he is only giving it
a turn that Sophocles had already rejected." In the last century the admiration of his artistry was intensified by the discovery of Sophoclean irony, which gave currency to the terms
"dramatic" or "tragic" irony, and the "irony of fate." Nevertheless classicists continued to stress his famous piety. They
are still pleased to cite Plato's story of the aged Sophocles,
who, so far from complaining about the ills of old age, rejoiced at his escape from the tyranny of sensual passion.

Their pleasure is rather odd. So far from proving the self-
restraint of Sophocles, the story suggests that he had long
been subject to this tyranny. A contemporary admirer, Ion of
Chios, in fact remarked upon his sensuality as well as his sophistication, and what little else is reported about his life indicates that the most god-fearing of Greeks was given to what
pious people would now consider immoderate, godless behavior. He is known to have had a mistress and several illegitimate children. He was also notoriously fond of handsome boys;
on a campaign Pericles is said to have rebuked him for attending to them instead of to his business as a general. But apart
from such evidence one might naturally doubt that so pious,
tranquil, perfectly tempered a poet as the Sophocles of tradition could have written so harrowing a tragedy as *Œdipus
Rex*. One might likewise doubt that an innovator, credited
with the addition of a third actor, could have instantly and
perfectly mastered a new technique, written plays incapable

of the slightest improvement after centuries of experiment in technique.

Sophocles remains a very great dramatist—to my mind, the greatest of the Greek tragic poets. By the same token, he was not a simple or conventional one. His plays are so varied, indeed, that it is difficult to speak of "Sophoclean tragedy." Those who speak of it most confidently give basically different interpretations of his plays, separately and as a whole. On the face of their testimony, the intentions of this master of clarity are much less clear than the intentions of either Æschylus or Euripides. So it is well to begin by stressing the troublesome questions raised by his vision and his artistry alike. We may better understand and appreciate him if we assume that he was mortal and fallible.

Taking the plays in the probable order of their composition, we immediately run into the puzzle of *Ajax.* It is essentially a two-actor play, with long speeches in the manner of Æschylus. Its most novel elements are "unclassical," including a gruesome scene of the crazed Ajax sitting among the bloody beasts he has slaughtered, and later his onstage suicide. The puzzle is that this suicide takes place long before the ending—in what would be Act III of a five-act play; what follows is a prolonged debate over his burial, which to modern readers seems like a letdown. It would appear that Sophocles regarded the death of his hero as less important than the final judgment of his character. It also appears, however, that even the ancients were puzzled by the structure of the play; for there is undeniably less tension after the suicide of Ajax, and the debate over his burial adds little or nothing to our knowledge of his character.

The judgment passed on him raises further difficulties. On its surface the play is a clear example of the punishment of *hubris:* the tragedy springs from the barbarous excesses of the hero when he is denied the weapons of Achilles. But it is Athena who directly brings on the tragedy by making him mad and then exposing him to ridicule. Both Ajax and his innocent wife complain about her "tyrannous" abuse of the power she boasts of. What are we supposed to think of this Athena? Paul Shorey said that any objection to her was "a sure sign of a parlor pink"; and ordinary Greeks brought up on Homer would surely not be surprised by her behavior. Nevertheless there is reason to believe that Sophocles considered it ignoble and cruel. He renders sympathetically the frightful sufferings of Ajax, in his realization that "I have no hope of mercy from the gods, I am not worthy to ask the help of man." He contrasts the harshness of Athena with the wisdom and humility of Odysseus, who argues for an honorable burial, appealing to the Greek principles of moderation and respect for the dead, in the name of "God's laws." And the final judgment of Ajax is clearly favorable. All the sympathetic characters are on his side, declaring with Odysseus that he was brave, noble, and good. Against him are only the insolent, vengeful Menelaus and Agamemnon—and Athena.

In *Antigone* the protagonist again disappears from the play well before the end; so it must be presumed that Sophocles was as much interested in the tragedy of the tyrannical Creon, who is responsible for the death of Antigone. At least he gives Creon more lines. Also he drags in his wife, to make a single appearance before killing herself, and then exhibits only her corpse and their son's—not the corpse of Antigone. But the trouble remains that Creon is much less interesting than Antigone to a modern reader. Even the Greeks must have thought him a pretty poor hero; he has nothing like the stature of Antigone or the other heroes of Sophocles and Æschylus, and little force or dignity in his last struggle—he simply caves in. It seems possible that Antigone ran away with the play because Sophocles too was really more interested in her. Or Professor Waldock may be right in his heretical suggestion that Sophocles ran out of material for the story of Antigone, and dwelt upon the tragedy of Creon for appearance's sake.

The chief issue that has concerned critics, however, is the

moral judgment to be passed on Antigone. The most popular of Sophocles' heroines, she has also been the most abused. Devotees of the tragic flaw have justified Providence and Aristotle by pointing out that she is self-willed, harsh to her gentle sister, arrogantly contemptuous of constituted authority. They are right at least in that the tragic issue here is not a simple conflict of right and wrong. Although Antigone appeals to a higher law when she buries her brother in defiance of Creon's decree, this brother was a proved traitor; Creon upholds the principle of obedience to law and duty to the State that was sacred to the Greeks. Still, one might expect her Christian judges to be the most impressed by her devotion to a higher duty, above the law—a significant innovation in Greek ethical thought; or if they justify her tragic fate they should also defend the execution of Socrates. And some contemporaries, who know more about women than Sophocles did, have been still harsher to Antigone. Edmund Wilson described her as a psychopath "fixated" on her brother.[6] Moses Hadas is almost as unsympathetic on the grounds that ordinary Greeks would have had more respect for Creon's position than for Antigone's. "Only the chivalry of a more romantic age," he writes, "could make one woman, and a woman who disregarded the rule of obedience appropriate to her sex, as important as the welfare of the state."

This comment illustrates the constant danger of the historical approach to the classics—the tendency not only to limit but to coarsen their meaning. One should expect a great poet to have finer perceptions, if not loftier ideals, than the man on the street. One should at least study his text before pinning it down to the conventional thought of his age. And Sophocles' text is distinctly sympathetic to Antigone. Creon is made a

[6] The only excuse for this fantastic misreading of Sophocles' text is another incidental puzzle—the grotesque argument of Antigone that she would make the sacrifice she did only for a brother, not a husband or a son, since the latter are replaceable. This passage seems so unworthy of her and her author that some translators omit it as spurious. But the same argument is found in a story told by Herodotus; so for some reason it may have impressed Sophocles.

tyrant who identifies the law with his own will, asserting the principle—obnoxious especially to Athenians—that "the State is the King." By contrast, the pride of Antigone is noble and selfless. If she should have been gentler to her sister and more respectful to Creon, she could not have avoided death except by sacrificing her principles. She expresses the feeling of most unindoctrinated readers as she goes to her tomb, the only bridal chamber she will know: "And yet, as men's hearts know, I have done no wrong, I have not sinned before God." As for the gods, they seem to vindicate her by punishing Creon, but their justice is somewhat tardy and still uneven or unclear. The others who die in the play are the innocent wife and son of Creon. While Antigone chooses her death, both she and the Chorus remind us that she is ultimately a victim of the curse upon the house of Œdipus, decreed by the gods in the dark old days before they had been reformed by Æschylus.

Much more perplexing is *Women of Trachis*. The question of what this play is about is confused even by its title, which comes from its Chorus—the least important chorus in Sophocles. The first half of the play is dominated by Deianeira, the wife of Heracles and the unwitting cause of his tragic death; the last half, after her suicide, is all Heracles, who then enters for the first time. Apparently the play belongs to Heracles, since he is the sole concern of Deianeira and his death agony concludes the play. The cause of his agony is a captive woman for whom he had developed a passion; although his wife did not blame him she sent him a philter to recapture his love, not knowing that it was a deadly poison. Hence a moralist might draw from the tragedy the lesson that men should not have concubines. No Greek audience, however, would ever see in this sufficient reason for the hideous sufferings of Heracles, nor does anybody in the play suggest such an idea. What, then, is the point of the play?

To a modern reader Heracles is a repulsive hero, quite apart from his infidelities. He dashes out the brains of the innocent herald who brought him the love-charm; he expresses no feeling whatever when he hears that his wife has killed herself because of her tragic error; he makes his appalled son swear to marry his concubine—he seems a monster of egoism. Gilbert Murray therefore concluded that the purpose of Sophocles was to expose the greatest of Greek heroes as a ruffian and brute. If so, he was assuming the impious role of Euripides as a debunker. But then he wrought his play strangely. The plot is an arbitrary affair, defying Aristotelian precepts of logic and probability; its tragic outcome is directly due to black magic. As for character, Heracles remains a great hero to his wife, his son, and the Chorus; and Sophocles gives no suggestion that they are stupid or insensitive. He does give weight to the question asked by the tortured hero. Heracles had finally completed his heroic labors, "toiling through forests and seas to root out evil," ridding Greece of its monsters; and is this, O God, his reward? The rest of the cast agree that his tragedy was fated by the gods. At the end his son states the most apparent moral: "Let all men . . . mark the malevolence of the unforgiving gods in this event." This unwholesome moral is borne out by the fate of Deianeira, an innocent victim. Some scholars have been pleased to endow her with a tragic flaw, saying that Greeks would condemn her use of a love-charm; but they prove only the callousness of this effort always to save the face of the gods. No heroine in Sophocles is portrayed with more evident sympathy.

The plain reader might think that the divine malevolence is still more marked in *Œdipus Rex*, where the gods decree at the hero's birth, or even before it, that he shall murder his father and marry his mother. Most critics have thought otherwise, however; and since this play is by common consent the masterpiece of Sophocles, the quintessence of "Sophoclean tragedy," discussion of it may be put off until the end. Meanwhile I see no reason to dissent from the general opinion that it is a marvel of dramatic technique, in its amazingly convincing development of a preposterously unnatural situation. Under close analysis, admittedly, its exposition is somewhat awkward.

Œdipus displays an ignorance about the past that implies a strange incuriosity: he has to be told all about the murder of the king whose place he took; and he also has to be rather slow-witted, so that he may be the last one in the theater to realize the awful truth. But such flaws become apparent only upon close study; they would not be noticed by an audience. They should remind us that Sophocles wrote his plays for a single performance, not for generations of analytical readers. They should put us on guard against the supersubtle interpretations that scholars produce after close study—interpretations that are often at variance with the plainest meanings of the dramas, and that imply that the most popular dramatist of his time, and reputedly the most proficient in his art, either failed to make his meanings clear or took pains to bury them.

This warning is especially pertinent to *Electra*. Although here the intention of Sophocles seems clear enough, the immediate problem is that in defiance of Aristotle, and perhaps of logic and morality, the tragedy comes to a happy ending. Critics have therefore argued that the ending is really tragic, since Electra and Orestes are bound to suffer for the murder of their mother. Still, the text fails to bear out this idea. The only hint of possible sorrows to come is Orestes' remark after the murder that all is right—"if Apollo was right." And nowhere does Sophocles suggest that Apollo may have been wrong. If anything, he studiously avoided the theological issue by playing down the fact that what the god commanded was matricide. Orestes expresses no qualms about his bloody duty, and then no remorse whatever. Neither does Electra, to whom the play belongs; when she hears her dying mother appeal for mercy she says only: "Strike her again!" Nobody mentions the Furies. At the end the Chorus simply rejoices:

> Now for the house of Atreus
> Freedom is won
> From all her suffering,
> And this day's work well done.

Upon closer study, indeed, the moral issue may seem more confusing. Electra has all the "flaws" of Antigone. She too speaks harshly to a timid, gentle sister; she is as self-willed, fiercely rejecting the authority of the rulers of the state; she is as immoderate, rejecting as well the familiar wisdom of restraint counseled by the Chorus. From beginning to end she is all pride, passion, excess. (Edmund Wilson sees her as another fixated neurotic.) Yet she is not punished by the gods, or by Sophocles. We may deplore this apparent reversion to an archaic morality, or doubt her future happiness in "real life," or hope that Sophocles wrote a sequel; but as far as this play goes, Electra is heroic and triumphant. If the tragic fate of Antigone was just, the gods were absent-minded here.

Philoctetes, which also has a happy ending, is otherwise much different. It is a new kind of drama, a departure that is more remarkable because Sophocles was well over eighty years old when he wrote it, and that might rejoice his admirers more if it did not blur the idea of "Sophoclean tragedy." It is a tragedy without violent death or serious threat of death, and without tragic import about the human condition. On its face it seems to be primarily a psychological study of the abnormal, tormented Philoctetes, who lives alone on a barren island to which the Greeks have exiled him because of his incurable, malodorous disease, and then of his effect upon young Neoptolemus, who has come with the unscrupulous Odysseus to get his invincible bow, now needed by the Greeks in order to win Troy. The major "reversal" is a change of heart, not of fortune. It comes when Neoptolemus, after getting the bow out of loyalty to the Greek cause, restores it to the helpless, embittered invalid; in his better nature he recognizes the higher claims of justice, or simple humanity. The triumph of moral over physical strength becomes still more edifying at the end, when Heracles enters as the emissary of Zeus to bid Philoctetes rejoin the Greeks at Troy, where he will be cured and win glory. Heracles bespeaks a pure piety—"the thing our Father holds most precious." Unfortunately, he also represents the inartistic *deus ex machina,* for which Euripides is condemned. His intrusion is more of a jolt because up to this point the play is a sensitive, realistic study of character, giving less impression of fated events than any other of the plays of Sophocles.

In *Œdipus at Colonus* the final apotheosis of Œdipus, and the blessings he invokes for Athens, are more appropriate to the theme and the occasion. Composed when Sophocles was about ninety years old, and Athens was facing defeat in the long, catastrophic Peloponnesian War, this play constitutes his last testament. For Athenians it must have been especially poignant because it was enacted posthumously, after Athens had fallen to Sparta. To us the blessing upon Athens may seem an arbitrary addition, of historical interest but doubtful artistic value. Nevertheless it is a magnificent play, a sublime conclusion to the story of Œdipus. We too may bring to it some sentiment, in the knowledge that it marks the end of Greek tragedy. We may feel still more reverent as we read the last lines, spoken by the Chorus:

> Now let the weeping cease;
> Let no one mourn again.
> These things are in the hands of God.

Then we may add that these things remain a mystery. The lines recall the pious, god-fearing Sophocles of tradition; but who is this God? What are his purposes for man? Sophocles does not say. His plays as a whole give a surprisingly vague, confused impression of the nature of the gods he feared. Nor have scholars made much of a possible change that came over his thought as he grew old, reflected in the more or less happy endings of his last plays. There are signs, especially in *Philoctetes,* that he may have been influenced by Euripides; otherwise we cannot trace a clear development in the few plays we have, and from other sources have no evidence that there was a marked development. The ancients seem to have taken for granted that essentially the same man wrote *Ajax* and *Œdipus at Colonus.* Most readers, I believe, still feel likewise. But what, then, was his vision of life?

Scholars are now less disposed than the Victorians to hunt out tragic flaws as a proof that God's in his heaven and Sophocles was really Robert Browning. They discount, too, the comments of his choruses, who habitually express a conventional piety, the wisdom of submission to the gods. The Chorus is not always the "ideal spectator" and does not necessarily speak for Sophocles; usually it is a chorus of average folk, bespeaking a conservative, prudential, often timid "citizen ethic" that sets off the heroic ethic of the protagonist. Most critics, however, still stress Sophocles' awe of the gods, and ultimately his faith in their justice. C. M. Bowra represents the traditional view in its somewhat more complicated form. While admitting that Sophocles raises difficulties, by appearing to ask questions without answering them, Bowra argues that there is no real uncertainty about his thought. Finally he permitted no doubts or criticisms of the gods. "The gods are always right and should not be opposed. . . . Sometimes indeed they are hard to understand, but none the less men must assume that all is as it ought to be." Tragedy in Sophocles results when men fail to assume this: the heroes suffer because they "have resisted their destinies," upset "the divine order of the world." In short, the main effort of Sophocles was to justify the ways of God to man.

To test this interpretation, let us now return to *Œdipus Rex.* The moralists have no trouble finding the tragic flaw of Œdipus. He is a proud and passionate man, too sure of himself, rash, and in his anger unjust to the blind prophet Tiresias, his friend Creon, and even his loving wife, Jocasta. He is really the blind man—and at the end acknowledges his fault by literally blinding himself. Bowra grants that the dreadful fate of Œdipus is not clearly deserved, but none the less finds a "salutary lesson" in his failings in piety. The essential conflict in the tragedy is "between divine truth and human illusion." Man must realize his "utter insignificance," and above all must never doubt the divine governance of the world, as both Œdipus and

Jocasta did in expressing skepticism about oracles. The lesson that Œdipus finally learns is that the gods are always right, and that "man must humble himself before them and admit that he is nothing and that he knows nothing." It would appear that Sophocles, not Æschylus, had the Hebraic spirit, and was indeed considerably to the right of the author of Job. And in this view *Œdipus at Colonus* is suffused with sweetness and light. Purified by his suffering, Œdipus dies a wonderful death and is received by the gods he has learned to submit to. They not only prove their justice and benevolence by forgiving him his crime, but show their power to exalt as well as punish. Bowra admits that Œdipus himself, rather strangely, says nothing of all this, apparently still not understanding the gods, and that the Chorus and other characters likewise miss the real point of his apotheosis; but he explains that the divine significance would naturally elude them because of their "limited human perspective."

As is already apparent, I suffer from the same limitation. Bowra himself confesses that the salutary lesson he finds in *Œdipus Rex* "may seem a little tame" for so horrible a fate; it strikes me as tawdry. The whole action of the play demonstrates only the power, never the justice, of the gods. Who can blame Œdipus for "resisting" the hideous destiny they had decreed at his birth? At that, he did not simply resist. The tragedy results from his fierce insistence on finding out the truth, at whatever cost to himself—from his integrity and nobility of soul, not his flaws. His heroic temper makes possible the quickening tempo and deepening irony that make the drama technically so impressive. His wife-mother, Jocasta, is as innocent a victim of "the divine order of the world." If she was "impious" in expressing doubt of the oracle, she had good reason to cry out against oracles that had made a horror of her own life; it was in respect for them that she had consented to the exposure of her infant son to die. The tragic theme of indiscriminate punishment is borne out by the minor characters as well: the kindly Messenger, happy to be the bearer of good news, which turns out to be fatal news; the Shepherd who had disobeyed his orders to make away with the infant, only to save him for this far more dreadful fate; and above all the young daughters of Œdipus and Jocasta, who are doomed to bitter, barren lives. If, as Aristotle said, we are simply shocked by the suffering of the innocent, the ending of *Œdipus Rex* is shocking.

The religious lesson is still confused in *Œdipus at Colonus*, where the gods make amends for their harshness. Œdipus has not become humble and submissive. Although he enters as a worn old man who declares that he has learned contentment by "suffering, time, and kingliness," he displays chiefly his old kingliness, and is as proud, violent, and "rash" as ever. His anger flares out at Creon, who now wants to bring him back to Thebes. He is even fiercer toward Polyneices, his eldest son; although Sophocles presents Polyneices sympathetically, Œdipus curses him as a scoundrel and invokes his death. The main development in the episodic action is the growing strength of Œdipus: a suppliant at the beginning, he completely dominates the cast at the end—but by force of character, not saintliness. And throughout he declares flatly that he has not sinned, and that his "crime" was due only to "God's pleasure." Sophocles goes out of his way to let Œdipus argue his innocence in a long monologue. When he learns the latest word of the oracle—that the gods have given him a special strength and will sustain him now—his only comment is: "Slight favor, now I am old! My doom was early." What Sophocles most plainly justifies by his apotheosis is the ways of Œdipus, not of the gods.

This apotheosis suggests a different approach to tragedy that has recently become popular—the "mythic pattern," drawn from the ancient ritual dramas. Francis Fergusson sees the main theme of *Œdipus Rex* as the perennial tragic quest of well-being, in the perennial terms of myth and ritual. The familiar moral, religious, or philosophical interpretations are all relevant but partial; Sophocles "preserves the ultimate mystery by focusing upon the tragic human at a level beneath, or prior to any rationalization whatever." [7] Specifically, Œdipus is the ritual scapegoat. Addressed by the priest as "foremost of living men," King Œdipus takes it upon himself to save Thebes from its terrible plague and blight, and learns from the oracle that Thebes must purify itself of a defiling thing it has cherished—the murderer of its former king Laius. His discovery that he himself is the defiling thing is ironic but profoundly appropriate: the King *must* be the scapegoat. Hence Passion leads to Perception; Thebes is purified; order is restored. And in *Œdipus at Colonus,* one might add, the ancient role of Œdipus becomes more prominent. "These things are mysteries, not to be explained," he tells Theseus; but by his miraculous death he achieves a kind of divinity and brings a blessing to the land of Athens.

So conceived, the tragedy evokes more pity and terror than in Bowra's interpretation. There remains a painful mystery, with no simple lesson of submission; the greatest men have to suffer and die for their fellow men, just because of their greatness. Hence the profound ambiguities in the drama of Œdipus. As Fergusson observes, he both flees and seeks his true destiny, tries to escape the gods' decree and to discover what it is; a puppet of fate, he yet wills his every move; and his success is his undoing, his undoing another triumph of heroic will. Such ambiguities are the essence of the tragic action: "triumph and destruction, darkness and enlightenment, mourning and rejoicing, at any moment we care to consider it."

Now we need not worry too much over the historical question of whether or not the mythic pattern derives from the Year-Dæmon. The important question is whether the pattern is in the plays, and if so whether it is the basic or essential pattern. In *Œdipus at Colonus* it is unmistakably there, and in

---

[7] My citations are from Fergusson's distinguished book *The Idea of a Theater* (Princeton, 1949). Since I shall keep returning to his thesis chiefly to express my disagreement with it, let me say at once that I consider his book the most stimulating and impressive work on drama of our time.

Œdipus Rex at least in the background. But it is not, I believe, the key either to Sophocles' intention or to the deepest meanings of his tragedy for us.

Knowing *Œdipus at Colonus*, devotees of the ritual pattern may forget that *Œdipus Rex* is a complete work in itself, written thirty years before its sequel and not intended as an introduction to this sequel. Sophocles gave up the trilogy form that Æschylus had found so suitable for effecting a final reconciliation. And in *Œdipus Rex* he does not actually "focus" on the mythic pattern. We may assume that Thebes was purified by the tragedy of Œdipus, and that henceforth its citizens will suffer no more from the plague; but who, in seeing the play, actually gives them a thought at the end? One who does is bringing it to the play himself, for Sophocles makes no reference to the happier state of Thebes. The concluding scene is given to Œdipus and his daughters. Œdipus rises above his own misery only to ask for his daughters, to express the hope that Heaven will be kinder to Creon for bringing his daughters to him, and to weep in the knowledge that Heaven will not be kind to them. The Chorus adds only the customary comment: "Call no man fortunate that is not dead." There is no note of "rejoicing" amid all the mourning. As for the audience of Sophocles, who might be expected to be more alert to the theme of purification, and to whom Fergusson attributes a "ritual expectancy," they knew that what actually lay in store for Thebes was more calamity—the famous war of the Seven Against Thebes as the sons of Œdipus fought over its kingship. They might therefore have detected still another note of tragic irony in the conclusion. As Œdipus brings up the subject of his unhappy daughters, he explains: "My sons are men and can take care of themselves."

These daughters continue to complicate the ending of *Œdipus at Colonus*. If we take literally the ritual pattern of the dying god-king who restores order, we must note that Œdipus was King of Thebes, and no good will come to Thebes from his purification or sacrificial death; for his own city he

has only curses. It is Athens he blesses, and Athens is represented as a city already strong, just, and pure; his blessing is
typical of the patriotic compliments that the poets were accustomed to work into their plays. Thus as Ajax prepares to
kill himself he is careful to say: "And great Athens too, farewell, whose folk are kin to mine." Nor does the miraculous
end of Œdipus resolve all the discords, constitute a message
of peace on earth. The Chorus chants one ode on the recurrent
melancholy theme:

> Not to be born beats all philosophy.
> The second best is to have seen the light
> And then to go back quickly whence we came.

(Bowra, incidentally, is troubled that a great artist should have
included a passage so "irrelevant" and so inconsistent with
"the care which the gods have for men.") There remain the
lonely, unhappy daughters of Œdipus, facing a tragic future.
Their lamentations take up most of the final scene.

At any rate, the ritual pattern is not the typical pattern of
the tragedies of Sophocles. Although one might make it out
in *Philoctetes*, where the god finally arranges for the hero to
bring good to the Greeks, this contrivance seems like an epilogue to the drama. *Electra* is focused on the fortunes of the
heroine, who is no scapegoat; the townspeople of Mycenæ
will presumably rejoice at her triumph, but their stake in the
drama is never dwelt on. The tragic conflict in *Antigone* takes
place on the level of "rationalization"; the sacrificial role of the
heroine is in the name of a principle above the State, and its
consequence is the punishment of King Creon. There is no
trace whatever of the ritual pattern in *Ajax*, where the hero's
death brings good to no one except his hateful enemies.
Women of Trachis might be interpreted as an ironic inversion
of the pattern, since the tragedy begins *after* the hero has purified Greece by slaying monsters and rooting out evils. His sufferings are more frightful because they purify neither him
nor anyone else in the drama, and so far from restoring order,

appear only to confirm the malevolence of the existing divine order.

This play more than any other forces the question that is still unanswered: what were the views of Sophocles about man and the gods, the meaning of man's life? Given the diversity of his plays, his refusal to be explicit, and the basic disagreements among his admirers, it would be impertinent to declare that the answer is clear or certain. Some would say that the very question is impertinent. Professor Waldock, who writes with refreshing good sense about the plays and their problems, objects to the notion that great plays must contain profound truths, or even "mean something"; to him *Œdipus Rex* is simply a wonderful story, about a highly exceptional rather than a universal situation. The whole uncertainty about the "meaning" of these plays would seem to indicate that their greatness does not depend on any specific meaning. Yet Sophocles was manifestly a thoughtful writer, concerned with major issues of human conduct and human destiny. Almost all readers feel that his plays positively do "mean something"— that he was expressing, however obliquely, some "philosophy of life." And almost all commentators agree on certain qualities that are clues to his thought, notably his irony and his refusal to declare himself in so many words. In our own world these might imply a devotion to art for art's sake. In the Greek world they imply a measure of philosophical skepticism. Sophocles was at least saying that the ways of deity are mysterious, and often painfully so.

This does not mean that he was an atheist, or even an agnostic in the modern sense. Since we are always prone to read our own attitudes into our favorite authors of the past, equip them with all the conveniences of modern thought, it should be stressed that the skepticism of Sophocles was fundamentally different from most contemporary skepticism. Nowhere in the plays is there a suggestion that he doubted the *existence* of the gods. All the plays testify to their power, all give a sense of a sovereign order above mere chance or happenstance. The very point of the most outrageous coincidences, as in the fate of Œdipus, is that they are not accidental but preordained; they were foretold by oracles—and the oracles are invariably right in Sophocles. Nor is there in *Œdipus Rex* the deep sense of outrage that modern readers may feel. None of the characters, including the Chorus, complains that Thebans are suffering for no fault of their own, in this plague sent by the gods; they simply assume that Thebes must be properly purified of its defilement. Although technically innocent, Œdipus accepts his "guilt": he is the defiled one, and must make amends. Like most Greeks, Sophocles apparently took for granted that innocent and guilty must suffer alike when the gods punish. While troubled by such divine injustice, he does not make an indignant issue of it. He was never so severe a critic of the Olympians as Euripides was.

Both gods and oracles might have been mere symbols for Sophocles, or dramatic conveniences. Yet they were evidently real to him, in a sense hard for us to understand and impossible to define exactly. What can we make of the apparently authentic report that when the new cult of Asclepius came to Athens, Sophocles entertained the god in his own home while a suitable shrine was being prepared? We cannot imagine Euripides inviting a god to his home—or Æschylus either, for that matter. We might say conscientiously that Sophocles was hospitable because he was public-minded and open-minded, or skeptical of his own skepticism, but we really feel that he was strangely naïve. We can hope to understand his apparent superstition only if we keep in mind a basic assumption that very few Greeks questioned before the time of Epicurus—the assumption that the powers that rule the universe, whoever or whatever they be, are not indifferent to man. For better or worse, these powers are concerned with his fate.

But the tragic fact remains that it might be for worse, for no intelligible reason. Given the assumption of a supernatural order, the crucial questions are: What is its relation to man? What are its purposes? The answer of Sophocles is in effect that its purposes are inscrutable. His plays do not represent the rule of the gods as always reasonable, just, and beneficent, but neither do they represent it as merely unreasonable or unjust. In the face of the ultimate mystery he could entertain different possibilities—or more simply, might express different moods. *Œdipus Rex* reflects a pessimism that in *Women of Trachis* approaches despair; *Philoctetes* and *Œdipus at Colonus* suggest a pious acceptance that approaches serenity. From his work as a whole, however, what comes through to us unmistakably is neither pessimism nor piety but the deep sense of mystery that underlies both.

One sign of this is his distinctive irony. In Sophocles irony is more than the dramatic device that Æschylus had learned to employ, and that Aristotle discussed under the labels of Discoveries, Reversals, etc. It becomes a way of viewing life that most clearly distinguishes him from Æschylus, and that Aristotle ignored. It is a philosophical perception of "the irony of fate": an awareness that heroes are by their nature built for ruin, and that their fate is incongruous, "wrong," but also in some sense appropriate, in any case natural. It is an awareness that the tragic situation, as Northrop Frye has said, is "primary and uncaused," a condition rather than an act—the condition that Œdipus was born into. The irony of Sophocles was not so comprehensive as that of Shakespeare, nor so conscious and consistent as that of such modern writers as Joseph Conrad and Thomas Mann. (Judging by Plato and Aristotle, the Greeks of the classical period never grew conscious enough of irony to discuss it.) But it was sufficient to give him his characteristic detachment and reserve. It explains why he committed himself to neither the exalted affirmations of Æschylus nor the indignant protests of Euripides. It also explains why he did not commit himself to the simple meanings of the ritual dramas; for no dying king can take away the basic evil, or restore more than the transient appearance of harmony.

Nevertheless ironic detachment is a way of viewing life, not a sufficient way of living—at least in the Greek *polis* for which

Sophocles wrote, and to which he was devoted. It brings up a further question: how should man bear himself under so mysterious and hard a dispensation? Again Sophocles gives no one definite answer. He evidently respected the conventional wisdom of resignation so often expressed by his choruses. Pride may aggravate the woes of man, who is not the measure of all things; patience, piety, and purity may help him to endure. Yet the heroes of Sophocles live by a different code. If they must be proud and willful in order to be protagonists of tragedy, he treats them with a more evident respect. He does not plainly condemn their pride unless, as in the Creon of *Antigone,* it is purely selfish or tyrannical. He creates timid foils for Antigone and Electra to set off their heroic spirit, or "noble excess." Among the functions of his choruses is an ironic role, for by their typical counsel of "Play it safe" they too set off this noble excess. Most of all, it seems to me, Sophocles honors the heroic spirit.

Thus Ajax in his unendurable shame surrenders only his life. He will not "huddle over the coals of flickering hope"; deprived of honor in life, he will still have it in death. He denies flatly that he now owes "any duty or service" to the gods. His dying prayer is not for forgiveness but for the punishment of his enemies.[8] The Chorus remarks that he died as he had lived, "a willful man"; and the rest of the play is a tribute to him. In *Electra* the climax is another revelation of the heroic spirit. The report of the death of Orestes provides an ironic cross-scene, as Clytemnestra rejoices, Electra despairs, and the audience knows that the news is false; but it is also the crucial test of Electra's courage, since Orestes has represented her one hope of freedom and revenge. She meets the test by resolving to carry out her duty anyway. When her sister tells her that she is only a helpless woman, who must learn "the wisdom of

[8] Bowra prefers to believe that he here relapsed into madness, saying that Sophocles "would not send this great being to his death in an unchastened, unrepentant spirit"; but in fact the tone of his last speech gives no suggestion of madness or hysteria—the great being speaks as one in complete control of himself.

bowing," and the Chorus chimes in that "prudence and caution are the only things worth having," she answers simply: "Then I must do the thing myself, alone." The rest of the play brings her reward. And most emphatic is the vindication of Œdipus in *Œdipus at Colonus.* The gods, we are told, have given him grace; but what the play shows is a proud king defending his past, maintaining his own ways, earning his apotheosis by integrity and strength of mind. We are not given to see the gods who receive him, but only the god-like element in Œdipus himself.

Cedric Whitman, one of the few critics to stress the humanism instead of the god-fearing piety of Sophocles, was inspired by the apotheosis of Œdipus to assert that "for sheer audacity and defiant insistence on human dignity, this vision of 'divine man' puts to shame all doctrines of the soul's immortality." Sophocles would probably have thought this language too proud, as well as a little strange; his vision seems no more audacious or defiant than Homer's, and somewhat sadder. Yet he was in the Homeric tradition, where ancient critics placed him. If he seems to have had more reverence for the gods than Homer had, and perhaps more fear, he had the same respect for the heroic spirit, the excellence that man can attain by his own efforts. The religious belief remains uncertain; the belief in human dignity is all the clearer for such uncertainty. This humanistic faith, I should say, was the soul of his art.

It illumines as well his major technical contribution to dramatic art—the drama of character. We might assume that someone was bound to add a third actor (though we should remember that the Greeks stopped short of a fourth one); but the most apparent reason why Sophocles did so was his interest in the soul of man. Unlike Æschylus, he made considerable use of this actor, to affect the other two actors, provide ironic contrasts, intensify or complicate the conflict. The result was not merely a more lifelike action, but more stress on human wills than on the will of the gods. As Watling puts

it, Sophocles made drama three-dimensional by adding the
depth of human character to the length and breadth of mythical narrative. "What had hitherto been a frieze of more or
less static figures confronting one another in profile became
a perspective of living human beings reacting on one another
and shaping their own destinies by the interplay of their contrasted characters."

Although Aristotle saw in this achievement mainly the perfection of Plot, it could be said that—excepting *Œdipus Rex*—
the soul of Sophoclean tragedy is Character. After critics have
exercised their wits on the structure of *Ajax* and *Antigone*,
most readers continue to be impressed chiefly by the heroic
figures of Ajax and Antigone themselves, not the complete action. In *Electra*, which is admirably constructed for its limited
purposes, the principal contribution of Sophocles to the old
story is the invention of characters and incidents to isolate and
test his heroine, reveal her character more fully. I am unable
to make a satisfying tragedy out of *Women of Trachis*, but
Kitto has done about the best for it by making its theme the
study of an exceptional rather than a symbolic character—the
great hero Heracles, who by the exigencies of his heroic career,
and by his nature as a great man, is ruthless, completely self-
centered, unconcerned about his family; so it is a fitting irony
that a loving wife should innocently cause the death of such
a man. And only in the light of this growing psychological interest can one understand *Philoctetes*, a play that otherwise
might seem as un-Sophoclean as it is un-Aristotelian. As a psychological drama it takes on wider meanings. It can support
the symbolism that Edmund Wilson reads into the incurable
wound and invincible bow of Philoctetes: an exiled, alienated
man representing the type of genius who by virtue of his great
gifts is unhealthy, abnormal, at once inhuman and superhuman,
apt to scorn and need his normal fellow men as much as they
distrust and need him; and who finally learns that "he shall be
cured when he shall have been able to forget his grievances
and to devote his divine gifts to the service of his own people."

Wilson's interpretation grows dubious when he concludes that "in the fortunate Sophocles there had been a sick and raving Philoctetes." If so, it was not for the kind of grievances suggested in this play; for from the beginning of his career he had been highly honored by his fellow Athenians, winning more prizes than any other dramatist. Yet the drama of Sophocles invites such speculation. It is worth pausing to consider the light he may throw on the psychological sources of Greek tragedy. Assuming a decent caution, we may dare to consider the inevitable text—*Œdipus Rex.*

Here Sophocles was of course not making a study of the Œdipus complex; there is no suggestion of abnormality in his hero. Nevertheless the Œdipus dream that Jocasta mentions was also reported by Herodotus, Plato, and other writers; evidently it was not uncommon for Greeks to dream of marrying their mother. They also had strange stories about the murder of the father. They hung on to the ghastly myth about Cronus, who castrated and killed his father, Uranus—a myth whose popularity is still more surprising if, as seems likely, the Greeks borrowed it from the Hittites. That the older god should be killed is a familiar idea in religious history, and readily understood on historical grounds of supersedence; but why must he be castrated? And Aphrodite born from the severed member? From such evidence Dodds has argued plausibly that among the tensions that gave rise to Greek tragedy was the deep resentment of the father, in a patriarchal society that was becoming increasingly individualistic. By tradition the father had absolute rights and the son only duties; hence the peculiar horror of the father's curse. Now the sons were asserting their own rights, which the Sophists taught included a natural right to disobey the father.

Sophocles was not necessarily conscious of the anxiety resulting from this conflict. The father-son relation is only an incidental theme in his tragedy, and one on which he took no clear position. (While he sympathized with Hæmon in his refusal to obey the autocratic Creon in *Antigone,* he did not

condemn Œdipus for exercising his paternal right to curse his
sons.) But since his interest in character reflects the growing
individualism of Athens, it is reasonable to assume that his
tragedy reflected the problems inevitably created by this individualism. To this extent, the Marxist interpretation of
George Thomson may also be pertinent. As a patriotic Athenian, Sophocles was naturally affected by the social disorder of
his time, and therefore sounded a more tragic note than
Æschylus. Æschylus, the old soldier who had fought at Marathon, lived in the glow of the national victory, and to the end
retained his vision of the glorious promise of Athens; the conflicts in his drama usually end in reconciliation and reaffirmation. Sophocles, who as a boy had danced in a procession celebrating the victory of Marathon, knew this glorious promise,
but he lived through the Peloponnesian War, the political and
moral tragedy of Athenian imperialism; his drama stressed the
tragic conflict more than the final reconciliation. "The Œdipus
of Sophocles," Thomson concludes, "is a symbol of the deep-
seated perplexity engendered in men's minds by the unfore-
seen and incomprehensible transformation of a social order
designed to establish liberty and equality into an instrument
for the destruction of liberty and equality."

So it might be—up to an unknowable point. We cannot make
very much of Sophocles' concern over the issues forced by imperialism and the war when, unlike Euripides, he remained
silent on these issues in his plays. Whatever it symbolized,
Œdipus Rex is about rather different issues. The "deep-seated
perplexity" that it directly reveals is over the contradictions in
the destiny of man, not in the Athenian state. And whatever
the tensions that gave rise to the drama of Sophocles, our final
concern remains his creative response.

The diversity of his plays indicates that it was not a simple,
direct, single-minded response. It befitted an age of intellectual adventure, and the ultimate uncertainty implied by this
adventure. But his most comprehensive response, as fittingly,
is *Œdipus at Colonus*. In his last testament Sophocles did

effect a clear reconciliation, in a perception that still embraced
the impenetrable mystery of man's life and the abiding reasons
for pity and terror. The sublime ending of the play is accordingly a quiet ending, much less sonorous and spectacular than
that of *Eumenides*, much more subtle and complex in its
harmonies, but also richer for its somber overtones, and finally
more stirring because it is not so obviously stirring. Although
paraphrase must be lame, I venture to review it as the supreme
example in Greek drama of how tragedy may provide "perhaps the most general, all-accepting, all-ordering experience
known."

The prelude to the ending is the exit of the doomed Polyneices, going "with open eyes to death," praying only that his
sisters may escape the evil. The Chorus comments on the
"new forms of terror working through the blind, or else inscrutable destiny." Œdipus then goes to his death, summoned by
the voice of God. Symbolically, it is now he who guides his
daughters, firmly, and in the same sovereign spirit tells Theseus
of the appointed blessing for Athens. When he leaves, the
Chorus reminds us of his tragic life by praying that "some just
god" will grant him eternal sleep, "because his sufferings were
great, unmerited and untold" and he is going down into the
dark, ghostly underworld that all men fear. The Messenger
who reports his death begins by emphasizing that what happened "was no simple thing." How and where he died only
Theseus was permitted to see, under pledge of secrecy, and
Theseus held his hands before his face, "shading his eyes as if
from something awful, fearful and unendurable to see." To the
Messenger the end of Œdipus was nevertheless most wonderful, since "he was taken without lamentation, illness or suffering." His daughters, however, see only the "bewildering mystery" of his lonely death; they continue to lament that they
were not permitted to join him, and now must look forward to
more suffering. The Chorus offers the obvious consolation,
which seldom consoles: in a world where none is free from unhappiness, they must bear with courage whatever God brings

about. Antigone is more comforted by the proud thought that
Œdipus "did as he had wished!"—he died where he chose to
die. She also promises that even in his eternal darkness he
shall not lack the love of his daughters. And here she echoes
the sentiment he had expressed as they clung together before
his death—a very simple sentiment, but one rarely found in
classical literature:

> You shall no longer
> Bear the burden of taking care of me—
> I know it was hard, my children.—And yet one word
> Makes all those difficulties disappear:
> That word is love.

Still, the difficulties do not actually disappear—else there
would be no tragedy. It is love of her brothers that impels
Antigone to reject the offered haven of Athens: her one hope
now is to stop the bloody war between them. She is consoled
by the promise of Theseus to help her return to ancient
Thebes; and the audience knows the fate that awaits her there.
Yet the audience too may find comfort. In his last words to
his daughters Œdipus had told them to show courage and
nobility (not meekness or piety); and Antigone is now showing these heroic qualities. Like Œdipus, she will do as she
wishes, choose her death. They both add nobility to the conventional wisdom of the Chorus—let the weeping cease, man
must endure; for man can endure, grandly. So the contrasting
themes of evil and heroism, loneliness and love, anguish and
exaltation, terror and wonder—all the major discords that arise
from human purpose and passion—are included and resolved
in the tragic perception that "ripeness is all."

History was to add a jarring note. The prayer of Sophocles
was not answered: the blessing that Œdipus imparted to
Theseus failed to save Athens. But there is at least a truly
poetic justice for us in the thought that Greek tragedy ends
with this play, in the holy grove of Colonus, the birthplace of
Sophocles.

4. EURIPIDES, THE REBEL

Although Euripides is by all odds the most troublesome of the Greek tragedians, his distinctive qualities seem plain enough. By common consent he was the most "modern" of the poets. He moved closer to realistic, secular drama, presenting the traditional subjects in the language and the guise of everyday life. He anticipated Ibsen by making drama an instrument of social criticism. He was a rationalist and free thinker who openly attacked the traditional gods. In his technique, too, he was heretical. He reduced the Chorus to a mere appendage, a means of lovely but incidental, sometimes irrelevant interludes between the acts; he made lavish use of such arbitrary theatrical devices as the *deus ex machina;* he was indifferent to the purity of tragedy, sometimes treating his hallowed materials lightly or humorously, and introducing a form that for want of a better name is called tragi-comedy. As might be expected, the general agreement on these qualities still leaves ample room for misunderstanding; the "rationalism" of Euripides, for instance, is by no means a simple attitude. Nevertheless his main position seems much clearer than that of Sophocles.

His merits, however, are much more controversial. As a radical, Euripides was unpopular during his lifetime; a favorite butt of the comic poets, he won the prize only five times, and ended his life in voluntary exile from Athens. He has been called the first great example of the type of "misunderstood artist," the rebel in advance of his time. But if so, the ancients soon caught up with him. In the century following his death Euripides became by far the most popular of the tragic poets, and remained so to the end of the Greco-Roman world. (Hence we have at least eighteen of his plays—more than of Æschylus and Sophocles together.) Since then his reputation has run the critical gamut. Following Aristotle, most classicists have been critical of him. On different grounds Nietzsche was still more critical, damning him as the destroyer of Greek tragedy.

Historians are generally agreed that he at least represented tendencies that were to prove fatal. Meanwhile he remained popular with Western poets, including such diverse ones as Milton, Racine, Alfieri, Byron, and Goethe. Simple readers were likely to feel as the Brownings did about "our Euripides the human, with his droppings of warm tears." As a rationalist, a liberal, and a humanitarian, not to say a great lyric poet, he is a sympathetic figure to moderns. He is so to me.

And yet he remains troublesome. Granted that he had aims different from those of Æschylus and Sophocles, and cannot be judged fairly by the same standard, his plays are full of faults by any common standard, Greek or modern. The notorious *deus ex machina* is only symptomatic of the mechanical quality that pervades his drama, and that appears as well in the mere cleverness, the rhetoric, the sensationalism, the artificial or illogical actions, the extreme or inconsistent characterizations. These faults are more disturbing because they appear to be due to sheer perversity rather than incompetence.

Let us consider what the modern defenders of Euripides say in his behalf, leaving aside the simpler ones who praise him merely because his heart was in the right place, and the sentimental ones who lap up his warm tears. Kitto, the most spirited and forthright, explains away all his seeming faults as deliberate effects "required" by his special purposes, or modes of his special kind of form. If his action is violent and sensational it is because he chose to write melodrama, aimed primarily at theatrical effectiveness: "Euripides will have no nonsense about tragic restraint, for he knows perfectly well that tragic restraint is for tragedy." If in writing tragedy he still depends upon mechanical contrivance and makes his action and characters extreme, it is because "he has a vision beyond these," or "thought it better to be vital than academic." Always he wanted to state his ideas as clearly and forcibly as possible, at any cost; for him the play was not the thing. Kitto has a simple formula to cover all apparent violations of dramatic form or logic: "When we see that Euripides is not putting together a play but presenting a tragic idea, the explanation is obvious."

The obvious rejoinder is that Euripides should be judged primarily as a dramatist, since his chosen business was putting together plays. But first let us see what can be said for one of his serious plays that looks like a hodgepodge—*Andromache*. Moses Hadas and J. H. McLean, following Gilbert Norwood, tried to make artistic sense of it by asserting that its real unity is unfortunately obscured by its misnomer—it should have been entitled *Hermione*. The first half of the play portrays Hermione's thoughtless cruelty to Andromache, the last half her equally thoughtless and hysterical remorse. Finally the full horror of her situation is revealed by the news that she is to be the wife of the scoundrel Orestes, the murderer of her husband, Neoptolemus.

The plain reader, however, might still complain that if the play does belong to Hermione, Euripides chose an odd way to tell her story. She appears in only two scenes, which take up less than a fifth of the play. The first half is in fact dominated by Andromache, and her persecution by both Hermione and Menelaus; these are the most poignant scenes. We might therefore rejoice when Peleus suddenly enters to take her part and presently save her life, only she then drops out of the play. She is followed out by Hermione after a scene with Orestes, who does not enter the play until this point. The rest of the tragedy belongs to Peleus, as he learns of the murder of his grandson Neoptolemus and laments over the corpse, which is dutifully brought in. The audience might lament less because it has not seen Neoptolemus alive. Finally the goddess Thetis, the mate of Peleus in years past, enters to announce that she will deliver him from all mortal ills and make him a god. The Chorus concludes with a comment that Euripides often appended: "That which was expected has not been accomplished; for that which was unexpected has god found the way. Such was the end of this story." It would seem an appropriate comment on this play, whose action looks like a defiance of all artistic expectation, and whose ending has no apparent relation to the story of either Andromache or Hermione.

In a later study, accordingly, Hadas gave up the effort to justify *Andromache* as "a story with plot and characterization." He took over the argument of Kitto, declaring that its unity lay simply in its theme, which is an attack on Spartan *Kultur*; in his "severely functional treatment" of this theme Euripides scorned "the ordinary amenities of the playwright." Kitto himself repeats that as usual Euripides was driving home a tragic idea, not merely making a play, but he also admits and defends its melodramatic glare. All the characters either typify or suffer from the revolting arrogance, ruthlessness, and brutality of Sparta, and because of this burning idea they are quite properly as extreme as Euripides can make them. His primary aim was to make our blood boil. Consequently he did not have to observe the limits of probability, and indeed could not afford any shading, any suggestion of complexity, anything but the most elementary character-drawing, for such distractions might keep us from coming to a boil. He could risk giving us a happy ending in recompense but only by making it arbitrary, throwing it in as a consolation prize, since a logical ending might be fatal to his purposes by effecting a catharsis—the last thing he wants here.

Now this may well have been the way Euripides thought as he wrote *Andromache*. Clearly he was very much concerned about the Spartan theme, little concerned about probability, and not at all concerned about unity of action. Yet there is no getting away from it: *Andromache* is a bad play, an almost incredible botch. In spite of his violent simplification Euripides failed to drive home his main intention, since other defenders have made out other themes (such as the evil of two wives in a household); but anyhow his intentions by no means settle the issue. On Kitto's basis one may justify the crudest melodrama or propaganda art. Indeed, it is hard to see how any artist could be legitimately criticized for anything, since a writer can always claim some peculiar purpose for whatever he does. And the provinces are full of inglorious Miltons who are not mute because they think that expressing their beautiful ideas is more important than making a work of art.

My immediate reason for laboring this issue is that the faults of Euripides are not only serious in themselves but historically important. We must perforce return to them because they signal the end of Greek tragedy, and because they account for his largely unfortunate influence, especially on Seneca, through him on the Elizabethans, and to some extent on neo-classical drama. My chief motive, however, is finally to do justice to a complex, fascinating artist. For me the greatness of Euripides as a tragic poet rests on a small but sufficient body of work, in particular *The Bacchæ*. But his best work recalls us to the puzzle of his work as a whole. As Kitto remarked in his defense of *Andromache*, any tyro could suggest obvious ways of giving the play at least the appearance of unity and logic; and Euripides was no tyro. The question, then, is why he chose to write as he did. It may lead us to a better understanding of a restless, energetic, highly original writer who was in some important respects, as Aristotle said, the "most tragic" of the poets, who is especially pertinent for us because he is the closest to us in spirit, who was yet an ardent Athenian and very much a man of his time, and who is altogether a profoundly ambiguous figure. Euripides is not, after all, so easy to label and place.

Most conspicuously he was a man of ideas: radical, heretical ideas, likely to be not only unpopular with his audience but uncongenial to the dramatic form in which he had to express them. Kitto is unquestionably right that Euripides was often more interested in putting across his ideas than in putting together sound plays. As Kitto also observes, however, he was as often content to be merely an effective showman. In his theatricality he might be considered the least realistic of the tragic poets. The most apparent link between his melodramas and his serious tragedies is the external, mechanical quality, suggesting the aloofness and coldness of an intellectual. Nevertheless Euripides is celebrated for his portrayal of sentiment and passion, and though some of his arias seem contrived for theatrical effect, others obviously sprang from his own emotion. He was more compassionate than either Æschylus or Sophocles, and more indignant about injustice; one reason for considering him the "most tragic" of the poets is that he stirs more pity. This likewise belies his reputation as a mere sophist or cynic, who "questioned everything and believed nothing." And always this intellectual remained the most lyrical of the tragedians.

Even the inescapable description of Euripides as the most modern of them needs to be qualified. Although he was indeed an innovator and a rebel, the conventional idea of the classical spirit makes him appear more radical than he was. Æschylus and Sophocles were bolder, more adventurous, and more realistic in their art and thought than their reputations would suggest. Euripides inherited from them much more than he repudiated. In particular he carried on the tradition established by Æschylus, taking seriously his role as educator of the community. Aristophanes has him agreeing with Æschylus that the principal merits of a poet are "the improvement of morals, the progress of mind"; they were alike more didactic than Sophocles. When he scandalized his audience by reinterpreting the hallowed myths and legends in contemporary terms, he was still doing essentially what Æschylus had done. One may doubt that he was actually a "misunderstood artist."

At least Euripides was no solitary adventurer. He had behind him a long tradition of free thought, and about him a company of fellow adventurers. The main reason why Aristophanes attacked him was his popularity with the bright young men of Athens. The immediate clue to his innovations, and to his faults, is the different climate in which he lived.

To begin with, his audience had changed. Such later plays of Sophocles as *Women of Trachis* and *Philoctetes* imply an audience that had grown more secular and sophisticated, perhaps somewhat jaded, and that no longer came to the theater to be elevated but was content to be intelligently interested, or even merely excited or entertained. Sometimes Euripides offered little but sensational or sophisticated entertainment, comparable to Broadway fare. His best in this vein is the strange, unclassifiable *Alcestis*: a sympathetic picture of a devoted wife who offers up her life for her husband without expressing a single word of endearment, coupled with a somewhat satirical study of her conventional, complacent husband, who is decent enough to be grateful for her sacrifice and embarrassed by it; and finally a happy ending arranged by the boisterous Heracles, who earlier had provided a comic interlude by getting drunk. But in his most serious plays Euripides was still likely to strain for effects, in the "modern style." Seeking to stir tragic pity and terror, he might verge on mere pathos or mere horror.

A major source of the changing climate was the Greek "Enlightenment," which may be traced to the rise of philosophy in Ionia, but in Athens became a revolutionary intellectual movement during the last half of the fifth century. Euripides was reputedly a disciple of Anaxagoras, who was banished from Athens for such heretical teachings as that the divine sun was a body of incandescent matter. He was also a friend of Socrates, and of the Sophists Prodicus and Protagoras. Protagoras, author of the famous statement "Man is the measure of all things," read in the home of Euripides the treatise on the gods that caused his expulsion from Athens. Euripides himself was once indicted for impiety.

Lovers of Greece have been troubled by these witch-hunts, which culminated in the execution of Socrates, and so far as is known, occurred only in Athens, the citadel of freedom. But they are understandable as symptoms of a national crisis—as was the Enlightenment itself. Athens was displaying an energy hardly to be matched in all history, alike in economic, political, artistic, and intellectual activities; it was running an empire, building the Parthenon, speculating about everything under the sun; only the ends of this extraordinary energy were no longer clear, or clearly ideal. Athens was turning to new gods, and especially to the Bitch Goddess. It was also conducting the Peloponnesian War, treating other Greek cities with increasing arrogance and ruthlessness. Although Euripides was only a dozen years younger than Sophocles, he belonged to a different generation: one that had no memories of Marathon and Salamis, the heroic sources of Athenian idealism, but had a vivid consciousness of the corruption of this idealism. Almost all his surviving plays date from the period of the Peloponnesian War.

Hence the rationalism of the Greek Enlightenment never became so optimistic as the rationalism of the Eighteenth-Century Enlightenment. It induced Euripides to question or condemn many accepted beliefs, but not to give answers or propose an alternative faith in pure reason. It made him more aware of the severe limits to human rationality. It led him to write tragedy, based on precisely this theme. And it then raised a fundamental difficulty that had not troubled Æschylus and Sophocles. As a tragic poet, he inherited a tradition of high seriousness, and a body of myths that he could not take with entire seriousness. He respected the tradition enough to base all his plays on the myths, which at least provided him with characters who did and suffered grand and terrible things. Sometimes he took them straight, expressing through them his deepest insights into the nature and destiny of man. At other times his main purpose was to explode them, show how ridiculous or revolting they were; his faults as a playwright may be partly explained by his contempt for his materials. At all times, however, he was self-conscious, and at no time single-minded or wholehearted. The unity that the age of Æschylus had known—of the individual and the state, ethics and politics, religion and poetry, thought and feeling—had broken up.

Now I do not conceive Euripides as the romantic artist torn by inner conflict, forever at war with his audience or with himself. Even his poorer plays give the impression that he was in command of himself, aware of what he was doing, and more or less content to do it so. Yet he was also aware of a changing world, with which he was not content. A critic of traditional beliefs, he was still devoted to old Athenian ideals; a herald of a new age, he was critical of it too. At the heart of his work is not pure rationalism or radicalism but ambiguity. This explains why he has fascinated so many of his detractors, and disturbed so many of his admirers; and why he has perhaps been more widely misunderstood or misrepresented in our time than in his own.

Thus the most conspicuous and persistent theme in Euripides, his criticism of the gods, is not mere atheism. He attacked the immorality of the traditional gods—especially Apollo, whose oracle at Delphi was prone to shady politics and at the time was favoring the Spartan cause. He raised no question of their existence. He seems to have entertained the possibility of a higher power that was making for righteousness, for his choruses and his most sympathetic characters sometimes appeal to such a power. He did not attack Zeus, the supreme god; on this score he was a more orthodox pagan than the author of *Prometheus Bound*. On the whole, however, he was disposed to pessimism. All his tragic dramas imply that the ruling powers of the world are irrational, or positively evil by human standards. His attitude was perhaps summed up by the Chorus in *Hippolytus*:

> I have a secret hope
> of someone, a god, who is wise and plans;
> but my hopes grow dim when I see
> the deeds of men and their destinies.

Ultimately men know nothing of these matters:

> Unpiloted we're helplessly adrift
> upon a sea of legends, lies and fantasy.

But we cannot say just what Euripides believed, because he himself does not plainly say. All we can safely say is that his scandalous "impiety" sprang from a humane moral sense—and that, alas for the humanist, it had an unfortunate effect upon his dramatic art. It helps to explain his fondness for the *deus ex machina.* As Kitto remarks, the gods in the machine serve less to cut the knot than to cut their own throats, by accentuating the evil role they have played in the action. Or sometimes —as in *Electra, Orestes,* and *Andromache*—they do not really cut the knot at all. The human drama as Euripides conceived it has reached its logical, tragic conclusion; now he offers an alternative ending, a happier one drawn from tradition, as a sop to his audience. From the ritualists' point of view, accordingly, there is an apparent paradox: Euripides turns out to be more conservative than Sophocles in that the form of his tragedy more nearly resembles that of the ancient ritual dramas, retaining their "epiphany." But the resemblance is clearly superficial. The essential thing here is a new kind of irony, more subjective and intellectual than that of Sophocles, springing from the author's self-conscious superiority to his subject, and anticipating the irony of Socrates.

The traditional stress on the impiety of Euripides has tended to confuse or obscure the issues that most concerned him. For the essential conflict in his drama is not between man and the gods or Fate. It is between man and man, or within man. The essential evil is human injustice, human irrationality, human folly. The gods may symbolize this evil, or the traditional beliefs may intensify it, but the real cause of tragedy in Euripides remains the passions of man. His realism, his pessimism, and his idealism alike sprang from his abiding concern with the nature of man: a creature with a god-like power of reason, who was so often mastered by unreason; a creature with a terrible capacity for passion, which could also be god-like. As a student of passion Euripides made his most original contributions to tragedy. In this light his greater plays remain diverse and complex, and may not be uniformly satisfying; but they have universal, enduring tragic interest.

The simplest and saddest of his tragedies, *The Trojan Women,* was inspired by the behavior of Athens, not Athena.

Such earlier plays as *Andromache* and *The Children of Heracles* show that Euripides was a patriotic Athenian, naturally hostile to Sparta and the Spartan way of life. This one, produced in 415 shortly after the infamous Melian episode described by Thucydides, expresses his revulsion against the atrocities of the Peloponnesian War. For once he dispensed with his customary theatrical effects, and virtually with Plot itself, to portray the sufferings of the "enemy" women at the hands of their cruel Greek conquerors. The tragedy is a prolonged lamentation that breaks almost all the rules of Aristotle, or any manual of dramatic technique. There is no reversal of fortune, no denouement, no real conflict—there cannot be a dramatic conflict, since the very point of the play is that the Trojan women are helpless. Neither is there a tragic rhythm or a logical development in its episodes; the episodes might be interchanged. Nevertheless *The Trojan Women* is a deeply moving play, quite apart from its historical interest as the first major literary protest against war. It has thematic unity, with sufficient variety of character and incident to make it more than a monody.

If some critics have felt otherwise, the text at least refutes those who find in it only a rain of warm tears. The play was an appeal to the civilized ideals of Athens that Æschylus had upheld, and that Euripides must have felt were still alive; the Athenians at least partially vindicated his faith by allowing it to be performed in the midst of the war. (One wonders whether a comparable play could be produced on Broadway today.) It demonstrates the superiority of the helpless women over their conquerors. "Greeks!" exclaims Andromache. "Your Greek cleverness is simple barbarity"; and Hecuba later adds that they are not even clever, since they are prey to unreasoned fear. Hecuba in particular demonstrates that the Trojan women are not simply helpless. The dominant character in the play, the aged Queen embodies the compassion, loyalty, and love that may soften the grief, but above all the fortitude that can endure the worst, the heroic capacity for suffering greatly.

"Forward: into the slave's life," she says as she leaves the stage; but in slavery she will still be a queen in spirit. She makes the drama tragic, not merely sad.

In *Agamemnon* Æschylus too had condemned the atrocities of war. Euripides went further, attacking the whole cult of the hero and the heroic ideal that the old soldier of Marathon had glorified. He anticipated Shaw by his habit of cutting down the traditional heroes to life size, making them talk and behave as ordinary Athenians would in their situation; and sometimes he simply gutted them. Of such debunking, *Electra* is typical. The scene of the play is not a palace or temple but a peasant's hut; the prologue is spoken not by a god but by the peasant, the husband of Electra; and the peasant is the noblest character in the play. Euripides presents the main action for what it is in everyday life—murder, of a mother. He treats Clytemnestra sympathetically, endowing her with a mother's desire to make peace with her daughter. He represents Orestes as a timid butcher, who murders Ægisthus when his victim has his back turned and is offering a sacrifice to the gods. In *Andromache*, we are reminded, Orestes is a scoundrel pure and simple—foreshadowing the type of the stage villain, who would live tenaciously and tediously ever after.

Even some admirers of Euripides (including Kitto) accordingly describe the heroine of *Electra* as a monster, whom he blackened in order to show up the moral naïveté of Sophocles' treatment of her. But if this was his initial intention, he accomplished much more. His Electra is the most sensitive, acute psychological study in Greek drama, and subtler than some modern studies made with benefit of Freud.

In part she suffers from an "Electra complex." Clytemnestra remarks that she had always loved her father best, adding that "it is often so." Essentially, however, Electra is a hysteric, a victim of the barren life to which she has been condemned. The passion for revenge that obsesses her, fills her with fierce determination, and also makes her liable to sudden panic, springs more from hatred of her mother than from love of her father. The hatred feeds on sexual jealousy of Clytemnestra, who has a lover and lives in luxury, while she herself lives with a peasant who in decency has not consummated his marriage with the princess. Her sick mind is most fully exposed when she stands over the corpse of Ægisthus. She hungers to pour out her hatred of this man who had "killed her soul," but she is also ashamed, fearful of the hatred she might incur by such impiety to the dead; she nevertheless gloats over the thought that he had been known only as "the Queen's husband," not "the King"; she is then struck by a poisonous suspicion, wondering whether he had found consolation in other women; finally she turns away in loathing from his "girl-like face," to express the prayer that God will grant her a real man. Needless to add, there is nothing heroic about this Electra. Yet Euripides makes her pitiable, giving glimpses of a latent decency and dignity in her warped soul. When she breaks down after the murder of Clytemnestra, her remorse is a genuine horror, not mere hysteria; and she then tries to shield Orestes by taking upon herself the whole blame for the crime.

Medea is another study of passion, but a more elemental passion, more universal in its implications, and both grander and more terrible. Here again a hero is debunked. Jason of the Argonauts turns out to be a smug, cowardly, ignoble bourgeois, who in order to improve his social position by a royal marriage, is divorcing and exiling his wife, Medea, even though she has sacrificed her family for him, saved his life, and enabled him to win his fame as a hero. He thereby gives Euripides an excuse to attack the bondage of women, whose plight Medea dwells on in her opening soliloquy.[9] But chiefly

---

[9] Ironically, Euripides' studies of passionate women—in particular Medea—earned him a reputation as a woman-hater. Actually, almost all his memorable characters are women; their woes are one of his favorite themes. Similarly all but three of his choruses are made up of women, and one of their common functions, as in *Medea*, is to express a sympathy for the heroine that a Greek audience might not feel. But in this sympathy Euripides was again not wholly untraditional. The Clytemnestra of Æschylus and the Antigone and Electra of Sophocles also dominate the plays in which they appear. Although their stature may be a heritage of Homeric society, it has led some recent scholars to question the traditional

the meanness of Jason serves to set off the towering passion of Medea. Wounded love and pride swell into the fury of jealousy and hatred that culminates in her horrible revenge, as she murders not only his bride and the bride's father but her own children. And Euripides allows her to triumph. Exulting over her revenge, she leaves for the haven of Athens.

Hence this tragedy is another defiance of Aristotelian principles. It is a shocking play, whose catastrophe is a slaughter of the innocent and hardly seems designed to effect a cartharsis of pity and fear. Ancient critics, however, were troubled for a different reason—the "inconsistency" in the character of Medea. They were not accustomed to a tragic conflict *within* the protagonist. The characters of Æschylus and Sophocles may struggle against fear and may doubt, falter, waver, repent; but they are never torn as Medea is torn by hatred, love, pride, and pity when she resolves to murder her children, recoils in horror, weeps over her darlings, recoils against her softness, gives way to pure anguish again, and finally decides that she must kill them just because she is their mother. Since such "inconsistency" strikes us as perfectly natural, even a psychological commonplace, we are likely to underrate the originality of Euripides, and to overlook a severe limitation he exposes in his high-minded predecessors. The classical conception of character—alike in drama, epic, and history—stopped short of unsuspected depths, basic contradictions, split personalities, the darkest mysteries of character. Neither did it permit significant development through experience. It restricted the tragic theme of purification by suffering; for the Orestes of Æschylus himself is not purified in heart, but legally exonerated.

Modern readers are troubled chiefly by the theme of *Medea* —the frightful destructiveness of passion. The whole play may seem simply frightful. Euripides does not build up the emo-

---

view that Athenian women were little more than household slaves, confined to the home. Contemporary allusions indicate that at least they attended the theater.

tion but makes it almost unbearably intense from the outset; and he could have made his point without all the gruesome detail in the Messenger's long report on how Medea's poison worked on her victims. Yet at least he aimed at more than blood-curdling melodrama, endowing Medea with a grandeur as compelling as awful. She is neither blind nor crazed as she makes her dreadful decision. Her passion also culminates in a clear perception: she sees "the full evil" of what she plans. Nevertheless she is prepared to accept the consequences of her crime.

In *Hippolytus* the story of Phædra illustrates the same basic theme. Aphrodite announces in the Prologue that the tragedy is all her work: to punish Hippolytus for his scorn of her, she has made his stepmother, Phædra, fall in love with him. But if Euripides relished this opportunity to attack the immoral Olympians again, we need not take Aphrodite seriously. She symbolizes the human passion of love. Phædra has "fallen in" love, as we aptly say. When she finally gives in to her hopeless passion, only to be scorned and reviled by Hippolytus, and then takes revenge on him, she is still acting out a realistic drama. It is more realistic, indeed, than most later tragedies of "romantic love," a theme whose popularity may be traced to Euripides. As a Greek, he did not regard such love as the supreme value, something for which a world is well lost. He regarded it as a passion: an elemental, non-rational power that in the words of the Nurse is "something stronger than God if that can be," and that is as likely to be a curse. As in *Medea*, it is here a terribly destructive power, bringing ruin to Phædra, Hippolytus, and Theseus, again without discrimination between innocence and guilt. The chief difference is that there is less horror in *Hippolytus*, and more pity. "All too well I know that I am a woman," says the wretched Phædra.

The structure of the play, however, brings us back to the troublesome aspects of Euripidean drama. While Hippolytus is the nominal hero and has more lines than Phædra, she remains the chief source of interest. Many readers feel a let-

down after she kills herself, well before the end, and all have
to recognize a shift of interest to the tragedy of Hippolytus
and Theseus. Critics have therefore had the usual difficulty in
unifying the play. The most attractive solution is to view the
devotion of Hippolytus to Artemis, the goddess of chastity, as
a complementary theme; his fate deepens the tragedy by showing that it is futile to deny the elemental passion of love, or as
wrong to try to suppress it entirely. Thus the wise servant
warns him at the outset against his haughty disdain of Aphrodite. The difficulty with this interpretation is that Hippolytus
has no clear, stable character. He first appears as a naïve young
man boasting of his chastity; call him innocent or priggish,
his boasts would seem even sillier to a Greek audience than
they do to American males who know their Kinsey. When
he hears of Phædra's love for him, he seems positively neurotic
in his frenzied hatred of women: "I'll hate you women, hate
and hate and hate you, and never have enough of hating."
When he hears from Theseus that the dying Phædra has
accused him of rape, he turns into an accomplished rhetorician,
defending himself in a sophisticated style to which all the
characters of Euripides have been bred, but which seems
more out of character because he continues to refer to his
"maiden soul." And when he is brought in dying, all bruised
and battered by the sea monster, he becomes a noble youth,
generously forgiving his father, still adoring his holy Artemis,
who enters to assert his entire innocence. It is hard to believe
that Euripides had his mind on the characterization of Hippolytus.

But there is no question of his interest in Phædra. It is her
story that has made *Hippolytus* one of the most popular of his
plays. And it recalls his special problems as a playwright.
Many Athenians were scandalized by Phædra; to them her
love was only incestuous. In *The Frogs* Aristophanes has
Æschylus protest against the desecration of the Athenian stage
by "filthy, detestable Phædras." We might assume, then, that
Euripides could get his story of her on the stage only by put-

ting it into a play ostensibly about Hippolytus. In his half-hearted job on Hippolytus he perhaps took most pleasure in exposing the neurotic purity of the "hero."

Furthermore, the Greek dramatic form was ill-suited to these novel interests of Euripides. *Medea* and *Hippolytus* are both essentially domestic tragedies, focused on individuals who in no sense represent the community. The choruses of Euripides never make the magnificent entrances that they do in Æschylus, and usually fall short of the role of "ideal spectator," but in these private dramas it is awkward for them to enter and look on at all. Medea and Phædra are both required to swear the Chorus to secrecy. The Corinthian women obligingly do nothing when the foreigner Medea reveals to them her plan to kill their king and his daughter, and still refrain when she enters the palace to murder her children. It is as embarrassing when Phædra reveals to fifteen strangers the dire secret that she has not dared tell to anyone. And in another drama, *Orestes*, the Chorus becomes simply a nuisance. When the women file in, as Orestes is trying to get some much needed rest, Electra begs them to stop singing and go home; and since in a Greek play they cannot, she must add, let them at least, for God's sake, sing quietly.

These incidental difficulties lead us back to the major issues raised by Euripides' realism, and the ambiguity of his total achievement. Only a pedant could condemn him outright for being loyal to the thought and experience of his own time, instead of to a purely classical ideal since defined by pedants. With his original interests and insights, he unquestionably widened the scope of Greek tragedy. In his studies of passion he explored new depths in the nature of man, new sources of tragic experience. In *The Trojan Women* he presented a more strictly universal, timeless drama than the *Oresteia* or *Œdipus Rex*, introducing the most common theme in the history of civilization—the inhumanity of man to man. His "advanced" thought brought him closer to the most immediate sources of misery, the evils that are more tragic because men either do not regard them as evil or attribute them to the will of the gods. Hence he was the first known Greek writer of importance to attack the institution of slavery; the first to take up the cause of women; the first to democratize tragedy by translating it into everyday language and giving common men a dignified role in it.

Yet by the same tokens Euripides also narrowed the scope of tragedy. His characters were mostly smaller in stature than those of his predecessors, seldom heroic or symbolic figures; his audience could feel intimate with them, even superior to them, but seldom elevated or awed by their fate. Likewise the scene of his drama was more constricted: not yet a private chamber, still open to vistas of an older, greater world, but no longer symbolic of the community or the cosmos. He introduced affairs with the gods mainly to belittle them, dispel all feeling of awe, and emphasize the discontinuity between man and the cosmos. In the life of man he had a clear vision of the elemental power of the non-rational without a deep intuition of underlying patterns, rhythms, and renewals. As an earnest Athenian he spoke out eloquently on matters of communal interest but chiefly as a sharp critic; he could not supplement his criticism with either a *Eumenides* or an *Œdipus at Colonus*. In the summary of Nietzsche, his drama was "a thing both cool and fiery, equally capable of freezing and burning," but incapable of achieving either Apollonian harmony or Dionysian communion.

Historically, the cool rationalism of Euripides was the major immediate threat to the art of tragedy. Since his thought is no longer shocking we are disturbed only by its obtrusiveness, coupled with his indifference to the amenities of drama. Thus his plays typically begin with a monologue of pure exposition, addressed point-blank at the audience; his endings are typically epilogues, outlining the future history of the main characters. Together they make for a literally more complete action, but a less profoundly suggestive one. Similarly his characters are fond of abstract speculation and formal argument.

A notorious example is the aged queen in *Hecuba,* who in the midst of her heart-rending lamentations pauses to inquire whether virtue is due to education or to birth, and to wonder why men neglect the most important of arts, Persuasion. The Greek audience evidently delighted in this sort of thing, which is not far removed from the set debates and the mechanical *stichomythia* in Æschylus and Sophocles. Nevertheless Euripides heralded a significant change. Although his predecessors were philosophical poets, philosophy in his drama became more conscious, independent, and detachable. Werner Jaeger noted the historic sequel: "Liberated from poetry, it turned to attack it and to dominate it."

The final comment of Euripides himself, however, was to a very different effect. At the end of his life, in exile, he wrote the extraordinary *Bacchæ*—as if to mock the whole critical effort to label and place him. This tragedy is wholly traditional in form, and exhibits a perfect, seemingly effortless mastery of the form. The Chorus is again a real actor, participating in the drama and orchestrating its themes in the manner of Æschylus. The tragic issue is again a public issue, involving the whole community, enacted on a public stage. The protagonists are the King of Thebes and the god Dionysus, the patron of Greek tragedy; they face each other in scenes that recall Æschylus and may have been suggested by his trilogy on the same theme. The story is a popular legend that to the Greeks was an actual historical event, and that for us has an added interest because it in fact reflects a major historic event—the coming of Dionysus to Greece. But in spite of all these old-fashioned elements *The Bacchæ* could have been written only by Euripides. Whether or not he conceived it as his last testament to Athens, it is the supreme testament of his genius as a tragic poet.

Critics have therefore disagreed more radically over its meaning than that of any other of his plays. Some have read it as the last word of Euripides the rationalist and rebel: the tragedy of King Pentheus, a good Greek who opposed the barbarous orgiastic religion of Dionysus, is the crowning exhibit of the injustice of the gods. Others have read it as a recantation: the tragedy is the punishment of a stubborn king who refused to welcome the radiant, joy-giving Dionysus. Of these some conjecture that Euripides was trying to overcome his scandalous reputation, some that he had had a genuine religious conversion. Still others have been frankly mystified. "No one will ever be able to say what this strange drama intends," says Allardyce Nicoll; though he adds that "no one can deny its power, its intensity, and its beauty." But this very disagreement gives the clue to the profoundest of Euripides' dramas. Its power and intensity spring immediately from the wild, eerie passion contained in a severely classical form. Ultimately its secret is again ambiguity, or specifically the ambivalence of Dionysus.

King Pentheus is not a pure martyr. He is arrogant and harsh, never reasoning with the new god or his worshippers, meeting them with brute force, displaying the "strict pitiless mind" that "is death unto godliness." He is plainly mistaken in his belief that the new religion is merely a worship of lust. For Dionysus, the "God of many names," is a many-sided symbol of "Heaven's high mysteries." He is a "Joy-bestower," liberating men from care by his gifts of wine, music, and love. He is nevertheless "Immaculate," somehow a symbol of holy purity. He is also a Savior, a Son of God on earth who has given his blood for man and who literally dwells in the hearts of his worshippers, enabling them to become one with him. He has indeed a Christ-like aspect as an adorable god, born of a mortal woman, who is despised as a god of the lowly people he welcomes, and who can inspire his followers to "walk humbly in God's sight." At times the Chorus of bacchantes speak like St. Paul about the foolishness of the Greeks: "The world's Wise are not wise." Historically, this Dionysus symbolizes the spiritualization of the primitive fertility god who had come from the East and swept all Greece.

Yet he remains a terrifying god, as he seemed to civilized

Greeks when he first invaded their land. He is a god of Darkness, whose rites are held mostly at night; he tells Pentheus that the darkness is a majestic thing. If he inspires ecstasy he also inspires a mad frenzy. Both may lead to orgy (in his defense the prophet Tiresias can say only that he "compels no woman to be chaste"), but the common climax is tearing animals to pieces. Here his intoxicated devotees tear King Pentheus to pieces, limb by limb. In the awful revenge that Dionysus takes on the King he reveals that like Jehovah he is a jealous god, terrible in his wrath. Or rather he is more awful because he does not display any wrath: he maintains a smiling calm that at first seems gentle, soon becomes disturbing, and grows steadily more sinister. At the end even his Chorus is appalled when Agave enters, still ecstatic and mad, bearing proudly the head of her son Pentheus, whom she has slaughtered on this most "blessed" of days—and then gradually comes to her senses. No scene in Euripides is more horrifying than this one, but here pity and terror are not numbed by the horror. By this time we have nothing but sympathy for King Pentheus, and especially for Agave, who with her father is punished so cruelly even though they have accepted the new god. The terror arises from the knowledge that all this was the god's doing, and that the god is pitiless, wholly unmoved, still imperturbable in his smiling calm.

In *The Bacchæ* Euripides dramatized the ambivalence of the actual, historic, many-sided Dionysus—"God, Beast, Mystery." His greatest gift to man was a sense of liberation, by which he also robbed them of their freedom, made them slaves to unreason. He was a "Light in Darkness" that led them back to the primeval darkness; his Truth made them free and made them mad. We know that the climax of his annual winter rites remained the tearing to pieces and eating raw of an animal, which presumably fascinated his worshippers as the ultimate in exaltation through revulsion. We find the same fusion of the holy and the horrible in the mystery religions that Euripides rightly associated with the cult of Dionysus, not-

ably the cult of Cybele: a Great Mother who with her dying
lover-son Attis inspired ecstasies of self-transcendence or self-
abandon that often terminated in self-castration.[1] Ultimately,
Euripides dramatized the profound contradictions in religion
itself. He showed the best and the worst of the religious spirit,
and how the best becomes the worst. He anticipated the observation of Radhakrishnan: "If we believe absurdities, we
shall commit atrocities." He anticipated the tragic contradictions in the religion that grew up in the name of Jesus: the
Christ who proved his gospel of universal love by dying for
man on the Cross, and whose Cross then became the symbol
of an uncompromising, ruthless idealism that inspired Christians to war on his own people, on heathens, and most fiercely
on fellow Christians who had incorrect opinions about their
Redeemer.

The immediate theme of *The Bacchæ*, however, is the familiar theme in the tragedies of Euripides—the elemental
power of passion. Both Pentheus and Agave are tragic victims
of this power, one by trying to oppose it, the other by giving
in to it. The most obvious point of the drama is the impotence
of reason. But the tragic wisdom of Euripides goes deeper
than this. Reason must realize not only the naturalness but the
necessity of this elemental passion, which is akin to the elemental forces in the natural world. Thought cannot penetrate
"Heaven's high mysteries"; it must recognize the "wisdom old
as time" incorporated in the mystery religions, and their deep
connections with the life of nature. As the god of Nature,
Dionysus is wild and lovely; he is majestically calm and still,
he offers peace and joy, he brings new life—he is prodigal in
his blessings; and he is completely amoral. There is no more

[1] A somewhat different newcomer was Orpheus, whose cult probably
helped to spiritualize Dionysus even though Greek legend had him destroyed by Dionysus in anger. He offered the Greeks positive immortality. The Dionysus of Euripides does not hold out this hope for man—
nor did any of the tragic poets. Tombstones indicate that it did not become a common hope until after 400 B.C., when the great period of
Greek tragedy was over.

love, pity, or justice in him than there is in nature. No wise man can be simply for Dionysus, or simply against him.

With the ancients *The Bacchæ* became the most popular of Euripides' plays; and we may wonder what they saw in it. Common men may have seen a celebration of the majesty and power of Dionysus, since they were pensioning off the Olympians and turning to savior-gods. We may wonder, too, whether Euripides foresaw that the future belonged to the mystery religions. Quite possibly he did, for in his last years Athens was invaded by a number of Eastern gods, including Cybele, Attis, Bendix, Adonis, and Sabazius—the latter an un-hellenized form of Dionysus. In any case, his last great play is still more haunting in a historical retrospect. It harked back to the coming of Dionysus, in whose name Greek tragedy arose. It heralded the mighty historic drama of the future, the eventual triumph of the Eastern religions, or specifically of the dying-god of the ancient ritual dramas, with which Greek tragedy died.

5. EPILOGUE: THE DECLINE TO SENECA

"Greek tragedy," wrote Nietzsche, "had a fate different from that of all her older sister arts: she died by suicide"—by the hand of Euripides. Hence "she died tragically, while they all passed away very calmly and beautifully in ripe old age"; and according to Nietzsche her death left an immense void that was deeply felt everywhere. The Greeks themselves seem to have been unaware of this tragic event. Aristotle gives no hint of the suicide or the void. Tragedy became popular all over the Greek world; theaters sprang up everywhere and guilds of actors rose to meet their needs. New plays were written down to the Christian era. (Even a Hellenistic king—Ptolemy IV—wrote a tragedy.) And though the great period ended with Euripides, its ending was hardly so shocking as Nietzsche made it. We have only thirty-three of the roughly one thousand plays performed in Athens during the century. The lost plays, which doubtless included considerable mediocre work, probably reflected the gradual exhaustion of the traditional form. Such exhaustion is the invariable fate of great forms and styles. For the historian of drama the surprising fact is not that Greek tragedy died but that it flourished for a whole century. In later history no great period of drama was ever to last so long.[2]

Yet the death of Greek tragedy, like its birth, was not strictly fated. We might get a fuller understanding of tragedy by inquiring into the causes or conditions of its decline, and the reasons why it never revived in the eight centuries of high culture before the Greco-Roman world of the West went down into darkness. For this world long continued to be creative. Although the Hellenistic Age ushered in by the conquests of Alexander the Great is commonly labeled "decadent," since it follows the classical peak on the historic curve, it was actually a vigorous age. The Romans in turn made important contributions when they took over Greek culture. As they produced a great epic poet in Virgil, so one might have expected them to produce a great tragic poet. As it was, they produced nothing better than Seneca, whose drama now seems an unconscious caricature of Greek tragedy.

According to Nietzsche, the arch-villain of the piece was Socrates. Euripides spoke for this "new-born demon" who destroyed both Apollo and Dionysus, annihilated myth itself. Socrates taught that knowledge is virtue and virtue is happiness, that ignorance is the only source of misery and sin, that only the intelligible is beautiful—in sum, a rationalistic faith that was fatal to tragedy. As usual, Nietzsche exaggerated: it is grotesque to imply that the faith of Socrates became the living faith of Athens. Yet Greek philosophy did become inimical

[2] Alfred Kroeber's *Configurations of Cultural Growth,* a survey of the major historical growths in all forms of culture, indicates how uniformly short-lived they have been in drama. In painting and philosophy they usually last for several centuries; in drama they average about fifty years. Notable achievement in drama seems to be more dependent on other institutions, and to require a rare set of artistic, economic, and social conditions.

to the tragic spirit. Plato, the pupil of Socrates, singled out Homer and the tragic poets as among the worst influences on the young. While Aristotle had much more respect for them, he was a rationalist who had nothing of their tragic sense of life. His confidence in the power of reason was shared by the dominant schools of thought in the century following him. Epicurus was skeptical about the gods but taught that by meditating on philosophy one could live "like a god among men"; the Epicureans sought happiness by suppressing all passion, denying any reason for terror. In this respect they were akin to the great rival school of Stoicism, with its ideal of imperturbable calm. The Stoics tried to attain their ideal by willing things to be as they were, and buttressed this effort by a metaphysics that taught that things were in fact just as they should be. They identified Reason with Nature or God, insisted that the universe was perfectly rational and good.

But there was something irrational, even desperate about this insistence. The Stoics evidenced no real love of Nature or God, they could never demonstrate the rationality of the universe, and they were always vague about the nature of its goodness. Their very emphasis on stoical endurance was a confession that man had to endure a lot, for cosmic reasons that were not at all clear. A touching example of their illogic is the cry of Posidonius when he was in misery: "Do your worst, pain, do your worst—you will never compel me to acknowledge that you are an evil!" Although Stoicism was a product of the elite, not a popular movement, it reflected the spiritual insecurity of the Greek world, the growing irrationalism among ordinary men—an irrationalism to which they were more liable because since Socrates intellectuals had become aloof from public life. The Greeks could no longer endure the spiritual freedom that Homer had won for them. One sign was the increasing popularity of the mystery cults. Another was the universal worship of Tyche, or Chance. And in time philosophy became infected by this popular irrationalism, or "failure of nerve." About 200 B.C. the slow decline set in, with the Stoics leading the way. Chaldean astrology became the vogue; all the schools except the Epicurean became cults, dedicated to the pursuit of salvation rather than knowledge or truth. Eventually Greek thought ended in the superstition and theurgy from which it had sprung.

In the long run, the tragic spirit suffered more from such irrationalism than from Socratic rationalism. Socrates did not "annihilate" the myth; Nietzsche himself later remarks that what followed the death of tragedy was "a pandemonium of myths and superstitions." More precisely, it was a return to the myth *as* superstition—the myth taken literally, really believed. Likewise the ancient ritual dramas were revived, not killed; the mystery cults presented these dramas in their pure form, as means of escaping mystery. All the old bottles were still there—but without "the new wine of reasoning and rebellious humanity."

There remains the question of underlying causes: why philosophy came to monopolize the high seriousness that tragedy had once assumed, why it withdrew from the communal life to establish schools for the few, and why it eventually succumbed to the low superstition of the many. For once the immediate cause seems plain: it was the decline of the Greek *polis* itself. History has rarely exhibited a more appropriate coincidence than the end of tragedy and the fall of Athens.

Although Athens recovered, to become an important power for a time, and to remain the nominal "school of Hellas" for centuries, it never recovered the collective ideal and the independent, abundant collective life that had nurtured its splendid drama. After it put Socrates to death its greatest son was Plato, who immortalized his disillusionment with Athenian democracy in the *Republic*—an ideal republic of and by the elite, and for the people as long as they were content to have no say in their government. Presently Athens succumbed to the rising power of Macedon; it had responded tardily and half-heartedly to the impassioned pleas of Demosthenes, who tried to awaken its old ideals. Its failure signaled the end of Greek independence. Everywhere Greek cities came under the domination of Macedon, and then of Rome. The *polis* retained a considerable degree of self-government and civic pride, it was still an "open" society that encouraged vigorous and varied activity, it maintained the old traditions of high culture—to the end it was Greek enough to enjoy tragedy. But it was no longer in control of its destiny, it could no longer give or demand of its citizens what Athens had in its prime, it could no longer inspire an art concerned with great ideas—no longer create tragedy.

Unable to fulfill himself completely as a citizen, the individual accordingly turned to his business, his domestic life, his private interests—at his most exalted, his private salvation. The ruling spirit of the Hellenistic Age was a bourgeois spirit, troubled in its depths, not really sure of itself, but complacent on the surface, typically resolving its uncertainties in ostentation. Like the Victorian Age, it preferred sentiment to passion; it cultivated the new theme of romantic love. It produced the new form of the idyl, which expressed a sentimental fondness for nature and the pastoral life, and revealed that it was cut off from these elemental simplicities. It was devoid of tragic irony; instead it took to wit, satire, epigram. And now that great public issues were no longer being debated, it developed the rage for oratory and rhetoric, the art of eloquence for its own elegant sake, that remained a blight to the end of the Roman world. In a similar spirit its poets played with the ancient myths and legends, preparing the way for Ovid. They made classical mythology what it has been for most readers ever since: a collection of pretty fairy tales, a rich source of literary ornament, but no longer a vehicle for religious thought or any serious thought.

In drama the characteristic expression of the Hellenistic Age was New Comedy. The Old Comedy of Aristophanes was an extravaganza that had developed out of the bawdy, phallic elements of the folk festivals: a medley of fantasy, obscenity, poetry, farce, satire, and burlesque that was often coarse but never commonplace, and was usually centered on public issues. The New Comedy of Menander was a comedy of manners, overlaid with sentiment and mild philosophical reflection. Its plots were conventional intrigue, usually involving heart-interest, usually resolved by coincidence (the great god Chance). Its characters were stock types drawn from bourgeois life; there was no Chorus. Its scene was an ordinary street. This type of comedy may seem more commonplace than it was because it has held the stage ever since.

New Comedy clearly stemmed from Euripides, who now held the tragic stage. After the fourth century there are no allusions to the performance of a play by Æschylus, and only one to a performance of Sophocles. Although we cannot be sure just what the Hellenistic Age found in Euripides, there is little doubt that it was impressed by his bourgeois realism, his interest in the individual, his sentiment, his rhetoric, and his theatricality. It was no longer scandalized by his "impiety," or his breaks with tradition. The performance of tragedies was still reserved for religious festivals or great national occasions, but essentially it became a great theatrical show, staged with ever more splendor as it lost religious and communal significance. The theater itself became a playhouse. It now had a high stage on which the actors performed; they stood out above the orchestra below—the dancing-place of a Chorus that could contribute to the spectacle, but no longer represented the community. The star actor was a professional who could achieve more fame than the playwright. In fourth-century Athens a law had to be passed prohibiting actors from tampering with the classical tragedies, which they had been altering to give themselves fatter parts.

In this retrospect we may better appreciate the incomparable theater of classical Athens: a theater that represented the City, with an audience that constituted the City, assembled on a major occasion of the civic life. Never since have dramatists had the habitual privilege of addressing such an audience, on such an occasion, with the freedom to use a hallowed form for expressing their own thoughts. And we may better understand why Rome, the dramatic creator of a great empire, failed to create a great drama.

As they built their empire, the Romans took over the bulk of Greek culture. By the end of the third century B.C. they had performed plays by Sophocles and Euripides and also developed a popular theater, under Plautus, that was influenced by Greek comedy; in the second century they produced several tragic dramatists of their own (Ennius, Pacuvius, and Accius) whose plays became classics and were performed for many years after their death. By the end of the Republic, in the following century, drama had become so popular that at least fifty annual festival days were devoted to plays. All over their empire the Romans began building the massive, well-designed theaters that are among their most impressive architectural achievements. By this time, too, they had produced poets of genius, such as Lucretius, Horace, and Virgil. In their own history they had great themes, heroic and tragic. In general, they appeared to have all the prerequisites for a great drama—except an audience that could inspire and appreciate it.

From the beginning the Roman populace displayed the coarse tastes that were eventually to be gratified by the brutal gladiatorial shows. They could enjoy the rowdy farce of Plautus, but their preferences ran to rope dancers, acrobats, boxers, and wild beasts. Their tastes were not improved by a self-conscious elite that prided itself upon its polite culture; for this audience Terence wrote his polished, genteel imitations of the New Comedy of Menander, introducing such types as the prostitute with a heart of gold. The ruling class prided itself upon sensational displays of its power and munificence. Thus Pompey's theater was opened by a performance of *Clytemnestra*, a tragedy by Accius, which featured a prodigious spectacle: the fall of Troy was an excuse for a trophy-bearing procession that included five hundred mules, three thousand chariots, and an unspecified number of elephants and giraffes. Rome itself was a cosmopolitan city that became increasingly splendid as it was adorned by the emperors, and increasingly parasitical and soulless. Its splendors emphasized the spiritual void, the want of the rich communal life that Athens had known. The Roman masses, who had no voice in their government, demanded only bread and circuses. Among the cultivated classes it was fashionable to write—everybody wrote; but writers were literati, addressing a coterie instead of a community. In time they wrote chiefly for one another. It seems almost certain that Seneca, the most famous of Roman tragedians, wrote his plays not for performance but for recitation before an invited group.

At any rate, the tragedies of Seneca are essentially declamation rather than drama. Although his kind of rhetoric has gone out of fashion, we may still find it occasionally effective, appreciate the neatness of some of his famous "sentences." For the rest, almost all readers today are struck by how crude his drama is, and how invincibly abominable his taste. It is hard to understand why for centuries Western critics and poets had so high an admiration of Seneca, installing his plays among the great classics; so it might become us to acknowledge that some of our own judgments will no doubt seem as foolish to later generations.[3] At least we must reckon with the considerable heritage of Seneca. Directly and indirectly, he passed on to Elizabethan drama the "sentence," the monologue, the ghost, the supernatural machinery, the theme of revenge, the villain who freely declares his villainy, the glut of horror for its own sake. And at least it is instructive to see what he made of his own heritage of Greek tragedy.

Seneca retained all the traditional appearances. He took his plots from the Greek legends, and emphasized such themes as

[3] I venture the opinion that most of the gods of contemporary criticism—Henry James, Joyce, Yeats, Proust, Rilke, Kafka, Lawrence, Eliot, and Pound—suffer from marked eccentricities or perversities that will trouble critics much more once they have got over the excitement of "explicating" their texts.

the power of Fate, the punishment of *hubris*, the danger of all extremes; he kept the Chorus and the Messenger, observed the unities, restricted himself to three actors. His tragedy seems more formal, indeed, than Greek tragedy, and throws into relief its basic realism. He does not so much observe the unities of time and place as neglect to create any sense of time or place. He treats the Chorus as a pure convention, making little or no effort to motivate its presence; it is typically an anonymous group that suddenly appears out of nowhere, for no apparent reason, and recites on whatever theme Seneca has a mind to expound, often without regard to the action going on. Sometimes he does not bother to provide an audience for his Messenger. Often his characters drop the pretense of addressing other characters, directing their monologues at nobody in particular. His dialogue is as formal, consisting chiefly of rhetorical repartee or an exchange of apothegms. In general, he carried to the extreme the worst tendencies of Euripides, his obvious model. Yet "formal" is not really the word for Senecan tragedy. He was indifferent to form, and had little or no idea of economy, purity, symmetry, appropriateness of any sort. He had as little notion of a "complete action," or concern for a "probable" one. His main object, apart from the display of his rhetoric, was to raise the hair and curdle the blood.

Seneca was most at home, accordingly, in the story of Medea, though he felt the need of intensifying it; his chief innovation was to have her kill her children onstage. What he could do with a grander theme may be illustrated by his *Œdipus Rex*. About half of one of its five acts is devoted to the main action, the hero's discovery of his guilt. As much space is devoted to an ode to Bacchus, recited by the Chorus while the prophet Tiresias prepares to consult the infernal host of the Styx. Seneca spreads himself still more on the horrible vision raised by Tiresias: the dead king Laius, "his limbs still smeared with his own blood, his hair squalid with dreadful filth," etc. The irony of the drama is effectively dissipated in the long opening monologue, in which Œdipus dwells on his awful misgivings about what the Fates have in store for him, and ends by contemplating flight. He is not endowed with a heroic character, or in fact any character to speak of; he is merely the excuse for the necessary horrors and the rhetoric to go with them. After he has blinded himself, dutifully providing "abundant streams of gore," his wife-mother enters to add a characteristic fillip. Resolved to kill herself, she considers the problem of just where to plunge the blade and finally decides that her "ample womb" is the appropriate place. It recalls the scene in Seneca's *Hippolytus* when, after the hero has been torn to pieces, Theseus begins to collect the pieces, speculates on one he is unable to identify, and settles his problem by fitting it into a gap in his jigsaw puzzle.

We must assume that Seneca had no thought of staging such scenes. Even in recital, however, they betray the hollowness of his tragedy. He had no idea of catharsis, no capacity for pity and awe. His melodramas exhibit as little sense of human dignity as piety. His most serious deficiencies spring not merely from his incompetence as a craftsman but from his basic unconcern with his tragic characters. And in this respect Seneca is more than a symbol of decadence. He is a lurid exhibit of a fundamental reason why the Romans in their prime did not write great tragedy.

As a people, the Romans lacked a tragic sense of life. At their best they were pious, grave, high-minded, dignified, responsible; but by Greek standards they were also insensitive, incurious, unimaginative. Their ideal hero, the Æneas of Virgil, reveals the defects of their virtues. He has a much higher sense of duty than the Homeric heroes, and as much less warmth, zest, and simple humanity. His "mighty bosom" shakes with grief, we are told, when his patriotic mission requires the sacrifice of Dido and her love; but we seldom shake with him, we feel that that bosom is as well armored against pity as against fear. When the Romans took to Greek philosophy most took to Stoicism, with its ideal of absolute self-possession, absolute acceptance of Necessity and obedience to Duty—an austere kind of wisdom that may seem akin to the tragic spirit, but is essentially different in its resolute refusal to challenge the universe, and its effort to suppress pity, fear, wonder, and all other emotion. As Seneca wrote, "To feel pain at the misfortune of others is a weakness unworthy of the wise man." His tragedies betray the basic illogic of Stoicism by implying that the Necessity he worshipped as a philosopher is not really right or good; his choruses sometimes dwell on the evil of Fate. But his most painful spectacles were not designed to arouse compassion.

At the end, however, let us not be too solemn about the decline of tragedy. One who values the tragic spirit ought to have a more complex, ironic sense of history than Nietzsche displayed when he wrote of the immense void left by the suicide of tragedy. Socrates, the alleged villain, contributed much more to the quest of the good life than Sophocles did. The Hellenistic Age filled the void with a great deal of still more influential enterprise, in art, philosophy, science, and religion. The Romans were no less vigorous and creative because they were unaware of the void. The *Pax Romana,* with its ideal of a universal commonwealth, has meant far more to the Western world than has Greek tragedy. And the theater itself gained as well as lost after the end of the great period in Athens. It became a cosmopolitan institution, one of the major traditions of the Greeks. The Romans preserved the tradition. Even the corrupt form that Seneca handed down to posterity had its value. It is doubtful whether the Elizabethans were ready for Æschylus and Sophocles. Seneca they could understand, and his rhetoric was at least a discipline, as his prestige was a stimulus.

In his own world, meanwhile, the decline of serious drama had an ironic aftermath. The theater was taken over by vulgar farces and pantomimes, performed by mimes who had fallen so low in the social scale that they included women, and were ranked with prostitutes. Although one of them became the famous Empress Theodora, wife of the Emperor Justinian, she could not restore the dignity of a profession that had once included Æschylus. But it was these despised mimes who kept alive the tradition of theater during the Dark Ages in the West.

CHAPTER IV

ELIZABETHAN
TRAGEDY

1. THE MEDIEVAL AND RENAISSANCE BACKGROUND

The Elizabethan Age was once pictured as a radiant dawn. At first historians interpreted it as a distinctively English affair, inspired by such national achievements as the defeat of the Spanish Armada. Then they recognized it as the English Renaissance; the key to it was the spirit of the Italian Renaissance, which was defined as an ardent, exuberant humanism. The typical hero of the Renaissance was Marlowe's Tamburlaine, drunk on dreams of power, beauty, splendor, glory. The ideal expression of its faith was the apostrophe of Hamlet:

> What a piece of work is a man! how noble in reason! how infinite in faculties! in form and moving how express and admirable! in action how like an angel! in apprehension how like a god! the beauty of the world, the paragon of animals!

In recent times, accordingly, scholars have been pleased to discredit this romantic Renaissance, and to dwell instead on the medieval heritage of the Elizabethans. The ruling ideas of the age, they insist, were still the orthodox Christian ideas. Its universe was the medieval theocentric universe, a "great chain of being" that extended from God through the angels to man and thence to animals, plants, and stones; though the lord of this earth, man was wretched as a creature of original sin, at the mercy of his senses and lower passions; and the morals drawn from his life were the medieval morals, particularly the sin of pride. It appears that Marlowe himself—the reputed arch-rebel and "atheist"—wrote conventional morality plays. One scholar ranks *Tamburlaine* among "the most grandly moral spectacles in the whole realm of English drama."

By now, however, it is easy enough to find a middle way be-

tween these views. Conventional Elizabethan thought undeniably did retain medieval ideas, as a historian might expect;
the Middle Ages could hardly die so expeditiously and completely as the romantic accounts of the Renaissance implied.
Nevertheless the spirit of the age was not simply or essentially
medieval—else there would be no distinctive Elizabethan Age.
The world of Marlowe and Shakespeare is obviously far removed from the world of Dante; no medieval writer could
have written *Tamburlaine* or *Hamlet*. As Tillyard observes
(and he is among the most influential scholars to stress the
neglected medieval aspects of the age), one cannot dismiss the
English Renaissance as a fiction by finding its characteristic
ideas in medieval writings. The *tone* of its utterances was different; familiar ideas were expressed with a new intensity and
fervor, or ideas that had been bold or marginal became commonplaces. The most evident stimulus of Elizabethan tragedy
was the tensions of an age of transition, the conflicts between
the old faiths and the new enthusiasms, which led to disillusionment and brought back the old fears. So Hamlet concluded
his apostrophe to god-like man on a note of despair: "And
yet to me what is this quintessence of dust? Man delights not
me. . . ."

Now, medieval men themselves knew plenty of tension, as
appears in the instability of Gothic art. They had to live in two
worlds: a City of God, an ideal universal order that was represented by the Church and the Holy Roman Empire; and a City
of Earth, a perpetual disorder that was neither holy nor Roman
nor imperial. As men they were cut in two. They were immortal souls, next to the angels, the lords of creation, who
could hope to rejoin their Creator in an eternity of heavenly
bliss; and they were fallen creatures of flesh, next to the beasts,
living on a corrupted earth at the very bottom of the universe,
and having much better reason to anticipate an eternity of
infernal torture. The vivid sense of both the angel and the
beast in man, and of God and the Devil, Heaven and Hell,
was intensified by the "Gothic" spirit, the willfulness and pas-

sion of a vigorous, youthful civilization. Medieval men were given to a reckless immoderation, violent extremes in piety and blasphemy, asceticism and sensuality, chivalry and atrocity. Their lust for life led to a horror of death unparalleled in all history. By the end of the fourteenth century Christian Europe was swept up in a *danse macabre*. Its art portrayed in ghastly detail the corruption and putrefaction of the flesh; the skeleton and the death's head became universal symbols; the *memento mori* was inscribed even on articles of daily use, from winepots to rings worn by whores. The horror was due in part to the fear of hell, but mostly it seemed due to the thought of mortality, the melting of this not too solid flesh. The Middle Ages bequeathed to Elizabethan drama its obsession with the theme of death.

Yet the "Age of Faith" wrote no tragedy itself. It produced dreary tales, like the Monk's Tale of Chaucer, about men "y-fallen out of heigh degree into miserie": tales complicated only by a simple idea of the rule of fortune that might not be clearly consistent with its faith in Providence, but that did not shake this faith. In so far as tragedy is "an affair with the gods," the Christian God discourages such affairs; he is always in the right, man always in the wrong. Later Christians, such as Pascal and Dostoyevsky, could have tragic affairs in their torment over the paradoxes of the true faith, the mystery why a perfect, self-sufficient God should have created so poor, perverse a servant. The Age of Faith, however, was very literal in its faith. As Loyola later wrote, if the Church "shall have defined anything to be black which to our eyes appears to be white, we ought in like manner to pronounce it to be black." Medieval men saw everything as black or white, and faithfully pronounced it black. They took their pessimism and their optimism straight, in alternation, with little sense of paradox. The great Pope Innocent III could write very calmly, almost smartly, about the unspeakable misery of the human condition.

As inconsistent, and ingenuous, were the willfulness and

passion of the Middle Ages. Machiavelli wrote that Christianity trains men "to endure evils, not to perform great actions"; and so it should if one takes seriously the Sermon on the Mount. In fact, it inspired medieval men to devote themselves to very great actions—prodigious feats of energy and valor on Crusades against the heathens, or in battle against fellow Christians. The hero was never more admired than in the Middle Ages. As a hero he might have a tragic fate—and often did. Yet he was never a tragic hero, comparable to Prometheus, Ajax, or Œdipus. He never challenged God's plan for man. In his pride, he might make inordinate demands on himself and his fellows, but he would not assert the value of pride. He suffered, and might learn by suffering, but what he avowedly learned was a sense of man's unworthiness, which made him worthy of heaven.

So it was even with Dante—by all odds the most comprehensive, complex, and mature of medieval writers. In the *Divine Comedy* he embodied all the strains of medieval life, the contradictions of its spirituality and its worldliness, the extremities of its hopes and its fears. A devout believer, dedicated to the supreme business of salvation, he was also a patriotic Italian and fierce political partisan, engrossed in the business of this life. A humble believer, often quaking in fear, he was also a proud individualist who made himself the hero of his supernatural epic, elected himself to the company of the greatest poets of antiquity, and introduced himself into heaven, even into the presence of God. He included so much in his epic that Francis Fergusson has called it "the most complete imitation of action" in our tradition, the only work that embraces "all the modes of human action." All, I should say, except the strictly comic and the strictly tragic. Dante transcends tragedy, without going all the way through the reasons for doubt and despair. He is innocent of the skeptical spirit. For all his earnest inquiry into the details of the divine scheme, his epic is essentially neither a challenge nor a quest but a demonstration, of a faith that in its fundamentals is never questioned. For all its incidental ironies, as of popes burning in hell, there is no ironic reserve. For all its multiple meanings—literal, allegorical, moral, anagogical—there is no real ambiguity. One may even find some suggestion of naïveté in this "Comedy," as when Dante gloats over the torture of his political enemies in the Inferno, on the gates of which it is written that not only Power Divine and Highest Wisdom but Primal Love designed these hellish tortures.

In general, one who comes to the Age of Faith from the world of Greek tragedy is struck by a naïveté that accentuated its basic incongruities and involved it in tragic dramas, but that also made it unaware of these incongruities, incapable of writing such dramas. The naïveté is most pronounced in the drama it did write. Although the mystery and miracle plays represent several centuries of growth, none of them approaches in artistry or maturity the earliest work of Æschylus. They are often quaint or touching, but the best are crude and the bulk is simply monotonous. Primarily they are of historical interest—which is to say, of little intrinsic or living interest to anyone but specialists. For the student of tragedy, however, they throw light on some basic issues.

As in Greece, this drama grew out of religion. Medieval men still realized that the Christian Mass is itself a drama of salvation. From the representations of the passion of Christ at Easter there developed the cycles of mystery plays, and with these the miracle plays representing Biblical stories or the lives of saints. Later came the morality plays, typified by *Everyman*. In almost all this drama one may make out the ancient ritual pattern of the Year-Dæmon. It survives in the conclusion of Knowledge in *Everyman*: "Now hath he suffered that we shall all endure." It is plainest, of course, in the passion of Christ. But medieval drama therefore raises difficulties for those who see in the ritual pattern the "essence" of tragedy; for none of this drama is really tragic.

Its dramatic potentialities lay in the human aspect of Jesus, which in their naïve realism the authors of the mystery plays were disposed to emphasize.[1] The *N. Towne Betrayal*, for example, represents Jesus as saying: "My flesh quaketh for fear and pain"; three times he begs his Father to take from him "this great passion," deliver him from the awful death in store for him. The playwrights might also have exploited the tragic possibilities in the anguished last words of the dying Jesus on the Cross, as reported by Mark and Matthew: "My God, my God, why hast thou forsaken me?" Yet there is little passion in the Passion plays, and no real occasion for terror. In the end, their authors always stressed the divinity of Jesus. They made no tragic point because the preordained end of the drama was pure triumph—the Resurrection. Similarly the miracle plays never give any suggestion that the saint might suffer in vain. And though *Everyman*, dealing with an ordinary mortal, is more nearly tragic, and must have stirred both pity and terror in an audience for whom salvation was still a vital concern, the tone of the play soon becomes edifying rather than tragic; long before the end it is clear that Everyman is going to be saved. In general, the Christian ritual pattern has no tragic potentialities until some element of uncertainty or doubt enters—some sense of actual *mystery* in the mysteries. Tragedy would not be written in Europe until a critical, skeptical spirit had got abroad.

Likewise medieval drama throws light on the uses of Myth. The Christian story is a grand myth, in the best sense of the word, and the youthful Gothic imagination was fired by it; it inspired the glories of medieval art. Nevertheless its potentialities were sharply limited by the literalness of the true faith. The basic Christian myths were regarded as historical truths, and reduced to dogma. With the Protestants such literalness would become explicitly hostile to Christian representative art, as a form of paganism. Meanwhile Christian poets could not treat their myths with as much intellectual and imaginative

---

[1] Incidentally, the plays were also spiced with ribald humor. Medieval piety, like Greek piety, permitted a degree of irreverence that would scandalize the lukewarm believers of our own time.

freedom as the Greek tragic poets displayed. They succeeded in creating a great drama only when they gave up subjects drawn from the Christian story, and had won a degree of freedom from the myth.

Ultimately, such emancipation was the work of the Renaissance. But first we have to deal with the usual complications. In the last century the Renaissance was commonly idealized as a golden age, a glorious rebirth of humanism and individualism, which unfortunately but understandably encouraged a deal of immorality and irreligion. In this century the Renaissance has gone the way of all the conventional "ages." It has been attacked as pagan, worldly, grossly sensual, swaggering in sinful pride; it has been defended as genuinely Christian, approaching an ideal of Christian humanism; it has been attacked again as academic, backward-looking, indifferent to science; it has been dismissed as essentially medieval, less glorious and original than the renaissance of the twelfth century; and recently there has been talk of a "counter-Renaissance," a second phase of pessimism and anti-intellectualism, represented by the works of Machiavelli, Montaigne, and Copernicus. In the face of such confusion some authorities wish to drop the whole concept of a Renaissance, as an artificial period made by historians rather than by history. Clearly it is not a well-defined period.

As clearly, however, something very important went on between 1400 and 1600, something that made a decisive difference in Europe. The Renaissance humanists were themselves conscious that they lived in a new age. "Immortal God," exclaimed Erasmus, "what a world I see dawning!" The arts in particular express an unmistakably new spirit, which has made them distasteful or reprehensible to devotees of medieval art. As Wylie Sypher points out in his provocative *Four Stages of Renaissance Style*, Gothic art had created very human figures but no stage or space for them, no humanized perspective. Now the architect, sculptor, and painter united to create "an adequate theater for the image of man" by restoring the wall,

reintegrating space, adding a third dimension, providing a new
perspective and new focus. Similarly the Renaissance humanists in effect created a new world for man. While the natural
man had been lively enough in the Middle Ages, he was always told that he was a proud, sinful man, and that his natural
business on earth was the salvation of his immortal soul. Now
the humanists gave him much freer play by declaring that his
interests and powers were valuable for their own sake, and by
making him aware of the rich possibilities of value in this life.
They stressed the "excellent dignity" rather than the natural
depravity of man, who had been created, after all, in God's
own image. His soul, wrote Marsilio Ficino, "will sometime be
able to become in a sense all things; and even to become a
god."

Hence the conspicuous enthusiasm and turbulence of the
Renaissance. "Its great achievements," as Ernst Cassirer
summed them up, "lay much less in the new *content* it created—although that too is infinitely rich—than in the new
energies it awakened and in the intensity with which these
energies acted." It produced many great personalities, men
more original than their ideas. Most conspicuously, it awakened a spirit of intense individualism. Art was no longer
anonymous or folkish: it was the work of self-conscious artists, who might be glorifying God or their patron, but who
also had a passion for earthly fame. Benvenuto Cellini even
wrote his autobiography—a performance unthinkable in the
Middle Ages. It is as unthinkable, indeed, in ancient Greece.
While this passion for fame recalls the Homeric heroes, the
men of the Renaissance were more individualistic than Greek
artists were, more conscious of their own creative power, and
above all more confident and willful. "DO AS THOU WILT,"
Rabelais inscribed on the gates of the Abbey of Thélème, his
ideal academy. The great men of the Renaissance, Burckhardt
observed, typically declared that men could do all things if
they would. Leonardo da Vinci proved it.

Now, this Renaissance individualist was bound to get into

trouble. Even if he was not worsted by other individualists he would in time discover the limits of his powers; frustration or disillusion was his natural fate. But his troubles were aggravated because he was seldom actually a pagan worldling. The conscience of the Renaissance remained medieval, haunted by the old fears. From the beginning its brilliant tapestry was shot through with a black pessimism, the blacker for its optimism. After heralding the dawn, Erasmus was also given to exclaiming at "this marvellously corrupt world," especially the growth of tyranny and avarice. Almost all the humanists took time off from the celebration of their golden age to deplore its evils of tyranny and avarice, its passion for gold. Although the contrasts between the ideal theory and the actual practice of the Renaissance were no more shocking than they had been in the Middle Ages, they created more tension because of its intoxicating new hopes, and also its growth in consciousness, its loss of innocence. And confusion and disorder were intensified because old institutions were breaking up. The city-state and the feudal kingdom were giving way to the modern nation; the feudal economy, based on the manor and the guild, was being disrupted by the rising capitalism.

Meanwhile the medieval conscience had erupted in the Protestant Reformation. As rebels against the central authority of Christian Europe the Reformers unwittingly contributed to the growth of individualism, but immediately they condemned the humanistic ideals of the Renaissance and reverted to the medieval themes of the world, the flesh, and the devil. No medieval cleric drew a blacker picture of human nature than John Calvin:

The mind of man is so entirely alienated from the righteousness of God that he cannot conceive, desire, or design anything but what is wicked, distorted, impure, and iniquitous; that his heart is so thoroughly envenomed by sin that it can breathe out nothing but corruption and rottenness; that if some men occasionally make a show of

goodness, their mind is ever interwoven with hypocrisy
and deceit, their soul inwardly bound with the fetters of
wickedness.

At the same time, Calvin made salvation harder for this corrupt creature by requiring much more individual effort of him,
doing away with the sacramental means of cleansing him of
sin, banishing the Virgin and the saints who had been inter-
ceding for him, leaving him alone to fight the Devil. And immediately the Reformers intensified religious strife, which
soon became bloody. "Christendom" had remained the supreme ideal of the Renaissance humanists, the most comprehensive symbol of the unity, order, and excellence to which
they aspired. Now Christendom was torn and bleeding.

In art, these tensions appear in what Wylie Sypher calls the
"mannerist" phase, preceding the grandiose reaffirmation of the
baroque. It is a restless, uneasy, disturbing art, given to distortion or discontinuity, unresolved tension, ambiguity, "de-
cisiveness of gesture within a fluid or dissonant context." It
is illustrated in the work of Tintoretto, Michelangelo, and El
Greco; its literary counterpart is the essays of Montaigne, the
tragedy of Shakespeare, the poetry of Donne. And it suggests
that the so-called "counter-Renaissance" was not so much a
reaction as a natural fulfillment: a clearer perception of the
contradictory purposes and passions, a fuller consciousness of
what had been going on all the time. Machiavelli's *The Prince*,
for example, was a highly original analysis of power politics,
but was not at all revolutionary in intention. As Machiavelli
said very plainly, he was merely trying to be realistic: describing the actual practice of successful Christian princes, recognizing it as unscrupulous, but concluding that unfortunately
it had to be so, human nature being as untrustworthy as it is.[2]

[2] Scholars have counted 395 references to Machiavelli in Elizabethan
drama as a symbol of villainy. But while Catholics and Protestants alike
condemned him as an arch-fiend, they testified to their Christian conscience, and to his realism, by continuing to read him in fascinated horror,
sending his work through many editions.

Still clearer evidence that the humanism of the Renaissance was approaching maturity was the irony of Montaigne. In his *Apology for Raimond de Sebonde* Montaigne dwelt at tedious length on man's capacity for folly and evil, and on the utter incapacity of reason to arrive at any certain knowledge of God, or any kind of ultimate truth. Ostensibly designed to prove that man must rely on faith alone, his treatise undermined faith by making it seem wholly unreasonable, ridiculing the notion that the universe was created for the sake of so wretched, vile a creature as man is, by the testimony of God's own ministers. What Montaigne was mainly attacking, however, was the Christian presumption and self-righteousness that already had embroiled Catholics and Protestants in atrocious religious wars. Other essays, such as "Of the Education of Children," express a much more cheerful view of human nature and the possibilities of life on earth, the positive goods that man may know and enjoy through catholicity, tolerance, and reasonableness. Essentially, Montaigne perceived at once the potentialities and the limitations of the human spirit, and their natural, incongruous, and inextricable commingling.

Copernicus, who has been linked with Machiavelli and Montaigne in the "counter-Renaissance," might symbolize rather the anomalies of the whole age. He expressed the optimism of the Renaissance. As he saw it, his theory revealed "a wonderful symmetry in the universe," a more perfect "harmony in the motion and magnitude of the orbs"; it confirmed the marvelous orderliness and excellence of the creation. His follower Kepler contemplated its beauty with "incredible and ravishing delight," as did Bruno. Churchmen, of course, were not ravished by the Copernican theory; the martyrdom of Bruno recalls how devastating its implications were for the medieval system of thought. Later John Donne got the point of the "new philosophy," which "calls *all* in doubt." But in the Renaissance the revolutionary Copernican theory had little apparent influence on thought. Elizabethan poets, including

Shakespeare, were either unacquainted with it or indifferent
to it; the pessimism reflected in Elizabethan tragedy sprang
from less distinguished sources. The humanists in general displayed little interest in science or natural philosophy, looking
instead to antiquity for their authority.

This authority they got primarily from Hellenistic and Roman sources, rather than classical Greek; and it helps to explain the anomalous Renaissance achievement in drama. When
the Greek tragedies were printed in Italy, early in the sixteenth
century, scholars and poets at once began to study, translate,
and imitate them. These imitations, which were performed
throughout the century, never rose above an earnest, academic mediocrity. Meanwhile scholars were diligently studying Aristotle's *Poetics*, erecting the more casual, incidental of
his observations into formal laws. Italian architects developed
from Roman models the modern theater, with its picture-frame
stage. The end product of all this labor was the neo-classical
drama of the seventeenth and eighteenth centuries—a drama
utterly foreign in spirit to the drama of Athens.

Hence the first significant achievement in drama was an
indigenous growth on the fringes of Renaissance Europe, in
Spain and in England. Probably it owed more to classical influence than appears on the surface. Indirectly, it owed something to the desire to emulate the achievement of the great
poets of antiquity; for the English playwrights, as for Sidney,
"climbing to the heighth of Seneca his style" was about the
ultimate in style. From Seneca, too, they got their ghosts, revengers, and assorted horrors. Nevertheless he was not the
father of Elizabethan drama. It had evolved independently,
out of medieval drama, and as it grew up, it became more
independent. When young Christopher Marlowe left his university and set about writing plays to earn his living, he wrote
for a popular theater that was a national institution. However
crude, it was essentially closer to the national theater of Athens
than was the classical theater of the Renaissance.

Yet it had caught the bold, humanistic, individualistic spirit of the Renaissance. The popular drama of Spain makes plainer that the spirit of the Elizabethan Age was not essentially medieval. For Spain remained orthodox, Catholic, hierarchical; and Spain wrote no tragedy. Its greatest dramatist, Calderón, presented some nominally tragic actions but always arrived at a pious or patriotic conclusion, resounding with devotion to God, king, or country.[3] Calderón's most thoughtful play, *Life Is a Dream*, is still free from serious doubt, irony, or tragic sense of life. In developing the theme that life may be "dreaming but a dream within a dream," he includes some nightmarish elements in his fantasy, but he stirs little terror. His main point is that we are sure to wake up in another life. If Spaniards might have worried about their destination in the afterlife, given their passion for gold and earthly glory, it appears that they were sufficiently assured by their freedom from heresy and religious doubt. England was coming up, at Spain's expense; but its greater poets were less complacent about their destiny.

2. THE BEGINNINGS: MARLOWE

By common consent, Christopher Marlowe was the first poet of genius to write for the Elizabethan theater. Famous for his "mighty line," he made a more important contribution by learning to write passages, making of blank verse the supple, nervous medium that Shakespeare was to exploit so superbly. Full of "brave translunary things," he also passed on to Shakespeare a drama of magnitude and magnificence. He is famous as well as a Byronic figure, whose brief, stormy career involved mysterious doings, charges of blasphemy and atheism, and finally his murder in a tavern brawl. To me he is much more fascinating as a symbolic figure: a lonely wanderer between the medieval and modern worlds, in a sense the tragic hero of

---

[3] His piety was so pure, or purely medieval, that it is not always edifying. In *The Devotion of the Cross*, for example, his hero is a scoundrel guilty of innumerable crimes, who at length is tardily caught and shot; then the print of the Cross is found on his body, the curses of the spectators melt into adoration, and his remains become holy relics.

his age. But it should therefore be said at once that Marlowe's plays are pretty bad plays.

His first work, *Tamburlaine,* is in Aristotelian terms all Spectacle and Diction, with only the rudiments of Plot, Character, and Thought. In time it struck even the Elizabethans as bombastic. Thereafter we can see Marlowe learning something about how to build a dramatic action, through dialogue instead of declamation, but at best he achieved only the potentials of great drama. Although the texts of *The Jew of Malta* and *Dr. Faustus* are extremely corrupt, with extensive additions by hack writers, there is no reason to believe that these writers butchered masterpieces. As we have them, at any rate, none of his plays belongs on the same shelf with Sophocles and Shakespeare. None deserves inclusion in a modern repertory, except as a novelty or a token of piety.

It is not surprising, of course, that a youthful pioneer failed to master his art. But the serious defects of Marlowe's plays are more significant because they remained the typical defects of Elizabethan tragedy. The great bulk of the tragedies, excluding Shakespeare's, are depressingly bad plays—much worse than one would gather from the many books on Elizabethan drama. We need to be on guard against the inveterate tendency of literary scholars to overrate the literature of the past, and then to look down their noses at modern literature as unworthy of serious study; for if we suffer enough from the deficiencies of our own culture, we suffer still more from contrast with a glorified, mythical past. Immediately, however, our task is to understand the relative immaturity of Elizabethan drama. In a historical perspective this drama takes on more interest— an "extrinsic" interest, as the formalists would say, but still a legitimate one. The plays of Marlowe in particular become more fascinating when considered in relation to his age. And finally this perspective may illumine the intrinsic merits of Elizabethan drama, the reasons why it is still worth studying.

T. S. Eliot declared that the basic fault of Elizabethan drama was the want of a convention, and its great vice an unlimited aim of realism. Other scholars have answered that it was in fact a highly conventional, stylized drama. Muriel Bradbrook has dwelt on its many conventions, though granting that they were not formulated, and excluding Shakespeare as not representative. Thus it regularly drew on stock themes and stock characters, including the hero of overweening ambition, the conscious villain, and the revenger; women were mainly of two types, the chaste and the unchaste. The dramatist was expected to have a moral aim and make clear-cut distinctions between right and wrong. He was also expected to incorporate a good deal of non-dramatic material, such as song, spectacle, apothegm, and comic interlude. Hence he was not required to observe formal unity or logical sequence; he was commonly indifferent to time, place, or even causality—murder or suicide did not have to be motivated. (In one of Rowley's plays a wife stabs herself saying: "I must die sometime and as good die this day as another.") Among the many incidental conventions were the disguise, usually with a flimsy motive and always impenetrable, and the habit of having characters die with a rhymed couplet, usually sententious. But Miss Bradbrook insists that all this is not to be regarded as a primitive technique—it is merely a matter of convention, which we must accept as we accept the Greek Chorus. The plain objection remains that most of these conventions encouraged a crude, immature drama. They did not constitute a discipline or impose a form. In tragedy they made for melodrama.

Although Marlowe set the pace for some of the extravagances of Elizabethan drama—providing, for example, sixteen corpses in *Tamburlaine*—a more influential model was *The Spanish Tragedy* of his contemporary Thomas Kyd. Its offerings included a ghost, the revenge theme, madness real and pretended, a dumb show, and a celebrated exhibit of horror: to avoid confessing, the hero bites off his tongue and spits it out on the stage. Some authorities have managed to praise Kyd's plotting and characterization, in which he shows some advance over his predecessors, but both are elementary. His play is pure melodrama, ranging from the lurid to the ludicrous. Its intellectual and moral tone is typified by its conclusion. The Chorus of Ghost and Revenge who had introduced the play enter to gloat over the nine killings ("Ay, these were spectacles to please my soul!") and to summarize the heavenly aftermath—the eternal bliss that awaits the revengers and the revenged, the infernal torments that await the five villains. For us the one cause of rejoicing is that the successors of Kyd dropped this obscene relic of the Greek Chorus.

Now it is conventional to blame the faults of Elizabethan drama on its audience—the "wretched beings," as Robert Bridges called them, for whom Shakespeare had to write. The scholar-poets of the time had worse names for them, and Shakespeare himself had Hamlet describe the groundlings as mostly "capable of nothing but inexplicable dumb shows and noise." Certainly these groundlings demanded their penny's worth in low entertainment. They reveled in rant, violent action, bloody deaths, crude horrors, vulgar humor, the antics of clowns and madmen. Still, it is too easy to get sentimental over the indignities suffered by the not too gentlemanly Elizabethan poets. Shakespeare managed to write great plays for this audience, with popular success and little evidence of self-pity. The others seldom give the impression of merely prostituting their talents, or hiding them. Thomas Kyd was evidently doing his level best in *The Spanish Tragedy*, however low the level. Christopher Marlowe wrote *Tamburlaine* with obvious *élan,* to please himself as well as his audience. When the other "university wits" had the opportunity of addressing a more exclusive, sophisticated audience, in the private theaters, their plays remained full of much the same faults, and were often the worse for a snobbish or cynical tone.[4]

All in all, the playwrights had to satisfy popular tastes, but in so doing they still enjoyed considerable freedom, as the

[4] Alfred Harbage has made a detailed comparison of the popular and the private theaters and their repertories in his *Shakespeare and the Rival Traditions* (New York, 1952). I shall return to his thesis in connection with the decline of Elizabethan drama.

variety of Elizabethan drama indicates. The plainest trouble remains that they enjoyed their freedom too much. If their audience did not hold them up to high standards, they themselves failed to develop such standards, or any clear standards. They were wildly confused about forms, if concerned at all; they could mix anything, up to the "tragical-comical-historical-pastoral" mentioned by Polonius. T. S. Eliot notwithstanding, they had no passion for "realism" in any strict sense of the word; realism would at least have been a discipline. Their passion was rather for sweep, pomp, copiousness—for including everything they could get away with.

As for tragedy, they apparently had no clear consciousness of what they were doing, and why. The Prologue to Part I of *Tamburlaine* (published as "Two tragical Discourses of Mighty Tamburlaine, the Scythian Shepherd") invites the reader to "View but his picture in this tragic glass and then applaud his fortunes as you please"; whereas Part I is a parade of triumphs by Tamburlaine, involving plenty of bloodshed but ending with the announcement of the hero's marriage, and with no foreshadowing of tragedy to come. We must wonder just what "tragical" meant to young Marlowe. His successors (always excepting the inscrutable Shakespeare) were more explicit but hardly penetrating. They echoed the popular idea that tragedy was a "mirror for magistrates," showing how vices are punished. The play was literally the thing to catch the conscience of the king; as Sidney said, it made kings fear to be tyrants. Chapman summed up the avowed intention of the playwrights by declaring that the soul of "authentical tragedy" was "material instruction, elegant and sententious excitation to virtue, and deflection from her contrary." Nowhere in Elizabethan criticism is there an adequate account of the tragic effect, or of the tragic spirit as it actually appears in the plays of Marlowe, Shakespeare, Webster, and others.

Yet those acquainted with neo-classical drama may not simply deplore the fact that Elizabethan drama grew up without the blessing of critical theory. As a natural, organic growth it was akin to Greek drama, which also preceded theory. And though it suffers by comparison with Greek tragedy, its underlying similarities as a national drama point to the reasons why it merits study in spite of all the sins committed in the name of "elegant and sententious excitation to virtue."

The theater was a major interest of the Elizabethans. Many troupes of actors kept touring the provinces, performing on village greens, in inns, and in the courts of nobles; those that settled down in London attracted proportionately far more playgoers than does Broadway today. The audiences were not purely plebeian but a cross-section of the general public. (Lords often commandeered performances of popular plays.) While they came to the playhouse in no solemn religious spirit, the heritage of medieval drama had prepared them for the serious treatment of great themes. If their expectation that serious drama would be about persons of exalted rank reflected mere class distinction, it at least encouraged the dramatist to deal with man's life at its heights and depths, or in its fullest manifestation. They also encouraged drama of magnitude and resonance by their natural love of poetry, even if it was a love more of the noise than of the thought. They were in some important respects more mature than the nominally more literate Hollywood audience today. They wished to be stimulated, not drugged or soothed; they did not demand sugar coatings or happy endings; they had more stomach for life.

Likewise their seemingly primitive open-air playhouse, with all its rowdy goings-on, resembled the Greek theater in that it symbolized their commonwealth. Its outer stage could be a street, a field, a royal court; its façade a house, a castle, a church; its inner stage a chamber or a tomb; its upper stage the walls of a city or the roof of a palace. And it was crowned by the hut or "heavens," with a canopy literally representing the heavens. It was an admirable theater for the sweep and stir of grand affairs, including affairs with the gods.

This is an idealized account of the Elizabethan theater, scarcely appropriate to many of the plays produced for it. But

Marlowe took advantage of its ideal possibilities, however unconsciously. His expansive genius was at home in this theater; he could play out more or less freely his stirring affairs with the gods. For such affairs were his paramount interest, and the immediate source of his originality and his intensity as a tragic poet. He introduced the serious treatment of the theme of death. His heroes were the first to die dramatically, significantly, revealing in their deaths the deepest meaning of their lives. Above all, he contributed the tragic hero—the man built grandly, and built to suffer and to die. If all his tragedies may be reduced to the theme that pride goeth before a fall, all are drastically reduced if this is made their essential meaning. To Marlowe the hero's pride was not simply evil, his downfall not simply right.

This youthful Master of Arts was more complex than the Renaissance firebrand of romantic tradition, but he was also much more complex and genuinely tragic than the medieval moralist that some scholars now make of him.[5] They dwell on the commonplaces of Elizabethan thought, such as the veneration of Seneca for his "tragedies of great morality" in which he "beateth down sin." Hence they again illustrate the nemesis of the historical scholar: the habit of limiting writers to the conventional thought of their age, forgetting that geniuses and mediocrities do not necessarily think alike, that both may be critical of their age and sometimes rebellious, and that the greater writers who accept conventional beliefs are still likely to transmute or transcend them. If we stick to the historical evidence, it indicates that Marlowe was not conventional; he had a scandalous reputation as an "atheist." We might therefore suspect that the show of Christian morality in his plays was a gloss to make them popular, or to protect himself. But the final appeal, of course, must be to the texts of his plays; and these do not bear out any simple, uniform interpretation.

---

[5] Roy Battenhouse, for example, argues that *Tamburlaine* is a grand morality play, in which the hero punishes sinners and is himself punished as the Scourge of God.

In *Tamburlaine*, Part I, Marlowe's poetry flouts whatever moral purpose he may have intended, or pretended. Again and again the mighty lines end with the sonorous name of Tamburlaine. The most eloquent, resplendent passages are not those which preach Christian morality, but those which glorify the "Faustian" spirit of Tamburlaine. The most quoted passage sounds the keynote of the play:

> Our souls, whose faculties can comprehend
> The wondrous Architecture of the world:
> And measure every wandering planet's course,
> Still climbing after knowledge infinite,
> And always moving as the restless Spheres,
> Will us to wear ourselves and never rest,
> Until we reach the ripest fruit of all,
> That perfect bliss and sole felicity,
> The sweet fruition of an earthly crown.

In the depths of his imagery, Kenneth Burke observed, a poet cannot lie; and there is no mistaking Marlowe's characteristic imagery. He has countless allusions to air, fire, sun, sky, the spheres—celestial images but in an astronomical rather than a religious sense, connoting vastness and brightness rather than holiness. His favorite verbs include climb, mount, soar. Among his most typical image-clusters, Harry Levin noted, are "topless towers" and "quenchless fires." Although his constant use of hyperbole led to bombast, it was at least in keeping with his conception of Tamburlaine, the "nonpareil." Tamburlaine wants an earthly crown most of all, but with its power he will have everything else under the sun: beauty, love, bliss, even poesy—"the highest reaches of a human wit." And in Part I he gets away with all this. Wherever he comes and sees, he conquers. He fulfills the Renaissance dream that men can do all things if they will.

The French humanist Le Roy remarked how appropriate it was that "the marvels of this age should begin with the great and invincible Tamerlane, who frightened the world by the terror of his name." While the Elizabethans must have known that he was the Scourge of God, the popularity of the legends about him suggests that they were as fascinated as horrified by him. Marlowe, himself proud and poor, was dazzled by this "Scythian shepherd" who rose to become the conqueror of Asia, "Fortune's master." And this is the trouble with his play. Una Ellis-Fermor wrote that it demands "eternal youth" to understand Marlowe, appreciate his bold defiance of the wisdom of the ages; but we cannot play wholeheartedly at being young and innocent. For us his hero is a barbarian, whose boastfulness sounds like pure megalomania. Even a youthful reader today may find the play monotonous and naïve. In any case it is essentially undramatic. The ludicrous battles, consisting of Alarms and Parades, only emphasize the lack of dramatic complication and conflict; for there are no complications in the nature of Tamburlaine, and the ostensible conflicts are merely a parade of his triumphs, which are as preordained as those of Superman.

With Part II, however, the complications begin. Whereas the main incidents of Part I had been taken from history, this play is almost entirely Marlowe's own invention; and it might be taken for a conventional morality play. Tamburlaine, who has become much more fanatical, cruel, and bloodthirsty, now repeatedly declares himself to be the Scourge of God. He is also less sure of himself, boasting in frenzy rather than calm assurance; for the Scourge of God is going to die. Early in the play his divine Zenocrate dies, lamenting that she fares like other empresses with "this frail and transitory flesh." In his outrage at this heavenly insult to his majesty, Tamburlaine commits still more abominable and senseless atrocities, but to no avail. Death comes to him too.

Nevertheless the morality of the play remains equivocal. The "atheistical" Marlowe goes out of his way to invent one episode in which Christian princes break their oaths and are made to appear less honorable than their Turkish conquerors. Even the climactic blasphemy scene might disturb the pious.

Tamburlaine burns the Koran, ridiculing the vain worship of Mahomet, taunting the god to come down and work a miracle if he has any power; whereupon he feels "distempered suddenly," coming down with the sickness that is to cause his death. So he is punished—but presumably by the heathen Mahomet. At that, his punishment amounts to no more than the realization of his mortality, which is shocking to Tamburlaine but to an orthodox Christian would hardly seem hellish enough for the Scourge of God. And the eloquent lines still express his unconquerable heroic spirit:

> Come let us march against the powers of heaven,
> And set black streamers in the firmament,
> To signify the slaughter of the Gods.

Tamburlaine dies giving lofty counsel to his sons, lamenting that their sweet desires will be deprived of his company, but expressing neither horror nor remorse. There is little suggestion that he is a damned soul, going straight to hell.

One clue to this apparent ambiguity is the texture of the play. While Part II has more variety and drama than Part I, it is still a sprawling, episodic play with little logical sequence or mounting intensity, and with much the same combination of poetic splendor, theatrical sensationalism, and silliness. But it has less *élan*, less verve and glow. Possibly it was a product of will, written to cash in on the popularity of Part I. Possibly Marlowe felt obliged to take a more conventional line in order to safeguard his reputation. More likely, he was simply growing up. He was no longer spellbound by his Tamburlaine, no longer could surrender himself wholeheartedly to boyish heroics. He was beginning to realize the elementary facts of life—and of death. At the same time, he was still far from maturity. The irony of the play is all on the surface, in the elementary idea that the mighty Tamburlaine is marching to his death. One has only to put *Tamburlaine* beside a Greek play to realize how youthful Marlowe was.

In short, his attitude toward his hero seems not so much

complex or deliberately ambiguous as uncertain or equivocal.
The play is significant chiefly as a biographical and historical
document, revealing a phase in the thought of its author and
his age. Marlowe is discovering that men cannot do all things
that they will, cannot master Fortune. He is realizing that the
glorious Renaissance individualist may be a ruthless egoist, a
source of great mischief to both his fellows and himself. This
individualist will become the villain in many Elizabethan
plays. In Marlowe he will become more evil, as Barabas in
The Jew of Malta and as Mortimer in *Edward II.*

At his most dazzling, the Renaissance hero is unlike the
Greek tragic hero in that he is more of an individualist, and
stands out not only above the community but often against
it. It is hard to make a ritual scapegoat of him. Thus there is
no sacrificial pattern in Marlowe's tragedies, no idea of renewal through death. Those who make this pattern the essence
of tragedy will have to exclude from the canon the plays of
Marlowe; and they may feel unhappier when superficial readers find their pattern in such tawdrier plays as *The Spanish
Tragedy*, in which the revenger looks like a scapegoat remov-
ing evil and restoring order. For Marlowe's refusal to offer
such consolations was not mere blasphemy, but fidelity to his
own tragic vision of man's fate. It is most pronounced in *Dr.
Faustus*, his most mature work. The appearances of a medieval morality play—the Good and Evil Angels, the Seven
Deadly Sins, the devils, the theme of the damnation of Faustus
—only accentuate how profoundly different Marlowe was from
the simple, pious author of *Everyman*. Here he most fully
realized the tragic potentialities of his Renaissance hero.

As it stands, *Dr. Faustus* is still a poor play. Presumably it
was the underlying conception that inspired Goethe to exclaim: "How greatly it is all planned!" Dramatically, the great
conception is realized only in a few scenes at the beginning
and the end. The middle is mostly trivial. Dr. Faustus fulfills
his dream of superhuman power by such stunts as playing
tricks on the Pope and getting grapes out of season for a lady.

The main action is also burlesqued by a still more trivial sub-plot, with wretched attempts at humor. Much of this dreary action is believed to be the work of hacks or clowns. Perhaps Marlowe left it to them to fill in, perhaps he planned it so to serve an ironic purpose; in either case it remains labored and dreary, and detracts from the greatness he clearly intended his hero to have. And it has a further unconscious significance. There is no reconciliation in this tragedy, no balance of good and evil, no feeling of final acceptance. In *Œdipus Rex* the mastery of form itself creates the impression that Sophocles has come to terms with man's fate, however critics may disagree about the nature of these terms. Marlowe's failure to master his form deepens the impression that he was unable to come to acceptable terms.

While Dr. Faustus is nothing like Everyman, demanding not only wealth, power, honor, and beauty but god-like omnipotence and omniscience, he is never so brilliant a figure as Tamburlaine. At the outset he is miserable in the realization that in spite of all his knowledge he is "still but Faustus and a man." Thereafter he is tormented by conscience, knowing that "the God thou servest is thine own appetite." At the end he is terrified, as Tamburlaine never was. He is damned from first to last because it is impossible for him to enjoy a heaven in either this life or the next. Everyman can repent, and feel saved. A Dr. Faustus cannot truly repent, but only know fear; there is no salvation for him except by a complete surrender of his aspirations, which would mean an annihilation of his personality—the only thing worth saving. And Marlowe knew his hero intimately. The poetic dramatization of his last anguished hour on earth, through the symbolic images of fire, blood, water, and the heavens that recur throughout the play, and especially the fire image that takes on an ironic meaning in his last futile cry, "I'll burn my books!"—this is no dutiful teaching of a moral lesson, but an intense realization of what it is to be a damned soul. There is no suggestion of rejoicing at the punishment of the sinner Faustus.

Marlowe also speaks through Mephistopheles. This is no conventional Devil, a spirit of pure evil. He is a sad devil, who instead of tempting Faustus tries to warn him:

> O Faustus! leave these frivolous demands,
> Which strike a terror to my fainting soul.

Likewise he tries to enlighten him about hell, which Faustus thinks is a mere old wives' tale; Mephistopheles comments wryly that experience will change his mind. But the hell he describes is not Dante's hell, a circumscribed region below the earth. "Hell hath no limits"; it is within him, wherever he goes; it is everywhere where heaven is not. So it is within all men who have lost the hope of heaven. It is the hell that Marlowe himself already knew, on earth.

Such knowledge may lead a man back to orthodox faith. To doubt that it did so with Marlowe we need not believe that he was literally an atheist. "Atheism" in Elizabethan usage might denote merely unorthodox belief, much as "socialism" today may denote mere liberalism; it appears that the atheistical notions charged to Marlowe amounted to some questioning of the divinity of Christ. In the plays the spirit of blasphemy that informs some scenes suggests a rebellion against God's decrees rather than a denial of his existence. Primarily, however, the tragedy of Dr. Faustus suggests that Marlowe was no longer proud of his free thought, whatever it was. He evidently could not share the hopes inspired by Christianity. Although the Good Angels tell Dr. Faustus to "think of heaven and heavenly things," and assure him that God will pity and forgive him, they sound perfunctory; nowhere in the play is there a vivid realization of the joys of heaven, or of a God of love. But Marlowe had not outgrown the fears inspired by Christianity. The eloquent passages express defiance, and then despair. The best-known lines invoke the earthly beauty of the pagan Helen of Troy:

> Was this the face that launched a thousand ships
> And burnt the topless towers of Ilium?

Immediately this radiant vision is followed by the most dramatic scene, of the final damnation of Faust. So the Renaissance dream ends in the nightmare of the medieval conscience.

The historical implications of *Dr. Faustus* have since grown more meaningful, especially in view of Goethe's *Faust*. Faustus may be regarded as a symbol of the rising scientific spirit. He was not an up-to-date scientist, to be sure, even for his own time. Marlowe was apparently either unfamiliar with the Copernican theory or afraid to mention it; the astronomy that Mephistopheles teaches Faustus is medieval. (The geographical and historical knowledge that Marlowe flaunts in *Tamburlaine* is also inaccurate—alas for the proud young Master of Arts!) But like Francis Bacon, Faustus worships knowledge as power, specifically as a means to controlling nature. In a broader view he symbolizes the distinctive "Faustian" spirit of Western civilization—the restless, willful, dynamic spirit that has led it to seek to convert and control, explore and exploit the whole world, and has made its history a series of revolutions, religious, political, scientific, and industrial. In either view, Faustus anticipates the tragedy of our century. Science has conjured up a power that surpasses his dreams, and now gives us nightmares. The Faustian spirit has brought on world wars and world revolutions, which may destroy the West.

Hence Marlowe's vision may seem profounder than Goethe's. The epical adventure of Goethe's Faust ends in a technological feat; his last work on earth is building dikes to reclaim land. Finally he is saved, not damned, just because he has never ceased to aspire to all the possible earthly goods that Dr. Faustus sold his soul for. He symbolizes the basic optimism of Goethe, which included a faith in technological progress. We cannot call this optimism simply shallow if we cherish the values of knowledge and free thought, the humanistic effort to make the most of life on earth. We can say that Goethe had too little tragic sense of evil. He himself once said that he could not write tragedies because he could not tolerate discords unresolved. We have to put up with discords grown more violent, both in the world of thought and in the world of action.

But I do not read Marlowe as a somber prophet who foresaw the dangers lying in wait for the whole humanistic enterprise, or anticipated the calamities of our century. He did not actually have a more profound, complex vision of life than Goethe. He was much less mature, and essentially more romantic. I see him as a young poet who experienced most intensely the conflicts between the new hopes and the old fears of his age, but was unable to view them steadily, much less to resolve them. Intoxicated by the Renaissance dream, he was still too close to the Middle Ages to appreciate that the Faustian life of aspiration might be its own reward, or "salvation." Whatever he thought, his feelings told him that salvation was of another world. Likewise they told him that his aspirations in this world were sinful pride, and meant damnation. For him the conflict was irreconcilable; he was incapable of either the Christian humanism of Erasmus or the calm, ironical skepticism of Montaigne. And since Dr. Faustus was destined to have an extraordinary career in science, technology, and business, gaining the whole world and then coming to fear that he had lost his own soul, while Erasmus and Montaigne remained on the shelves of libraries, Marlowe wrote more prophetically than he knew.

In this view *Edward II* takes on some added interest. Generally considered the last of his plays, it is unquestionably the most mature in dramatic technique. Marlowe has learned to develop his action through nervous dialogue, suited to character and situation, with fewer set speeches or exercises in rhetoric. It is a more complex action, in which tragedy does not spring from mere villainy and involves more than death or damnation. Marlowe has also learned to keep his eye on the dramatic object. He presents a sober, objective account of political struggles that reflect the growing individualism of the

Renaissance but not so much his own hopes and fears. He succeeds in building up sympathy for Edward II, a weak, self-indulgent monarch who, like Shakespeare's Richard II, brings about his own ruin but takes on dignity as he is dethroned, and struggles desperately to maintain this dignity as he is humiliated, tortured, and finally murdered. For the first time Marlowe stirs considerable pity.

But *Edward II* is still far from a masterpiece. Technically, its most conspicuous weakness is a break in the middle, with a too abrupt shift in sympathies. A soliloquy or so is enough to transform the loyal, forlorn queen of Edward II into a scheming adulteress; her lover, Mortimer, who has been a high-spirited, hotheaded rebel, as suddenly turns into a pure Machiavellian. More important, the play never reaches the heights of the final scene of *Dr. Faustus*. The gains in dramatic skill are offset by a loss in poetic intensity. The mighty lines, the images of air and fire, the visions of brave translunary things are fewer and fainter; the tragedy evokes less terror and less wonder. One may be reminded of Thomas Wolfe, who had the Faustian spirit of Marlowe and as an artist was guilty of similar extravagances, and who also lost in power as he learned to be more impersonal and restrained. One may fancy an unconscious prophetic note in the last words of the ambitious Mortimer, who goes to his death with tragic dignity:

> Base fortune, now I see that in thy wheel
> There is a point, to which when men aspire,
> They tumble headlong down: that point I touched,
> And seeing there was no place to mount up higher,
> Why should I grieve at my declining fall?
> Farewell fair Queen, weep not for Mortimer,
> That scorns the world, and as a traveller,
> Goes to discover countries yet unknown.

Marlowe, who was himself soon to travel to the unknown countries, might have welcomed these lines as his epitaph. He had not reached the heights, his work as a poet was not yet done; there is no sign here that he was world-weary, exhausted, broken in spirit. Still, I doubt that his premature death cost us dramatic masterpieces.

3. SHAKESPEARE

"I know not," wrote Sam Johnson in an editorial note on Shakespeare, "why our editors should, with such implacable anger, persecute our predecessors"; and let us remember, he added, that "we likewise are men." This is not an easy thing for devotees of Shakespeare to remember. After two centuries of intensive study of his works critics are still announcing the "real" or "true" meaning of a passage or a play, the more triumphantly when it is a meaning that all other critics have somehow overlooked. "The imaginative study of Shakespeare has not yet properly begun," begins an eminent specialist; but as a solitary pathfinder he feels no less confident, declaring that this study must "certainly" begin with the symbolic meanings he has found. So it is with some pride that I disclaim any intention of offering an original or definitive interpretation of Shakespeare. I have nothing really new to say about his greatness as a poet and a dramatist. Although I am concerned only with his tragedies, I do not pretend to do full justice to these— for instance, to his extraordinary command of language, which deserves all the close study it has elicited. I am concentrating on his tragic vision of life, and its relation to Western history.

"Shakespeare excepted," I have been tagging to generalizations about Elizabethan drama. It is a valid exception, which in turn needs to be qualified. The excesses of "bardolatry," including the supersubtle interpretations of careless or routine passages, periodically call out a return to the view that Shakespeare was essentially a popular showman, working on the same level as his fellow playwrights; yet on the face of it he gave something like his best in his greater plays, and his best is inimitable. He is so far superior to his fellows that he cannot be considered the natural fulfillment of Elizabethan drama, the apex of the familiar curve. As a tragic poet, he alone achieved artistic mastery of a most difficult form, a drama of sweep, copiousness, and limitless variety.

But this is also to say that Shakespeare was an Elizabethan. First of all he was a playwright, and a popular one. He observed most of the "conventions" of Elizabethan drama, introducing plenty of villains, ghosts, madmen, and fools, with plenty of action, spectacle, and declamation. He was so little concerned with posterity that he made no effort to preserve all his plays, though in his will he was careful to dispose of his second-best bed. He was so much at home in the Elizabethan theater that one wonders whether he realized the greatness of his plays. What little is known of his life—his reputation for gentleness and geniality, his busyness as actor, play-doctor, and all-around man of the theater, his return to Stratford as a prosperous bourgeois, his interest in getting himself a coat of arms—indicates that at least he was more content with his vulgar profession than were the "university wits," and took his art with nothing like the solemnity that literary critics do today. In some respects, moreover, he was a provincial Elizabethan, who as a patriot displayed a limited interest in the rest of Europe. He was indifferent to some of the major social and intellectual developments of his time. Apparently he did not share, for example, the scientific interests of Francis Bacon that heralded the world to come.

Yet Shakespeare was without question the most comprehensive dramatist of his time, or of all time. His vision was so broad, his sensibility so quick and acute, that his abundance and variety pose the immediate problem for critics. As T. S. Eliot has said, "We must know all of Shakespeare's work in order to know any of it." Fully to understand the work of his tragic period, more specifically, we must know that it was preceded by romantic comedies and chronicle plays, punctuated by such bitter comedies as *Measure for Measure*, and followed by *The Tempest*. And the tragedies themselves are so varied— even disregarding *Romeo and Juliet*, the romantic tragedy of his youth—that we cannot properly speak of a "typical" Shakespearean tragedy. Each has its own climate, marked by distinctive imagery; together they conform to no one pattern or tragic formula. We might have a rather different impression of Shakespeare if, as with Æschylus and Sophocles, only a few of his plays had survived. As it is, what remains most "typical," apart from his poetic command of language, is the breadth of vision and abundance of life.

This may at least help to dispose of one question that has especially worried critics—Shakespeare's ideas about God. Given the breadth and abundance, critics have succeeded in identifying him with every major variety of Christian belief. The Ghost in *Hamlet* alone can support several different versions of his belief; for Hamlet's thoughts about it reflect the contemporary Catholic view that ghosts came from purgatory, the orthodox Protestant view that they were evil spirits, and the skeptical view that they were hallucinations. But the endless disagreement among his religious interpreters itself reveals that Shakespeare did not plainly commit himself to any definite belief. Whatever Christian faith he may have had is certainly not so clear as that of Dante before him, of Calderón in contemporary Spain, or of Corneille and Milton after him. While his plays give no impression of "atheism" or rebellion, they do suggest that he was much less concerned about God and Satan than Marlowe was. The wide-ranging thought of Hamlet barely touches on the religious problem. Shakespeare's other tragic heroes seldom express specifically Christian hopes and fears, and they go to their deaths with no chorus of Christian sentiments. And the orthodox must always be troubled because he wrote in an unmistakably tragic spirit. "If this be our end, what boots it to be Virtuous?" complained Rymer of the ending of *Othello*. His attitude may now seem naïve; but T. S. Eliot has been as disturbed by the thought that the greatest of English poets lacked a Christian philosophy.

Just what Shakespeare believed in these high matters remains uncertain. He is the most noncommittal and elusive of the world's great poets. For that matter, we cannot assume that he had a settled belief, since everybody recognizes the deepening pessimism in his tragic period. For the same reason, however, we cannot dismiss the whole matter by regarding him as a mere "spectator of genius," or wholly disinterested recorder. However comprehensive his sympathies, his moral judgments are generally clear enough; good and evil may be mixed, but for the most part they are sharply distinguished— his villains are even too plainly labeled; and his later tragedies make it evident that he felt intensely about these matters. This feeling, together with his breadth and abundance, points to the most apparent element in the thought of Shakespeare— Renaissance humanism.

It is not an explicit creed, of course, much less a formal philosophy. Essentially it seems more a matter of feeling or sentiment than of concept or doctrine. But there can be no question of Shakespeare's keen interest in the nature of man, in all its diversity and incongruity, its capacity for good and evil. Character is more central in his drama than in Greek drama. His action springs more directly from character, and then in turn affects it more decisively; his tragedy more clearly illustrates the Aristotelian principle of the tragic flaw. In particular Shakespeare reflects the individualism of the Renaissance. It appears concretely in his host of individualized characters, by far the most widely diversified assembly that had yet appeared on the stage, and still unsurpassed for variety and uniqueness. It appears above all in his many great personalities, all endowed with splendid powers of self-expression. Shakespeare's heroes have the stature of the Greek heroes, and together give a much ampler, more vivid impression of the possibilities of the human spirit.

Immediately, these great personalities embody the spirit of the Elizabethan Age, which was an age of lusty individualists. And the tragic end of many of these individualists, such as Marlowe, Raleigh, and Essex, suggests an immediate source of the increasingly dark vision of life expressed in the plays of Shakespeare's tragic period. Probably this vision reflected the political disorder that darkened the last years of tyrannical Queen Bess, and that was dramatized by the execution of Essex. Probably, too, the "dark lady" of the sonnets had something to do with it; there is little question that Shakespeare suffered from some personal tragedy. But in any case he went much deeper and further in his plays. His tragic vision is impersonal and all-inclusive. Its most significant, if not its ultimate, source is the tension of the late Renaissance.

In one of his sonnets Shakespeare wrote:

> Most true it is that I have look'd on truth
> Askance and strangely. . . .

To begin with, he may be associated with Sypher's "mannerist" stage of Renaissance art. The gulf that separates him from Spenser and Sidney is that which separates Michelangelo from Botticelli. The ambiguity of mannerist art—the vivid immediacy and the intensity coupled with final imprecision or indecision—was a natural consequence of the new focus on man in all the arts; for as one sees him in perspective, in depth, this is likely to become a tragic focus. It followed as naturally from the early Renaissance vision of perfect harmony, a "beautiful Whole" that Alberti declared the laws of art and nature alike conspire to form; for nature does not so conspire, the harmony was formal and forced, and the result was an art often rigid and cold—less poignantly human than Gothic art. The early humanists were likewise given to a formal celebration of Man that was not conspicuously humane; or when they became sensitive to the evils of tyranny and avarice they tended to an alternation of optimism and pessimism, both simplified and in a sense abstract. They seldom looked on truth askance or strangely. Montaigne was the first to take a complex view of man in all his concreteness, and to hold it steadily.

But Montaigne was seldom intense. His wisdom found little room for the heroic spirit that dares, defies, risks all. It was Shakespeare who most comprehensively embraced, and deeply felt, the contradictions of the Renaissance. They began with the exhilarating new sense of the ideal potentialities of man, and then the more acute awareness of his limitations, his capacity for evil. They were magnified and intensified by the inherited sense of a universal order, natural, social, political, and religious, and then the growing sense of the disruption and corruption of this order. While Shakespeare's vision was focused on the individual, it placed him as the Greek poets did, in relation to the community and the cosmos. The evil he saw was most conspicuous in the nature of man, and likely to take the form of political ambition or corruption; but it was also in nature itself—in the whole universal order that somehow engendered evil. At best, as A. C. Bradley wrote, "We remain confronted with the inexplicable fact, or the no less inexplicable appearance, of a world travailing for perfection, but bringing to birth, together with glorious good, an evil which it is able to overcome only by self-torture and self-waste."

Now this is neither a novel nor an entirely adequate view of Shakespearean tragedy. *Othello* and *Coriolanus*, for example, both lack cosmic implications; whereas *Antony and Cleopatra* is made spacious by cosmic imagery that supports the imperial lovers, and gives no sense of inexplicable evil. To repeat, Shakespearean tragedy is too diverse to be encompassed by any one critical method or formula. Nevertheless an approach to it as Renaissance tragedy, a reflection of a major phase in Western history, can take us close to the heart of most of the plays, may at least illuminate the others, and need not reduce any of them. This approach leads through their significant imagery, including the tempest-music antinomy in which G. Wilson Knight finds "the only principle of unity in Shakespeare." It may embrace the "symbols" with which he and others now prefer to replace "concepts" (though I am not always sure just what "symbol" means in contemporary discourse, and suspect that concepts are always being smuggled in again). I therefore propose to follow out the development of Renaissance tragedy by concentrating on three plays in chronological sequence—*Hamlet, Troilus and Cressida,* and *King Lear.*

In the first, the immediate issue is the famous problem of Hamlet himself. Now that hundreds of critics have had their say about him, studying him as if he were a living person instead of a character in a play, it is a commonplace that they have neglected the complete action, confused the issue of what the play is about. Yet there is good excuse for their obsession with the character of Hamlet. Shakespeare's characters in general call for more attention than those in Greek drama because he was more interested in character for its own sake, and at more pains to individualize it. Hamlet in particular is the most highly individualized, complex, self-conscious character in drama up to his time. He not only speaks more lines than any other Shakespearean hero but has a greater command of language, to express a much wider range of thought and feeling. He is unique in that his tragedy is focused not on his fatal deed but his prolonged inability to perform the deed. Hence one cannot decide what the play is about until he has decided what Hamlet is like. Without him the play would be a sensational melodrama, as it was in Kyd's version.

The main objection to the innumerable readings on the character of Hamlet is the confidence with which critics have "plucked out the heart" of his mystery. Some of the readings have been simply absurd (for instance, that he was a woman in disguise, in love with Horatio). Others have been absurdly simple, reducing the problem to such yes-or-no questions as whether he was "really" mad. Even the best-known interpretations are oversimplified. "A too pure, noble, most moral nature, but without the energy of nerve which constitutes the hero, sinks under a burden which it can neither bear nor throw off," wrote Goethe; while Coleridge saw in Hamlet another Coleridge, given to "a great, an almost enormous, intellectual activity, and a proportionate aversion to real action consequent upon it." Shakespeare's Hamlet was neither so hyper-sensitive nor so hyper-intellectual. He was a heroic personality who could perform violent, even brutal actions, killing Polonius with no sign of compunction ("I'll lug the guts into the neighbor room"), boarding the pirate ship like the soldier he was reputed to be, and callously arranging for the execution of Rosencrantz and Guildenstern.

Other critics have accordingly stressed the legitimate excuses for Hamlet's delay in carrying out his revenge, such as doubts about the honesty of the Ghost or the external difficulties in killing a king. He has been "scolded," remarked J. M. Robertson, "as never hero was before, by literary persons conscious of their own consummate fitness for killing a guilty uncle at a moment's notice." But the trouble remains that Shakespeare's Hamlet cannot himself accept such excuses for his delay. "O, what a rogue and peasant slave am I!" he exclaims in one soliloquy; and in a later one he declares more soberly:

> I do not know
> Why yet I live to say 'This thing's to do,'
> Sith I have cause, and will, and strength, and means
> To do't.

Each noun knocks a pretty theory on the head; and Shakespeare emphasizes Hamlet's bafflement by giving Laertes a similar cause, with nothing like his advantages, and showing how easily he breaks into the palace and has King Claudius at his mercy. Likewise Hamlet gives the lie to the hard-boiled commentators who point out that the so-called problem of his procrastination was overlooked for two hundred years, and assert that it was invented by critics, not by Shakespeare. He himself announces the problem.

Dover Wilson, whose Shakespeare is a consummate craftsman who can do no wrong, therefore concludes that "we were never intended to reach the heart of the mystery"—Shakespeare deliberately made Hamlet unfathomable. This would seem an odd intention for a popular playwright who, as Wilson insists, always wrote for an audience, not for readers. On the face of the critical record, we can never be sure what Shakespeare intended. The only certainty is that he did create a mysterious character. The mystery may well have been deepened by some uncertainty in his intention, or carelessness of detail (as in the matter of Hamlet's age); or it may have been clarified by his leading actor, whom he could coach. Yet mystery is of the essence of Hamlet, as it is of no other of his heroes. To me it is a natural kind of mystery, not a puzzle designed to tantalize his audience.

As early as 1711 Lord Shaftesbury called *Hamlet* "that piece which appears to have most affected English hearts," and it has since affected other peoples as well. Its universal appeal is plainly due to Hamlet himself, who remains perhaps the most living character in all drama. For we always know him, even if we do not clearly understand him; and as we know him better he may seem both clearer and more baffling, as do some persons we know best in our own experience. It is only strangers or simple types who can be labeled and pigeonholed. The complete reality of Hamlet would alone explain why he cannot be completely explained.

More precisely, he is Montaigne's man, *"ondoyant et divers."* As Montaigne wrote, "I have nothing to say entirely, simply, and with solidity of myself, without confusion, disorder, blending, mingling, nor in one word." Hence almost everything that has been said about Hamlet is true, or partly true. He is the rare, gentle, sensitive spirit pictured by Goethe, a "sweet prince," finely attuned to fine issues; yet he is mostly ungentle in action, coarse or savage in his humor, merciless to all but Horatio. He is Coleridge's intellectual, "sicklied o'er with the pale cast of thought"; yet he is forever doing, from first to last dominating a play crowded with action. He is shrewd, subtle, and acute, and histrionic and reckless in a madness that is both feigned and real. He hates and loves life, he fears and courts death. But it is his thought and feeling, not his action, that makes him superior to everyone else in the play—his action is mostly a spur-of-the-moment reaction, even in his final triumph. He represents a landmark in the growth of self-consciousness. And this naturally includes a consciousness of the mystery of man's being, the limits to self-knowledge.

A specific reason for the contradictions in Hamlet is that his mind is disordered. When he first greets his old friends—Horatio, Rosencrantz and Guildenstern, the Players—we catch glimpses of the "normal," genial Hamlet; but his first soliloquy reveals a man suffering from a profound shock, due immediately to the "incestuous" marriage of his mother with his hateful uncle. While he is never literally mad, neither is he quite sane; at times he verges on hysteria. Bradley and others have noted in him the symptoms of the sickly "melancholy" in which Elizabethans were interested. Ernest Jones was able to make out a strong case for regarding him as a victim of an Œdipus complex.[6] The sexual sources of his unconscious feeling of guilt would explain, for example, his ambivalent attitude toward his mother, and in particular the savage obscenities he addresses to Ophelia.

Since most readers feel that Shakespeare put much of himself in Hamlet, many have speculated that he suffered from a similar disorder. The mystery of Hamlet might be explained by inferring that he put more of himself in his hero than he intended, or something of himself that he did not understand. Dr. Jones inevitably concludes that he too was torn by an Œdipus complex; and other critics have noted a sex-nausea in the plays of his tragic period. Yet such theories, even if true, can never account for the greatness of Shakespeare, or immediately for the extraordinary richness of *Hamlet*, the greatness of its hero. Like his author, Hamlet is much more than a neurotic. In his disordered state he becomes acutely conscious of a deeper disorder in the state of man. As Caroline Spurgeon

[6] So regarded, the play is "a highly elaborated and disguised account of a boy's love for his mother, and consequent jealousy of and hatred toward his father." In replacing his father, his uncle Claudius incorporated the deepest, buried part of his own personality, became tied up with his own moral fate; so Hamlet "cannot kill him without also killing himself." This psychoanalytical interpretation may disgust lovers of the play, and surely does not give us its "essence"; but it does illumine the text, which Dr. Jones reads sensitively.

first pointed out, the dominant imagery of the play is of infection and disease. "To Shakespeare's pictorial imagination," she concludes, "the problem in *Hamlet* is not predominantly that of the will and reason, of a mind too philosophic or a nature temperamentally unfitted to act quickly: he sees it pictorially *not as the problem of an individual at all*, but as something greater and even more mysterious, as a *condition* for which the individual himself is apparently not responsible, any more than the sick man is to blame for the infection which strikes and devours him, but which, nevertheless, in its course and development, impartially and relentlessly annihilates him and others, innocent and guilty alike. That is the tragedy of *Hamlet*, and it is perhaps the chief tragic mystery of life."

This brings us, finally, to the play itself—the complete action. It is an extraordinarily abundant, varied action, full of ironic parallels and contrasts, as many-faceted as the personality of its hero. The fullness of life represented in it, and represented in such concreteness, with such vigor and brilliance, justifies Tillyard's description of it as "the greatest display of sheer imaginative vitality in literary form." Hence it has inspired as remarkable a diversity of interpretation. We should not feel humiliated by the sensible conclusion that we cannot hope to define its theme with precision and assurance, and need to be on guard against the constant tendency to restrict or impoverish its significance.[7]

One of the most provocative approaches is that of Francis Fergusson, which harks back to the strange underlying similarities between the stories of Hamlet and Orestes. While recognizing the multiple meanings of the play, Fergusson defines

[7] An eminent example of this tendency is T. S. Eliot. Having decided that the play is essentially about the feeling of a son toward a guilty mother, Eliot decided that this feeling is excessive, and also discovered that some important scenes do not bear on this theme; so he pronounced the play "undoubtedly" an artistic failure. The feeling will seem less excessive if one remembers that to the Elizabethans Hamlet's mother was guilty of not only adultery but incest. But given a play so rich and universal in appeal, a baffled critic might first suspect some failure in himself.

its main action or "ultimate meaning" as "the attempt to find
and destroy the hidden 'imposthume' which is poisoning the
life of Claudius's Denmark." All the characters are involved
in this action; all in their different ways illustrate that something is indeed rotten in the state of Denmark. In Toynbee's
phrase, Claudius is the primary source of "Schism in the
State," Hamlet the major example of the consequent "Schism
in the soul." Among the foils to Hamlet is the healthy young
Fortinbras, another son of a wronged king, who at once swings
into vigorous action. The tragic rhythm of the drama leads to
the perception of Hamlet's ancient role as ritual scapegoat. In
killing Claudius he roots out the evil, but at the cost of his own
life; and in his dying words he awards the throne of Denmark
to Fortinbras, who symbolizes the "new faith," "a new hope for
a new, purged state." Fergusson grants that the ritual pattern
may be obscured by the possibly excessive richness and complexity of the play, and particularly by the modern ironic
awareness of Hamlet and his author, but the historical significance of the play is thereby heightened. While Shakespeare's
theater was still close to the ancient roots of drama, the great
tradition of comprehensive order, he anticipated the break-up
of this order. *Hamlet* mirrors the historic process that led to
the chaos of the modern world, and its "fragmentary theaters."

Now it seems to me that the play does conform to the ritual
pattern, and that this pattern has both more artistic and more
historical significance than modern playgoers realize. To an
Elizabethan audience the state of Denmark would naturally be
a major issue of the drama. They still had the traditional feeling for the king as symbolic father of the community, upon
whom its welfare depended. This feeling is reflected in all
Shakespeare's chronicle plays, which are concentrated on the
evil of civil war. Most of the tragedies also indicate his concern with political order. Their resonance is due in part to the
reverberations of evil throughout the State; the communal welfare is involved in the fate of the hero. And in all his plays the
ritual aspect is accentuated by the many ceremonial scenes.

Yet the ritual pattern is too faintly sketched to be the core
of *Hamlet*. Fergusson distorts the play by the "major importance" he is obliged to assign the role of Fortinbras. The young
prince is the subject of some undramatic exposition at the
outset, as Claudius gives instructions to ambassadors and a
little later gets their report, and he then makes only one brief
appearance before the final scene, speaking six lines as he
marches across the stage. When Fergusson declares that "he
is felt as a constant, though off-stage, threat to the corrupt
regime," one can only say that this is not so. More to the point,
no one who knows Hamlet can hale Fortinbras as a savior. It
impoverishes the tragedy to see "a new faith and hope" for
Denmark in this simple prince who leads an army to war
"even for an eggshell." Shakespeare's histories and tragedies
both show that he saw through this naïve idea of honor and
glory, which was far from being a new faith. Hamlet himself
manifests no more concern for the state of Denmark as he
grows calmer and more assured toward the end; he is not exalted but stoically resigned—"the readiness is all." Through
Hamlet we know that the evil is ineradicable, that there is no
sure hope for the future, that there will always be something
rotten in the state of Denmark. Simple men will be insensitive to it, or content with simple pseudo-solutions. The finest
spirits will suffer more because they are more finely attuned,
and among other things realize that a Fortinbras is more fit
for life in the everyday world.

The Elizabethan audience may well have seen *Hamlet* as
Fergusson does, since Shakespeare did make a point of giving
them Fortinbras as the new king. But the generations of readers since have been much more interested in the tragic soul
and fate of Hamlet than in the purification of Denmark; and
so, I believe, was Shakespeare himself.[8] Fergusson acknowl-

---

[8] That he had become more interested in the winning or losing of
souls than of kingdoms is indicated even in *Henry V*, the climax of his
histories. Henry is ostensibly the ideal image of the statesman-king; but
he is hardly an interesting character, or even a real individual. He is all
king, a simple figure in a simple action that could stir only a simple pa-

edges that Fortinbras represents no solution to Hamlet's "problem," serving rather to return us to "the wider mystery of life
in the world at large." Actually, we get our deepest sense of
this wider mystery through the being of Hamlet, which is set
off by the sharply limited perspective of Fortinbras. His problem—which significantly is not of his own making—is ultimately
the problem of the whole human condition. This is for me the
core of a play that in our immediate experience is a sufficiently
unified, completed action.

   Mystery is again of the essence of the whole action. The
play begins with questions, about the strange apparition of the
Ghost. Its hero is constantly asking questions about the life of
man, now in meditation, now in anguish, while he himself is a
puzzle to the court around him because of his riddling language and strange behavior. The questions are focused on the
infirmity of man, but also on the problem of appearance and
reality. Maynard Mack has noted the emphasis throughout on
the ambiguities of "seem," set against the idea of "seeing";
other recurrent key words are "assume" and "put on," "show"
and "play." Appropriately Hamlet brings the action to a head
by staging a play within a play—a burlesque ritual. And he
fascinates us more than any other hero because he not only
broods over the problem of the human condition but so completely embodies it. Contending against a "mighty opposite," he
exemplifies the dualities in man, the conjunction of savagery
and sensitiveness, obscenity and idealism, madness and insight—the apparent incongruities that are natural to the paragon of animals who is also the quintessence of dust. "A little
more than kin, and less than kind," he speaks to and for all
thoughtful mankind. Anatole France spoke fittingly in reply:
"What one of us thinks without contradiction and acts without
incoherence? What one of us is not mad? What one of us does

---

triot: it stirred Shakespeare's imagination to little but rhetoric and spectacle. Shakespeare then went on to write *Julius Cæsar*, in which the
noblest character, Brutus, is an ineffectual political man. And there is no
trace of the ritual pattern in this play, which immediately preceded
Hamlet, or in *Coriolanus*, a later political tragedy.

not say with a mixture of pity, comradeship, admiration, and horror, Goodnight, sweet Prince!"

Hamlet finally comes to accept the human condition, and then to settle his personal problem. But he does not thereby dispel the mystery. He continues to ask questions, about mortality: Where now are the jibes and songs of poor Yorick? May not the noble dust of Alexander be stopping a bung-hole? And these raise the further question of man's relation to the cosmic order, a sense of which pervades the play. In his disgust with life Hamlet has lamented that "this brave o'er-hanging firmament, this majestical roof fretted with a golden fire," now seemed to him only "a foul and pestilent congrega-tion of vapors"; upon his recovery he remarks soberly the "divinity that shapes our ends, rough-hew them how we will." The ironic disjunction between human designs and the over-ruling design is summed up by the Player-King:

> Our wills and fates do so contrary run
> That our devices still are overthrown;
> Our thoughts are ours, their ends none of our own.

What, then, is the nature of this unspecified divinity that shapes our ends? What are its ends?

In *Hamlet* Shakespeare does not press this question. The most thoughtful of his heroes fails to accommodate those who would equip him with either medieval or ultra-modern atti-tudes. Hamlet never asks the question raised by Job. Appar-ently he believes in the Ghost who returns from purgatory, and in the black hell to which he hopes to send the soul of Clau-dius; it is fear of the afterlife that dissuades him from suicide:

> To die—to sleep.
> To sleep—perchance to dream: ay, there's the rub!

Perchance: apparently he is neither a devout Christian nor a resolute skeptic. Unlike Claudius, he never turns to God in prayer. As he leaves this "harsh world" his only concern is his "wounded name," not his soul. "Report me and my cause aright to the unsatisfied," he begs Horatio.

Since the good Horatio did not understand him either, the immense commentary he has inspired might be regarded as a work of piety. It is a tribute to the plainest manifestation of divinity in his tragedy, which is the divinity in Hamlet himself. He gives us no reason to take literally the pious hope of Horatio that flights of angels sing him to his rest; for him "the rest is silence." But it is not the silence of despair. We accept his fate, as he accepts it. His death is right—any other ending is unthinkable. It is also right that he does not speak of personal immortality. In his suffering he bears the cross of self-conscious man; in his acceptance he perceives the universal fate of man; in his triumphant death he redeems the infirmity of man. He is immortal as a great personality, symbolizing the powers of the human spirit that may reconcile us to the fact of our mortality.

In achieving this equilibrium on humanistic grounds, Shakespeare transcended the common thought of his time. There is no sign in him of the medieval horror of death or fear of hell. There is no sign either that he had been dazzled by the Tamburlaines, or had made such exorbitant demands on life as Dr. Faustus. Yet the intensity of *Hamlet* reveals that Shakespeare was by no means impervious to the shocks of his age. The tragic equilibrium is always precarious. In his following play, *Troilus and Cressida*, Shakespeare failed to maintain it.

This strange play is not strictly a tragedy. Shakespeare's editors were uncertain how to classify it, since it ended neither in death nor in happiness. Critics who feel no compulsion to label are still troubled by its inconclusiveness, and the violence of its unresolved discords. Possibly Shakespeare intended a comedy but wrote in a savage mood; possibly he intended a tragedy but could not respect his subject. Anyhow *Troilus and Cressida* is an unsatisfying play. If this were the only work

of Shakespeare that had come down to us we might still recognize a genius, but we would hardly conceive him as a "universal poet." When viewed in relation to his entire work, however, the play is much more suggestive. It becomes in a sense
more tragic than *Hamlet*.

In general, its theme is a far worse corruption. Shakespeare
reduced the famous love story to a sordid affair by reducing
Chaucer's Cressida to a pure wanton. She is the quintessence of
sex as exploited by Hollywood:

> Fie, fie upon her!
> There's language in her eye, her cheeks, her lip,
> Nay, her foot speaks: her wanton spirits look out
> At every joint and motive of her body.

The story of her perfidy is played out against the background
of the Trojan War, which is as wanton an affair, fought over
another glorified slut. The Homeric heroes come out as badly,
from the "dull brainless Ajax" to the cowardly Achilles, the
"idol of idiot worshippers." The coarseness of the entire action is emphasized by the imagery, with its many references to
beasts, food, and merchandising. The tone of the love affair is
set by the lewd Pandarus, who when not on stage with the lovers is always in the wings. The Greek heroes are provided with
an obscene chorus by Thersites, who in his own words is "a
bastard begot, bastard instructed, bastard in mind, bastard in
valor, in everything illegitimate." The most extraordinary
scene in the play is a bastard operatic quintet. Cressida se-
duces her new lover, Diomedes, pledging her troth by giving
him the sleeve with which Troilus had pledged his; the scene
is viewed at a distance by the horrified Troilus, desperately
repeating "I will not speak a word," and the worldly-wise
Ulysses, as vainly counseling patience; and farther in the background stands Thersites, offering his usual cynical commentary.

"All's done, my lord," says Ulysses when Cressida leaves the
stage. Troilus answers simply: "It is." The remaining action

proves him right. Hector, the noblest character in the play, is butchered by the myrmidons of Achilles when he is alone and unarmed, whereupon Achilles puts in his claim to deathless glory. Troilus rages over the battlefield, performing pointless deeds of valor, left alive only to be denied a glorious death. He could not in any event assume the heroic role of scapegoat; we know that Troy is doomed. No good comes of anything— nothing can come to any good in the world that Shakespeare has pictured here. The field is left to Pandarus, groaning with venereal disease, who concludes the play by offering the antithesis of catharsis. He bequeaths his diseases to his fellow "traders in the flesh," and in effect to the audience—to the world, which, as he points out, affects to despise panders but keeps them busy.

Wilson Knight sought to redeem his Shakespeare, whose heart is a "grand positive," by making the Trojans represent the beauty and worth of human nature, the Greeks its stupidity and evil. But the play defeats every effort to read it as a genuinely tragic conflict. The wise Ulysses is on the Greek side; only he is a mere commentator, who achieves nothing and suffers nothing. The Trojans, who incidentally include the ridiculously affected Æneas, lack the stature of tragic heroes. Troilus himself is Fortinbras in love. He is full of passion, "plain and true," but expresses it with nothing like the radiant imagery of Romeo; he realizes his fondest dream by going to bed with his fair Cressida, no less happy because they are tucked in by Pandarus. Although Hector is nobler and more mature, he is ineffectual even before his ignoble death. At a Trojan council he calls for an end of the senseless war, pointing out that the "moral laws of nature and of nations" require the return of Helen to the Greeks; but he suddenly gives in, concluding that he will fight to keep her. The issue is dropped for good. Nothing comes of what had promised to be a significant debate over standards of value.

Nothing comes, either, of the often quoted speech of Ulysses on the supreme importance of order and degree:

The heavens themselves, the planets, and this centre,
Observe degree, priority, and place,
Insisture, course, proportion, season, form,
Office, and custom, in all line of order:
And therefore is the glorious planet Sol
In noble eminence enthron'd and spher'd
Amidst the other. . . .
          O, when degree is shak'd,
Which is the ladder to all high designs,
The enterprise is sick! How could communities,
Degrees in schools, and brotherhoods in cities,
Peaceful commerce from dividable shores,
The primogenitive and due of birth,
Prerogative of age, crowns, sceptres, laurels,
But by degree, stand in authentic place?
Take but degree away, untune that string,
And, hark, what discord follows! Each thing meets
In mere oppugnancy: the bounded waters
Should lift their bosoms higher than the shores,
And make a sop of all this solid globe:
Strength should be lord of imbecility,
And the rude son should strike his father dead:
Force should be right; or, rather, right and wrong,—
Between whose endless jar justice resides,—
Should lose their names, and so should justice too.

This speech sums up the medieval conception of universal order, the whole logic of hierarchy. But I have quoted it at length
(though at that less than half of it) to emphasize that it *is* a
speech, and not a high order of poetry. It represents the kind
of oratory that Shakespeare habitually used in his routine
court scenes. The carefully ordered march of the rhetoric—the
parade of wooden abstractions—suggests that Shakespeare's
imagination was not really working on the theme of degree.
Anyway the play scarcely bears out the warning of Ulysses.
The untuned Greeks are going to win the war; the well-ordered

Trojans are going to lose. Still less are the heavens implicated. Although Troilus once begs the gods who are frowning on Troy to make their plagues mercifully brief, the plagues are not their doing; there are no blows of Fate, no tempests, no suggestions of disruption in the cosmic order—glorious Sol is in his place. And that this Trojan War is medieval, not Greek, further confuses any effort to draw a medieval moral from the play. The chivalrous knight, devoted to war and his lady, stood near the top in the medieval hierarchy; here Shakespeare represents him as either fraudulent or futile. Thersites sums up the sordid reality beneath the medieval ideal: "Lechery, lechery; still wars and lechery; nothing else holds fashion: a burning devil take them!"

What can we make of this play? Although scholars think that Shakespeare may have written it for a special audience of law students, it cannot be dismissed as merely a work written to order. There is too much energy and feeling in it, and a similar feeling runs through other plays of this period. The heart of it is a total revulsion. "Man delights not me—no, nor woman neither," said Hamlet. The disillusionment that he finally overcame has in *Troilus and Cressida* become downright disgust. Most conspicuously it is a disgust with sex— lechery, lechery! [9] The many allusions to merchandising suggest that it may have been due as well to the growing commercialism, the unashamed greed that other Elizabethan playwrights emphasize much more. But it is all-embracing and all-pervading. Every appearance of idealism is countered by Pandarus and Thersites. No other character speaks so pungently as the cynical Thersites, in his vulgar prose. "I would thou didst itch from head to foot, and I had the scratching of thee," he tells Ajax. His author allows him to do plenty of scratching.

Shakespeare himself was not wholly cynical. He displays

[9] Inevitably this recalls the unhappy love affair sketched in Shakespeare's sonnets. The indications of a homosexual relationship are also borne out by the sordid relationship of Achilles and Patroclus, "his masculine whore."

some sympathy for Troilus and Hector, as a Thersites would not. He writes as a Hamlet, one aware of ideal values and still devoted to them; he represents the corruption as in fact a corruption, not the norm of human nature. Yet his ideal values are not embodied in any character comparable to Hamlet, or exhibited in any significant action. In this drama they are never given a real chance. Here lechery is the one touch of nature that makes the whole world kin. The ending of the drama is distinctly cynical, and it makes plain how fatal cynicism is to the tragic spirit.

The comedies that Shakespeare now went on to write are further evidence that *Troilus and Cressida* was not merely a technical failure, due to an uncongenial or refractory subject, but a symptom of Hamlet's melancholia. In *All's Well That Ends Well* all goes with little mirth, and ends mechanically. *Measure for Measure* is memorable chiefly for its vivid evocation of the rottenness in the state of Vienna; its remorselessly chaste heroine is the least delightful or convincing of Shakespeare's heroines. *Othello* begins against as sordid a background, with an obscene clamor about the love of the blackamoor, and its whole action depends upon the machinations of Iago, the complete cynic. With *Othello*, however, Shakespeare returned to high tragedy. It was followed by *King Lear* —the mightiest of his dramas, and the climax of his vision of evil.

"The bonds of heaven are slipp'd, dissolv'd, and loos'd," cries Troilus when he discovers the falsity of Cressida. "When I love thee not," Othello says in the same Elizabethan vein, "chaos is come again." Only a romantic would associate disappointment in love with cosmic disorder, and the heavens in fact appear undisturbed in these plays. But in *King Lear* the heavens do crash, chaos does come. The storm scenes on the heath represent a universal cataclysm, a fury of all the elements—of nature, human nature, and supernature. This is by all odds the most terrible of Shakespeare's tragedies. In no other is suffering so intense, evil so cruel and monstrous. The adolescent heartbreak of Troilus would seem mere silliness in the world pictured here, but even the woes of Hamlet might look like growing pains when compared to the torment of King Lear.

For many, indeed, this tragedy is almost intolerable. Their final impression is stated by Kent: "all's cheerless, dark, and deadly." To me *King Lear* is a sublime drama, which affords the essential tragic pleasure. But to appreciate it one must put aside any cheerful notions of piety or justice, and first go all the way through the dark and deadly experience that Shakespeare was at such pains to render.

The immediate theme of the play is the tragedy of old age, due especially to the heartlessness of the young. The tragic rhythm is uniquely terrible. In the opening scene King Lear divides up his kingdom; his "purpose" is the ironic hope that he may "unburden'd crawl toward death." Thereafter his drama is all passion and anguished perception. He simply suffers—his actions have no influence on the course of events. Although he has brought this suffering on himself by his ungovernable, despotic temper, we feel long before the end that he is a man "more sinned against than sinning." And Shakespeare reinforces this theme by adding the sub-plot of Gloucester and his sons—an action that parallels the main action instead of providing the customary contrast or relief. Another old man pays a terrible price for the frailties of his age, through the monstrous ingratitude of another child.

This sub-plot overcrowds the play, which is full of improbabilities, inconsistencies, and loose ends. It also makes the play too schematic; the major characters represent the extremes in selfishness and unselfishness, cruelty and kindness, almost like figures in an allegory. Nevertheless all are carefully individualized, each speaks with a characteristic accent. Even the many villains—Goneril, Regan, Edmund, Cornwall, Oswald—have distinct personalities. The tragedy is more painful because it is so poignantly real, in some respects the most lifelike of Shakespeare's tragedies. When Lear thunders at his daughters and the elements, he rants more magnificently than any other character in Shakespeare; but he also speaks with a heartbreaking simplicity that sets him apart from all the other heroes. So do Cordelia and Kent. The last acts are studded with plain little speeches that are commonplace in themselves, sublime in their context.

The imagery of the play, as noted by Caroline Spurgeon, further intensifies and amplifies the theme of evil. It is predominantly of physical pain—the human body flayed, scalded, wrenched, racked, contorted in agony. It also includes many bestial images, to emphasize the "unnatural" cruelty of the wolfish children. But Shakespeare most obviously universalizes his theme by direct statement. The mad Lear is obsessed by the theme of injustice. The Fool harps on the idea that everything is topsy-turvy. All the characters point to the wide, deep correspondences that make this the most comprehensive and resonant of Shakespeare's tragedies. Immediately the violent disorder in the nature of man is reflected in political disorder; the humiliation of the royal Lear leads to civil war, not only between his supporters and his daughters but between the daughters. And though Shakespeare is too busy to do more than sketch this latter theme, he dwells from beginning to end on the cosmic implications of the evil. He forces the anguished question asked by Lear: "Is there any cause in nature that makes these hard hearts?"

When humiliated by his daughters, Lear appeals to the gods above:

> O heavens,
> If you do love old men, if your sweet sway
> Allow obedience, if yourselves are old,
> Make it your cause; send down, and take my part!

The heavens are not deaf, but what they send down is the dreadful tempest; and Lear can only rant, bid them then to let fall their "horrible pleasure," but still protest their "high-engendered battles 'gainst a head so old and white as this." It appears that the gods do not love old men. Even the mild-

mannered Albany, who has faith in the "justicers" above, expresses the fear that unless they quickly assert their justice,
"Humanity must perforce prey on itself." The other virtuous
characters express diverse views. Kent, the stoical old soldier,
knows only the amoral power of Fortune:

> It is the stars,
> The stars above us, govern our conditions.

Edgar is more optimistic, but his cheerfulness also has a stoical
quality:

> Men must endure
> Their going hence, even as their coming hither:
> Ripeness is all.

In his agony Gloucester takes the gloomiest view:

> As flies to wanton boys, are we to the gods;
> They kill us for their sport.

The medieval-minded in the Elizabethan audience might have
taken comfort from the thought that in all this there is no
question of the Christian God, since Shakespeare had been
careful to move the familiar legend of "King Leir" back into
heathen times. (In a previous chronicle play Lear was a Christian king.) Today devotees of the medieval heritage might be
upset by the absence of a Christian frame in the tragedy that
represents the fullest manifestation of Shakespeare's powers.

He is at the peak of his powers in the tempest scenes on the
heath. There is no paraphrasing the tremendous orchestration
of these scenes, which has no parallel in the world's dramatic
literature. But two themes in particular reveal Shakespeare's
incomparable genius as a tragic poet. These are the incongruous themes of humor and madness—materials that were forced
on him by popular taste, and that were commonly among the
crudest conventions of Elizabethan drama.[1]

[1] Thus the title page of the first edition of *King Lear* featured, together with Lear and his daughters, "the unfortunate life of *Edgar,* son

Out of the stock type of the clown, Shakespeare created Lear's Fool, to deepen immeasurably the tragic irony of the drama. He is a "bitter fool," who is pining away for the loss of Cordelia and incessantly reminds Lear of his folly; an innocent fool, who wounds his royal master even when he is patently trying to cheer him; a devoted fool, who suffers miserably from the tempest but remains by his master's side, laboring heroically "to out-jest his heart-struck injuries"; a pathetic fool, evidently himself touched in his wits and almost frightened out of them by the apparition of Edgar as the mad Tom of Bedlam. Most daring is the grotesquerie of the scenes that follow when Lear, now mad, sets up court to try his daughters, appointing the Fool and the mad Tom as "most learned justicers." This is grim humor indeed, so ludicrous that it might seem fatal to the dignity of the hero. The Fool has all along set off the utter lack of humor in Lear—a common limitation of the tragic hero, and a subtler suggestion of his pride or folly. Now we are shown that the royal hero can be an utter fool. Still it all rings true. Lear's obsession is a natural consequence of his suffering; he is made ridiculous only to appear more tragic; and even so he retains his majesty, remaining the grandest figure on the stage.

Although the Greek dramatists never risked such Gothic grotesquerie as this, they did introduce the theme of madness, as in the Ajax of Sophocles. The passion of the tragic hero is always likely to verge on madness. Again, however, Shakespeare's treatment of this theme is much more varied, subtle, and profound. Clifford Leech has pointed out how he sounded the full tragic implications of madness. He characteristically made it realistic; for different reasons and in different forms, it is natural to Hamlet, Othello, Ophelia, and Lady Macbeth, as to Lear. It represents a positive disorder in the hero, another sign of his human limitations. At the same time, his comments are still relevant to the tragic issue, even sharper

and heir to the Earl of Gloucester, and his sullen and assumed humour of *Tom* of Bedlam."

because of his disorder. In revealing a world out of focus they add another perspective, while also revealing that no other character sees the world whole. And always madness is the most dreadful affliction of the human spirit, the ultimate threat to its dignity. It is a reminder, Leech writes, "that our capacity to suffer has a breaking point, that our powers of comprehension are dim"—that the exaltation of high tragedy had better be earned by facing up to the very worst.

The worst, finally, is sounded by the devoted Kent. As Lear enters with the dead Cordelia in his arms, Kent speaks one of the plain, poignant little lines that characterize this tragedy: "Is this the promised end?" The end brings some consolations, to be sure. The evil characters have all been destroyed, the forces of good have triumphed, order has been restored, and Lear dies happy, in the illusion that Cordelia is alive. Nevertheless this is an illusion; the good have also been destroyed, and those who remain must still suffer. When Lear dies, Kent speaks as his truest friend:

> O, let him pass! he hates him much
> That would upon the rack of this tough world
> Stretch him out longer.

Shakespeare also undercuts Lear's kingly role as ritual scapegoat. As he goes off to prison with Cordelia he is happy simply in the thought of being alone with her and rid of the vanities of kingship:

> So we'll live,
> And pray, and sing, and tell old tales, and laugh
> At gilded butterflies, and hear poor rogues
> Talk of court news; and we'll talk with them too,
> Who loses and who wins; who's in, who's out;
> And take upon's the mystery of things,
> As if we were God's spies: and we'll wear out,
> In a wall'd prison, packs and sects of great ones,
> That ebb and flow by the moon.

The tragedy is still more heartbreaking because Lear is denied the very little he now asks of life. Upon his death only
God's spies can take much comfort in the thought of who's in
and who's out in his kingdom now. Although Albany tries to
carry out the ritual pattern by offering the kingdom to Edgar
and Kent, Kent declines the role of Fortinbras. He states his
intention of joining his master in death. Albany then drops the
subject as he concludes the play:

> The weight of this sad time we must obey:
> Speak what we feel, not what we ought to say.

Not what we ought to say. After all we are made to feel in this
play, it would be inhuman, even blasphemous, to say that now
all will be well.

Yet we need not feel despair. In this dark and deadly world
it is fitting that Lear and Cordelia should die—but the more
so because in death their beauty of soul is more radiant.[2] The
monstrous evil in the play is not only defeated: in the final
impression it counts for less than the goodness of Lear, Cordelia, Kent, and the Fool. In no other tragedy did Shakespeare
create such radiant goodness as this. It does not really triumph, since the evil is primarily self-destructive and in defeat
exacts an awful cost of the good; yet it is inextinguishable. It
is sufficiently triumphant in the mere fact of its persistence in
so dark a world.

And through suffering it grows brighter. Both Gloucester
and Lear die of hearts broken " 'Twixt two extremes of passion, joy and grief," and die better men, with a clearer perception of the grounds for both joy and grief in man's life.
The purification of the autocratic Lear is a continuous theme,

[2] One who feels otherwise should consider Nahum Tate's version of
King Lear, which displaced Shakespeare's on the English stage throughout the eighteenth century. Tate preserved the lives of Lear and Cordelia, also throwing in a marriage between Cordelia and Edgar. On
realistic grounds his happy ending is plausible enough—even more
plausible than Shakespeare's ending, since the death of Cordelia is poorly
motivated and mechanically contrived. But it is a sickening letdown from
the plane of Shakespeare's drama.

beginning in the first act as he tries to learn patience. In the storm on the heath, the climax of his sufferings, he not only takes thought of the shivering Fool but learns sympathy for all the "poor naked wretches" of his kingdom. "O, I have ta'en too little care of this." In his madness his speech is a fierce mixture of "matter and impertinency"; the matter concerns the frailty and evil of all mankind, and again the injustice to the poor. When he recovers his wits he is all gentleness and sweetness: "You must bear with me; pray you now, forget and forgive: I am old and foolish." The evil of man's life remains strictly irredeemable; Lear redeems us only in the sense that Kent and Cordelia do, by showing that man can be at his best when his condition is at its worst. But his story has the tragic beauty that the story of Jesus has for those who do not believe in his divinity, and take literally his dying words: "My God, my God, why hast thou forsaken me?" One cannot simply despair of a race that can produce a Jesus.

To many readers *King Lear* may still seem intolerably tragic. One should not be dogmatic about his feelings in these matters, and assume that all sensitive readers ought to feel precisely as he does. But at least it seems clear to me that life on these terms was not intolerable to the author of this tragedy. If the violent disorder in the play reminds us of the deep disorder that apparently threatened Shakespeare's mental health during the tragic period, or in particular of the sex-nausea,[3] *King Lear* was not the product of a disordered or diseased mind. However dark, this is a controlled vision, and finally a balanced vision. The extraordinary splendor and power of Shakespeare's dramatic writing would alone suggest that he was master of his feeling, able to accept the human condition,

---

[3] The mad Lear gives the most lurid expression to this disgust:
  Down from the waist they are centaurs,
  Though women all above:
  But to the girdle do the gods inherit,
  Beneath is all the fiends'; there's hell, there's darkness,
  There is the sulphurous pit, burning, scalding, stench,
  Consumption;—fie, fie, fie!

but his ideal values are plain, and at the end no Thersites or Pandarus enters to mock them. The most terrible of his tragedies, this is also the most compassionate, and the one that most clearly displays a reverence for the human spirit at its best. It is the most complete fusion, in the white heat of intensity, of the dualities of good and evil, in man and in the universe, and of the many possible ways of looking at both. Since Shakespeare does not clearly resolve the dualities, or commit himself to any one view, each reader may find grounds for the final word he believes he "ought to say," in keeping with his own faith; yet he ought not to say that Shakespeare was saying simply this.

If this judgment is colored by a knowledge of the rest of Shakespeare's work, at least it is supported by the tragedies that followed. The disillusionment apparent in *Troilus and Cressida* culminated in the utter misanthropy of *Timon of Athens*, the bitterest of Shakespeare's plays—and a remarkably poor one; but the others indicate a renewed faith. *Macbeth* again plunges us into a stormy, sinister, chaotic world in which even animals are given to violently unnatural behavior. "Fair is foul, and foul is fair"; nor is it always clear which is which, since the weird sisters are somehow in touch with the controlling powers, able to prophesy both fair and foul. Macbeth himself is the most deeply flawed of Shakespeare's heroes. At the end, however, all is fair. Macbeth is punished for his crimes, Malcolm and Macduff are completely victorious. And in *Antony and Cleopatra* there is nothing foul or unnatural. Although the love of Antony brings disorder to the Roman Empire, Shakespeare consistently glorifies it by cosmic images of an ordered world, radiant and harmonious, without tempest. Even in death the lovers have "immortal longings," expressing little sorrow and no remorse; Octavius, who ostensibly restores order to the Empire, is by contrast an insignificant, almost contemptible politician. Critics of all schools might therefore find fault with this tragedy, which lacks a Christian frame, a tragic lesson, a ritual pattern, a sense of mystery. But all might agree that it is the most spacious and gorgeous of Shakespeare's tragedies.

It accordingly foreshadows the "brave new world" of the comedies with which Shakespeare ended his career—*Pericles, Cymbeline, The Winter's Tale, The Tempest.* The theme of all these plays is reconciliation, regeneration, rebirth; winter gives way to spring, tempest to "heavenly music." If Shakespeare was following the current fashion in turning from tragedy to romantic comedy, he was manifestly expressing a changed state of mind as well. *The Tempest* most of all is a work of love. A beautiful play in its own right, it is a sublime postscript to the tragedies. One can hardly help reading this last of Shakespeare's plays as a conscious farewell to the stage. "I shall miss thee," Prospero tells Ariel, his "delicate spirit," when he is about to release him from his labors. Having raised many a tempest, waked many a sleeper from the grave, by his "so potent art," Prospero now abjures his magic. "I'll drown my book," he concludes; and possibly he had in mind the agonized words of another magician, Dr. Faustus—"I'll burn my books!" He is serene, having no reason to feel remorse for his works, but he is also a little sad, as becomes one who has known much tragedy. He has to confess his utter failure with Caliban, the brute in man; there is no hope of redeeming this monster. Once he has retired, "Every third thought shall be my grave." He knows how insubstantial is the pageant of man's life:

> We are such stuff
> As dreams are made on, and our little life
> Is rounded with a sleep.

We need not get sentimental over this aspect of *The Tempest.* If Shakespeare was taking a bow before posterity, he was still an impersonal, noncommittal, ironic dramatist, speaking his last word in the form of a play that is deceptively simple on its surface, and as rich and haunting in its depths as *Hamlet.* "Any set of symbols, moved close to this play," wrote Mark

Van Doren, "lights up as in an electric field." But there is no mistaking the harmonious ending. We may assume that Shakespeare had no illusions about the "brave new world" of the Renaissance, or man as a paragon. When Miranda exclaims about this world "that has such people in't!" Prospero says simply: " 'Tis new to thee." Still, he forgives the villains in it. Shakespeare had made his peace with it. "Ripeness is all."

4. THE DECLINE TO THE RESTORATION

Elizabethan drama officially came to an end in 1642, when the Puritan-controlled Parliament closed down the theater. This action is seldom pictured as a literary calamity, for drama had been dying of itself. Tragedy had long since given way to plays of romance and sentiment. Poetry, like feeling, had become conventional and was mostly on the surface. In general, the signs of decadence are unmistakable, and raise the usual depressing questions. But they may seem less puzzling or depressing if we remember that the great period of tragedy was very brief, covering less than a score of years at the turn of the seventeenth century, that its greatness was mostly due to the work of Shakespeare, and that except for him it never reached maturity.

Let us consider Tourneur's *The Revenger's Tragedy*—a play given high praise by Elizabethan specialists, even called "noble in its austerity." At first glance, it contains all the makings of tragedy by most standards, aside from the Elizabethan standard of wholesale slaughter. Tourneur treats with deadly earnestness the theme of evil. He sustains the macabre atmosphere that he establishes in the striking first scene, when the hero, Vindice, stands in the darkness, holding the skull of his betrayed mistress, while her murderer, the Duke, and his horribly evil family cross the stage with torchbearers. The best-known passage, which illustrates the poetic power of Tourneur, is Vindice's soliloquy on the vanity of life, inspired by the skull of his beloved:

Does the silkworm expend her yellow labors
For thee? For these does she undo herself?
Are lordships sold to maintain ladyships,
For the poor benefit of a bewitching minute?

The play is full of Aristotle's *peripeteia;* someone has counted twenty-two of these ironic reversals. A ritual pattern may be made out in the final purification of the kingdom, when a virtuous nobleman succeeds the evil Duke and promises to rule under Heaven's sway. Vindice heroically accepts the penalty for his bloody revenges: "We die after a nest of dukes. Adieu!"

Nevertheless *The Revenger's Tragedy* is a preposterous play. The action moves by purely mechanical contrivance, through the creaky devices of disguise, misunderstanding, and coincidence. The characters are mostly drawn in black or white; they include the most loathsome and incredible set of villains in Elizabethan drama. The climax is brought about by what Vindice's brother calls the "quaintness" of his malice. The lecherous Duke, who had hired him to bring in a lady for seduction, is presented in the darkness with the skull of Vindice's betrothed, "dressed up in tires," and kisses its poisoned mouth; in his death agony he is then forced to witness the adultery of his duchess with his bastard son. After this horror Tourneur can build up to a last act only by introducing a holocaust, arranged by having Vindice suddenly induce the company to join him in murdering the rest of the monsters. (One named Supervacuo, incidentally, is unaccounted for—apparently overlooked by the cast or the author in the excitement of the slaughter.) All this distortion is so consistent that T. S. Eliot has remarked the "amazing unity" of the play in its representation of "an insane and unique and horrible vision of life." But these are words for nightmare, not for a tragic vision. Tourneur shows no pity, no sense of complexity in evil, no sense of mystery. What he conveys most vividly is an absolute loathing.

For the critic, however, there remains some perplexity.

Whence and wherefore all this sound and fury? For the violence of Tourneur does not seem merely sensational or immature. Neither was his nightmarish vision actually "unique." A mysterious figure, he leads us into the background of his age, the shadows into which he disappeared, and immediately to a similar playwright of considerably greater stature—John Webster.

Webster's performance is in many respects as crude as Tourneur's. His plots are creaky and his technique is often childish, as in the many explanatory asides that spell out the dramatic meaning in words of one syllable. He exploits the "conventions" for purely sensational effects. Ghosts stalk in to no purpose except to raise gooseflesh; characters go mad or play mad only to please the groundlings; dumb shows illustrate or repeat the horrors. His plays are full of gruesome scenes and loathsome characters, whose villainy may be poorly motivated. The atmosphere is as nightmarish as in Tourneur. Webster often expresses a comparable loathing for man and his life: a deformed creature who insults the animal world by calling his deformity brutish, and who bears about his "rotten and dead body" in the continual fear of being put in the ground "to be made sweet." An admirer of Webster has described his plays as "the feverish and ghastly turmoil of a nest of maggots."

But there is much more in Webster than this. *The White Devil* and *The Duchess of Malfi* are not only powerful plays but truly tragic ones, rising above horror to a somber grandeur. His vision is more complex than Tourneur's, and is rendered with more poetic and dramatic intensity. He displays pity as well as disgust. His villains are not simple Elizabethan monsters; they ponder as well as proclaim their evil motives, and are capable of self-loathing, a remorse beyond the exigencies of winding up the plot. His nobler characters have a heroic spirit. After her horrible ordeal the Duchess of Malfi says proudly: "I am Duchess of Malfi still." She faces her executioners in the same spirit:

> I would fain put off my last woman's fault,
> I'd not be tedious to you.

Webster's tense, ambiguous vision of life is summed up in his treatment of death. No Elizabethan playwright seems more obsessed with the theme, or insists so morbidly on the earthworms whom man lives to feed. None strews the stage with more corpses, at less provocation. The often weak motivation for the killings emphasizes the irrational evil that makes his world so nightmarish. Yet it is in death that Webster's characters realize themselves, summon up the best of their humanity. Even his villains usually meet it with dignity. As one says,

> I do glory yet
> That I can call this act mine own.

A nobler character states the essential faith of tragedy:

> Though in our miseries Fortune have a part,
> Yet in our noble sufferings she hath none:
> Contempt of pain, that we may call our own.

Altogether, Webster's tragedies are second only to Shakespeare's. *The Duchess of Malfi*, produced shortly after Shakespeare had quit the stage, made a grand enough swan song for Elizabethan tragedy. It is the more mournful, however, because the death of this tragedy seems premature. The qualities of greatness in Webster throw into sharper relief the serious faults that he never outgrew. His crudities make him seem irresponsible in spite of his basic sincerity, even his desperate earnestness. And his qualities of desperation point to his limited command—intellectual or imaginative—of a tragic condition that made him feel so intensely. He was shocked, obsessed, by an evil that he could not transcend in a larger frame or a longer perspective.

Although this sense of evil may be traced to the medieval heritage, the pessimism of Webster does not seem medieval. The many references to heaven and hell sound as conventional as the many to Fortune; they are not tense with religious feeling. The hell that concerned him was here on earth, and heaven was evidently no compensation for it. Ultimately, his pessimism—and that of Tourneur—seems due to disillusionment with Renaissance ideals. It signified a loss of faith rather than a reassertion of the traditional faith, and so took the form of a violent revulsion. Its most apparent source, or symbol, was the growing rule of money, in a society that was shifting from a feudal to a capitalistic economy. Like other Elizabethans, Webster and Tourneur attacked the Machiavellian politician, but they harped most of all on the theme of greed, the evils of gold. As most Americans know, "Business and sentiment don't mix." Many Elizabethans were still naïve enough to believe that sentiment was more important.

In such attacks on contemporary evils, the playwrights were hardly anticipating modern sociological tragedy. They were not analytical enough to study the causes of social evil, nor optimistic enough to preach social reform. But they call for some discount of the popular notion of the glamorous Elizabethans, which may make an Ibsen seem wholly alien to the great tradition, and make unhappy writers today feel that their own sense of alienation is unprecedented. According to T. S. Eliot, for example, Elizabethan dramatists were blessed in that they lacked a sense of a "changing world," or of corruptions and abuses peculiar to their age. "We feel," he wrote, "that they believed in their own age, in a way in which no nineteenth or twentieth-century writer of the greatest seriousness has been able to believe in his age. . . . We can partly criticize their age through our study of them, but they did not so criticize it themselves." Actually, the morbidity of Webster and Tourneur appears to have been due in part to the feeling that the corruptions and abuses of their age *were* peculiar.[4]

[4] In another essay Eliot himself felt rather differently. Here he declared that "the philosophical basis, the general attitude toward life of the Elizabethans, is one of anarchism, of dissolution, of decay."

The later dramatists were less critical of their age. Beginning with Beaumont and Fletcher there was an obvious falling off in intensity and seriousness, as tragic drama declined into romantic story and symbolic imagery became merely decorative. This decline is somewhat puzzling, since it did not reflect an era of increasing order and security. Rather, there was more reason for tension. Political, economic, and religious strife was to culminate in the beheading of Charles I. In the world of thought, men were catching on to the implications of what Galileo had discovered with his "fantastic glass" (mentioned by the wicked cardinal in *The Duchess of Malfi*). Sir Henry Wotton reported to King James that Galileo "hath overthrown all former astronomy—for we must have a new sphere to save the appearances." John Donne despaired of the appearances. As a result of the "new philosophy," he wrote in his "First Anniversary,"

> 'Tis all in pieces, all coherence gone,
> All just supply, and all relation. . . .
> The world's proportion disfigured is.

Such tensions help to explain why he and the other "metaphysicals" wrought their poetry of paradox.[5] And although this cerebral poetry was ill-suited to drama, it forces the question why both thought and feeling grew more superficial in contemporaneous drama.

[5] Donne is commonly praised today for his union of thought and feeling, by contrast with the "dissociation of sensibility" from which poets have suffered ever since; but in fact he was a conspicuous example of such dissociation. The resolution he achieved in his poetry was primarily verbal, the "union" of the pun. It amounts to casuistry or equivocation, and reveals his deep anxiety—in particular his fear of death and hell. The "Jack Donne" who privately wrote an unorthodox essay in defense of suicide was never reconciled with the Dr. Donne who ended in the arms of the Anglican Church; and neither was capable of the harmony achieved in *The Tempest*. I should question both the thought and feeling of the strained metaphor that Cleanth Brooks calls probably the most celebrated metaphor of our time:

> Such wilt thou be to me who must
> Like th' other foot, obliquely run;
> Thy firmness makes my circle just,
> And makes me end where I begun.

The childish conventions of Elizabethan drama, once more, naturally impeded the development of mature tragedy. Only the sovereign genius of Shakespeare could work such materials into great drama. Lesser writers, even such potentially great ones as Marlowe, Tourneur, and Webster, were always prone to melodrama. Among the particular liabilities were the conventional villain and the commonplaces about moral instruction, which alike obscured the idea that "in tragic life no villain need be." But in the light of subsequent history, the limitations of popular Elizabethan drama seem less significant than the limitations of the more sophisticated drama that replaced it.

In *Shakespeare and the Rival Traditions*, Alfred Harbage dwells upon the private "coterie" theater that grew up early in Shakespeare's career. This was an indoor theater, artificially lighted, in which companies of boy actors performed for a much smaller audience at considerably higher prices of admission. Its audience was naturally exclusive—an urban smart set rather than a representative national audience. The playwrights who wrote for it often expressed their contempt of the popular theater. Their plays were typically licentious and satirical, lacking the moral, religious, and patriotic sentiments that appealed to the despised common people. They sought to debunk rather than elevate; they presented many more evil characters than good ones; they were given to pessimism, cynicism, diabolism—a self-indulgent kind of gloominess, which revealed no more depth or complexity of vision than appeared in the popular drama. Harbage insists that much generalization about "Elizabethan" drama is vitiated by neglect of these rival traditions.

He somewhat exaggerates both the wholesomeness of popular drama and the decadence of the coterie drama. (One of these decadents was Ben Jonson.) Nevertheless he points to an important difference, which essentially was between not a plebeian and a patrician theater, but a public and a private one. The private theater was naturally less suited to the purposes of tragedy, and in fact produced fewer tragedies. Whereas about thirty per cent of the known plays in the popular repertories until 1613 were tragedies, with twenty per cent histories and the rest comedies, the private repertories over the same period show only fifteen per cent tragedies, all the rest being comedies. And the future belonged to the private theater. We may now make out a turning-point in the year 1609, when Shakespeare's company moved into Blackfriars. Perhaps they foresaw the future; possibly this is one reason why Shakespeare quit the stage shortly thereafter. In any case the trend continued. "The Muses chatter, who were wont to sing," an actor complained in 1638. By 1642, when drama was suppressed, all the major theaters were private ones.

The question then arises why this change took place. An immediate reason was the growing Puritan hostility to the playhouses and their crowds of happy customers; the players sought refuge in the less conspicuous private theaters, closer to the indulgent court. A deeper reason, indicated by this very hostility, was that the drama was not so deeply rooted in the communal life as it had been in Athens, and never achieved the dignity of Greek drama. It was more susceptible to mere fashion—as tragedy itself became the fashion, for a mere decade. But essentially the change was in keeping with the change that came over European art and literature with the Renaissance. Gothic art, the work largely of anonymous artisans, had been close to the folk. Renaissance art became highly self-conscious, and consciously aloof from the ignorant, vulgar folk; it was of, by, and for an elite. Thus literary critics distinguished tragedy from comedy primarily in terms of class: tragedy was about the affairs of kings and nobles, comedy was about common people and ordinary life. In general, "culture" became what it means to most people today: interests associated with leisure and privilege, above and apart from everyday life.

Restoration drama, which historians used to picture as a new growth due to French influence, is best understood as a logical result of this whole development. Although it owed considerable to the French, it stemmed directly from the Elizabethans. Its characteristic innovation, the "heroic play," was implicit in late Elizabethan drama, which had begun to exploit the themes of love and honor. Ideally, this was to be the noblest form of drama, raising tragedy to the plane of epic. Actually, it was an operatic entertainment for a small audience of court followers who had little feeling for either tragedy or epic. The courtly ideal it celebrated was no longer the living ideal that it had been for the early Elizabethans, such as Spenser, Sidney, and Raleigh. The dramatists concentrated on "painting the passions," especially love; but the passions were essentially fashions, the painting a rhetorical exercise. If romantic love is at best a doubtful subject for high tragedy, not to say epic, the increasing concentration on it in Restoration drama was plainly a constriction. It did not signify that the poets had come to recognize any primary significance in the relation of man to woman. It signified that as poets they had lost interest in the larger relations of man to society and the cosmos, the problems of his destiny.

Artificial as the heroic play was, we must pause over it if only because it was written and defended by so great a poet and critic as John Dryden. Dryden was an ambiguous figure, in his own words

> betwixt two Ages cast,
> The first of this, and hindmost of the last.

Often he was pleased to dwell on the superiority of his age, in manners, taste, and above all "wit." Its art was more polished and refined as well as more regular; it had cultivated that "most pleasant form," tragi-comedy; it had brought into drama "the sweetness of rhyme"; it had raised "love and Honour" to a high degree, painting gentle and noble passions instead of the rude, violent ones that obsessed the Elizabethans. "To please an Age more Gallant than the last" was sufficient praise for a poet, Dryden concluded in one epilogue. Nevertheless it was not really sufficient for him. In his prologues and epilogues he was constantly railing at the audience that sat in judgment of his plays; evidently these paragons of wit had poor taste, after all. He felt that the foremost honors went to the "barbarous" Elizabethans. His pride gave way to a "secret shame" whenever he thought of Shakespeare, the poet of Nature. Although Shakespeare was uneven, he was always great when dealing with the great occasions. By contrast, his own contemporaries were dealing with "Weak, short-liv'd issues of a feeble Age."

Still, Dryden himself expended a great deal of time and talent on these issues. Essentially he was a man of his age, not a victim of it. The fairest text for comparison is his *All for Love*, based on *Antony and Cleopatra*. This was the best suited of Shakespeare's tragedies for retelling in the Restoration manner, and Dryden's performance is quite respectable. His play is better constructed than Shakespeare's, much more dignified and mature than the common run of Elizabethan plays. By general consent it is Dryden's best play, as he himself regarded it. It was the only play, he once remarked, that he wrote for himself. And it therefore makes plainer that he was not a great *tragic* poet.

The subtitle of the play, "The World Well Lost," points to Dryden's shortcomings. He makes more of the love affair, adding the complications of jealousy and misunderstanding, but he fails to create a vivid impression of the "world" that is its stage and stake. Although he opens the play with a speech about the dreadful prodigies and portents that have visited Egypt, implying a convulsion of nature such as Shakespeare was wont to introduce, he then drops this subject for good; it was merely a rhetorical device, a bit of "atmosphere." The frequent reference to the Roman Empire, the "vast" character of Antony, the "transcendent" passion of Cleopatra, likewise emphasizes his failure to render the vastness and transcendence. Dryden excites chiefly pity, which at that is sometimes facile. (Thus he brings in Antony's children and prompts a character

to remark: "Was ever sight so moving?") He excites little terror, little sense of the wonder of man's passion or the mystery
of his fate. If the constriction of the drama is partly due to his
confining his world struggle to a single court on a single day,
primarily it is due to Dryden's feeling for his subject, the limits
of his imaginative reach. He gives himself away in a prefatory
remark that not all poets had "a taste for tragedy." He had
some "taste" for it as a literary mode. But he had no tragic
sense of life.

Neither did any of his important contemporaries. The one
possible exception was John Milton, who had been isolated by
the Restoration. His *Samson Agonistes* is a singular work, more
truly classical in form and spirit than French drama. Its action
involves some doubt and despair, reflecting Milton's own fate
as a solitary outcast, "blind among enemies." Samson, his
"hopes all flat," is eloquent in his despair. The Chorus pointedly
raises the tragic issue, in irregular verse:

> God of our fathers! what is Man,
> That thou towards him with hand so various—
> Or might I say contrarious?—
> Temper'st thy providence through his short course:
> Not evenly, as thou rul'st
> The angelic orders, and inferior creatures mute,
> Irrational and brute?

God mysteriously elects to abase the greatest of men; "just
and unjust alike seem miserable," alike "come to an evil end."
Yet there is nothing evil, or really tragic, in the end of Samson.
His sacrificial death is not merely a reconciliation but a resounding triumph, demonstrating the theme that the Chorus
has announced at the outset: the ways of God are just, and
justifiable to men. "Nothing is here for tears," says Samson's
father, ". . . nothing but well and fair." "All is best," echoes
the Chorus, dismissing us with "calm of mind, all passion
spent." *Samson Agonistes* is a noble religious drama, and may

remind us that great religious drama is even rarer than great tragedy; but it emphasizes the essential difference between them.

At any rate, Milton's drama was as unsuited as Elizabethan drama to the Restoration Age. Both were outmoded by not only the growing sophistication and gentility but the growing rationalism, derived from science. In the light of this rationalism, which we have inherited, we feel a kind of naïveté in the intensity with which the early Elizabethans responded to the thought of death, and to the contradictions of their experience. As we rejoice in the genius of Shakespeare, who transcended this naïveté, we should remember that he shared the intensity, of which Dryden was incapable. We might also rejoice over the accidental, or providential, fact that he was born at just the right moment. Had he appeared a generation earlier or a generation later, he might not have realized his genius. As it was, he had a tradition, a playhouse, and an audience that made it possible for him to write his masterpieces. For similar reasons he could not breed followers worthy of him, found an enduring school.

CHAPTER V

NEO–CLASSICAL
TRAGEDY

1. THE AGE OF LOUIS XIV

Although French classical tragedy was held up as a model during the Restoration and eighteenth century, it has always seemed more or less alien to the English-speaking world. Dryden himself had some harsh things to say about his French tutors. "Their heroes are the most civil people breathing," he wrote, "but their good breeding seldom extends to a word of sense; all their wit is in their ceremony; they want the genius which animates our state; and therefore it is but necessary, when they cannot please, that they should take care not to offend." In particular he ridiculed Racine, who had brought the Hippolytus of Euripides to Paris, taught him to make love, turned him into "Monsieur Hippolyte." Following Dryden, English critics generally admired the regularity and decorum of French tragedy but complained of its lack of vigor. Following the Romantic Movement, most had a much lower opinion of Corneille and Racine, if they discussed them at all. There are modern books on tragedy that do not even mention them.[1] It is hard for us to think of them as in a class with Shakespeare. Nevertheless we should suspect that this attitude is provincial—as provincial as we know Voltaire was when he described *Hamlet* as a "vulgar and barbarous drama, which would not be tolerated by the vilest populace of France." The French still rank Corneille and Racine among their greatest writers; and nobody denies that theirs is one of the great literatures. Certainly those who are able to put up with the barbarities of *Tamburlaine* and *The Revenger's Tragedy* are not entitled to be supercilious about French classical tragedy. With Racine especially we are dealing with mature, civilized drama. It is at

[1] For example, Mark Harris's *The Case for Tragedy* and William Van O'Connor's *Climates of Tragedy*.

least the best that the post-Renaissance had to offer in tragedy, down into the nineteenth century. And it was at this time that France took over the cultural leadership of Europe. The Age of Louis XIV, which produced Corneille and Racine, symbolizes a major phase in Western civilization.

Essentially it was an age of consolidation, whose most conspicuous symbols were order, authority, and propriety. Cardinal Richelieu had brought order out of feudal and religious turmoil by strengthening the authority of the monarch. Under Louis XIV, who took all power in his own hands, France became a highly centralized modern state, and the strongest power in Europe. While there is considerable question about his greatness as a man and a monarch, at least no king was ever a greater actor of kingship, or worked harder at being every inch a king, throughout the longest reign in recorded history. He and the palace he built at Versailles set the style for absolute monarchs all over Europe. Versailles also set the tone for art and literature, as well as the ideal of *politesse* in the salons.

The characteristic style in art was baroque, or late-baroque. In Sypher's terms, it was a formal reintegration, a resolution of the uncertainties of the "mannerist" phase; without equivocation it sought elegance, elevation, the "grand style." The spirit of order and obedience to authority was most apparent in literature. The French Academy, set up under Richelieu, soon began to lay down the law. The law was regularity, propriety, decorum. The consolidation of literature was in part a reaction against the exuberance and license of the Renaissance, as typified by Rabelais, but it was also a fulfillment of the authoritarian tendency in Renaissance literary criticism, which had looked to the classics for rules. Now critics succeeded in imposing the famous rules. Poetry was rigidly bound by them until the nineteenth century.

As for drama, France had had a popular theater much like the Elizabethan, if not so full-blooded. During the Elizabethan period it produced a form of tragedy almost as irregular. But at this time it produced no Marlowe. One reason, aside from the element of sheer chance in the appearance of genius, is that its audience was purely plebeian, not representative; the upper classes remained aloof from so vulgar a theater. By the time a genius did appear, in the person of Corneille, the theater had grown fashionable, but in the process it was being cut off from its roots in folk tradition. It attracted a sophisticated audience like that which attended Restoration drama. Hence it too was made subject to the classical rules. Among the first acts of the French Academy was an attack on Corneille for the irregularities of his first major play, *The Cid*.

All this concentration on order and authority was effected in the name of reason or good sense. In literature the classical mode was rationalized as a return to the good sense of the ancients, and also as a correct imitation of Nature. In thought generally, the rationalism of Descartes was a significant influence, or at least symbolic. As he made "clear and distinct ideas" the criterion of truth, so all writers sought clarity and objectivity. As his philosophical ideal was the order and certainty of mathematics, so the age sought to reduce all spheres of experience to a comparable order, or in the words of Daniel Mornet, "to organize a sort of social and esthetic geometry." It put its trust in formulas, maxims, rules. Another symbol was the formal gardens of Versailles—"Nature methodized."

Now to us this is a naturally unattractive age, whose political order seems conspicuously unreasonable. The rule of Louis XIV was despotism, marked by a steady decline in municipal liberties, and by as steady and successful an effort to reduce self-reliant noblemen to servile courtiers. While Louis was proud to conceive himself as the "Sun King," from whom the whole national life emanated, his primary concern was always the welfare of the monarchy, not the people. With Versailles he created a glittering, parasitical, irresponsible court that was further removed from the commonwealth. At best the atmosphere of Versailles, and of the salons that imitated it, was not conducive to the creation of high tragedy; and this was the atmosphere breathed by Racine, an intimate of

Louis and constant attendant at court. "Why," asks Professor A. F. B. Clark, "should not the manner of a Louis of France be as good a model for a tragic poet as that of an Elizabeth of England or an Œdipus of Thebes?" An immediate answer is that tragedy was created by free Athens, not royal Thebes, and that in England it was not produced by or for the court of Elizabeth. One can hardly imagine the performance of an *Œdipus Rex* or a *Hamlet* at the grandiose palace of Versailles. And as unattractive is the literary despotism, the absolute rules, which among other things killed lyric poetry.

Yet this seventeenth century is one of the very great centuries in the history of human thought. It is Whitehead's "Century of Genius": of Descartes, Hobbes, Locke, Spinoza, and Leibniz in philosophy; of Kepler, Galileo, Boyle, Harvey, and Newton in science. In the arts its famous names include Milton, Molière, Velasquez, Rubens, and Rembrandt. And though all this great achievement gives an absurd air to the pomp of the little "Sun King," in his chilly palace, it should remind us that the Age of Louis XIV was nevertheless a truly brilliant, creative age.

In general, it had the virtues of its defects. In its drive to reclaim, consolidate, and formalize, it succeeded in ordering a great deal of experience, creating a circumscribed, indoor world but a coherent, well-lit one. The rationalism that limited its imaginings was also a discipline that made for an admirable clarity, economy, and precision. Its tyrannical ideal of *"le goût,"* or good taste, was at least a civilized ideal, and a civilizing influence; Elizabethan drama reveals the real need of standards of taste and judgment. For such reasons France now became the cultural leader of Europe. At home a sufficient example of the glory of the age was La Fontaine. In our own century or the last, Lytton Strachey remarked, La Fontaine would naturally have been a café-drifter; but the Age of Louis XIV "took this dreamer, this idler, this feckless, fugitive spiritual creature, kept him alive by means of patrons in high society, and eventually turned him—not simply into a poet, for he was a poet by nature, but into one of the most subtle, deliberate, patient, and exquisite craftsmen who have ever written in verse."

The inimitable fables of La Fontaine also oblige us to begin qualifying the conventional descriptions of French Classicism. They were a highly original creation, not the product of authority, formula, or rule; they cannot be adequately described as classical or baroque. Neither can Molière be pinned down, nor even Corneille and Racine. Neo-classical drama was by no means a mere imitation or anachronism—it was a new form, developed to meet new needs. In developing it, each in his own individual way, all three quarreled with the rules, all declared repeatedly that the chief rule was to please. Likewise critics kept talking of *force* and *éclat* as well as clarity, propriety, and correctness. They fought out the famous battle of the Ancients and the Moderns, in which the Moderns had the better of it. Something of the individualism of the Renaissance survived the resolute efforts of the authorities to impose law and order.

Similarly the absolutism of the age failed to smother the tradition of free thought that stemmed from the Renaissance. Louis XIV could not be attacked openly, but he lacked the power over the minds of men that Oriental monarchs exercised; thinkers of the time generally remained critical of his rule, in effect not regarding him as divinely appointed or inspired. The Church was not the power it was in Italy or in Spain, where the Inquisition largely succeeded in stifling free thought; the French were proud of their "Gallican Liberties," privileges peculiar to France that limited the power of the Pope over them. In particular the tradition of Montaigne remained strong. All the writers of the century studied Montaigne and quoted from him; almost all owed something to his skepticism and his humanism. The clearest testimony to the strength of his influence is the attack made on him by Pascal, who recognized him as the symbol of the growing skepticism—and who himself had much of Montaigne in him. And Pascal failed to stem the tide. The Age of Louis XIV terminated in the work of Fontenelle and Bayle, forerunners of the Age of the Enlightenment.

This underlying freedom in thought is hardly surprising in an age devoted to rationalism, under the ægis of Descartes. But it brings up the usual complexities. An age as creative as the Age of Louis XIV could never be so simple and uniform as it appears in the unavoidable generalizations. Its incessant effort to impose order and rule itself testifies to the existence of disorder and uncertainty, and in writers might create more tension than it resolved. One does not have to go deep beneath the formal, elegant surface to discover striking incongruities.

Its famed *politesse,* to begin with, was still on the surface. Daniel Mornet observed that some fifty editions of books of etiquette were published, with repeated injunctions against what would strike us as the grossest breaches of etiquette. (And we might pause a moment to pity the court of Louis, living amid the glitter, the cold, and the stink of the unsanitary palace of Versailles.) The morals of the age were no better than its manners. The police archives of Paris have revealed a sinister underworld of crime, which came to light in the trial of La Voisin: a woman who provided love philters, poisons, and Black Masses for the highest personages in France, including friends of Racine and possibly Racine himself. As Brunetière wrote of his Paris, "every day some Phaedra was poisoning some Hippolytus"; Racine did not have to go to Euripides or Seneca for his subject matter. His religiosity, and that of Louis, points to another anomaly. "Boileau is devout and malicious," wrote Fontenelle; "Racine is more devout and more malicious." Both the religious spirit and the classical spirit of the age were belied by the bitterness and malice that so often cropped up, as in the literary quarrel between the followers of Corneille and Racine, the vicious attacks on Molière, and even the controversy over quietism between Cardinals

Bossuet and Fénelon. Few ages have been less distinguished for charity and humility, or for moderation and tranquillity.

Such symptoms of anxiety suggest a degree of overstatement in the typical generalization of Mornet, that the age "had no sense of history, no sense of the instability and transitoriness of human societies and of a great number of human rules." If so, it had no tragic sense whatever; and one might wonder why it wrote tragedy at all. It indeed did its best to avert its gaze from the dark unknown. Nevertheless a strange melancholy pervades the literature of this allegedly complacent age. If this was in part a fashion, a means to a literary effect, and sometimes a reflection of the ennui of Versailles (as in the memoirs of Saint-Simon), it also sprang from a pessimistic view of human nature. Most of the greater writers of the century—notably Pascal, La Rochefoucauld, and La Bruyère—dwelt chiefly on man's folly and evil. They were typically more somber than Montaigne. They wrote like disillusioned rather than unillusioned men, recalling Molière's hero in *The Misanthrope*—a comedy that is not far from tragedy.[2]

The rationalism of the age was likewise not so clear and cool as the textbooks, or its own manuals, would have it. If writers were inclined to be more rationalistic than reasonable, they still had some awareness of the insufficiency of reason and rule. They were especially concerned with the problem of passion. The war between reason and passion was a major theme of the age. Most of the leading thinkers, especially among the churchmen, attacked the passions. The Jansenist Nicole, an austere theologian who could sound as cynical as La Rochefoucauld, proclaimed that everything that touches the heart is necessarily poisoned: "All men naturally hate one another. . . . We desire to be loved only in order to love ourselves the more." But some thinkers defended the passions,

---

[2] It is suggestive that when Émile Faguet discussed the pleasure of tragedy, in a book on the drama of the period, he located its primary source in man's malice, his tendency to enjoy the misfortunes of others.

pointing out that they could yield an ardor for the good. Pascal recognized the need even of excess. "Passion cannot be *belle* without excess," he wrote. "When one doesn't love too much he doesn't love enough." Literary men were naturally disposed to be kindlier to the claims of the heart; they celebrated the passion for honor, or *"gloire."* And at least they knew the tragic power of passion, which made human nature not so amenable to the rules they might still proclaim.

The tensions that gave the Age of Louis XIV its tragic potentialities are most clearly seen in Pascal. A stern Jansenist who had had a mystical experience and thereafter devoted all his genius to the service of God, Pascal was also a child of Montaigne. He knew that reason could prove nothing about the existence of his Creator. He saw, for example, the hole in the plausible argument from design: the traces of God's handiwork in nature were only traces, and the evils of nature gave as good reason for doubting His existence. Why, he asked in anguish, did not God say all, or say nothing? For he could not understand the "monstrous" attitude of many contemporaries who were content to rest in doubt and uncertainty. Neither could he despise reason, or like Martin Luther brand it as "the Devil's bride." "Thought makes the whole dignity of man," he declared, adding that the endeavor to think well was the basic morality.

His final appeal, however, was to the despised passions: "The heart hath its reasons, which reason knows not of." The heart of Pascal was a well of passion. He dwelt on the terror and despair he felt as he contemplated the "infinite immensity" of the "whole dumb universe," which science was now making known. Hence he insisted the more desperately on the absolute necessity of belief in God: there was no peace, no joy, no good for man except in the knowledge of God. The torment of spirit that permeates the *Pensées* leads many readers to suspect that in his heart of hearts Pascal suffered from doubt. At least his faith failed to give him abiding peace of mind. Himself blessed, or cursed, with a magnificent mind, he could never forget that reason was unable to demonstrate the all-important truth for man.[3]

From the horns of his dilemma Pascal made some cynical observations, and at times seems to echo the commonplaces about the vileness and utter insignificance of man. But what he saw most clearly, and expressed most eloquently, was the tragic paradox of the human condition. The terrible thing about man is that he is *not* a worm—worms never know his torment. He is an incomprehensible mixture of spirit and clay; he is an astonishing mean between all and nothing, the infinitely large and the infinitely small—extremes alike incomprehensible; and he is conscious of his impossible situation, incapable alike of absolute knowledge and absolute ignorance. He is the weakest reed in nature—but a "thinking reed." He is nobler than the whole universe that crushes him because he knows that he dies, whereas the universe knows nothing of this; he is also full of natural error, the most foolish creature in the universe. Nothing stays for him: this is his natural position; and nothing is more contrary to his natural inclination. He must forever seek the truth he can never know, burn with a desire for a certainty and a stability he can never hope to attain. He is a natural freak:

What a chimera is man! Strange and monstrous! A chaos, a contradiction, a prodigy. Judge of all things, yet a weak earthworm. Depository of truth, yet a cesspool of uncertainty and error; the glory and the scrapings of the universe.

Montaigne had said all this, but in a much calmer spirit. His conclusion was that man should accept his anomalous being, live "without wonder or extravagancy." Pascal, who devoted

[3] The most that reason could offer, he declared, was his famous wager: the skeptic should bet on God if only because he had everything to gain and nothing to lose. This wager seems less reasonable when one exposes Pascal's silent assumptions—that God requires belief, rewards it with heaven, and punishes doubt with hellfire. He himself narrowly escaped damnation as a heretic.

his genius to an extravagant and it would seem vain endeavor to live as a saint, felt with the utmost intensity the paradoxes that Montaigne found curious or fascinating. In France he was the most striking example of the tensions between the medieval faith and the modern mind. Both more medieval and more modern than Shakespeare, he might have written great tragedy had he been a playwright. As it is, he affords an illuminating perspective on the tragedy of Corneille and Racine.

2. THE "GREAT AND GOOD" CORNEILLE

With the production of Corneille's *The Cid* in 1637 modern drama may be said to begin; but it is hard for moderns to understand the intense excitement it roused in its day, or the literary fame it has enjoyed to this day. What most readers now see in it is a cloak-and-sword melodrama, celebrating preposterous heroics. In the course of one day the hero fights two duels, wins a great victory over the Moors, and at odd moments keeps offering his life to his beloved, whose father had unfortunately been the victim of his first duel; his king finally arranges a happy ending that satisfies the claims of both Love and Honor. This action is played out to the accompaniment of incessant rodomontade. The characters never get off their high horse to make a natural remark or engage in ordinary conversation; in every passage they parade their sentiments about Honor, with a dreadful lack of reticence. Their self-consciousness is more oppressive because they declaim in a strangely impersonal manner. "Honor demands this victory o'er my love," one says—and any one of them might have said. They are forever talking *about* their emotions, instead of expressing them; they are mouthpieces for abstract qualities that all share, and that seem arbitrarily differentiated as "my" honor or "my" love. They are heroic personalities without any personality to speak of.

The storm raised by this brassy drama may make it look still sillier. At first enthusiastically acclaimed by both town and court, *The Cid* soon came under violent attack. Its critics were disturbed by its improbabilities but outraged by its improprieties. The French Academy, formally called in to settle the furious controversy, published their *Sentiments*, which were mostly as foolish as unfavorable. They found, for instance, that the high-flown sentiments of the heroine were not high enough: she should never have allowed her love of the hero to cloud her duty of avenging the death of her father. And that Corneille bowed to the will of the Academy, thereafter writing plays more classical and correct, hardly makes him nearer and dearer to us. I can think of no major writer, indeed, who appears to have less to say to us, and in a manner less suited to our taste. As we try to be catholic and humane, the fairest judgment on his work would seem to be that of Brunetière: "It is beautiful, admirable, sublime; it is neither human nor living nor real."

Yet we must reckon, as always, with the fact that Corneille's drama once did seem very human, living, and real, and that he is still ranked among the major writers in Western tradition. In his own time so good a critic as Dryden preferred him to Racine. Down to our time he has been praised by such diverse and sophisticated writers as Nietzsche and Sainte-Beuve, T. S. Eliot and Sartre. He has even been defended by a disciple of the new criticism, Martin Turnell. And these oddly assorted admirers may challenge our interest for a further reason. Almost all who write about Corneille stress his simplicity, whether grand or naïve. He is "the great and good" Corneille, an honorable old soldier; he represents what is undying, or what is dead, in the heroic tradition; he remains "firmly frozen in the ice of honor and duty." As critics thaw him out, however, they give contradictory accounts of him. It appears that the same old Corneille is an ambiguous figure, and perhaps as controversial a one as he was in his own age.

Most commonly he is pictured as a romantic individualist, an Elizabethan type who survived into the classical age. Lytton Strachey remarked his natural kinship with Christopher Marlowe, as another romantic and rhetorician whose poetry de-

mands to be read aloud; others have called him the French
Shakespeare. Corneille was accordingly a victim of his age,
which cramped his natural style. And there is unquestionably
some truth in this view of him. The exciting action and the
strut and éclat of *The Cid* were better suited to the Elizabethan theater, whose audience would not have been at all
troubled by its improbabilities. When forced to confine his
drama, Corneille continued to focus it on the heroic individual,
a type drawn from the Renaissance rather than the court of
Louis XIV. That he suffered from his confinement is revealed
by the many Prefaces and Discourses in which he wrestled
unhappily with the problem of the rules, now honoring the
sacred authority of Aristotle, now protesting against its tyranny. He was even so bold as to assert that the subject of a
"belle tragédie" ought not to be "probable." Often he declared
that the primary aim should be to please the people and the
court, not the savants, and his impulse was to please by éclat.

Those who sympathize with Corneille, however, tend to
overlook a further paradox. The rebel in him was also a reactionary. As his heroic ideal was a throwback to an earlier
age, so his apparent liberalism in art was a reversion to the
popular romance. The academic attacks on *The Cid* represented a vital concern for the future of French drama, which
Corneille might have given a reactionary turn by the power of
his genius. At least his liberalism was no aspiration to breadth,
variety, and fullness. He never displayed Shakespeare's vivid
interest in all forms and conditions of life. Only those who
lament the loss of a series of *Cid*'s can deplore the discipline
to which he was subjected. And from the outset Corneille had
a neo-classical aspect, in that the world of his thought was
severely limited and severely ordered. In this respect he was
at the opposite pole from Christopher Marlowe.

Thus his heroes include no Renaissance individualists of the
type of Tamburlaine or Dr. Faustus. Their ruling passion was
not the will to power that Nietzsche read into them, mistaking
them for his supermen. While the men in *The Cid* resemble

the Homeric heroes in their passion for personal honor and fame, they have taken on not only the chivalrous ideal of romantic love but a supra-personal ideal of duty that may require the sacrifice of their love or their life. The Infanta is already talking of the claims of Reason. Thereafter Corneille's tragedies are centered on the theme of a heroic Will, disciplined by Reason, contending against Passion. Essentially they embody the Stoic morality exemplified by the Roman character. It is generally agreed that Corneille's best plays are his Roman plays, *Horace, Cinna,* and *Polyeucte.* The reason why *The Cid* may still be regarded as the ancestor of most modern drama is that it introduced the drama of psychological action, focused on the conflict of will and feeling within and between the characters, the physical action taking place offstage.

The neo-classical rules were therefore not simply a nuisance for Corneille. They helped him to concentrate on his major interest, from which he might have been distracted had he been free to represent all the spectacular and exciting goings-on of Elizabethan drama.[4] But always the severest restriction on his drama was self-imposed. For Corneille a *"belle tragédie"* was the struggle of heroic wills, triumphing over passion, adhering to their resolution at any cost, and thereby exciting "admiration" instead of mere pity and terror. We can see at once that this was a narrow conception of tragedy, likely to become mechanical and monotonous. So let us try to see its dignity, its loftiness, its possible grandeur.

---

[4] It is no longer necessary to debate the famous unities of action, time, and place. They obviously make for concentration, forcing the dramatist to take his action at the moment of crisis, and preserving him from the clutter and sprawl of Elizabethan drama; hence modern dramatists, from Ibsen on, have often chosen to observe them. As obviously it is foolish to require the unities; dramatists would then be debarred from themes that require a ranging movement or development in time, as do *Hamlet, Macbeth,* and *King Lear.* The argument that the unities were necessary to preserve the illusion of reality rested on a complete misunderstanding of the conventions of the theater and the psychology of the audience. Since they were not an organic development, as in Greek drama, but an artificial requirement, dramatists had to waste considerable ingenuity to observe them, or get around them.

There is little question of Corneille's sincerity. Some find him cold, as even his contemporaries complained; others, like Croce, feel that his ideal of the "deliberative" will was the living passion of a poet otherwise devoid of passions; but almost all agree that he really meant what he wrote about honor, duty, the great soul. He was closer than Dryden to the heroic age, at his best able to make its emotion seem genuine. His drama was never so false as to call out such burlesque as Buckingham's *Rehearsal*, which fairly killed Restoration heroic drama. If his ideal seems naïve today, one reason is the pervasive indignity of bourgeois materialism, which makes talk of honor sound like sheer pretense. (We may recall the cheerful words of Jim Fisk—one of the more honest scoundrels who made good—when his Erie coup failed: "Nothing is lost save honor!") Even so, it still has some force—or so we must hope. Something like the spirit of Corneille animated the legendary American sergeant as he led his "sons of bitches" over the top.

That Corneille would never have stooped to such vulgarity is not wholly to his credit, but it suggests another difficulty in appreciating him that is not wholly to our own. For us his "grand style" is rhetoric. As Sainte-Beuve observed, it is a style to please "statesmen, geometricians, soldiers"—and one might now add, to appall devotees of metaphysical and modern poetry. It comes down to bald, ringing statement, with little power of suggestion except sound effects. Nevertheless the rhetoric of Corneille is not the bombast of the Elizabethans at their worst. It is energetic debate, vigorous assertion of will, grand assertion of faith—it is impassioned argument, not a direct expression of passion, but it is under control, not a mere verbal flow. And it ought not to be simply alien to the many of us who rose to the old-fashioned eloquence of Winston Churchill during the war. Given the vast confusion of our times, and the incessant blare of cheap, false simplicities in print, on screen, and over the air, we may understand why many poets and critics are painfully self-conscious, morbidly fearful of rhetoric or forthright statement; but we should deplore this as indeed a painful, morbid condition. The great writers of the past typically had no such fear of speaking out or singing out, were at no such pains to cover their tracks or hedge their sentiment. Like Corneille, they felt free to be as eloquent as they pleased about the platitudes.

This defense of Corneille, however, is itself too self-conscious, and finally more than a little futile. I do not believe that his drama can be made moving to a contemporary English-speaking audience.[5] Granted the genuineness of Corneille's heroic ideal, one may still weary of the incessant, strident declamation of it. The invariable dramatic attitudes or postures naturally tend to pseudo-drama, and give the passion the semblance of protocol. He himself complained of the "weakness" of Racine's characters, who are apt to give in to their love. His own characters always run true to form; so one may feel that their passions are straw men, set up to provide the necessary show of inner conflict before the final triumphant show of sovereign reason and heroic will. A typical example is Pauline, the heroine of *Polyeucte*, who loves her lover, her husband, and above all her duty as a Roman wife. "My reason, it is true, controls my feelings," she says; hence she can "avow without confusion" both her feelings and her virtues. She avows them tirelessly from beginning to end: "Pure I will remain," "Truth is my guide," "Let Duty still be queen!" Sainte-Beuve reproached the French for their failure to glory in their possession of Pauline, but I assume that they may feel toward her as her lover did when he cried: "One faintest flaw reveal, to give my soul relief!"

Even the admirers of Corneille generally admit that he is the most limited of the masters in the range of his thought and feeling. To me his baroque art is essentially mechanical, ex-

[5] I speak mournfully as a teacher who has tried to do his best for Corneille, but has yet to discover or awaken the least enthusiasm for his plays. And though Martin Turnell does much better by him in *The Classical Moment*, a sympathetic study of French classical drama, the most he could say for Corneille made a chapter of only 26 pages in a 250-page book.

ternal, and however sincere, neither deeply imagined nor deeply felt. It is a controlled but not a restrained art. Its lack of restraint is more oppressive because there is little tension beneath the metallic surface, little suggestion of strong emotion or wild impulse that had to be restrained. While his characters are full of sound and simulated fury, they are always under too perfect control. They have no life of their own. We can size them up completely at a glance, or from the instant they open their mouths; they never surprise us, as they never surprised their author. The actions they are engaged in are as synthetic. Plot Corneille conceived as "invention"; he described his additions to the legend of Polyeucte as "theatrical embellishments." And though his "grand style" is suited to his heroic drama, it seems painted on—as if he first wrote the play and then versified it, adding the embellishment of Diction to Character. The style remains essentially uniform, from character to character and play to play. Its monotony is not relieved by Martin Turnell's observation that the "regular thud" of the end rhymes helps to suggest a stable order; for this order is gone, it was not in fact stable, and there remains only the thud.

If this judgment of Corneille is temperamental or provincial, one may at least say flatly that his drama is not great *tragedy*. None of his admirers, to my knowledge, has argued that he had a tragic sense of life. He himself called his plays tragedies in good faith, taking for granted that he was writing a modern equivalent of Greek tragedy; but he was also conscious of having different purposes, proud of exciting "admiration" instead of the unmanly emotions of pity and fear. However desirable, admiration is scarcely a "tragic" emotion. Anyway there is nothing to fear in his world, except the show of unmanly emotions. If the characters are placed in ironical situations, the ironies are "theatrical embellishments" and involve no paradoxes or insoluble dilemmas. There is no moral complexity, no religious uncertainty. There is no shadow, no mystery, no sense of depths or darkness. Corneille is wholly uncritical of his simple faith, never brooding, yearning, doubting, challenging.

Polyeucte, which is generally considered his greatest play, is the best proof of how completely he lacked the tragic spirit of Pascal. Here he introduced an apparent complication in the struggle between reason and passion by centering it on the hero's newborn Christian faith, which looks like a passion. Polyeucte might recall Pascal when he exclaims: "Faith—*faith* —not reason, shall see light at last." But he remains the typical hero of Corneille, differing only in that he has found a new mode of *gloire.* Torn between love of his loyal Roman wife and duty to Christ, he resolves his dilemma by embracing martyrdom—a seeming renunciation that is not actually a tragic sacrifice. As the hero says (rather unheroically), "It saves me from the risks I might have run." Relieved of all risk, he goes to his death ecstatically, in the certainty that he is going straight to heaven. Neither is his pagan wife a tragic victim: his death immediately inspires her to give her great heart to Christ. Corneille then removes all trace of evil by having her father—the one character in the play who was as concerned about saving his skin as his honor—suddenly announce his conversion to Christianity. For modern readers, the sublime in Corneille is often clouded by a suggestion of the ridiculous; but at best it never embraces the tragic.

His own fate was more tragic. Although his plays held the stage to the end, in mid-career they fell off badly. His themes of high-mindedness and greatness of soul were not only ill-suited to the increasingly servile court of Louis XIV, but were bound to pall in time, given his simple formula. He could maintain interest in his unvarying type of hero only by inventing more extraordinary situations, with more striking embellishments. Hence he produced a series of melodramatic failures. Even as a pioneering dramatist Corneille had not offered fresh insights, created new values. Now he was too insensitive and inflexible to accommodate himself to changing times, or to feel a tragic tension—he could only grow morose. The best he could do was finally to give in and turn out the fashionable type of love play, even though he had declared that tragedy should involve "greater misfortune than the loss of a mistress." The most apparent reason for his surrender to fashion was not a change of heart but jealousy of the brilliant successes of his younger rival Racine; and his *gloire* was not enhanced when he tried to compete on Racine's own ground.

3. THE "TENDER" RACINE

"The difficulty we have with Racine," writes Francis Fergusson, "seems to be due to the fact that we do not want to accept as 'really' tragic the single moment of experience and the single angle of vision upon which the whole drama is based." Racine's theater is "the theater of reason," in which reason is the "sole value." He excites the passions, of course, but "only to enter the inimical realm of the mind." Although Fergusson has high praise for the clarity, precision, and formal and intellectual integrity of this drama, and grants that it can be extremely revealing, he finally emphasizes its extreme narrowness, especially by contrast with the much wider scene and the shifting perspectives of Shakespeare and Sophocles. Its rationalized plot or "intrigue," its purely ethical motivation, its perfectly balanced rhymed couplets, its alert, logical confidants who ask all the right questions—all contribute to a beautifully consistent image of human life, but one that may strike us as grotesquely inadequate for tragic life. For its rational principles no longer seem universally, eternally valid. They look baroque.

Martin Turnell presents a quite different Racine. His is no apostle of reason but "a reckless champion of the primacy of passion," who therefore shocked the followers of Corneille. He is the most subversive as well as seductive of the great classical writers; his true heirs were Stendhal and Baudelaire. And whereas Fergusson's Racine idealized a closed, stable society, Turnell's portrayed a disintegrating society blighted by despotism. "In making sexual passion the supreme value in a world of dissolving values, the last refuge of the man who has lost faith in all else, Racine anticipates the writers of a later age." Even *Athaliah*, the religious drama that concluded his career, is more compelling for its implied doubt than for its avowed faith.

Criticism of Racine has oscillated between these extremes. The soundest position, I should say, is as usual the unexciting one, somewhere in the middle. Fergusson makes his case too easy by basing it on *Berenice*—a play written on the model of Corneille, for a command performance, and the only play of Racine's in which honor and duty triumph over love. He makes only brief reference to the more famous *Phædra*, which might give him some trouble, and no mention at all of *Andromache* and *Athaliah*, which would give him still more.[6] Turnell's Racine, on the other hand, is naturally more sympathetic to students of tragedy, but looks too romantic for the author of *Berenice* and the man who began and ended as a Jansenist, or Calvinistic-Catholic. Love as portrayed in his dramas is hardly a supreme value, much less a refuge.

In other words, Racine is a complex figure. He is fundamentally different from Corneille, and much more ambiguous or equivocal. As a man, the "tender" Racine pictured by Taine and Sainte-Beuve has inspired recent critics to picture an implacable *méchant;* biographers adduce good evidence at once of his feminine sensitivity, his priggish insensitivity, his savagery and malice. As a playwright, he is in one aspect decorous and artificial, in another sometimes terrifying in his realism. His drama is not governed by so simple, invariable a formula as Corneille's, nor strictly by the ideal of simplicity that he was fond of proclaiming in his Prefaces, and realized in *Berenice*. He began by writing heroic drama in the grand manner of Corneille, later returning to it in *Mithridates*. His original genius emerged in *Andromache*, a tragedy of amour, but the

---

[6] In fairness to Professor Fergusson, it should be remembered that he was necessarily simplifying because he was concerned with representative types of drama, not trying to do complete justice to Racine.

intrigue of this play is not simple. (Orestes loves Hermione, who loves Pyrrhus, who loves Andromache, who loves the dead Hector.) *Phædra*, his masterpiece in this genre, is likewise more complicated than the *Hippolytus* of Euripides, on which it is based. Meanwhile he had written *Britannicus*, a study of imperial Nero and his imperious mother, and *Bajazet*, which with its Turkish setting has an Elizabethan flavor. He concluded his career with *Athaliah*, a drama so different in both form and content from these others that I shall discuss it separately at the end.

Essentially, Racine developed the psychological drama that Corneille had created, and that was better suited to his own genius. The action is internal, centered on the conflicting passions of the protagonists. But in Racine there is far more tragic tension, since passion is always likely to triumph over reason or duty. Santayana spoke of the moral censor in man, whose function is "to forbid the utterance, in the council chamber within us, of unparliamentary sentiments, and to suppress all reports not in the interest of our moral dignity." In the drama of Corneille this censor is always vigilant; in Racine he repeatedly falls down on his job. "I yield me blindly to passion," Orestes announces at the outset of *Andromache*. Hermione expresses still more freely the indignities of her jealous love, and of the hatred that springs from it. In a fury of hatred she commands the unhappy Orestes to murder Pyrrhus, who has rejected her love; when he obeys she turns on him as furiously for having killed the man she loved, and in her frenzy kills herself; and Orestes goes mad. Andromache, the other major character who is left alive, is left plotting bloody vengeance on the Greeks. Such is the "polite" tragedy, of the "tender" Racine.

Throughout *Andromache* the characters refer to Fate, or the "perverse" gods. Actually, all the "fatal turns" they lament are their own doing. Critics have therefore described the world of Racine as one deprived of "divine grace," and as a Jansenist he might have conceived it so. But he does not clearly suggest this Christian interpretation. Although his classical materials would naturally permit no reference to God, Devil, or Original Sin, there is little Christian feeling in this tragedy. Like the tragedies of Euripides, it displays the terrible destructive power of elemental passion. Racine is here no more a "champion" of love than was the author of *Medea* or *Hippolytus*.

Phædra is more ambiguous. On the surface, it is a still plainer demonstration of the evil of passion, in stricter Jansenist terms. The passion of Phædra is not a normal but a guilty love—for her stepson, Hippolytus; when spurned, she sends to a horrible death a wholly innocent man. In his Preface Racine emphasizes a stern moral intention:

> I do not venture to maintain that this play is the best of my tragedies. . . . What I can maintain is that I never wrote one in which virtue is more emphasized than in this one. The slightest errors are severely punished here. The mere thought of sin is regarded with as much horror as sin itself. The weaknesses of love pass for real weaknesses; the passions are presented to the eyes only in order to show all the havoc of which they are the cause; and vice is depicted everywhere in colors which cause its deformity to be recognized and hated. That is properly the goal that any man who labors for the public should set before himself.

Hence no one expresses the least pity for the dying Phædra at the end. The fatality of her passion is accounted for by the pitiless logic of Jansenism, which denied man free will and made salvation wholly dependent upon divine grace. In his Preface Racine also declares that Phædra's crime was a punishment by the gods rather than a movement of her own will.

Yet he protests too much in this Preface, which was written some months after the play had failed and he had renounced the theater. The merciless treatment of Phædra suggests that through her he was punishing his own guilty loves, which he was renouncing with the theater. (He had had one mistress who was an intimate of the notorious La Voisin, another whom he shared with half a dozen lovers.) By the same token, we might expect him to have a covert sympathy for her; and the text bears this out. He provides her with all the excuses that Euripides had given her. Phædra is no wanton, but a middle-aged woman who has long struggled desperately against her hopeless, humiliating passion, even to pretending hatred of Hippolytus; she reveals her passion only when she hears a false rumor of her husband's death; she is then concerned with her reputation for her children's sake as well as her own; and each fatal step is instigated by her nurse, who is one of the very few confidantes in Racine to be endowed with a personality. The one important addition he made to the Greek legend, the introduction of Aricia as the beloved of Hippolytus, is an added extenuation of Phædra's crime. Her discovery of this love is the crowning humiliation, as she realizes that the coldness he professed was a mere show. "Hippolytus can feel—but not for me!"

Most of all, Racine's sympathy is revealed by the magnificent study he makes of her passion. If he sincerely intended a moral lesson, as a repentant Jansenist about to return to the fold, he felt differently as an artist. He did not actually emphasize virtue in dramatic terms; his virtuous characters—in particular "Monsieur Hippolyte"—are all pallid and feebly drawn. The greatness of his play derives solely from the greatness of its heroine, in her terrible love, shame, grief, and remorse. Admittedly we may pity her more than Racine's audience did, or than he himself consciously did—just as we may pity the Phædra of Euripides more than the horrified Athenians did. Nevertheless her play would not be a great tragedy—and a favorite role of French tragediennes down to our own time—if she were merely an exhibit of the hateful deformity of vice. The drama of Racine is so plainly limited in scope that there is little danger of distorting it to suit our tastes. The danger is rather that because of our different tastes we may under-

rate his achievement, fail to appreciate even the obvious virtues of his method.

Thus Phædra is not, like Hamlet, a haunting character with
a life of her own, outside the play. Neither is she a complex
character who calls for subtle analysis; Racine's subtlety lies
in his rendering of the nuances of passions that are immediately and completely intelligible. Similarly his poetry does
not lend itself either to quotation out of context or to "explica-
tion" in the modern manner. It is a direct, bare statement of
the character's immediate thought and feeling, with little imagery and as little lyrical generalization about life or dusty
death. Close analysis may reveal some symbolism, as in the
unconscious sexual desire suggested in *Phædra* by the many
references to night, shadow, forests, the Labyrinth, etc. Otherwise the critic can talk only of rhythm, ease, grace, melody—
qualities that make Racine notoriously untranslatable. We may
therefore complain that his art is not deeply or richly suggestive. But first we should acknowledge the purity and clarity of
this art and the intensity gained by elimination of all irrele-
vance.

"There are some who think that this simplicity is a sign of
little invention," Racine wrote in his Preface to *Berenice*.
"They do not reflect that, on the contrary, all invention con-
sists in making something out of nothing, and that a great
multiplicity of incidents has always been the refuge of poets
whose genius lacked either sufficient abundance or sufficient
force to hold the attention of their audience throughout five
acts by a simple action, sustained by the violence of the passions, the beauty of the sentiments, and the fitness of the expression." If Racine usually sustained interest by some intrigue
as well, he in fact never depended upon multiple, violent, or
spectacular incident; he also proved his assertion that "it is
not necessary to have blood and corpses in a tragedy." And in
Berenice he gave a marvelous demonstration of how much he
could make out of the simplest material.

The whole action takes place in an antechamber, over a few

hours, and involves only three main actors. The basic situation and the characters remain unchanged: King Antiochus loves Queen Berenice, who loves the Emperor Titus, who loves her but cannot marry her because she is a foreign queen. The action is simply the interaction among them as they explore the situation, work their way through false hopes and ironic misunderstandings. After a series of pairings, the three finally come together in the last scene, to realize that they are alike doomed to renounce their love, and then to accept their fate. Though all are devoted to Corneille's ideals of honor and duty, they never parade them as noisily and flamboyantly as his heroes do; they have more real dignity, and maintain it in the face of real despair. They may induce the feeling of "majestic sadness" that Racine here declared was the pleasure proper to tragedy.

This is a quite decorous pleasure, however, in which the majesty is less pronounced than the sadness. Shakespeare also wrote a tragedy about imperial lovers and the conflict of love and duty; and the striking contrast of *Antony and Cleopatra* emphasizes the severe limitations as well as the perfection of Racine's art. In structure *Berenice* is clearly superior to Shakespeare's vast, sprawling drama, and should remind us that Racine's technique of concentration has proved more fruitful; modern drama is in this respect closer to him. Shakespeare's drama is as clearly much more ample, abundant, and rich in texture. And if preference between these incompatible modes of art is ultimately determined by cultural tradition, or by temperament, there is little question for one concerned primarily with the tragic effect. Racine's tragedy is a play for limited stakes, on a narrow stage, in a decorous style, with no reference to man's position in the universe, the problem of his fate. It is far from an "all-accepting, all-ordering" experience.

Whether the scene of Racine's plays is Greek, Roman, or Turkish, we are always in the circumscribed world of Versailles: a world of ladies and gentlemen whose passions may be violent but are confined to courtly interests, chiefly love, and are uniformly expressed in the same elegant language. It is always an indoor world, shut off from the community, the earth, the cosmos, the gods. The privacy of the drama is accentuated by the confidant, a polite stooge who is perhaps suited to love intrigues but otherwise is one of the unhappiest conventions ever introduced into drama, the more depressing because it took the place of the Greek Chorus. The utmost in generality is represented by Berenice, who at the end remarks (somewhat too complacently): "We'll be example to all time of the most tender and unhappy love that ever was in dolorous history." In other plays the endings typically confine the implications of the drama to the particular situation, and give no suggestion of endlessness or of renewal.

⎣The constriction of Racine's world is due not so much to the formal unities, or even the ideal of "the theater of reason," as to the neo-classical ideals of gentility and decorum. The taboo against reference to the "vulgar" objects of everyday life (such as the button that the dying Lear asks to have undone), and against the introduction of common people in tragedy, was hardly a requirement of "reason." It sprang from a classy rather than a classical taste, and made for elegance more than austerity.⎦It tends to obscure the power that Turnell admires in Racine, "of discovering a common humanity beneath the refinements of civilization, of speaking of passion as directly to the flower-seller as to the intellectual." His characters speak directly enough, in a mode that may indeed impress the flower-seller, but that may also detract from their common humanity. Even French critics complain of their scrupulous obedience to the rules of elocution, in which they have alike been perfectly instructed. "However agitated they may be," Mornet commented, "they always think more of the public than of themselves." However infuriated, terrified, bewildered, or appalled, they always have the sang-froid "to 'invent,' to find the best arguments, to distinguish and define them clearly; to 'dispose' them in the most convincing order; to 'express' them in the tone, the style that is appropriate." By polish and refinement Racine gave this formal style a remarkable appearance of simplicity and ease; but it is scarcely an appropriate style for the expression of tragic experience. The paucity of its imagery and the conventionality of its infrequent metaphors ("the fires of love within us," "this serpent cherished in your bosom") are another indication of how sharply confined his world was. His tragic poetry has no deep connections with the life of nature, the eternities, the primordial images, the prophetic soul dreaming on things to come.

All this is to say that the interest of Racine, as of most writers in his age, was confined to man in the social world. But it points to the limitations even of his humanism. For one thing, this specialist in passion studied few passions, chiefly love and jealousy. He was also more interested in woman than in man; his memorable characters are almost all women, and his best plays are all named after women (as Corneille's were named after men). Most important, he exhibits neither a deep compassion nor a deep reverence for the human spirit, in woman or man. His heroic dramas are conscientious but unimpassioned exercises in the mode of Corneille; *Berenice*, the best of them, still has the air of a tour de force. The tragic dramas in his own mode deal with damned souls whom he intimately understood, perhaps sympathized with, but never endowed with heroic splendor. The Jansenist in him could not forget that they were damned souls, could not permit them the dignity of Œdipus or Hamlet. He never created a great tragic hero to challenge the gods or the proprieties. However ambiguous his attitude, moreover, his vision of life was not complex or ironic. The ironies in his drama are on the surface, or in the intrigue. He had little of Pascal's sense of the whole paradox of man's being. The immediate paradox is that this ideal representative of "the theater of reason," for whom reason was supposedly "the sole value," manifested less respect for the power and dignity of the human mind than did Pascal, who was tormented by its inadequacy.

As I see him, in short, Racine was a sensitive, somber spirit, aware of original sin and damnation, perhaps tormented by his own guilt; but not a profoundly tragic spirit, brooding over the problem of evil or the mystery of the human condition. Neither was he a tragic victim of his age, as his early desertion of the theater has led some to picture him. One can hardly imagine him in any other age. He gives no evidence of a naturally exuberant genius that was stunted or deformed by the rigorous requirements of classicism. Unlike Corneille, he was not a champion of outmoded ideals; he was more at home at Versailles, as a favorite of Louis XIV. He was not a creator of new values either, a pioneer like Ibsen or a rebel like Eurip-ides. If critical of the reigning ideals, he did not openly ques-tion or attack them. At his most critical he reflected the under-lying tensions and the growing disillusionment. His somberness was a common mood in an age that was brilliant and vivacious on the surface, but not lusty or gay.

As for his quitting the theater, the endless controversy over his motives has made it seem more mysterious or theatrical than it actually was; but it is worth considering for the light it throws on Racine and his age. The fact is that when only thirty-eight years old, at the height of his powers, he suddenly gave up writing plays, to remain silent for twelve years. He took himself a pious bourgeois wife, who brought him a hand-some dowry, gave him seven children, and never saw or read one of his plays. He settled down to the life of a good prosper-ous bourgeois, complaining of his poverty while enjoying the service of a coachman and two lackeys. He worried chiefly over one son who showed some inclination to become a literary man and attend the theater. "Your little brother wants to be remembered to you," his wife wrote the boy, "and promises that he will not go to the theater like you, for fear he may be sent to hell."

The most apparent reason for Racine's retirement was the shock of the *Phædra* fiasco. He was always extremely sensitive to criticism, certainly "tender" in this respect; and as a rival of Corneille, and favorite of Louis XIV, he had plenty of enemies. Controversy in this "polite" classical age was not mannered; critics defended their principles by calling their opponents vipers, drunkards, atheists. And *Phædra* was the object of an especially vicious attack. The story goes that when the news got out that Racine was writing it, a cabal of his enemies, led by a prominent duchess, hired a hack to produce another play on the same subject, bought up most of the seats in both theaters, and hired a claque to applaud his rival and hiss Racine. Although the story is probably exaggerated, it is certain that a cabal did go to work to bring about the failure of his play, and that they succeeded.

Another apparent factor was his Jansenist conscience. Racine quit the stage to return to his old teachers at Port-Royal, in avowed contrition. (As the Jansenist theologian Nicole wrote, "A poet is a public poisoner, and a writer for the stage should be considered guilty of the murder of innumerable souls.") How deep his remorse and his piety went is debatable. François Mauriac pictured his renunciation of the stage as a deliberate sacrifice, the greatest he could make to his God. Racine's contemporaries failed to recognize this sacrifice; most expressed doubts of the genuineness of his conversion. "He now loves God as he used to love his mistresses," commented Mme de Sévigné. At least his reborn piety was neither austere nor warm. He remained a courtier, with a fine apartment at Versailles; his letters reveal more concern with the management of his financial affairs than with the salvation of his immortal soul; and they are not notable for a spirit of love and charity (a comment one might also make on the public utterances of some prominent converts in recent times). When one of his former mistresses was dying, he commented only on "the obstinacy with which this unhappy woman refuses to renounce the stage."

This casualness brings up the most significant thing about the whole affair—that Racine's contemporaries were as casual about the loss of their greatest dramatist and poet. Nobody remarked the pity of it. The Age of Louis XIV evidently did not have the passion for literature that literary men are now apt to think, in their distress over the vulgar modern world. Like almost all aristocratic societies, the court of Versailles was much more concerned about courtly affairs, the favors of its Sun King. Contemporary gazettes refer as often to Racine the courtier as to Racine the dramatist. And Racine himself expressed no deep unhappiness over the disuse of a talent that was death to hide. His later letters give no indication whatever of an absorbing interest in literature, a feeling of aching void.

Another reason for his retirement may have been the feeling that he had exhausted the possibilities of his limited theme. He did not grow enough, after finding himself in *Andromache*, to suggest that he left great possibilities unfulfilled, deprived posterity of a series of masterpieces. It may be, indeed, that posterity gained by his retirement. For Mme de Maintenon, the pious new love of Louis XIV, finally requested Racine to write "some kind of moral or historical poem from which love should be entirely banished," suitable for performance by the young girls in her school of Saint-Cyr. Racine responded with his Biblical play *Esther*. Its triumphant success then inspired him to write *Athaliah*, a masterpiece in a mode essentially different from his earlier dramas.

The most lyrical of his plays, this is also the most obviously dramatic, and has the most amplitude and magnitude. Racine treats his Biblical subject in a manner reminiscent of both the Greeks and the Elizabethans. He makes natural and effective use of a Chorus of maidens, who are participants in the action. He also provides a stirring spectacle, at last dispensing with the confidant, individualizing a relatively large cast of characters, and in the climactic scenes bringing in a host of supernumeraries; his stage is as crowded as an Elizabethan stage. *Athaliah* is a grand synthesis of classical form and Christian content, grand enough to suggest a modern Æschylus. It even has some haunting suggestion of unsuspected depths.

On the surface, the play is a triumphant vindication of the Hebrew-Christian faith, based on the brief story in II Kings

viii–xi. The heathen Queen Athaliah, who has murdered the
royal children of the house of David and is now threatening
the Temple with destruction, is defied by the High Priest,
Joad, who has secretly brought up her young grandson Joas,
rescued from the attempted murder. Fierce and steadfast in
his faith in God, Joad brings about her death by revealing the
identity of Joas and having him crowned king. God, according to Sainte-Beuve and others, is the chief character in the
play. King Louis, however, might not have been simply edified by it. The play contains a number of pointed references
to despotic monarchs who put their own will above law, and
doom their subjects to toil and tears; the High Priest warns
young Joas against the dangers of uncurbed power and flattery.
In his Preface Racine reminded his audience that the triumph
of the Biblical Joas was not a pure blessing, for after some
years of good behavior he killed the High Priest in a fit of
temper. Readers might then recall that both the Temple and
the House of David were destined to be destroyed; God was
not going to save his chosen people. For such reasons Martin
Turnell feels that the power of *Athaliah* owes more to the underlying doubt than to the stated faith.

At least there is enough suggestion of complexity and mystery to give this religious drama a tragic quality. The God
whose presence is felt throughout the drama is a fierce, jealous
God, who was beginning to get out of date in Racine's time.
The Chorus and the loyal general Abner are deeply troubled
by his seeming indifference to his chosen people, and question
his justice. "Where, God of Jacob, is Thy goodness fled?" asks
the Chorus. Nor is the triumphant outcome clearly his handiwork. It is due to the craftiness as well as the heroism of the
High Priest, who tricks Athaliah into coming to the Temple,
to meet her death. And Athaliah herself is the most memorable
creation in the drama. Racine endows her not only with
majesty but with feelings of compassion and remorse that are
not suggested in the Biblical story. Strangely drawn to young
Joas, she rejects the advice of her own priest, who would have

the mysterious child killed; hence it is a good impulse that leads to her ruin. She is most majestic as she goes clear-eyed to her death, defying the "relentless god" who has triumphed over her. More than any other character in Racine, she has the force and dignity of the tragic hero.

Yet *Athaliah* is essentially great religious drama, not great tragedy. Its clearest import remains its purport, as a work of orthodox piety. However repellent the jealous God of vengeance may be to modern readers, he was the God of the Jansenists; they did not require of him justice or mercy by human standards. If we see reasons for doubt of Racine's God, the doubts expressed in the play are as completely resolved as in *Samson Agonistes*. Every choral ode ends in exaltation. The action ends in pure triumph, with no tragic or ironic undertones. The text of the conclusion gives no hint that Joas went the way of most other kings of Judah; readers unacquainted with Biblical history would hardly guess this aftermath. Racine himself may have felt some doubt, or even deliberately intended to imply it; but a truly tragic poet would have dealt with one of the many high priests and prophets of Israel whose faith was not rewarded with triumph on earth.

Hence *Athaliah* is an appropriate swan song for the *grand siècle,* which represented the end rather than the beginning of an epoch. As appropriate for the dying age was the ironic aftermath. The play was given only three performances. Thereupon Racine quit drama for good, though he was only in his early fifties and had eight more years of life. They were unhappy years because he fell into disfavor with Louis, who practically expelled him from Versailles. He worried himself sick; he had no real need of the prayers of his pious aunt, who daily begged God to humiliate him for the good of his immortal soul. His unhappiness emphasizes his mortal dependence on Versailles. He had early won a pension as a reward for an ode celebrating the recovery of King Louis from the measles; after his religious conversion he still dedicated his work to Louis, whom he pictured as a sort of Galahad in a

fawning inscription for *Esther*. It is a reminder that *Esther*
gave Mme de Sévigné one of the proudest moments of her
life, because Louis spoke a few words to her at the performance she was privileged to attend; while she dismissed Racine's
popularity as "a craze which would pass, like that for coffee."
We may therefore take pleasure in the thought that Louis XIV
has won more lasting fame as the patron of Racine than as the
military conqueror and defender of the true faith that he
fancied himself; and we may wish to think of Racine as primarily a somber critic of his society. Nevertheless he identified
himself with this society, he shared its limited aspirations, and
until the end he was at home in it.

4. THE AGE OF THE ENLIGHTENMENT

Although scholarly piety has preserved the work of the contemporaries and immediate successors of Racine in the theater,
it is a dreary memento. At best these playwrights were all
mediocre, inferior to the lesser Elizabethans. They serve to
emphasize again how rarely genius has appeared in tragedy,
and how inadequate are the studies of historical critics who
interpret the work of genius as merely the product or the reflection of the age. But they also emphasize the essential limitations of neo-classical tragedy, the reasons why the thousand
tragedies produced by this tradition in France would naturally tend to be mediocre.

They are typically genteel. Pradon (the author of the rival
Phædra) reproached the Greeks for the ferocity of their heroes,
and announced his preference for "an agreeable probability
to a shocking truth." Saint-Evremond was complacent about
the superior morality of modern tragedy, which took pains to
reward virtue; he admired "the agreeable sentiments of love
and admiration that are discreetly interwoven with a rectified
fear and pity," and that aroused a "tender admiration." The
theme of love in particular became the rage, in this supposedly
classical, rational theater. It was strictly a rage, for it was not
treated with real seriousness; the interest was primarily senti-

mental, not psychological.[7] Plot remained intrigue, with considerable complexity but no copiousness or variety; in time it would produce the "well-made" play. And the fashionable audiences that prided themselves on their tastes were often as enthusiastic about these synthetic plays as they were about the masterpieces of Racine. They also applauded the unclassical kinds of drama that were popular in the Age of Louis XIV, including pastoral, tragi-comedy, opera, heroic comedy, and *"tragédie à machines."* The best thing to be said about their uncertain taste is that it gave sufficient freedom to Molière, who remains the most vital playwright of the age, and the least classical and genteel.

It is therefore inaccurate to speak of a "decline" in French tragedy after Racine. Tragedy remained on the level that only Corneille and Racine had risen above. The early retirement of Racine, however, was symbolic of the decline of the Age of Louis XIV. The Sun King reigned too long. There was little radiance in the last half of his reign, during which he was engaged in almost constant warfare, with little success, at the cost of increasing misery for the bulk of his subjects. Fénelon summed up his achievement in a bitter letter: "You are praised to the skies for having impoverished France, and you have built your throne on the ruin of all classes in the State." The uses of life at Versailles grew weary, stale, flat, and unprofitable. In his later memoirs Saint-Simon dwelt on the "state of decadence, confusion, and chaos which has grown steadily worse until the most complete and universal ignorance has extended its empire everywhere." Louis made it worse by his growing concern for religious orthodoxy, which led him to revoke the edict of toleration of Protestants. His piety was chiefly superstition; its quality was defined by Mme de Main-

[7] Among the ludicrous aspects of French drama is that the great Homeric heroes—especially Achilles—all blossom out as great lovers. A typical performance was a play about Agamemnon in which he and his son, Orestes, are both in love with Cassandra. Racine himself, in his early *Alexander the Great*, represented Alexander as more concerned about winning the love of his mistress than conquering the world.

tenon, his devout wife, who told a cardinal that he would
never miss a sermon or a fast day, but was never able to understand what was meant by repentance or humility. At Versailles it made for still less spirit and spirituality. The outcome
was the cynical indifference under the Regent Orléans, who
succeeded him.

The growing disillusionment conceivably might have inspired a more tragic drama had not the despotism of Louis discouraged individualism and high seriousness. La Bruyère, one
of the few major writers to emerge in the last half of Louis's
reign, was still more somber than Racine; but his pessimism
remained a form of disillusionment. And at the outset of his
first work he remarked: *"Tout est dit."* All was said, that is,
within the limits prescribed by the classical tradition. "Every
great tradition has its own way of dying," wrote Lytton
Strachey, in sympathy; "and the classical tradition died of
timidity. It grew afraid of the flesh and blood of life; it was
too polite to face realities, too elevated to tread the common
ground of fact and detail; it would touch nothing but generali-
ties, for they alone are safe, harmless, and respectable; and, if
they are also empty, how can that be helped?"

This report of its death is somewhat exaggerated. The classical tradition did not die with the Age of Louis XIV: it continued to dominate French poetry and drama throughout the
eighteenth century. Although the battle between the Ancients
and the Moderns ended in a nominal victory for the Moderns,
literature was not emancipated. Boileau took over the authority of Aristotle, who had been misinterpreted anyway;
Corneille and Racine became the models instead of the Greek
tragic poets, who had never been understood. Tragedy wa-
vered between the heroic and the sentimental mode but remained regular, except for some timid innovations that failed
to revitalize it. Voltaire, the one considerable tragedian of the
century, conceived an ideal union of English genius and
French taste, but he lacked the English genius, or any real
genius for the theater. While he concentrated on Oriental

rather than classical subjects, and worked in some subversive ideas about religious bigotry, he wrote chiefly heroic tragedy, watered by some love interest. Today his plays are much less highly esteemed than they were by his contemporaries. Hence it is a somewhat doubtful tribute to Corneille and Racine that the tradition they molded reigned for almost two centuries, without producing any notable drama.

The rest of Europe also paid tribute to French classicism, which was a salutary influence on inchoate or disorganized literatures, but in time a yoke that had to be thrown off. Alfieri most nearly succeeded in bringing classical drama to life by infusing it with his ardor for liberty—a political enthusiasm that was impossible in the Age of Louis XIV. In England, French influence was offset by patriotic admiration of Shakespeare, who held the stage in mutilated versions such as Nahum Tate's; his influence was sufficient to confuse the intentions of some playwrights, but not to inspire a revolt against classicism. Nicholas Rowe and others followed Racine by writing sentimental tragedies about women. For the rest, there were such frigid academic exercises in tragedy as Addison's *Cato* and Johnson's *Irene*. The only memorable achievement of the century was in comedy.

Meanwhile a development that was to prove historically momentous was the rise of the bourgeoisie—the class to which Corneille, Racine, and Molière all belonged, but which only Molière represented in his drama. The citizenry was now flocking to the theater, which flourished and expanded. It was not an invigorating influence, however, at least on tragedy. The prosperous bourgeois liked to be edified and moved to tears, but they were not yet ready for anything so austere as tragedy. The chief token of their rise in the world was the emergence of bourgeois tragedy, represented by Diderot's *The Natural Son* in France, Lillo's *The London Merchant* in England, and Lessing's *Miss Sarah Sampson* in Germany. In their day these plays seemed revolutionary in their realism, and stirred tremendous excitement. Today they seem ludicrously sentimental

and unreal. A sample of their high-flown style is the answer
given by Lillo's hero when a temptress asks him what he
thinks of love:

> If you mean the love of women, I have not thought of
> it at all. My youth and circumstances make such thoughts
> improper in me yet. But if you mean the general love we
> owe to mankind, I think no one has more of it in his
> temper than myself. . . . In an especial manner I love my
> Uncle. . . .

Lovers of literature may again be distressed, and critics hum-
bled, by the historical record, that so preposterous a play as
The London Merchant was among the most widely admired
in a century which made a fetish of good sense and good taste,
and that so great a writer as Lessing wrote a play almost as
bad.

This leads us to another anomaly, as depressing to those who
like to think that poets are especially sensitive to the deep
trends of their time, and are therefore naturally in the van-
guard of culture. The highly formal, classical eighteenth century was in another aspect the revolutionary Age of the Enlightenment. The champions of the Enlightenment—including
Voltaire and Diderot as thinkers rather than as poets—carried
on the rationalistic and humanistic tradition of the Age of
Louis XIV, but to radically different conclusions. They were
more consistently and ardently devoted to Reason, and in its
light became critical of ancient institutions and authorities.
They proclaimed the ideal of freedom of thought. In religion
and government they rebelled against the authoritarianism
that still held sway in literature. They looked forward rather
than backward; they bred the faith in progress that became
basic in the liberal, democratic faith. Their work culminated
in the French Revolution—an event that a reader of the poetry
and drama of the century would seldom be led to expect. The
Enlightenment had far more influence than classicism did on
later history, and on later literature as well.

But its optimistic faith was no more conducive to the writing of tragedy. Reason was to dispel all mystery, as Newton had already unlocked the secrets of Nature. Reason had also exposed the main sources of evil, the tyranny of priests and kings. The champions of the Enlightenment made brilliant use of irony in their satire, but they had little of Pascal's sense of the inescapable paradoxes of man's nature, the inescapable ironies of his fate. They were brilliantly effective in their attack on specific evils, but had little sense of the ancient, irremediable evil. In literature their spirit is exemplified by Schiller, who declared that the purpose of tragedy is to arouse pity or sympathy; he made no mention of fear. For the men of the Enlightenment there was little to fear except the powers of ignorance, superstition, and prejudice. Their limitations may be summed up in the statement that they lacked a tragic sense of life.

1. THE PECULIAR ISSUES

Among the incidental oddities of our queer times is a question often discussed: is it possible for modern man to write tragedy? The common answer has been No; and literary men have then found still another reason for despairing of modern culture. Their worry may seem a little ludicrous in an atomic age. Most societies in the past managed to get along without writing tragedy, and never asked such a question. Yet it is a significant question, which finally involves the basic issues of our civilization. It must be considered, at any rate, in a chapter entitled "Modern Tragedy."

The gloomiest statement of the case is Joseph Wood Krutch's well-known essay "The Tragic Fallacy." Krutch argued that modern knowledge has killed the tragic faith, and all possibility of recovering it. Man can no longer believe that his fate makes the least difference to a universe he conceives as soulless. Worse, he can no longer believe in his own nobility; he knows that he is a creature of reflexes and complexes, determined by heredity and environment. The glory both of God and of Man has departed this world. Although Krutch later modified his rather melodramatic statement of our plight, his thesis is substantially borne out by the many poets and critics who stress only the vulgarity and barbarity of modern civilization, and can see no tragic dignity in the calamities that are signaling its collapse; if it now appears that we may end with a bang, we remain hollow men who can only whimper. Even John Dewey, the incorrigible optimist, provided a text for literary despair. The best we can do, he once remarked, is to venerate what we do not really believe, and to criticize what we really live by.

This side of despair, the possibilities of high tragedy are

most obviously limited by the characteristic realism of modern literature. As writers faithfully portray the life of their time, the scene dwindles into a parlor, the protagonist into a petty bourgeois. Some may focus on the ordinary, commonplace individual, the Bovary or Babbitt; others on the abnormal individual, the neurotic who we have come to realize is not so abnormal after all, but a brother in the unconscious. In either case the hero is naturally unheroic. If he stirs pity, he stirs little fear—except as we feel our own littleness and helplessness. He may then illustrate a deeper irony: with increased freedom, political and intellectual, modern man has come to realize that he is not so free, but a slave to custom, to economic necessity, to class consciousness, to unconscious desire, to irrational passion—to impersonal forces that cannot inspire the awe that the will of the gods once did. Hence the hero may suffer further in becoming primarily a guinea pig, an exhibit for sociological or psychological analysis. (In the fables of Kafka he is not even granted a name.) As the terms of our problems keep shifting, his tragedy becomes outdated. And it is naturally told in prose, the language of everyday life. It is deprived of the intensity and extensity, magnitude and lift, which poetry can give.

A still more common complaint, especially in America, is the commercial theater. How could a tradition of high tragedy ever take root on Broadway? The show business is precisely that: a business whose commodity is a good show. Granted that Shakespeare too was in the business, his Globe was essentially different from the theaters of Broadway. It was a national theater serving the general public, not a slick industry catering to the few. Hence the Little Theaters that have sprung up all over the land, in town and on campus, have also failed to create a living theater. Mostly they produce old Broadway hits; now and then they produce arty little plays, for arty little audiences. At best, serious drama attracts a small but heterogeneous audience that is not representative of the community, and may be self-consciously aloof from the community. Critics point out that it lacks a common faith, a common moral attitude, a common tradition in art or anything else. It has no deep sense of myth or ritual.

For such reasons Francis Fergusson sees no hope of restoring the comprehensive "idea of a theater" realized by Sophocles and Shakespeare. In his sensitive, sympathetic studies of the greater modern dramatists he demonstrates how all fall short of this idea, presenting diverse but always limited, partial, fragmentary perspectives. "And when the idea of a theater is inadequate or lacking," he concludes, "we are reduced to speculating about the plight of the whole culture."

As we speculate, we are immediately oppressed by the uniformity of a mass culture, and in particular its standardized, synthetic entertainment: manufactured by cynical professionals, disseminated by mass media, having none of the spontaneity and genuineness of folk art, but only endless variations on a few monotonous themes, such as boy makes good, boy wins girl. Lacking a folk tradition, the masses have no use for a tragic hero. They demand a successful hero, at their most exalted a Führer; their scapegoats are villains—the Reds, the Jews, the eggheads. In another aspect, we are oppressed by the multiplicity and heterogeneity of our civilization, the immense complexity and confusion. Underlying the uniformity is a profound disorder, disharmony, disunity. In the arts the great traditions have given way to a welter of changing fashions that at best represent a self-conscious experimentation, at worst a feverish strain for originality. And the most promising innovations are not likely to be promising for tragedy, which is naturally concerned with the permanent, elemental, and universal in experience.

Now I believe that modern writers nevertheless can write, and have written, drama worthy of being dignified by this name. It is my thesis that the realism which is the obvious source of the limitations of modern tragedy is also the chief source of its strength; or in other words, that this tragedy is at its best when it is most distinctively modern. For it is bound to be different from ancient tragedy, and in some respects is bound to suffer from the inevitable comparison with it. The responsible modern writer cannot escape the radical and continuous change that the political, industrial, and scientific revolutions have brought about. He cannot blink the new knowledge about the nature and history of man and the universe, cannot evade the terms of life in a mass society. He cannot write like Sophocles or Shakespeare. Nor is there any hope of realizing Fergusson's ideal theater. The magnificent theater of Athens was possible only because of the littleness of Athens, the intimacy of its civic life; and Shakespeare's England was still relatively cozy. Broadway can never be the focus of the national life.

Yet it is possible to take such news calmly. The inevitable comparisons should also remind us how few writers have written great tragedy, and how brief were the periods of its greatness. History does not indicate that the state of drama, or the idea of a theater, is a good index to the state of culture as a whole. It does indicate the need of qualifying somewhat the laments over the plight of the modern dramatist, with his restricted audience. For Athens was a rare exception in cultural history. In almost all other societies serious drama, like poetry, was addressed to the few; the rise of an elite is the norm in the history of literature. The *Divine Comedy*—Fergusson's *ne plus ultra*—was itself written for a very small audience.

We should also suspect possible sentimental exaggeration in the ideal picture of the Greek or Elizabethan theater, with a homogeneous audience united in a semi-religious experience. Although we cannot know just what the Athenian or Elizabethan man on the street thought and felt—we scarcely hear his voice—these were both ages of ferment, of lusty individualism, of underlying doubt and disillusionment, of conflict and change. An audience that gave prizes to both Sophocles and Euripides, or that applauded both *Tamburlaine* and *Hamlet*, evidently comprised considerable diversity of interest and belief; the common faith to which the dramatists appealed was more patriotic than ethical or religious. And some such faith underlies the heterogeneity of the modern audience. This audience is, after all, a group with some common interests, not an anarchic crowd. Its group spirit, as Henri Gouhier points out, is based on a common acceptance of the drama, not a common interpretation of it. Those who cherish a free society—and most of us still share this faith—should not be dismayed by diversity of belief. Those who conceive the ideal audience as a community of fellow believers, stirred by a uniform emotion, at a ritualistic performance, on a ceremonial occasion, might contemplate the crowds whom Hitler harangued. Or they might attend a revivalist meeting.

The plight of our whole culture, real as it is, is likewise oversimplified. As everybody says, we live in a revolutionary world; and it is therefore full of contradictions, still more complex than it appears. There is no mistaking, for example, the notorious pessimism that Krutch saw as the essence of the modern temper. Yet the decline of faith in the supernatural may tend to make man more self-important than he was as a fallen creature of original sin; those who display least faith in him are typically the traditionalists. Modern man has been given to as notorious a complacence about his progress. Religionists declare that the root evil of our time is man's sinful faith that he can get along without God's help. Particularly in America, optimism has smothered the tragic spirit more than has Krutch's kind of pessimism. Modern writers in general have been less given to despair of the human condition than to indignation over remediable social evils.

And so with science, the ultimate source of both the pessimism and the optimism. In its triumphant advance, it introduced grave complications into the drama of civilization long before it created the problem of how to live with hydrogen bombs. Unquestionably it has undermined the traditional faith that man is the main object of the whole creation, and has therefore led to gloomy views of the meaninglessness of his life, on an insignificant planet in which life itself may be "a

disease that afflicts matter in its old age," and is in any case
doomed to ultimate extinction. In dealing with man himself,
scientists have encouraged further indignities by their fear of
the horrid word "value," and their tendency to reduce complex organic phenomena to quantitative, material terms, in an
effort to improve their dubious scientific status.[1] As a result,
men have confused the physical basis of behavior with its essence, and so landed in the kind of "realism" reflected in
Krutch's essay. Love, we hear, is "nothing but" sublimated sex,
or a biological urge to reproduce the species. And in this century the role of science has become still more paradoxical. A
power that men of the Enlightenment believed would banish
all mystery, it has now made the universe more mysterious than
ever before in the history of thought—not only queerer than we
suppose, as one scientist wrote, but "queerer than we *can*
suppose."

Yet the new concepts represent a marvelous adventure in
thought. While the critics of science picture it as another form
of vulgar materialism, it remains a great imaginative enterprise that in its further reaches, as in the speculations of an
Einstein, is a more spiritual activity than what commonly
passes for spirituality today. It can inspire a much deeper sense
of wonder and awe than we get from most modern literature.
As the old story goes, the scientist said: "Astronomically speaking, man is negligible"; the poet replied: "Astronomically
speaking, man is the astronomer." But in fact the men of science have often had to tell this to the poets. The greater
scientists and philosophers of science have almost uniformly
reasserted the dignity of man, on the basis of the new knowledge. Perhaps the darkest view of man's nature, that of Freud,
is still a genuinely tragic view; for if man has to struggle constantly against the dark powers of the unconscious, by the

[1] The early behaviorists, for example, demonstrated the purity of
their science by basing it on the mechanistic concepts that physicists had
already found inadequate for the physical world. Because states of consciousness cannot be measured or objectively observed, they leaped to
an elementary fallacy, denying that they existed.

same token he is not at their mercy and may maintain his dignity.

By such considerations I do not mean to minimize the very difficult problems that the responsible modern artist has to contend with, often in the face of the massive indifference of his countrymen. I am merely suggesting that the problems are also challenges, which need to be seen in perspective and from more than one point of view. Neither supported nor restricted by a common convention, writers have responded to the challenge in such diverse ways that one cannot generalize so freely about modern literature as one may about Greek, Elizabethan, or classical French, and should not approach it with set presuppositions and expectations. As for modern tragedy, critics still argue that it is not "really" tragic by some canon derived from the practice—or more often the theory—of the ancients. The fair question is whether, in the new terms imposed by modern knowledge and conditions of life, it still affirms equivalent values and affords an equivalent pleasure.

In a previous work, *Modern Fiction,* I applied this test to a number of major novelists. The tragic spirit has turned to the novel for expression, since it is a form better suited than drama to a complex age, permitting both more amplitude and more inwardness. Only two or three dramatists compare in stature with the two or three dozen greater novelists over the last hundred years. But for the sake of consistency, or convenience, I shall here focus on modern drama. For the playwright the basic problems are complicated by the further need of a theater and an audience; he is not so free to write as he pleases. At the same time, he has a possible advantage in the very limitations of his form. He cannot indulge in the streams of consciousness or the involved analyses that may illumine character but blur the drama, obscure the elemental issues; he is forced to strip and come directly to grips with his theme. I propose, at any rate, to examine a number of diverse playwrights, not necessarily the best of our time, but representative of the major tendencies in modern tragedy, for better or worse.

2. ROMANTIC TRAGEDY: WAGNER

With the Romantic Movement that swept Europe at the beginning of the nineteenth century, one might have expected
the rebirth of a vital tragic drama. In fact almost all the
greater poets of the period tried to write such drama, and in
the manner of Shakespeare. Everywhere writers came under
the spell of Shakespeare: Schiller in Germany, Pushkin in
Russia, Hugo in France, even Polish and Hungarian poets.
The Romantics also had a deeper appreciation of Greek drama
than had the neo-classical writers, and with it of Gothic art,
Teutonic saga, and folk poetry. Goethe coined the term "world
literature." And it was a period of *Sturm und Drang*. The
French Revolution inflamed poets with high hopes, which were
disappointed by its tragic aftermath. With this and the American Revolution, the Napoleonic wars, the disintegration of the
feudal order, and the beginnings of the Industrial Revolution,
the modern world was born, amid sufficient tension.

But no great drama came out of this stirring historical
drama. Although there were many plays of some poetic distinction and a few of some dramatic merit, none could be
called great tragedy. The romantic tragedies that were successful on the stage, such as the plays of Victor Hugo, were
generally romantic in the popular, superficial sense; and this
flamboyant drama soon descended into pure melodrama. It survives chiefly in Italian operatic form.

The failure of romantic tragedy is no puzzle, however. One
obvious reason for it was that the poets were mostly incom-
petent or undisciplined playwrights. They were also overawed
by Shakespeare, inclined to imitate him instead of creating a
new form and style appropriate to their different age. In England all their faults were confirmed because they were cut off
from the popular theater, which had already sunk to melodrama and farce—a level considerably lower than that of
Broadway today. In Germany the poets were stimulated by the
rise of a new national theater, as well as the flowering of the

German genius in music and philosophy, but they therefore make plain a deeper reason why the Romantics failed to create a great tragic drama. Again I should say simply that they lacked the tragic sense of life. While rebelling against the classicism of the eighteenth century, they generally adhered to the optimism of the Enlightenment. At their most serious and original they wrote a drama of dream, aspiration, triumphant idealism, typified by Schiller's *William Tell*. The greatest work produced by the Romantic Movement, Goethe's *Faust*, remains the testament of a basically optimistic philosophy. Less divine than the *Divine Comedy*, this presents an otherwise more comprehensive image of human experience, with a profounder irony and a more searching realism; but it is little more tragic. Faust too ends in heaven.

For my purposes, romantic tragedy is interesting chiefly for the perspective it gives on modern tragedy, which with Ibsen began as a revolt against it. But immediately it leads to the monumental effort of a post-Romantic, Richard Wagner, to restore high tragedy on a different basis. He sought to create a really "grand" opera that would be the modern equivalent of Greek tragedy. He conceived the ideal of the "united artwork," a union of music and poetry, or specifically of Beethoven and Shakespeare. Let us forget for the moment his monstrous egoism, his bombast and extravagance, his ugly anti-Semitism, his later chauvinism. Let us put aside, too, Fergusson's plausible thesis that his theater is the theater of pure passion, in contrast with Racine's theater of pure reason; for if this applies to *Tristan and Isolde*, whose love music suggests a prolonged orgasm, it does not clearly apply to the much more ambitious and comprehensive *Ring of the Nibelungs*. Both the ideal theory and the actual achievement of Wagner raise fundamental, far-reaching issues.

As a young man, influenced by the revolution of 1848, Wagner developed his lifelong thesis that art should express the spirit of a free community, as Greek tragedy had done. He also set himself against the dominant tendencies of his age—

in particular the bourgeois money spirit. Hence he concluded that—unlike Greek art, which was a product of the community—modern art must be revolutionary, in opposition to a community whose religion was the pursuit of wealth. Traditional opera he scorned as a mere amusement or distraction for the decadent bourgeoisie. But beneath the money spirit still lived the spirit of the Folk, and by stirring this, Wagner dreamed of purifying his society. He accordingly went back to myth for his subject matter; the myth shows "what is eternally human and eternally comprehensible in life." Specifically, he revived the old Germanic myths, which Goethe once described as "gloomy old epics," too barbarous to have any vital meaning for modern Germans. All in all, his opera was to be a ritual, communal drama, national but also supra-national, expressing "the spirit of a free humanity soaring above all barriers of race." At Bayreuth he sought to create a modern Athens.

In this high enterprise Wagner was aided by the ardent young Nietzsche, whose first major work, *The Birth of Tragedy*, was in part designed as a manifesto for him. This "haughty and fantastic book," as Nietzsche later called it, has been largely outmoded by the historical research it helped to inspire; like most thinkers before him, he read his own philosophy into Greek tragedy and so found Dionysian passion everywhere—even in the Chorus. Nevertheless he was the first to ask the significant question about Greek tragedy: what is Dionysian? He rejected the conventional religious and moralistic interpretations that had dominated criticism to his time; as he later wrote, "What matters is not eternal life but eternal vivacity." He recognized the ritual basis of Greek tragedy, and its connections with the mysteries. He anticipated a great deal more in modern criticism, as in his attacks on "scientism" and his stress on the value of myth, the plight of the modern man in having no mythical home. He encouraged Wagner especially by his prophecy that through music, myth and tragedy would be reborn. Like Schopenhauer, he regarded music as "in the highest degree a universal language," which did not merely imitate phenomena but directly represented the essential reality underlying them; or one might now say, the "archetypal patterns" in the psyche.

Although Wagner probably did not need such encouragement, he was enthusiastic about *The Birth of Tragedy*. "I have never read anything more beautiful than your book!" he wrote Nietzsche. And he could do with some philosophical authority, which perhaps clarified as well as confirmed his intentions. In his own day his highly emotional music struck many people as cold, because the principles of its construction were not purely musical. Today purists still complain that it is based on literary rather than strictly musical ideas—as it would naturally be, given Wagner's concept of the "united art-work." But whatever the value of his music as music, the only question that concerns me is the quality of the total drama, and particularly its tragic quality, as a means to the social catharsis that was Wagner's lifelong dream.

Tristan and Isolde, glorious as its music may be, is the most dubious of his operas as a drama of purification, or a myth symbolizing eternal truth. Although the young Nietzsche described it as the "most chaste" work he knew, even lovers of Wagner would now agree with Fergusson that it is a drama of pure passion, of a distinctly unchaste kind. It is "Dionysian" in the darkest, unholiest sense. The love music is an endless hymn to Night: Night not merely as a time for the consummation of love but as a symbol of glorified darkness, the antithesis of light and "dishonest day," and finally a symbol of Death. "Let the Day to Death surrender!" runs the refrain of Tristan at the climax. These lovers are quite unlike Romeo and Juliet or Antony and Cleopatra, who associate love with images of brightness. Their love can be consummated only in darkness, and by death. It represents not a renewal of life but a yearning for death; a passion to escape not only the prosy bourgeois world but any world of responsible effort. And the orchestra, which Wagner conceived as a replacement of the Greek Chorus, serves a very different purpose here. Whereas the

Chorus typically expressed the "Apollonian" wisdom, the traditional sense of order, Wagner's orchestra is as Dionysian as the lovers, intensifying their sensual passion by its repeated crescendoes.

But the *Liebestod* at the end strikes a different note. In her death song, soaring in exaltation over the orchestra, Isolde no longer glorifies the Night but sings radiantly of her undying love. The music builds the same feeling of a triumph over death, falling away to a quiet close with "calm of mind, all passion spent." Nietzsche asked whether anyone could listen to this last act and "hear the re-echo of countless cries of joy and sorrow from 'the vast void of cosmic night' without flying irresistibly to his primitive home." Fergusson answers that when the curtain falls one catches the subway to his unprimitive home, "unutterably feeble and discouraged perhaps, but a wretched human individual still." I find it hard to understand how one could feel discouraged and wretched after the transcendent *Liebestod*. And though it is unprofitable to argue about such impressions, the case for Wagner is made much stronger by the *Ring of the Nibelungs*.

The ring itself symbolizes the lust for wealth and power, a curse that can be removed only by the self-sacrifice of Brünnhilde; her immolation ends the reign of the old gods and inaugurates a new era of human life on earth. The theme of this epic cycle, in other words, is the tragic theme of purification, by the ritual scapegoat beloved of the new school. The music has an appropriately primeval, heroic quality, and often creates a powerful impression of the superhuman—the death of the gods, the end of a world. Both the drama and the music excite passion for life's sake rather than death's sake. When Siegfried wakes Brünnhilde from her spell, she hails him as "thou sunshine," "thou wakener of life, thou sovereign light." Presently she gives in to a passion as tempestuous as Isolde's, but now the lovers jointly "Hail the light that from night hath burst!" And in the immolation scene that concludes the cycle Brünnhilde expresses her grief, and her tragic perception of the hor-

ror of the whole drama, before she rises to her defiant exaltation. She brings about the death of the old gods by her own
heroic spirit, without the aid of new gods.

Still, the *Ring* is no synthesis of Beethoven and Shakespeare. What moves us in this opera is the power of Wagner's
music, not the profundity of his myth or the reality of his
drama. As Nietzsche observed, it is an intermittent power; the
attention of the audience is not merely weakened by Wagner's
remorseless repetition but often distracted by the non-musical
elements of the opera. The distraction raises the immediate
question whether opera can ever achieve the effect of Shakespearean or Sophoclean tragedy.

Certainly it can never *replace* drama, as Wagner was proud
to believe. Aside from the conventionally poor acting of tenors
and sopranos running to fat, drama is always likely to suffer
when music is made its vehicle, instead of a choral interlude or
background; for the music tends to subordinate conceptual
thought, diction, characterization—elements that no admirer
of Shakespeare would willingly sacrifice. Hence few librettos
will bear reading. Their text may recall Voltaire's remark that
when a thing is too silly to be said, one sings it. I am disposed
to leave this question open, however, if only because at least
one opera, *Boris Godunov*, strikes me as an impressive tragic
drama. Its hero can stand on his own feet as a tragic hero, in a
credible and moving action to which the music adds grandeur.

But *Boris* thereby accentuates the serious shortcomings of
Wagner. The plainest reason why he failed to realize his ideal
synthesis of Beethoven and Shakespeare is that he was nothing
like Shakespeare. As a poet he had at best some flair for folkish effects; he was apt to become banal, even grotesque. For
him poetry was a mere versifying of the prose in which he first
wrote his dramas. "The poem is fully worked out," he once
wrote a friend; "nothing remains to be done but the simple
versification, which any tolerably skillful verse-maker could
do." Wagner had as little genius for the creation of character.
Although his heroes and heroines are musically alive, in the

libretto they are chiefly overgrown vocal cords, throbbing with passion but having little personality and no mind to speak of. Siegfried, for example, was intended to represent "the human being in the most natural and gayest fullness of his physical manifestation"; in fact the superman comes out as a superboy-scout, more than a little ludicrous in his mental and spiritual manifestation. And the deficiency here is not merely in techni-cal skill as a playwright. It is a shallow conception of the heroic and tragic—a deficiency in mind. It was a fatal defi-ciency for one who took himself so seriously as the unacknowl-edged legislator of the modern world.

In this view Wagner's extravagances take on more signifi-cance. They were a form of self-indulgence, sprung from the colossal conceit that appears to have been God-given but was confirmed by the romantic cult of genius. Before Nietzsche became disillusioned with the jealous god of his adoration, he privately observed: "No one can be wholly honest with him-self if he believes only in himself." In his later distress over Wagner's straining for all kinds of effects—"the magnificent, the intoxicating, the bewildering, the grandiose, the frightful, the clamorous, the ecstatic, the neurotic"—Nietzsche added: "He knows what our age likes." Ultimately, Wagner was a brother under the skin with the bourgeoisie whom he thought he despised. He had their penchant for size, upholstery, lux-ury, noisy ostentation. Nietzsche's disillusionment was sealed by his "Christian" opera, *Parsifal*, which he considered an act of apostasy, a surrender to the age; but Wagner had never been the true aristocrat that he was.

The establishment of the Bayreuth Festival, the climax of Wagner's career, dramatized its basic issue. In his notebook Nietzsche had jotted down the ideal of this modern Athens: "Union of all really creative persons; artists to come with their art creations, authors to produce their new works, reformers to present their new ideas. It will be a universal *soul-bath,* and a new realm of untold blessing will be revealed there." For years Wagner devoted all his energy to realizing this dream.

When, in 1876, the Festival was at last inaugurated with the performance of the *Ring*, to the applause of an international audience, he was naturally overjoyed. Nietzsche was as profoundly depressed, not only by Wagner's handiwork ("this volubility with nothing to say") but by his audience. Since only the wealthy could afford the high cost of tickets for the twelve performances, the Festival attracted the "leisure rabble of Europe"—uncreative persons, the least fit for soul-baths. At Bayreuth, which Wagner saw as his final triumph, Nietzsche saw "the death agony of the *last great art*."

His despair was melodramatic, of course. As a festival that still attracts music-lovers, Bayreuth remains a creditable institution. But in terms of Wagner's expressed purpose it was indeed a failure. The *Ring* did not mirror the "public conscience" or the deepest interests of his society: it was an operatic appeal to a strictly mythical spirit of the Folk. And in fairness to Wagner's achievement, which as opera remains impressive, I should say that the main conclusion to be drawn from Bayreuth is that no artist today—however lofty or profound—can *create* a communal, ritual drama comparable to the Athenian. Or at least not in a free society, comprehending "the spirit of a free humanity" that Wagner dreamed of expressing. George Thomson has said that he first realized the inspiration behind the *Oresteia* when he saw, at a dramatic festival in Moscow, an opera inspired by the emancipation of women, in a theater "packed with an alert and critical audience of workpeople." Nevertheless, no great tragic drama has come out of the Soviet; and I doubt that any will—until poets and workpeople are allowed to be much more alert and critical. In Germany Thomson might have realized a similar inspiration at the festivals of Hitler.

The chauvinism of Wagner's last years—his welcome of Bismarck's dream—suggests a related conclusion, about the uses of myth. In the political world the myth becomes a lie. In the literary world the cult of the myth is a reactionary cult, and it can become, as it did in Wagner, a cult of the positively irrational. Thus Tristan sang of "daylight's falsehood," which included not only rank and fame but honor—in effect all rational, responsible endeavor. Although critics from Nietzsche to Mann have commented on the "naturalism" of Wagner, he lacked the basic realism of Shakespeare and the Greeks. He was always an incurable romantic, prone to the "idealistic lies" that made Nietzsche weary with disgust. After this kind of soul-bath one may be refreshed by Goethe's ironic attitude toward Germanic myth and saga.

Today it is no doubt too easy to attack Wagner, and to underrate his originality and his monumental genius.[2] It is a sign of his greatness, as well as his failure, that he stands alone, with no successors in the form he created. For my purposes, however, the main point remains that this form had no future. Neither did romantic tragedy as a whole. At best it produced such offspring as the swaggering *Cyrano de Bergerac*, an effective stage piece that is only nominally tragic. For the student of tragedy, the most significant play produced in the romantic period is one of a very different type. This was *Danton's Death*, the work of Georg Büchner, a remarkable young radical who died in 1837 when only twenty-four years old, and was forgotten for almost a hundred years. With his *Woyzeck*, it was the first essay in naturalistic tragedy.

As a youthful play, *Danton's Death* is naturally faulty. It is jerky in composition, stilted in dialogue; it strains for profundity. Nevertheless it has scenes of surprising power, and actually is profound. Its theme is "the terrible fatalism of history," which Danton perceives when he is condemned to death for no fault of his own. That no good will come of his death is emphasized by street scenes showing the waywardness of the common people he has fought for. In jail he momentarily tries to assume the role of scapegoat, saying to a fellow victim: "If History once opens her vaults, Despotism may still suffocate

[2] To do him the justice that I cannot in this brief study, I should recommend Mann's essay on his "Sufferings and Greatness." Mann wrote lovingly of an art that he considered "as magnificently equivocal, suspect, and compelling a phenomenon as any in the world of art."

from the vapors of our corpses." The friend answers: "We stank
quite sufficiently in our lifetime.—These are phrases for posterity, aren't they, Danton; they have nothing to do with us."
The bitter truth is that by his death order will *not* be restored,
his society will *not* be purified. As he perceives, it is simply
that history has no further use for him.

To the modern realist this kind of perception has become
commonplace. Only the hero of popular fiction can save his
country by dying—and he almost never dies, or even fades
away like old generals. It is manifestly unrealistic to believe
that in modern nations any hero can restore social order or
redeem his fellows by a sacrificial death, any more than America was restored or redeemed by the assassination of Abraham
Lincoln. The most obvious tragedy of our times is that millions
of people have been helpless victims of still more terrible historic fatalities, in economic depressions and world wars.
Büchner accordingly forces the basic issue of modern realistic
tragedy: whether on such terms men can retain the essentials
of the tragic faith. And *Danton's Death*, I believe, is moving
testimony that they can. The hero may at least restore a spiritual order in his own mind, as to some extent Danton does. He
may face his fate with dignity, the more admirable because
it is clear-eyed and supported by no illusion. On the scaffold
one of Danton's friends pronounces his forgiveness of his
executioners. Another, habitually ironical, comments wryly on
this gesture, but then tries to embrace Danton, confessing: "I
can't even make a joke. The time has come." Yet none is broken
in spirit. If posterity was not redeemed by their death, it may
still be inspired by their example. Their ideals survived the
Reign of Terror, just as the ideals of Christ have survived the
often bloody, tragic history that his followers have made in
his name.

3. BOURGEOIS TRAGEDY: IBSEN

The Ibsen who thrilled and shocked all Europe, and had so
profound an influence on modern drama, is the Ibsen of

Ghosts, the first great bourgeois tragedy. This is not strictly a representative work. He was greater than any one of his plays, and himself declared that his poetry was to be found only in his plays as a whole, no one of which was complete by itself. Neither was *Ghosts* a sudden or complete innovation. We have seen the rise of bourgeois tragedy in the eighteenth century, and may find its beginnings in Elizabethan drama; in Ibsen's own lifetime Hebbel prepared the ground by his dramatic theory, as well as his play *Maria Magdalena*. In general, the time was ripe for Ibsen. Yet he was the genius who rose to the occasion—as genius does not invariably do. The originality of *Ghosts* is sufficiently proved by the sensation it caused. At its first performance in Berlin a Danish critic announced: "This day marks the beginning of a new literary era." Brandes wrote as truly that the play made Ibsen "the most modern of the moderns." And it was a conscious innovation, the product of a long, slow growth. Ibsen was over fifty years old when he wrote it.

He had begun by writing romantic drama based on Teutonic saga, the "heroic" past of Norway. His revulsion against the sentimental romanticism that Wagner never outgrew at first found expression in poetic dramas, *Brand* and *Peer Gynt*, but finally carried all the way to realistic prose drama about contemporary life. He rejected verse as "most injurious to dramatic art," and especially unsuitable for his new purposes because of his conviction that modern life did not permit grandeur. With *Pillars of Society* and *A Doll's House* he restricted his action to topical social problems, his scene to the bourgeois parlor.

These self-imposed limitations raise the immediate issues. *Ghosts* appears to be about an ordinary young man, Oswald, who falls victim to softening of the brain, due to syphilis inherited from a father who was a pillar of local society but secretly dissolute. As the play opens, the father has just died. Oswald's mother, Mrs. Alving, is resolved that after her long ordeal of keeping up false appearances, they shall now lead a life of freedom, joy, and truth. The plot thickens as she discovers that the son who she has proudly announced is hers alone, and who shall owe nothing to his father, is taking to the ways of the father. The denouement comes when she learns that he is doomed by syphilis, and wants of her only the promise of a killing dose of morphine when the next attack leaves him helpless. The play concludes with the onset of the fatal attack. Oswald tonelessly asks for "the sun, the sun." After shrieking "I cannot bear it!" Mrs. Alving stares at him in "speechless horror." The apparent thesis is the falsity of conventional bourgeois marriage—an idea that today seems less than revolutionary. This once shocking play is also dated by Ibsen's dramaturgy, which here leans heavily on coincidences, pat ironies, theatrical curtains—the tricks of the "well-made" play.

Krutch made *Ghosts* a prime exhibit of the "mean misery" that passes for modern tragedy. He contrasted the wretched Oswald with the tragic heroes of yore, describing his failure as "trivial and meaningless"; the upshot is simply despair, "intolerable because it is no longer significant or important." Fergusson also uses *Ghosts* as an exhibit of modern realism, and though he makes a much more acute study of it, he arrives at almost as melancholy a conclusion. Recognizing that the play belongs to Mrs. Alving rather than Oswald, he makes out a tragic rhythm comparable to the rhythm in *Œdipus Rex*: like Œdipus, she is "engaged in a quest for her true human condition," and as the action develops, attains to an ever clearer, fuller realization of the meaning of her past. But the all-important difference is that her tragic quest is not completed—it is "brutally truncated." Her shriek at the end drives home the thesis but in this deeper sense concludes nothing: "it is merely sensational." Neither is the action of the drama "placed in the wider context of meanings" that poetry demands. Ibsen illumines most brilliantly "the limitations of the bourgeois parlor as the scene of human life." And all critics add that the social-problem play is bound to become dated, lose point and force. Thus Nora thrilled or scandalized our parents as she slammed the door at the end of *A Doll's House*, leaving her selfish, petty husband after asserting her woman's right to a life of her own; but now we may wonder a little wearily why it took her so long to see through so transparent a husband and arrive at so elementary a decision.

Yet such losses are not wholly unprecedented—else scholars would be out of a job. We wonder often enough at the behavior of Greek and Elizabethan heroes, whose dramas likewise reflect topical interests and require historical understanding; the footnotes that explain the point do not restore the whole impact. Ibsen is actually no more dated than Dante. Before deploring sociological fiction and drama, in any case, we should ask the obvious question: *why* have modern writers turned to this genre? For with Ibsen, again, it was a deliberate choice. He was not by nature or nurture given to the realism that many lesser writers have since taken for granted.

To begin with, let us recognize the legitimacy and the value of timely drama. Posterity need not be the main concern of a responsible artist. He can still be respected if he speaks powerfully only to his own age, for the great majority of serious writers can hope for no more than this, and without the mass of honorable second-rate work we could not hope to have the "timeless" masterpieces. We should also acknowledge our lasting indebtedness to some dated work. "It seemed to me," wrote the Ibsen of *Ghosts*, "that the time had come for moving some boundary-posts." If the work that impressed Brandes as his "noblest deed" now seems commonplace in its thesis, the influence of Ibsen helped to make it commonplace. His sociological drama represented another landmark in the advance of consciousness. It was a stimulus to imagination, not a mere cramp. It gave writers more freedom and scope.

Above all, this is a wholly natural type of tragedy—given a serious concern with man's fate. Through the rise of science, writers have become more aware of the hereditary and environmental forces that actually determine the fate of most

men. The indifference of Shakespeare and the Greeks to such
forces was not wholly a matter of lofty artistic principle: it signified as well a limited understanding. In our vast, complex
civilization, moreover, the individual may be more at the
mercy of his social environment, or more conscious of his impotence. In short, Ibsen was telling a significant tragic truth
about modern life. He himself did not regard the doom of Oswald as "trivial and meaningless." Only a literary critic with a
thesis could do so.

Shakespeare and the Greeks also believed that they were
"holding up the mirror to nature," telling the tragic truth about
man's life. Modern realism is different in its closer literalness
→ and its common concern with the ordinary man, the familiar
and average in experience. But Fergusson confuses its issues
by defining its "essence" in terms of its most superficial aspects,
as a "strictly photographic imitation of the human scene," or
in the words of T. S. Eliot, reality as "perceived by the most
commonplace mind." Hence he declares that realism imposes
upon the writer the "necessity" of pretending that he has no
poetic purpose, but is aiming only at truth. The poetry he finds
in Ibsen is always "hidden" or "evident only to the histrionic
sensibility." It is a "triumph" whenever Ibsen transcends the
literal, reveals an intention "more philosophical than history."
Actually, all the greater realists have had such an intention,
none has confined himself to the literal. If the realistic method
has manifest dangers, anyone who knows Balzac, Flaubert,
Hardy, Turgenev, Tolstoy, and Dostoyevsky will not equate
realism with meagerness and superficiality. As for Ibsen, our
immediate concern is not the wonder that he managed to
smuggle some poetry and philosophy into his drama, but the
scope and depth of the vision that he naturally, unmistakably
did embody. Our final concern is the tragic values of a drama
that deliberately eschews splendor and grandeur.

Although *Ghosts* is no affair with the gods, many still find
it a powerful drama, and not primarily because of its demonstration that hereditary syphilis is a damnable thing. One ob-

vious source of its power is the tragic sense of inevitable doom, a fated action that may be associated with Greek fatalism, or with the Hebraic idea that the sins of the father are visited upon the children. In either case it may be called a "timeless" theme. Another means to wider connections is the symbolism indicated in the title (as in the typical titles of Ibsen's bourgeois dramas—*Pillars of Society, A Doll's House, The Wild Duck*). Underlying the surface thesis is the more significant idea that Mrs. Alving realizes in the course of her tragic quest:

> I am half inclined to think we are all ghosts, Mr. Manders. It is not only what we have inherited from our fathers and mothers that exists again in us, but all sorts of dead ideas and all kinds of old dead beliefs and things of that kind. They are not actually alive in us; but they are dormant all the same, and we can never be rid of them. Whenever I take up a newspaper and read it, I fancy I see ghosts creeping between the lines. There must be ghosts all over the world. They must be as countless as the grains of sand, it seems to me. And we are so miserably afraid of the light, all of us.

Such ghosts keep returning in Ibsen's drama, whose people are mostly fearful of the light or unable to endure it; and this theme has lost none of its point or force. It has always been true, though ancient writers were disposed to revere the ghosts. It is especially pertinent in a revolutionary world, when traditional beliefs are so often at variance with changed conditions and new knowledge. And Ibsen habitually set it in a still wider context. His bourgeois parlors, haunted by ghosts, are invaded by thoughts of the elemental wildness of mountain, fen, and fiord. Mrs. Alving's parlor looks out on snow-capped mountain peaks, which are lit by the rising sun as the tragedy comes to a close—the sun that Oswald begs for, the glow in which she has aspired to live with him.

Yet this vision of mountain peaks produces no exhilaration: it only intensifies the "speechless horror" of Mrs. Alving. And here again is the ultimate issue of realistic tragedy. Fergusson finds this ending literal, brutal, merely sensational. Others agree that it is merely depressing, effecting no catharsis. There is no reconciliation, no equilibrium of good and evil. The issue becomes more difficult if one feels, as I do, that Ibsen was not being sensational, but had good reasons for ending his bleak play as he did. Since the tragic spirit has always been fundamentally realistic, the modern realist says in effect: Let us tell the whole tragic truth. Let us admit that there is no apparent moral order governing the universe. Let us recognize that the "true human condition" may often be helpless and hopeless, strictly irreconcilable. Tragedy cannot serve the deepest needs of modern man unless it drops such pretenses as that a Fortinbras will restore the health of Denmark—an idea as naïve as the popular faith in the U. S. Marines. Let us not have "complete actions" at the expense of the tragic truth.

On this issue one must begin by speaking only for himself. Whether or not one derives the pleasure of tragedy from *Ghosts* is not primarily a matter of sure, fine esthetic taste, but again a matter of temperament, or philosophical predisposition. Neither can one dispose of the issue by an appeal to "truth." An utterly sordid or horrible story can be quite true— the newspapers are full of them. Ibsen's *Hedda Gabler* is another powerful drama, a realistic study of a neurotic, predatory woman who destroys her lover and herself; but it seems to me too abnormal and purely horrible to be a great tragic drama. Yet *Ghosts*, and Ibsen's drama as a whole, can provide an experience comparable in kind to the experience of Greek and Shakespearean tragedy, if less rich and deep. And having granted a temperamental factor, one may point to some objective qualities of Ibsen's drama that validate this experience, and with it the judgment that he belongs among the greater writers of tragedy.

For one thing, Ibsen himself clearly did not intend *Ghosts* as a message of despair. He was saying that men need not be so miserably afraid of the light. By the same token he was not the cynic or nihilist that horrified conservatives made of him. As a helpless victim of the ghosts, Oswald is a pitiable figure, far from heroic but by no means contemptible. His much more admirable mother arouses both pity and terror. Her tragic quest leads her to a belated perception of Ibsen's positive values. It bears out his explicit statement of the tragic faith that at least partly offsets the horror:

> It has been said of me on different occasions that I am a pessimist. And I am in so far as I do not believe in the everlastingness of human ideals. But I am an optimist in so far as I firmly believe in the capacity for the procreation and development of ideals.

Most of all Ibsen was devoted to the ideal of freedom. His bourgeois dramas illustrate his lifelong effort to emancipate the individual from bourgeois conventionality. Like Mrs. Alving, almost all his heroes are engaged in the tragic quest to realize themselves, discover in freedom their true human condition. In the light of human history, with its overwhelming preponderance of closed societies, this is not strictly a perennial, universal theme; but it is an appropriate theme for high tragedy, and surely has lost none of its pertinence for us today. And Ibsen treated it in a spirit not only liberal but tragic. He went deeper than the Marxists and other political reformers, once commenting that they wanted only liberties, not liberty. (Leftists had joined the bourgeoisie in denouncing *Ghosts.*) He was much more complex and ironic, aware of the evils that inevitably attend the quest for freedom.

One witness to both the depth and the loftiness of Ibsen is Thomas Mann, who coupled him with Wagner as "northern wizards" or "weavers of spells," among the giants of the century. (It is well to remember that this century which is conventionally divided into Romantic and Victorian, both epithets of disparagement today, was in fact a century of giants—artists like Balzac, Zola, Dostoyevsky, and Tolstoy, working on a grand scale.) The most striking witness is Nicolas Berdyaev, who testified to the enormous influence Ibsen had on him during the spiritual crisis following his emancipation from Marxism. He found in the reputedly cramped realist a prophet comparable to Dostoyevsky and Nietzsche, and was fired by his scorn of the bourgeois spirit, his concern for the heroic personality, the heights, the mountaintops. As a theologian, Berdyaev was obliged to add that Ibsen had lost sight of the living God, was ignorant of the final meaning of sin, and could not find the way to the heights—or in other words, was a tragic rather than a Christian poet; yet he linked him with Kierkegaard, in his contempt for the spirit of compromise. For Berdyaev, Ibsen's main theme was the eternal conflict between dream and reality, creativity and life, the heroic personality and the conventional collective.

Although this is most apparent in the later plays of Ibsen, he himself insisted on the essential unity of his entire work, as well as the need of viewing it as a whole. To do justice to his stature, and in particular to the breadth and complexity of his tragic vision, we have to consider some of his other plays.

Ibsen's major poetic dramas already complicate his gospel of the power and freedom of the human will. In *Brand* this will appears as spiritual arrogance; the tragedy reveals the inhuman aspect of Kierkegaard's uncompromising, all-or-nothing spirit. *Peer Gynt* satirizes the more common corruption of the ideal of individualism and self-realization, which becomes an excuse for self-seeking or mere flabbiness of will. Peer Gynt follows the motto of the Trolls: "To thyself be—enough!" He is good enough to himself to make a fortune in the slave traffic. At length he is hailed as Emperor—but in a lunatic asylum. "It's here that men are most themselves," the head of the asylum explains, "—themselves and nothing but themselves." At the end Peer is horrified to discover that he has no real self, and is not fit even for Hell. "Sinners in the true grand style are seldom met with nowadays," the Button Moulder tells him; "that style of sin needs power of mind."

Among the sociological plays, the most provocative after

Ghosts is *The Wild Duck*. This is a fantastic combination of
high comedy and pathos, in a *petit-bourgeois* milieu rendered
with thorough realism, and includes an ironic reversal of the
scapegoat pattern: it ends in tragedy when the young daughter
sacrifices herself in a vain effort to purify the household. It
recalls the persistent element of the grotesque in Western tradition, beginning with Gothic art; now the deliberate impiety
or impurity invades bourgeois realism. Ibsen wrote Brandes of
the "mad fancies" he was playing with, and took pleasure in
the thought of mystifying his critics. What mystified them, of
course, is that he here turns in on himself, satirizing the zeal
for social reform that had made him famous. Gregers, the
idealistic meddler who causes all the trouble, is a pitiless self-
caricature; he is the crippled "wild duck" that he is fond of
seeing in others. Ibsen mocks even his lifelong message, the
call for liberty and light. Dr. Relling, his spokesman, asserts
that the bulk of mankind will only suffer from such demands:
what they need above all is illusion. The tragic perception in
the drama is that men must be protected against such perceptions.

Nevertheless the play is not so cynical as some critics concluded. Dr. Relling speaks in a spirit of pity and love; he does
not despise unheroic humanity, but simply recognizes its
limitations. Liberals might still profit from his wisdom. For
Ibsen, at any rate, *The Wild Duck* was no repudiation of his
past. While now making a fresh start, he returned to his basic
themes. He concentrated on the individual for his own sake,
and finally on the heroic personality. In the process he moved
from the remediable social evil to the inherently tragic element of the human condition. The transition is illustrated by
Rosmersholm, which is essentially a re-treatment—still realistic
but more complex, subtle, poetic, and suggestive—of the underlying theme of *Ghosts*.

The hero, Rosmers, is struggling to get free of the puritanical
tradition of Rosmersholm, the ancestral homestead. Rebecca,
a strong-willed, emancipated woman who loves him, does her

best to help him so that they may be partners in a life of freedom and joy, the "happiness that ennobles." She fails when it
transpires that she has been more or less responsible for the
suicide of his unhappy, invalided wife. Then she submits to his
demand for expiation: together they drown themselves in the
millstream haunted by the "White Horse" of Rosmersholm—
the heritage of sin and guilt. This love-death is the most ambiguous ending in Ibsen's drama. In one view it represents a
tragic failure, even sheer futility. Rebecca has collapsed under
the strain, surrendered to Rosmersholm in despair; her sacrifice seems meaningless because Rosmers is not transformed by
it—he is at best pathetic rather than heroic. Yet it is also a
dignified acceptance of a real necessity, the claims of conscience. Rebecca has perceived her actual guilt, and with it an
ennobling aspect of the Rosmersholm tradition. It is hard to
say whether her sacrifice is chiefly noble or foolish; and one
may suspect some uncertainty in Ibsen's own mind. He wrote,
however, that the play deals with the struggle to live in harmony with one's convictions, and he noted the inevitable complications and uncertainties of this struggle. The modern
intellect is forward-looking, hurrying on from gain to gain; conscience is always conservative, deeply rooted in tradition. In
effect, Ibsen here recognized the hardest problem: that
"ghosts" have some valid claim upon our loyalty.

Ibsen concluded his career by bringing back the tragic hero.
His last plays, beginning with *The Master Builder*, are admittedly personal plays. Although they reveal some falling-off
in his powers, they are memorable testaments of the "northern
wizard" who had chosen to write bourgeois drama, and now
reflected on his career and his time.

The hero of *The Master Builder* may be taken for Ibsen
himself. He had started his career by building churches and
high towers, but had become famous when he turned to comfortable homes for ordinary human beings. To this end he had
sacrificed his own domestic happiness (as Ibsen had exiled
himself from Norway during most of his career). Now he is

sick in mind, desperately afraid of being shunted aside by the younger generation. He also wonders "whether there will be any use for such homes in the coming time"; since men are not happy in them, the upshot of his career is "nothing really built." The master builder is then stirred by Hilda, a young girl whom he had inspired years ago, and who returns to insist that he live up to her dream image of him. He resolves to build the "only one possible dwelling-place for human happiness," castles in the air—but "with a firm foundation under them." Meanwhile Hilda insists that he dedicate a tower on a new home of his own by climbing to the top and fastening a wreath on it. His wife is horrified, and the younger architects are contemptuously amused; they all know that he gets dizzy at any height. Nevertheless the master builder responds to the challenge, climbing to the top; and though he falls to his death, Hilda ends the play with a shriek of wild triumph—very different from the shriek of Mrs. Alving.

The younger generation might still claim the last word. Ibsen himself got a little dizzy writing this play, and neglected to put a firm foundation under it. Hilda is rather incredible; the young might comment cynically on the dream girl of the aging Ibsen (not to mention the Freudian significance of the towers and his inability to climb them). Though he had prided himself on never sacrificing realism to symbolism, here he did sacrifice it; the play cannot stand up as realistic drama. But the master builder himself is a compelling creation. If we are especially interested in him as a self-portrait, we may appreciate still more the irony of this portrait. He is a Nietzschean superman, ruthless in his will to power, who sacrifices both himself and others to this will, and appropriately dies of dizziness. He proves that modern man can still build high towers; or that he is unfit for them.

The hero of *John Gabriel Borkman* is another superman, or "sinner in the true grand style." An unscrupulous financier, he has for the sake of his career renounced the woman he loved and married her sister. Now financially ruined, he lives in solitude in his loveless home, like Napoleon on St. Helena, still dreaming of climbing back to the heights, but doomed to sterility. The woman he has rejected comes back to pronounce the fatal theme: "The great, unpardonable sin is to murder the love-life in a human soul"—as Borkman has done to her, and to himself. We know that Ibsen was a lonely giant in his old age, realizing that he had been unable to surrender himself to the love he craved. This tragedy, however, is memorable in its own right, to my mind one of his greatest. While the minor characters are sketched perfunctorily, the hero and the two sisters are as statuesque as characters in Greek tragedy. The Greek quality is most pronounced in the last act, when—the whole past disclosed, the action completed except for the iminent death of Borkman—the three comment like a Chorus on the meaning of their lives, aware that they are alike doomed to frustration. At the end the sisters are reconciled in their common fate: "We two shadows—over the dead man." It is a somber acceptance, with no suggestion of a communal order restored or a cosmic moral order vindicated. But this is not a cramped scene, and there is nothing trivial, mean, brutal, or sensational about it. Ibsen demonstrates that modern life does, after all, permit a kind of grandeur.

His last play, *When We Dead Awaken*, is subtitled a "Dramatic Epilogue," and by his own acknowledgment is an epilogue to the series that began with *The Master Builder*. The hero is again an artist (now a sculptor) who stands out from the common run; the theme is again the nemesis of creativity, in its conflict with life and apostasy from the common life. The hero reflects on "the fundamental duplicity of all ideal endeavor," which tends to separate the idealist from his fellow men and cheat him of his human heritage of sunshine, natural beauty, love. The woman he has sacrificed to his ideal mission as an artist repeats the main theme: "The love that belongs to the life of earth—the beautiful, miraculous earth-life—the inscrutable earth-life—that is dead in both of us." Then the dead awaken, try to recapture this life. Together they start climbing toward the mountain peak shining in the morning sun—the symbol in *Ghosts*. They die in the effort.

Unhappily, it is a weak play. By now Ibsen was losing his technical control, and in particular his grip on reality; the play is all ghostly symbolism. As a personal epilogue, however, it becomes moving. Although there was apparently no such woman in Ibsen's life, the sculptor Rubek is otherwise much like his author. Both won their fame abroad, and are unhappy upon returning to their native Norway; both are also unhappy about the bourgeois audiences that now applaud their work without understanding it.[3] Ibsen can still be ironic. Rubek makes lifelike portraits of the plutocrats, with their "respectable, pompous horse-faces"; and he takes a grim pleasure in the thought that his customers admire and keep ordering these "double-faced works of art." But chiefly he is despondent as he looks back to the enthusiasm of his prime, when he was sure of his ideal mission, and contrasts it with his present confusion and uncertainty of purpose.

The mournful, twilight atmosphere of Ibsen's last plays recalls his comment on his reputation as the creator of a new era. "On the contrary," he wrote, "I believe that the time in which we now live might with quite as good reason be characterized as a conclusion, and that something new is about to be born." Having no clear vision of the new age, he felt chiefly the decay of his own, the twilight of the old values. To revert to his image of the master builder, the homes he had built for human beings were scarcely designed for comfort and had provided little happiness. He never got around to building his castles in the air. As a realist, he felt that his age provided no firm foundations for them.

---

[3] There was nevertheless something of a disingenuous bourgeois in Ibsen. When the clergy rose to the outraged protests that he invited and expected in writing *Ghosts*, he defended himself by saying that the play "preaches nothing at all," and that he had taken good care that no single opinion expressed by his characters could be laid at his door. As a young man, he had been frightened into a timid aloofness by some trouble his radical opinions got him into. As an old man, he had a secret passion for honors—grand crosses and ribbons to stick in his coat.

Yet he might have remembered a passage in his *Emperor and Galilean*. "Do not reproach the age," Maximus told Julian the Apostate. "Had the age been greater, you would have been less." Ibsen came at the right time to do his work. In drama, at least, he was indeed the prophet of a new era. With him the theater again became a medium for serious literature, and a new movement got under way. It was a European movement, since he wrote as a European; this Norwegian bourgeois was less provincial than Racine. And in turning to realism he not only realized his own genius but pointed in the necessary direction. Romantic tragedy was clearly unsuited to his age, except as fancy entertainment. A vital drama had to be in vital relation to the actual problems of the modern world, reflecting the new knowledge, interests, attitudes, conditions of life. Knowing Shakespeare and the Greeks, we are at once struck by how severely Ibsen limited tragedy; so we may forget that he also widened its scope, enriched it by opening up new realms of experience. Taken as a whole, his drama is a solid and rather grand achievement.

4. NATURALISTIC TRAGEDY: STRINDBERG AND HAUPTMANN

"Zola descends to the sewer to take a bath," Ibsen wrote, "I do in order to scour it." Actually, he did not descend to the lower depths of society. He was indifferent to the working class, never dramatizing the problem of its welfare; he was hostile to the peasantry. His individualism was aristocratic, not egalitarian. In the light of the new naturalism he came to seem an old-fashioned optimist. Wedekind attacked him for representing men as higher rather than lower animals.

"Naturalism" is no longer a helpful term in critical discourse. It is commonly used as a synonym for realism, which itself is none too precise a term; in its familiar sense of an extreme degree of realism, with an emphasis upon the sordid, it leads to unprofitable controversy, since one man's sordidness is another's sober truth. Nevertheless we cannot avoid the term when dealing with the literature of the last decades of the nineteenth century. It then denoted a highly self-conscious, militant movement, led by Zola, which represented a much more violent revolt than Ibsen's against the romantic, genteel tradition. The naturalists concentrated on the life of the lower classes, who had entered realistic fiction only incidentally. They emphasized grim, squalid, brutal detail because the life of the poor was grim, squalid, and brutal. Most significantly, they made a point of taking over both the methods and the findings of science. In *The Experimental Novel* Zola argued that the novelist should give fiction the validity of a scientific experiment by operating objectively on his characters in a given situation, just as scientists operated in the laboratory. Although we need not take this theory seriously, the early naturalists did adopt the method of close, impersonal observation and analysis—"the modern method," as Zola proclaimed—and with it the mechanistic, deterministic doctrine of nineteenth-century science. Habitually they demonstrated that men were victims of their heredity and environment.

The theory of naturalism is plainly disastrous for tragedy. If man is merely a creature of brute compulsion, in no sense a free, responsible agent, his story can have no dignity or ideal significance of any sort. It is not clear why the naturalists should have had such a passion for telling this story. But as their passion suggests, their practice was often inconsistent and impure. The mixed consequences of naturalism may be illustrated by two playwrights—August Strindberg and Gerhardt Hauptmann.

Although Strindberg avowed that the immediate inspiration of his drama was Antoine's production of Zola's *Thérèse Raquin*, he was an exceptionally original dramatist who introduced a new type of characterization. "Because they are modern characters," he wrote, "living in a period of transition more hysterically hurried than its immediate predecessor at least, I have made my figures vacillating, out-of-joint, torn between the old and the new." He attacked the conventional idea of character, which represented it as a fixed, stable, consistent, readily describable thing. Anticipating the depth psychology of Freud, he stressed the multiple, confused, largely unconscious motives of behavior.

Thus in *Miss Julia*, the manifesto of his naturalism, a neurotic girl throws herself at a servile, brutal valet during a summer festival, only to be deserted by him after the nominal seduction when her father is about to return; he responds to her desperate appeal for help by hypnotizing her into the courage she needs to kill herself. Strindberg points out in his preface that the causes of her behavior, aside from the chance seclusion and the aggressiveness of the excited male, include the passions she has learned from her mother, the mistaken upbringing by her father, the influence of her fiancé, the festive mood of Midsummer Eve, the dusk, the aphrodisiac influence of the flowers, her physical condition, and her preoccupation with animals. Altogether, Strindberg concludes, she is "a victim of the day's delusions, of the circumstances, of her defective constitution—all of which may be held equivalent to the old-fashioned fate or universal law. The naturalist has wiped out the idea of guilt, but he cannot wipe out the results of an action."

More characteristically, Strindberg describes Miss Julia as a type of "man-hating half-woman" that may have existed in all ages, but has now come to the fore and begun to make a noise. In other plays, notably *The Father* and *The Dance of Death*, the battle of the sexes is still more desperate and elemental; man and wife fight to the death. Strindberg conceived this as Darwinian tragedy. To those who complained that it was too cruel and heartless he replied: "I find the joy of life in its violent and cruel struggles." A milder and perhaps fairer statement of his credo is this: "The true naturalism is that which seeks out those points in life where the great conflicts occur, which loves to see that which cannot be seen every day, rejoices in the battle of elemental powers, whether they be called love or hatred, revolt or sociability; which cares not whether a subject be beautiful or ugly, if only it is great." It was presumably the "greatness" of his conflicts that led Shaw to call Strindberg "the only genuinely Shakespearean modern dramatist."

For his distinctive purposes Strindberg originated a brilliant, if un-Shakespearean technique. Its essence is a fierce concentration. He reduced his cast to a minimum, usually three or four characters. He not only observed the unities but sought ideally a continuous action, without act intermissions. He confined himself to a single set on an almost bare stage, with the fewest possible props; in *The Father* he needed only a lamp and a strait jacket. Especially in this play he achieved a terrific intensity. In general, there is no denying the genius of Strindberg, and the unique power of his naturalistic drama. Within his range he was profounder and more original than Ibsen, who looks bourgeois by contrast. While Ibsen's preoccupation with disease, from *Ghosts* to *When We Dead Awaken*, may be taken as symbolic of a sick society, Strindberg pictured its nightmares, the convulsions that were to materialize a generation later in World War I. With Nietzsche—who was greatly excited by *The Father*—he stands out as one of the few writers of his time who sensed the horrors to come. Add the new forms he invented in his effort to express the chaos of modern experience, such as his later dream plays, and the many-volumed autobiography in which he analyzed his own strange experience, and we have one of the most extraordinary of modern writers.

But we do not have a great tragic dramatist. Strindberg's naturalistic drama is the clearest illustration of Krutch's dismal thesis. The neurotic Miss Julia is much too mean to be a tragic figure; at most she stirs some pity—more than Strindberg intended, if we take him at his own word—in her utter bafflement. The heroes of his other tragedies are generally stronger, or at least fiercer, but no more admirable. They fight the battle of the sexes with an insane violence and mercilessness. Their madness is not, as with Hamlet and Lear, the result of their tragic experience—it is the mainspring of the tragedy. Though they illustrate the pathological extremes to which men are liable, the hell men can make of life, they are much too abnormal to represent the tragic fate of Man.

Why, one wonders, should Strindberg have made such a pother over such repulsive creatures? The answer is suggested by *The Creditors*, in which he perfected his naturalistic technique. A woman who has gutted her husband is in turn gutted by her ex-husband, a ruthless intellectual who speaks for his author. Impervious to pity and terror, he represents the possible good to be won from these mad struggles. The time may come, Strindberg prophesied, when we shall stand utterly indifferent before the spectacle of life, by having "closed up those lower, unreliable instruments of thought which we call feelings, and which have been rendered not only superfluous but harmful by the final growth of our reflective organs." Briefly, the chief objection to Strindberg's pathological dramas is that he himself was pathological. He believed that he *was* telling the tragic story of mankind, and that the hell he created was the normal condition of man. This supposedly objective naturalist, free from illusion, was in fact an intensely subjective artist, a victim of obsession. Hence the fierce intensity of his drama becomes a violent monotony, suggesting monomania. The immediate key to his art is his mother-fixation, followed by three unhappy marriages; woman to him was one of nature's mistakes, unfortunately still necessary as a biological intermediary between the man and the man-child. In a broader view, he is significant mainly as a symptom of the sickness and potential chaos of his age, which he never succeeded in mastering.

Strindberg's autobiography traces his passage through various phases that have since become too familiar, including a youthful radicalism, a revulsion into a fascistic contempt of the common herd, an absorption in science, another revulsion into literary Catholicism. Following his nervous breakdown, which brought him close to insanity, he entered the "spiritual" phase that produced his fantasies and dream plays. Because of his genius these are often fascinating plays, of added interest to students of modern drama because in his restless experimentation Strindberg anticipated expressionism and surrealism. But finally they too are symptomatic.

The most striking is *The Ghost Sonata*. Its theme recalls Ibsen's favorite theme, the ghosts that return. As a character in another of Strindberg's plays exclaims, "Everything is dug up! Everything comes back!"—to create another nightmare. The play has a convincing dream quality in its fusion of grotesque fantasy and weird realism. "The characters split, double, multiply, vanish, solidify, blur, clarify," Strindberg wrote of these dream plays—yet they remain whole. "A single consciousness holds sway over them all—that of the dreamer; for him there are no secrets, no inconsequences, no scruples, and no law. The dreamer neither condemns nor acquits: he merely relates." In *The Ghost Sonata*, however, the dreamer does pass judgment. One of the more perceptive characters remarks that they are all miserable sinners but know it, and so are better than their misdeeds. The action bears out his Christian hope that suffering and repentance may wipe out the evil. It is a movement away from the "natural" world, into "reality" —first into the Round Room with a clock (Time), finally into the Hyacinth Room with an image of Buddha (Eternity). Here the Student appeals to the Savior who had descended to this madhouse, jail, and morgue on earth. When the innocent Young Lady droops and dies, he calls upon the wise and gentle Buddha to give them patience. With his final appeal for mercy the whole room disappears, and Böcklin's painting "The Island of Death" takes its place, to the tune of soft, "pleasantly wistful" music.

Strindberg had made the pilgrimage—back to the Absolute, to Rome, to the East, to Nirvana—that so many revolutionaries and sophisticates have made in our own time. And as with many of them, it is rather pathetically wistful. It looks more like a retreat than a regeneration. The ending of *The Ghost Sonata* is arbitrary and unconvincing, apart from the ludicrous

use of Böcklin as a *deus ex machina*. The play is not a product
of the Buddhistic patience and resignation that Strindberg
counsels. Its power, like that of his other dream plays, derives
more from its underlying realism than its spirituality or mysticism. Although he went considerably further away from the
natural world than Ibsen, into a realm of "reality" where mere
mistiness could pass for profound mystery, he never succeeded
in losing himself in the blue. The artist in him continued to
profit from a stubborn skepticism that denied the man real
peace of mind.

The Dream Play, Strindberg's most ambitious effort in this
genre, will do as his ambiguous testament. Its theme is the
woe of man's life, as discovered by a daughter of Indra who
comes down to earth, and the woe is presented with a compassion that even embraces women. The Daughter early announces the faith that love will overcome everything. But the
play fails to demonstrate this faith. The Daughter speaks more
truly when she becomes better acquainted with the bedlam of
the world: "Woe unto him who first recovers his reason!" The
Poet struggles against his reason:

> (Ecstatically) Man was created by the god Phtah out of
> clay on a potter's wheel, or a lathe—(skeptically) or any
> damned old thing. (Ecstatically) Out of clay does the
> sculptor create his more or less immortal masterpieces—
> (skeptically) which mostly are pure rot.

In the conclusion the Daughter explains to him the mystery
of life. Maya, the World-Mother, had persuaded Brahma to
propagate himself; so it was "Woman through whom sin and
death found their way into life." And so it is time to leave
Strindberg. This is where we came in.

Hauptmann's career was similar in that he turned from naturalistic to poetic drama and came to a dubious end, as the
only German writer of distinction to support Hitler. His naturalism, however, was utterly different from Strindberg's. One
of its animating principles was expressed by a character in *The*

Rats: "Before art as before the law all men are equal." Hauptmann points to the logical connection between naturalism and the rise of democracy.

His best-known play, *The Weavers*, is a slice-of-life in which the hero is a class—the workers, the poor. The source of their tragedy is neither pride nor fate but the power loom, with which hand workers cannot compete; the weavers are driven to rebellion by starvation wages. The play has the faults one might expect. It is sprawling, talky, and overinsistent, and its huge cast of characters includes many stock types. It suffers by comparison with *Germinal*, Zola's epical novel on a similar theme; the novel is a more suitable form for so big a subject. But like Zola, Hauptmann does justice to the tragic complexity of the issue. Though his play created a sensation because of his manifest sympathy with the weavers, he does not sentimentalize them. Their rebellion is a blind, frenzied, futile uprising from which everybody suffers.

More representative of Hauptmann's naturalistic tragedy is *Drayman Henschel*. A simple drayman promises his hysterical dying wife that he will not remarry; for need of a home he then breaks his promise and marries a woman who proves greedy and faithless, ruins his reputation, undermines his simple integrity, and finally drives him to suicide. Hauptmann tells this story with uncompromising, unsentimental realism, never suggesting that his hero is nature's nobleman. The tragic perception of Drayman Henschel is limited and confused:

> A bad man I've come to be, only it's no fault o' mine. I just, somehow, stumbled into it all. Maybe it's my fault too. You c'n say so if you want to. Who knows? I should ha' kept a better watch. But the devil is more cunnin' than me. I just kept on straight ahead.

Nevertheless he has dignity as he keeps going straight ahead, accepts the consequence of his misdeed, expiates in the spirit of a humble Othello. He kills himself without false heroics, off-stage. It is a moving play, the more so because of its quietness.

Now, that all men are equal before art is dangerous doctrine. The inequalities in men are supremely important, as the source of all ideals of excellence. The story of Drayman Henschel, told with compassionate understanding, is surely worth telling and knowing; but it cannot have the significance of the tragedy of an Œdipus or a Hamlet. Hauptmann recognized as much by dealing with loftier subjects in other tragedies. "The great failure," declares a spokesman in *Michael Kramer*, "can be more meaningful—we see it in the noblest works—can move us more deeply, can lead us to loftier heights—deeper into immensity—than the clearest success." The great failure requires greatness in the protagonist; a Drayman Henschel cannot lead us to the heights or into the immensities. As it is, we have had a surfeit of realistic stories about commonplace lives, or worse.

Yet writers in a democratic society, with a literary tradition of realism, will naturally write about the common man; and no believer in democracy can merely deplore such subject matter. The sentiment of equality has its own value, as a recognition of brotherhood in a common humanity and a common fate. The little man is not inferior in every respect; he may in simple decency be a better man than the hero or the genius. Other avowed naturalists—like Theodore Dreiser in *Jennie Gerhardt* —have managed to endow lowly lives with tragic dignity. And the writer who chooses to treat such lives has at least one advantage: he is likely to be closer to the elemental and universal than the aristocratic writer, who expresses the ideals of a privileged class in a particular society. *The Weavers* was a timely play, dealing with a kind of struggle that is especially characteristic of modern civilization; but it is also the timeless story of the poor, the life of most men in all civilizations before our own. If Hauptmann was not so great a writer as Corneille and Dryden, a tradition that still preserves their tragedies should find room for his type of tragedy.

At least the naturalists did not simply degrade man. Generally they tended to widen sympathies, create new values in literature. If the tragedy of low life has a limited significance, high tragedy may also limit our awareness by accustoming us to an exalted realm where is enacted not the story of Man but of the heroic few. "As for our grand sorrows," remarked a simple woman in Santayana's *The Last Puritan*, "they are a parcel of our common humanity, like funerals; and the Lord designs them for our good, to wean our hearts from this sad world. . . . And it's almost a pleasure to grieve, all hung in weeds, like a weeping willow. But the price of eggs, Mr. Oliver, the price of eggs!" Another reason why tragedy gives us pleasure is that it makes us forget the price of eggs, delivers us from all the petty, nagging, humiliating cares that we can never escape in life. No doubt this is all to the good, since we can count on having enough cares. But as Karl Jaspers observed in *Tragedy Is Not Enough*, the glamour of tragedy may obscure the appalling realities of human misery: the hopeless, helpless misery that the masses of men have always known; misery without greatness, without dignity, without any decent meaning whatever; misery that seems more intolerable because men have always tolerated it. We have no right to demand of artists that they treat such misery. As we value the tragic spirit and its essential humanity, we have no right either to condemn the naturalists who did treat it.

5. THE REALISM OF CHEKHOV

"The novel is a lawful wife," Chekhov once said, "but the stage is a noisy, flashy, and insolent mistress." For this mistress—for the modern audience of whose limitations we hear so much—he nevertheless managed to write a uniquely quiet, modest kind of drama, so unostentatious that it may seem not to be real drama at all. Let us consider, for example, *The Three Sisters*. The apparent theme is the unhappiness of three sisters who live in a dull provincial town and yearn to go to Moscow. There is really nothing to prevent their going, but they stay; their brother gets married to a vulgar girl; friends come and talk and go, over a period of some years; and the outcome of these aimless, pointless happenings is that the three sisters grow unhappier, yearn still more for Moscow, but realize that they never will go to Moscow. Throughout there is little real conflict or struggle. The play demonstrates no thesis, makes no clear predication of any sort. Even those who are moved by it may find it hard to say what the play is about. It has taken on some "social significance" because the futile society pictured by Chekhov has since crumbled and been reinvigorated by the Soviet; but he did not write as a prophet, and history alone could not make his play significant as drama.

As tragedy, *The Three Sisters* would seem to be still more wanting. About this time John Masefield wrote that tragedy is a vision of the heart of life, which "can only be laid bare in the agony and exultation of dreadful acts." There are no such dreadful acts in this or the other serious dramas of Chekhov. Here the fiancé of one of the sisters is killed in an offstage duel in the last act, but it makes little difference; she had consented to marry him only because he was "a nice man"—he was not the man of her dreams. Evil is not the main source of the suffering. There is no tragic denouement because no tragic conflict and no tragic hero. Neither is there a decisive tragic perception. At most the characters arrive at a somewhat clearer, sadder perception of their frustration, which they were aware of at the outset. Their sadness is not majestic, as in Racine's *Berenice*. They are not purified or regenerated by their suffering, nor does it bring good to their community. There is no trace of the ancient ritual pattern.

In short, *The Three Sisters* fits none of the familiar definitions of tragedy. And so much the worse for the definitions. It is an exceptionally rich, poignant, moving play. Chekhov has been called the greatest dramatist since Shakespeare. I would not defend to the death this invidious judgment, especially since he left only four mature, full-length plays at his early death. But I do insist upon the inadequacy of any conception of tragedy that excludes these plays, or any conception of modern realism that belittles them.

They are not really artless or formless plays, of course, nor is their art an ineffable one that defies all analysis. While learning to dispense with most of the familiar conventions of drama, Chekhov developed new conventions of his own.[4] He perfected an art as fine as that of Henry James, or even subtler. William Gerhardi noted that he managed to say subtle things simply, easily, directly, without James's "strings of definitions, qualifications, amplifications, ramifications, curtailments."

The "protagonist" of Chekhov's mature drama is always a group. It is a unified group, representing not a slice-of-life but a basic pattern, as of frustration, waste, or utter ineffectuality. Most of the more important characters illustrate the pattern directly; the rest serve as contrasts, by their complacence, indifference, or resignation. The group mood is orchestrated as they wander the stage, brush against one another casually, and touch off sudden bursts of feeling. The minor characters do not exist merely for the sake of the main action, but have a distinctive life of their own. All are like little Hamlets, apt at any moment to talk about the meaning—or meaninglessness— of their lives, often without attending to what the other characters are saying or doing. And all the characters are given to rushes of simple candor. How old you've grown! How ugly you look! How nice your fiancé is—but oh, how plain! Or as a departing soldier tells one of the three sisters, it's not *au revoir* —it's good-by. We shall never meet again! Or if we do, perhaps in ten or fifteen years' time, we won't really know one another.

All critics speak of the aptness of Chekhov's unobtrusive detail, in both his short stories and his plays. Most characteristic is the significant triviality, the relevant irrelevancy, the logical incongruity. As all the hopes of Dr. Astroff have been extinguished at the end of *Uncle Vanya*, he stares in silence

---

[4] Those interested in dramatic technique may see the development more clearly by studying his early, more explicit and conventional plays *Ivanov* and *The Wood Demon*, the latter a failure which he reworked into *Uncle Vanya*. Also pertinent is the work of Stanislavsky, whose Moscow Art Theater first became known for its productions of Chekhov and through them developed its celebrated ensemble playing, with minute attention to every detail of speech, gesture, action, tempo, mood, setting, atmosphere.

at a map of Africa on the wall, then suddenly remarks that it must be awfully hot in Africa now. The trivial, irrelevant thought breaking in on misery is psychologically true, it may convey a more poignant impression of the misery, and here it has a further implication: in setting his stage Chekhov noted that this map was obviously of no use to anybody. In *The Three Sisters* one of the three is sobbing in despair over her wasted life: "Where has it all gone to? Where is it? Oh God! I've forgotten. . . . I've forgotten everything. . . . There's nothing but a muddle in my head. . . . I don't remember what the Italian for 'window' is, or for 'ceiling'. . . ." Again the incongruous detail is true, poignant, and significant; for among her accomplishments is a knowledge of several languages, which in this provincial town she has no use for whatever. Elsewhere in the play a character tells an anecdote about a cabinet minister who was sent to prison, where he saw with delight the birds he had never noticed before, but upon his release never noticed them again. Chekhov's peculiar genius for detail may be exemplified by these birds: the "little" things that go unnoticed in ordinary realism, but may touch off thought and feeling about very large matters—the nature of man, of his society, of his relation to the cosmos.

By such detail Chekhov expands the scene of his drama, which nominally is confined to middle-class homes in the provinces. He gains poetic suggestiveness by some obvious means, such as garden scenes at twilight and guitars to provide a musical background, and also amplifies the drama by staging most of his action on ceremonial occasions, gatherings at anniversaries or for arrivals and departures—especially departures. His seemingly plotless actions contribute more subtly; by their form they deepen the sense of the fluidity of life, the endless coming, mingling, and going, the final inconclusiveness. The "recognition" in his dramas is not a surprising discovery, as in Ibsen and the Greeks—it is a realization that "the thing that hath been is that which shall be." But Chekhov constantly gives vistas of a wider scene through the aspirations of his characters. Almost all yearn for a richer life, in a greater world; all want to go to Moscow. While engrossed in apparent trivialities, all are given to philosophizing, and live imaginatively in a loftier realm of the spirit.

Hence they have dignity in spite of their futility. There is not a great soul among them; none is capable of heroic action, none can speak with firmness or authority. Dr. Astroff speaks for most of them when he says: "I am old, I am tired, I am trivial; my sensibilities are dead." Yet he could not say this if he were in fact trivial. Like him, the others suffer because their sensibilities are far from dead. They feel finely and deeply, if not greatly. Thus the three sisters suffer acutely from the vulgarity, callousness, and thoughtless cruelty that merely upset most people. They would not actually be happy in Moscow either. And a complacent bourgeois who now and then strays in among Chekhov's people, to accentuate their failure, serves as well to raise a question: what is success in life? Chekhov leaves it a question. "To divide men into the successful and the unsuccessful," he wrote, "is to look at human nature from a narrow, provincial point of view. . . . One must be a god to be able to tell successes from failures without making a mistake."

Once more I am led back to an old-fashioned approach. The ultimate secret of Chekhov's magic is not the subtlety of his artistry. It is the breadth of his vision, the strength of his spirit, the wholesomeness and sweetness—the wonderful, rare quality of his humanity. If this could be dramatically realized only by a suitable technique, it is the beginning and end of his art, it is what chiefly distinguishes him from the many fine artists in modern literature, and it is commonly neglected in the formal analysis of modern criticism. It also points to a neglected consideration in the complaints about modern tragedy and the disappearance of the tragic hero. The "great soul" in the drama of Chekhov is the soul of its author. Its presence is always felt even though he is scrupulously impersonal and has no spokesman. It gives his drama—at least for those temperamentally or philosophically attuned—a radiance that may do for splendor, or even touch sublimity.

A writer, Chekhov said, "must be humane to the tips of his fingers." This is not actually a requisite, else we would have to dismiss many great writers, from Milton and Racine to Joyce and Eliot; but in this spirit he always wrote. No great writer has manifested more reverence for life, in the feeling that it is the only life we can ever know or even imagine on earth. Dostoyevsky and Tolstoy were wont to preach that all men are brothers and we must love one another. Chekhov never preached; but he wrote with more love and charity than they.

In his humanity he was also more keenly aware at once of the ludicrous and the tragic aspects of man's folly and futility. Humor runs all through his serious drama. It is only slightly more pronounced in *The Cherry Orchard*, which he labeled a comedy, and which might be called the quintessence of tragicomedy. Behind the humor is a pervasive irony that never allows us to forget how ineffectual his people are, how absurdly wide the gulf between their aspiration and their performance. Hence he never falls into bathos, despite all the tearfulness that makes his plays perhaps the dampest ever written, and the easiest to parody. His characters can be as sentimental as they please because his own sentiment was a perfect blend of wonder, compassion, humor, and ironic reserve. This may not be the ideal blend for tragedy; one might wish for an admixture of some stronger emotion, such as anguish, indignation, or fear. But it helps to define the rare quality of Chekhov.

It also explains why the upshot of his tragic drama is not sheer futility or despair. Although he often declared his belief that nature is completely indifferent to man, he revered life too much to be simply pessimistic; pessimism and optimism may alike be arrogant and do an injustice to life. He pointed to a comforting aspect of nature's indifference to man, in that the individual will be forgotten—and forgiven. "And everything is forgiven," he wrote characteristically, "and it would be strange not to forgive." At worst, the final impression left by his tragedies has been finely stated by William Gerhardi:

> It is a sense of temporary possession in a temporary existence that, in the face of the unknown, we dare not undervalue. It is as if his people hastened to express their worthless individualities, since that is all they have, and were aghast that they should have so little in them to express: since the expression of it is all there is. And life is at once too long and too short to be endured.

But their individualities are not actually worthless—and they might be much more valuable. In every play one or more of the main characters voices a recurrent theme of hope. We must work, work; life is hopeless now, but in the future all men and women will work; they will know a happiness that our generation can't—and *mustn't*, for their sake. Such passages always have ironic undertones. ("Forward!" cries the "perpetual student" in *The Cherry Orchard*, who has been unable to graduate from his university.) Still, they reflect Chekhov's own hope, and meanwhile his humanistic faith. One implication of his insistent theme of frustration and waste is that life can be so much richer than it was for his futile generation, in a backward land.

Chekhov summed up his living faith in a letter: "My holy of holies is the human body, health, intelligence, talent, inspiration, love, and absolute freedom—freedom from violence and falsehood, no matter how the last two manifest themselves." He had no faith, however, in a divine order sustaining these human values. His tragic drama also exemplifies his repeated remark that there is no understanding the human condition. And so it does not satisfy many critics. Francis Fergusson again presses the final issue. After a characteristically sensitive analysis of Chekhov's art, and tribute to his "extraordinary feat" of revealing so much while predicating nothing, Fergusson ends by stressing the limitations of his drama. "We miss, in Chekhov's scene, any fixed points of human significance." He is aware of history and moral effort, but like Ibsen, and unlike Dante, he does not know what to make of them. Although he is a more perfect master than Ibsen of the "little scene" of modern realism, he as "drastically reduced the dramatic art."

It is unquestionable that Chekhov had nothing like Dante's assurance about the meaning of history and the moral order, and that many men miss this assurance. Yet the fixed points in Dante's scene are not actually fixed. Taken literally—as he and his age took them—his notions about history may seem as grotesque as his geography and astronomy; many men are also repelled by his moral order, in particular its fantastically disproportionate punishments; and his whole theater, which for his age was vital, complete, and essentially true, has for most men become antiquated, limited, essentially unreal. It is now an impossible theater for tragic drama conceived in Dante's own realistic spirit. The question, again, is whether on the conditions of modern knowledge and experience men can still come to satisfactory terms with life. And though Chekhov's terms manifestly cannot satisfy those who require fixities or religious certainty, they are at least honorable terms, they include Christian ethical values (notably more charity than Dante displayed), and they represent a positive acceptance. They foster a reverence for life, and for all possibilities of a richer, more humane life. They made possible the development of Chekhov's incomparably fine art. Unlike many modern writers, he was not a tormented spirit in search of a faith, a total solution. Unlike most of the major modern dramatists, he was not a restless experimenter, seeking new forms, turning from realism to symbolism, expressionism, or dream plays. He traveled a straight path, steadily, surely perfecting his form of realism.

To me this development looks more like an enrichment than a drastic reduction of the dramatic art. Admittedly Chekhov's tragedy is never high tragedy, nor is it a "complete action" in

Aristotle's sense, or Fergusson's. But in some important respects it is a more complete picture of life, a fuller "recognition" of tragic possibility, than we find in any ancient tragedy except Shakespeare's. Chekhov's "little scene" is the earth of Everyman. His drama is realistic tragedy in the widest, most universal sense: tragedy short of catastrophe and death, since catastrophe is not the normal lot and dying not the most painful experience; tragedy as all men know it and feel it, not merely an Œdipus or a Hamlet. It may make one aware of how much is excluded from the "complete actions" of the Greeks.

Among the more truly universal themes of Chekhov is the tragedy of attrition, the gradual frustration, the growing weariness, the final hopelessness. It begins as the old story of seeking and not finding; it ends as the worse story of no longer seeking. "What shall I do with my life and my love?" cries Uncle Vanya; and like millions of others he can find no satisfying answer. With the hopes unrealized comes the sense of waste, of opportunities lost—the sense of what "might have been," which no writer has rendered more poignantly than Chekhov. A related theme is the farewell, forever. In every play his people are saying good-by, not *au revoir*, to friends, to lovers, to family, to the homestead, as well as to the dreams of their youth. They accordingly have an acute sense of the transitoriness of life, and the ultimate oblivion. That the individual is forgotten is not just a comforting thought; it is a high price to pay for nature's forgiveness. Still another related theme is the inescapable loneliness of the individual. Chekhov's people seem lonelier because of the ensemble, even because of the sympathy of the other sensitive people about them. "We shall rest!" Sonya tells Uncle Vanya in the beautiful passage that concludes the play. "I have faith, I have faith." But Uncle Vanya is crying, he has no faith, there is no rest for him; and she can only repeat through her own tears: "We shall rest!"

For all these reasons Chekov's people voice the everlasting

question that torments even the faithful. Why must men suffer? Why are things so? At the end of *The Three Sisters*, as a band plays offstage to mark the departure of their military friends and the three sisters stand huddled together, the oldest summarizes the main themes that run through all Chekhov's dramas:

> How cheerfully and jauntily that band's playing—really I feel as if I wanted to live! Merciful God! The years will pass, and we shall all be gone for good and quite forgotten. . . . Our faces and our voices will be forgotten and people won't even know that there were once three of us here. . . . But our sufferings may mean happiness for the people who come after us. . . . There'll be a time when peace and happiness reign in the world, and then we shall be remembered kindly and blessed. No, my dear sisters, life isn't finished for us yet! We're going to live! The band is playing so cheerfully and joyfully—maybe, if we wait a little longer, we shall find out why we live, why we suffer. . . . Oh, if we only knew, if only we knew!

The music grows fainter; a drunken old boarder sings to himself: "Tarara-boom-de-ay. I'm sitting on a tomb-di-ay. . . . What does it matter? Nothing matters!" As the curtain falls, she repeats: "If only we knew, if only we knew!"

To some this conclusion is mere pathos. Certainly it is in a minor key, and indicates a measure of real reduction in Chekhov's tragic drama. His art could not encompass tempestuous experience, the passion of an Œdipus, a King Lear, a Phædra. No one would rank him among the giants of literature. He dwindles when set beside his own great countrymen. The tumultuous drama of Dostoyevsky in particular may make Chekhov appear a dabbler in emotion, a peddler of wan, wistful sentiment. Yet the nightmarish world of Dostoyevsky may also deepen our appreciation of the humanity and the truth of Chekhov. If not so profound as Dostoyevsky, he was saner as well as gentler. Despite his irreligion, he had a much more Christian spirit. Through the ages men have prayed to their gods for the compassion that he showed his creatures, though he had no illusions about their frailties.

Today his countrymen have partially realized the hope so often expressed by his characters: they are now all at work. If the rest of us are not too happy about their work, there is perhaps some reason for hope in the knowledge that they still cherish the works of Chekhov, even though he was patently not a good Marxist. One may wonder whether Stalin ever thought of him at Yalta; for Chekhov spent his last years at Yalta, where as a dying man he wrote his "comedy" *The Cherry Orchard*.

6. POETIC DRAMA: T. S. ELIOT

While a realistic impulse remains basic in modern literature and there is little sign of a flight to romance, dissatisfaction with the means and ends of conventional realism has led to widespread experimentation in drama. Some of the new forms came with shiny new labels, such as "Expressionism"; others are still nameless, except as modes of "symbolism"; but all might be gathered under Jacques Copeau's phrase, as an effort to create a modern "poetry of the theater." The effort has enlisted a great deal of ardor, talent, and technical ingenuity. Nevertheless—or therefore—the results have seldom been satisfying. The playwright's imagination is concentrated on the creation of his new form, or manipulation of his new technique; action and character are likely to be deficient in blood and bone, have little but a symbolical existence. Tragedy in particular is likely to suffer from the premium on originality and virtuosity.[5] Generally the new poetry of the theater has been most effective when the realistic impulse has remained strong,

[5] An example is Cocteau's highly praised *The Infernal Machine*, a modern version of *Œdipus Rex*. In this ultra-stylized drama a sophisticated Œdipus is suddenly transformed in the last act; we are told that he returns to the timeless myth, becomes "man," henceforth belongs "to the people, to the poets, to the pure in heart"; but in effect this Œdipus still belongs to the man on the Parisian boulevard.

as in the drama of Pirandello, or when the playwright has been able to draw on a living folk poetry, as were Synge and Lorca.

For my limited purposes, the most provocative effort has been that to restore a literally poetic drama, and with it a modern equivalent of the mythical, ritual patterns underlying Greek tragedy. This has been dignified by the theory and practice of T. S. Eliot, the greatest living poet in English. Yeats, who had a flair for the theater, was distracted by his inclination to mysticism and magic; he developed a drama of virtually pure myth and ritual, without plot or character, or realistic substance. Eliot, lacking his flair, has kept an eye on the practical requirements of the theater. "The ideal medium for poetry, to my mind," he wrote long ago, "and the most direct means of social 'usefulness' for poetry, is the theater." He has never been so fearful of moral or social usefulness as some of the critics he has inspired, he has freely confessed a desire to address a wider public, and he has succeeded in doing so, by honorable concessions.

Now the revulsion against the common notion that prose is the only really natural medium for drama has led to considerable exaggeration of its deficiencies. The greater modern realists have made imaginative use of language—more so than did Corneille, for example. Ibsen's dialogue is rich enough in double meaning and intricate cross-reference to reward a close rereading of his plays. Strindberg rightly boasted that the seemingly haphazard, fragmentary dialogue in *Miss Julia* "acquires a material that later on is worked over, picked up again, repeated, expounded, and built up like the themes in a musical composition." Chekhov could have said as much for his dramatic style, while he also permitted his characters to express themselves more or less eloquently in monologues. Yet poetry has manifest advantages, especially for tragedy. It permits a dramatist to make much freer, fuller use of all the resources of language, to illumine, intensify, enrich, and magnify his meanings. At the great moments it enables a lift and soar that would seem pretentious in realistic prose drama. Whatever we think of Eliot's plays as a whole, we must be grateful for many passages in them.

In his first major dramatic effort, *Murder in the Cathedral*, our indebtedness is primarily for the religious poetry and pageantry, not the drama. It has the ritual form of Greek tragedy, including a Chorus of Women of Canterbury voicing something like a humble citizen ethic ("living and partly living"), and a "pathos" and "epiphany" in which Thomas à Becket plays out his martyr's role of ritual scapegoat; but it has little conflict or character, and as little tragic effect. Thomas is presented with the temptations of worldly pleasure, power, and prestige, which he at once rejects. He suffers real anguish only briefly, when he is shown the worst temptation: in embracing martyrdom he might be succumbing to pride, seeking "spiritual power," doing the right thing for the wrong reason. After a choral interlude, however, he announces that he knows the right reason for martyrdom, which he has found by himself without the aid of the other characters; we are not shown the change taking place in him. Thereafter he preaches a sermon on the Christian mysteries and goes serenely to his death. Although the last half of the play is exciting as music and spectacle, it excites little pity or terror. Thomas is not a humanly tragic figure—we always know that he is headed for sainthood. The other characters, including the Chorus of Women, are all symbolic or abstract, not real persons in a real world. The most lifelike are the worldly Knights who murder Thomas, and at the end step forward to present their case to the audience—an ingenious conclusion, though possibly jarring in its sophistication.

Fergusson complains that the play rests upon no direct perception, natural faith, or analogies in common experience, but upon a theological concept that is beyond reason. Thomas even spurns the idea that his decision need be intelligible in terms of common experience:

Those who do not the same,
How should they know what I do?

This arbitrariness might be excused because Eliot wrote the play for a special occasion, the Canterbury Festival, and counted on a more or less devout, informed audience; but the question remains how meaningful his play would be for a general audience. Nor is its subsequent popularity in commercial and little theaters a sufficient answer. One may doubt that many in the audience deeply experienced either catharsis or religious exaltation; most obviously they responded to the pageantry. At any rate, Eliot himself has tacitly acknowledged the validity of such complaints. While he remarked in his early "Dialogue on Dramatic Poetry" that the Mass is the perfect drama, he also warned that "religion is no more a substitute for drama than drama is for religion." In his subsequent plays he accordingly treated religious themes in more realistic terms, presenting a veiled Christian drama for a secular audience—a "subversive" drama, as it were, for an audience of Tempters and Knights.

In *Family Reunion* Eliot attempted a synthesis of Greek, Christian, and modern elements. Harry, the hero, is hounded by a guilty conscience, owing to a childhood made unhappy by alienated parents. His resemblance to Orestes is emphasized by the appearance of mysterious Eumenides; other reminders of Greek tragedy include a Chorus, representing his worldly family. The basic theme of the play is Christian: the quest for salvation, through sin and expiation. Eliot is careful not to mention God, so as not to upset his secular audience, but he freights the drama with Christian terminology—sin (not crime), redemption, election, "two worlds," "The crossed be uncrossed," etc. Harry solves his problem in the way of the saint, by renouncing the world and taking upon himself the sins of the family. Nevertheless the play is essentially a realistic study of modern life. Most of the members of the family are conventionally proper or improper, affording an opportunity for satire and even some comedy. When they line up as a Chorus, their typical attitude is bourgeois: "Hold tight, hold tight, we must insist that the world is what we have always taken it to be." At their worst, they symbolize the sickness of the modern world, "a world of insanity." And Eliot takes particular pains to motivate his hero's behavior in terms of modern psychology. Harry is the product of his unfortunate upbringing; the development of the action is his gradual realization of the meaning of his past, upon which his future must be built. Eliot is true to both Freud and his God when he has Harry exclaim that "the things that are going to happen have already happened."

The result is a haunting play, of some dramatic as well as poetic distinction. It is not, however, a successful synthesis—as Eliot himself pointed out, with disarming candor, in his lecture "Poetry and Drama." [6] One may be incidentally jarred by a neat satirical or comic passage, in a household visited by the Eumenides; or by the sudden coalition of the Chorus, a sudden lift from prose to poetic aria; or by the too sharp contrast between the prosaic members of the family and an ultra-perceptive, spiritual Aunt Agatha. But especially troublesome is the hero, who seems more ambiguous than Eliot intended. We get through Harry the "very important" idea that his psychological troubles started with the lack of healthy freedom in his childhood, when the main rule of conduct had been to please a mother who otherwise made him feel guilty. We might therefore conclude that he would have been a better man had he been brought up in the progressive

---

[6] He discovered, for example, that his Eumenides would not go on the modern stage. "We tried every possible manner of presenting them. We put them on the stage, and they looked like uninvited guests who had strayed in from a fancy-dress ball. We concealed them behind gauze, and they suggested a still out of a Walt Disney film. We made them dimmer, and they looked like shrubbery just outside the window. I have seen other expedients tried: I have seen them signalling from across the garden, or swarming onto the stage like a football team, and they are never right. They never succeed in being either Greek goddesses or modern spooks."

school of John Dewey, and as he matured, been warned against the Christian guilt complex; only we must doubt that this was Eliot's meaning. Harry still looks unhealthy in the process of his "conversion," which is most intelligible in Freudian terms. "You attach yourself to loathing as others do to loving," one of the more acute characters tells him; and though he eventually appears to overcome his loathing, he hardly manifests a spirit of love. This might be a deliberate irony, implying that Eliot had some doubt of his spiritual message; but again we are evidently expected to believe that Harry is being really purified, "elected" to go the loftiest Christian way. His election is not too convincing.

When Eliot later confessed that his hero now strikes him as an insufferable prig, he did not take up the questions that a secularist might raise about the Christian theme of the play. In acting the role of redeemer, Harry fails to restore order or virtue in the family. He declares that his leaving will be "the best thing for everybody," but it brings little apparent good to anybody. Indeed, the immediate consequence is the death of his mother. The "Christian Orestes," in other words, kills his mother at the end of the play instead of the beginning, and after instead of before his purification. The most tragic, moving scene in the play is the despair and death of the forsaken mother, "an old woman alone in a damned house." Another significant difference from the Greek legend was noted by Maud Bodkin, in her laudatory comparison of *Family Reunion* with *Eumenides*. The salvation attained in the tragedy of Æschylus is collective and historical; the purification of Orestes brings good to the entire community. The salvation in Eliot is individual and spiritual; Harry purifies himself by deserting the community. If, as Miss Bodkin believes, a major task of religion is the realization of brotherhood, the deepening and strengthening of the human community, the Greek tragedy may be considered the more religious. Eliot conspicuously lacks the "religious sense of the common life" that she exalts, and that Æschylus was devoted to.

Once more, however, he went on to meet his critics halfway. In *The Cocktail Party* he not only wrote a consistently modern play, dropping the Chorus and the Greek ghosts, but tried to do justice to the common life—making the concessions to ordinary humanity, one might say, that the Church in her wisdom has always made. While he introduced another saint-like martyr who turns her back on "a world of lunacy, violence, stupidity, greed," his spokesman declares that in such a world a decent routine life is good enough. The play is designed to show that both these ways are necessary. Although it is not tragic, beginning and ending as sophisticated comedy, it is relevant for Eliot's new comment on the human condition.

This is concentrated in the second act. In Act I, at a high-comedy cocktail party, there appears among the worldlings a mysterious, rollicking Unidentified Guest, known only as One-Eyed Reilly. In Act II Reilly suddenly appears as his true self, a spiritual psychiatrist or father-confessor. ("In the kingdom of the blind the one-eyed man is king.") He is assisted by two of the guests, who as suddenly drop their worldly airs to form with him a little trinity. First he reconciles an estranged couple, the hosts of the party, by getting them to tone down their demands on one another:

> The best of a bad job is all any of us make of it—
> Except, of course, the saints. . . .

Then he deals with Celia, who has a strange sense of solitude and sin. When she is left cold by his account of the normal way of compromise, he tells her of the second way, the unknown, terrifying way of faith, and sends her to his "sanatorium," evidently a nunnery. In Act III Reilly's good works are justified at another cocktail party, which rounds out the play. Husband and wife are now happy together, if in the manner of a Noel Coward couple. The news comes that Celia, as a missionary nun, has died a gruesome death, crucified by natives near an anthill; but Reilly is neither surprised nor upset. "That was her destiny"—and it was a triumphant one. He absolves the hosts, who feel that if Celia was right they must be terribly wrong. It is right that the party go on.

One may appreciate Eliot's effort at charity, as well as his wit, and still feel that he has not brought off this difficult effort to blend cocktails and crucifixions. The shift in tone between the almost farcical first act and the semi-mystical second act is too abrupt, and the attempted harmony in the third act still jangles. But it is again the religious theme that is least convincing to the uninitiated. Celia never comes to life. Eliot does not adequately motivate and dramatize her conversion, much less her martyrdom; it seems still more arbitrary than the conversion of Harry in *Family Reunion*. And the quality of Eliot's charity is strained. He does well by the sophistication of his worldlings, but not by the positive virtues of the normal way, the decencies of the common life that it took him so long to condescend to. His third act might have come off better had he something of the spirit of Chekhov.

In short, the main trouble is still the exclusiveness and arbitrariness of Eliot's faith: "How should they know what I do?" While he habitually lays claim to *the* Christian tradition, he is committed primarily to the letter, the theological dogma, the established Church, and the ascetic tradition, rather than to the gospel of Jesus. An avowed aristocrat, he is temperamentally all faith, with little hope and charity. Nowhere in his drama is there an eloquent representation of simple Christian feeling, of love or compassion, such as one finds in *The Green Pastures*—a play suggesting that a direct treatment of Christian myth is still possible. (Obey's *Noah* is another example.) At the same time, Eliot's apparent complexity is more verbal than philosophical. On the surface he is all tension, irony, ambiguity, paradox—the classical text for contemporary critical theory. Beneath this appearance is a confirmed dogmatism that allows him to commit himself to simple formulas ("classicist in literature, royalist in politics, Anglo-Catholic in religion"), and to be as cool and untroubled in contradicting as in reaffirming himself. His irony is essentially an unambiguous attitude, playing easily upon the simple theme that the modern world is a wasteland, but seldom turning in on itself, raising any really disconcerting question about his own faith, revealing any really tragic sense of modern life. His drama lacks the profound tension that one feels in Donne, Pascal, Dostoyevsky, and Unamuno, and that one might expect to find in a modern religious poet. A Christian poet today might write great tragedy, by my humanistic standards. I doubt that Eliot can.

All this, however, is to judge him by high standards—his own standards. His drama has exceptional interest, as the effort of a distinguished poet who is still finding his way in the theater; his partial failures are more stimulating and potentially fruitful than the successes of most playwrights. And his popular success is encouraging, even though one must discount it as due in part to his pre-established reputation. Many in the audience have no doubt been disposed to attribute their bafflement to his profundity, while reviewers have been more lavish with their customary epithets ("an authentic masterpiece," "a major event in the theater") because they have no secure standards by which to judge his novel form. Eliot has been aided, too, by the popular religious revival: with Toynbee and Niebuhr he has made the cover of *Time* magazine. None the less he has demonstrated both the artistic and the commercial possibilities of poetic drama. If his dramatic poetry is occasionally too esoteric or cryptic for the stage, he has developed it into an admirable medium, close to the living language, never echoing Shakespeare as the Romantic poets did. He has shown the necessary way for modern poetic drama: aiming "to bring poetry into the world in which the audience lives and to which it returns when it leaves the theater; not to transport the audience into some imaginary world totally unlike their own, an unreal world in which poetry can be spoken." He has also proved the contention in his "Dialogue on Dramatic Poetry," that "if you want a thing you can get it, and hang the economic factors."

7. EXISTENTIALIST TRAGEDY: SARTRE

Although existentialism has caused considerable excitement, which lately has spread to psychiatrists, it still looks like a passing fashion in thought. Basically, it is a desperate restatement of humanism, whose novel elements are the most dubious. Yet it is a significant fashion. Its desperation is an outgrowth of the appalling actualities of our time, in particular World War II. By the very fierceness of its concentration on the elemental facts of solitariness and mortality, it is often penetrating. It is at least a useful corrective to the liberal optimism that has glossed the painful realities of the human condition. If existentialism magnifies the worst, it never blinks the worst. And in Jean-Paul Sartre, its chief literary spokesman, it inspired a fairly impressive drama.

Kierkegaard, the spiritual father of existentialism, bequeathed the cardinal doctrine of the paradoxical self. The self is the ultimate reality; and this is a wholly subjective truth, immediately and passionately known, but undemonstrable by reason, and self-contradictory from beginning to end. The self is free, and its freedom is logically absurd. It must assume absolute responsibility, which is logically impossible. For Kierkegaard its whole duty was to seek and serve God, rejecting all worldly compromise—sacrificing everything to its self-sufficient Creator, who logically needs no such service.

For Sartre, the first duty of the self is to deny God.[7] The basic irrational fact is the utter meaninglessness of the universe in which man must give his own life meaning. Human values are supported by neither God nor nature, have no logical use. The self is free—and alone; it is everything—and nothing. In this

[7] I am not attempting to do justice to the whole thought of Kierkegaard, or to the different thought of other existentialists. While Sartre has tried to reconcile existentialism with Marxism, Heidegger managed to reconcile it with Nazism; Jaspers and Marcel have brought God back. These wide divergences, which make it harder to define or defend the essential truth of existentialism, are illustrated in the popular jibe about a student of Heidegger. "I am resolved," he declared solemnly, "—only I don't know to what."

void the individual not only must seek to realize himself, but must assume complete responsibility for what he makes of himself. For he is not a product of his environment, any more than he is a child of God. He cannot blame the environment, however obviously and senselessly it may limit his choices, since his choice is still his own. If gangsters come out of the slums, so do poets and policemen, reformers and go-getters. Hence the "dreadful freedom" of existentialism. Hence the effort of almost all men to evade the dreadful truth, deny their individual responsibility, blame fate or society for their failures.

Out of respect for the basic earnestness of Sartre, I would dispose at once of a deal of faddishness that has gone with the inevitable manifestoes. He likes to play the *enfant terrible*. He can be merely clever, and therefore foolish. He has claimed a historic alliance with not only Sophocles but Corneille, making the preposterous statement that Corneille "gives us back man in all his complexity, in his complete reality." Sartre's drama in fact resembles Corneille's chiefly in its rhetorical passion, an abstract, schematic quality that would seem to be the unpardonable sin in a religion of the self. It also has a virtuosity that may immediately create a powerful illusion of reality but finally leaves the impression of contrivance, makes it seem to some extent remote and unreal.

Essentially, however, Sartre's drama is in the realistic tradition. Some of his plays are strictly realistic in technique; others that take the form of fantasy are in no sense romantic. He has proudly asserted that he is restoring to the theater the whole truth about man. His not too simple conception of this truth is pretty well summed up in the sequence of three plays, *No Exit* (also translated as *Vicious Circle*), *The Flies*, and *The Victors* (translated literally, *The Unburied Dead*).

In *No Exit*, three strangers—two women and a man—come separately to a mysterious chamber that presently they discover is hell. By the end of the play they have discovered that their hellish fate is to live together for all time with their eyes open, stripped of the lying pretenses by which they had lived on earth. The two women, one a lesbian, had been rotten to the core; the man had been a deserter, for good reasons that he had justified without succeeding in getting rid of a guilty feeling that the real reason was cowardice. Now they must confront the whole ugly truth about what they had made themselves. The man has all eternity to fight out the question whether he really had been a coward, with the odds all against him. Drama is added by his struggle with the lesbian over the possession of the other woman, whom neither can hope really to possess since the other will always be present. He realizes that they must forever go "round and round in a vicious circle." He concludes: "Hell is—other people!"

It is a logical conclusion, given such specimens as these. But it also points to a logically unnecessary doctrine in Sartre. Wishing to preserve at all costs the uniqueness, integrity, and solitariness of the self, he has asserted that its basic responses upon encountering other selves are fear and shame. Conflict is the normal relation; love he has described as simply the wish to be loved, and bound to fail simply because two are two. In *No Exit* he demonstrated his thesis by creating characters among whom decent relations are impossible. Eric Bentley expressed the obvious complaint, that the play has "no tragic dignity, no tragic protagonist, no tragic anything." I find in it a measure of dignity. One of the women is at least honest and courageous, frankly admitting to her evil, proudly declaring: "I prefer to choose my hell." The man is honorable enough to be concerned over the issue of his cowardice, and brave enough to fight it out; he is a better man for his tragic perception, at least fit for hell. Still, none but a disciple of Sartre would call *No Exit* an inspiring play. Others may admire its devilish ingenuity, but add that this hell is by no means representative of the human scene.

In *The Flies*, however, Sartre dramatized his positive values. This is another tour de force, as an existentialist version of the Orestes legend, and like other modern French versions of the Greek tragedies (Cocteau's *The Infernal Machine*, Giraudoux's *Electra*, Anouilh's *Antigone*) it is talky and synthetic. It includes much cynical detail. The Furies are swarms of Flies; instead of a stately Chorus there are Old Women in Black, spitting, with such supernumeraries as an Idiot Boy; and the whole community, whose salvation was the concern of Æschylus, is made up of miserable cowed wretches who are beyond saving. But from this mean background Orestes emerges as the existentialist hero. Although an unorthodox type of tragic hero, he is in his way a grand and terrible one. The main action is his realization and acceptance of his fearful mission.

Zeus, the god of flies and death, has enslaved the entire citizenry except Electra through fear and remorse. He announces that he delights in the torment of guilty consciences; he confesses that he loves nobody, and himself committed the first crime by making man mortal. He also confesses to a secret torment of his own—the bitter knowledge that men are free: "Once freedom lights its beacon in a man's heart, the gods are powerless against him." Orestes wins his way to this knowledge. "From now on," he declares, "I'll take no one's orders, neither man's nor god's. . . . I say there is another path—*my* path." He will take this even though he must say farewell to all happiness. It is wholly his own deed when he kills Ægisthus and his mother, who dies cursing him. And thereupon he begins to pay the whole awful cost. The citizens, whom he was trying to restore to a sense of human dignity, turn on him savagely—thirsty for the blood of the scapegoat. Electra, at first drunk with joy at their revenge, succumbs to remorse and turns on him in hatred. Orestes is utterly alone. Zeus tries to frighten him into penitence, pointing out logically that "the universe refutes you, you are a mite in the scheme of things." Still Orestes refuses to repent or to be refuted. Again he asserts that man must find his own way, just because nature and the gods abhor him. "Human life begins on the far side of despair." As the play ends, Orestes strides into the light, into a new life, "a strange life," with the Furies shrieking and flinging themselves on him.

This drama would seem tragic enough. Even the loveless Zeus expresses some pity for Orestes; and we mites know that there have been such lonely exiles, know in ourselves the feeling of insignificance in the cosmic scheme of things. Yet it is indeed a "strange life" that Sartre creates in *The Flies*. It is never clear enough, in either dramatic or philosophical terms, why Orestes *must* assume so terrible a burden. Earlier he had declared his human need of belonging to a place and having comrades, and his tutor, a smiling skeptic, had introduced him to a decent place. The people of Corinth lived a joyous Epicurean life, free from fear and remorse. Admittedly this is not a heroic life, but it reminds us that there are many tolerable ways this side of despair, and that the horribly guilt-ridden community of Argos is no more representative than the trio in *No Exit*. Given such a community, it is still less clear why Orestes must murder his mother and Ægisthus, who because of their remorse are already as dead as his murdered father. The only consequence of his deed is the breakdown of Electra. Though Orestes expresses some pity for her, he refuses to lament this consequence, on the grounds that her suffering is self-inflicted. Sartre reveals a kind of terror *of* pity.

More clearly he reveals the fundamental distortions of existentialism. Many will agree that the universe is indifferent to man and his values; but it does not follow, as Orestes asserts, that nature abhors man and is positively hostile to his values. Nature is bountiful as well as amoral; it provides the conditions under which man has realized his values. In a naturalistic view, these values are the product of an evolutionary process that has culminated in the conscious life of man. Most of them have an evident biological value, springing from his requirements as a social animal and enabling him to achieve more control over his environment.[8] The whole process re-

---

[8] Biologists point out that death itself has a biological value. It is apparently not inherent in the properties of protoplasm, but developed

mains mysterious, and the human spirit unique and ultimately inexplicable; but it is surely possible for man to feel at home in the natural world that produced him.

Nor is his freedom so dreadful. It is made dreadful by Sartre's conception of the separate, solitary self that bristles at the intrusion of others. This existentialist self is a pure abstraction. The conscious self—above all, the ideal self as conceived by Sartre—is a social product. It becomes self-conscious only through its relations with other selves, it can realize itself only in a community, it can achieve a high degree of individuality and freedom only in a civilized community. Its oneness is also a many-ness. If it is naturally self-centered, its interests as naturally include the interests of some others; only a freak is wholly indifferent to others, or feels merely shame or fear at their approach. Such values as sympathy, loyalty, kindness, and love are rooted in social life, or in biological terms, the co-operative behavior that extends down into the animal world. Universal brotherhood may be an impossible ideal; a measure of human solidarity is a fact, and a crucial one. Sartre's implicit denial of solidarity might be called the absolute crime against our humanity.

But for the same reasons he cannot freely commit this crime. Existentialists always have to struggle with the problem of getting their separate selves into some kind of satisfactory relation, logical and moral. Sartre in particular had to reconcile his doctrine with his active Marxist sympathies, which led him to proclaim that the theater ought to be "a great collective, religious phenomenon." One of his arguments is that the revolutionary act is the free act par excellence. Another is that the self must identify itself with all the oppressed and try to destroy the oppressors in order to create a free society. Still,

---

in the course of evolution; it enormously facilitates the process of natural selection, which could hardly continue if all living creatures lived indefinitely. I do not advance this as a thought to comfort one on his deathbed. I mention it only because of the inverted religious idea expressed in *The Flies*: that death was the first and dirtiest trick played on man by the gods.

Sartre keeps squirming because his artificial definition of the self provides no firm ground for supra-personal obligations. In a communistic society the supremely free act would be the counter-revolutionary act; in a free society it might well be the Nazi act, out of contempt for the fear-ridden masses who persecute an Orestes. Meanwhile "collective" and "religious" are hardly the words for the theater of *No Exit* and *The Flies*.

Sartre's inconsistency becomes more understandable, however, when we consider the conditions of life in the French Underground, which was the matrix of his existentialism. In his essay "The Republic of Silence" he gives an eloquent account of these conditions. "At every instant we lived up to the full sense of this commonplace little phrase: 'Man is mortal!'" The fighters in the Underground had made their choice in the knowledge that capture meant not only death but torture. Each had to face the ultimate dread: under torture, would he be able to keep silent? They were united in an equality of solitude, risk, and dread:

> And this is why the Resistance was a true democracy: for the soldier as for the commander, the same danger, the same forsakenness, the same total responsibility, the same absolute liberty within discipline. Thus, in darkness and in blood, a Republic was established, the strongest of Republics. Each of its citizens knew that he owed himself to all and that he could count only on himself alone. Each of them, in complete isolation, fulfilled his responsibility and his role in history. Each of them, standing against the oppressors, undertook to be himself, freely and irrevocably. And by choosing for himself in liberty, he chose the liberty of all.

Hence the cardinal principle of existentialism: "Total responsibility in total solitude—is not this the very definition of our liberty?" The answer is No; but at least Sartre has earned his belief. And in *The Victors*, the most powerful and realistic of his plays, he dramatized the experience by which he earned it.

The protagonists are a group of Underground fighters who have been captured by the Vichy French—their fellow countrymen—and face the ordeal of torture, to make them reveal the hiding-place of their escaped leader. Their main concern is that a man can never know in advance how much he can endure. As one of them remarks, "It's not fair that a single minute should be enough to ruin a whole life." To make matters worse, they had botched their assignment, which was an idiotic one anyway; the village they had been ordered to attack could not possibly have been taken. Their deaths will serve no one. The most hopeful of them says: "With a bit of luck I can maybe tell myself that I'm not going to die for nothing." Although they manage not to break down, the further complications of the drama tend to destroy this hope, or any chance for easy heroics. Among other things, a youngster goes mad with fear as his turn for torture approaches; so one of them strangles him, with the consent of his sister. The outcome is sheer futility. In the hope of obtaining their release, one pretends to give in, directing their captors to a corpse they will mistake for that of the escaped leader. The torturers rejoice in the illusion of their success, but know that they will have to live with this ugly memory. An underling with a trigger-itch orders all the prisoners to be shot anyway. Everybody loses.

It is an almost unbearable play. For many, the scenes of physical torture are too painful, the final effect is chiefly horror. Yet there can be no question that these protagonists do have tragic dignity. Immediately, their suffering and death serve no purpose whatever—any more than did the death of almost any one of the millions who were slain in the war. The example of their heroism, however, does have meaning and force, as it did in the historic Underground. For the spectator, their idealism is not futile, even if he does not know that their cause finally triumphed. It is more stirring because they have no illusion that any immediate good will come of their sacrifice. In this play Sartre displays the lofty possibilities of the

human spirit that in *No Exit* he ignored, and in *The Flies* confined to the not too convincing figure of Orestes, and that may
justify his pitiless insistence on human freedom and responsibility.

It is therefore regrettable that in spite of the overpowering
realism, *The Victors* has the air of unreality that clings to all
Sartre's drama. Its passions still have an abstract, rhetorical
quality. After the strangling of the fear-crazed youngster, for
example, the survivors worry and argue over whether the deed
was done in pride, to save themselves for a heroic death; the
man who did it finally decides that it *was* out of pride, and
that he cannot live with this thought. They are here acting
like good hundred-per-cent existentialists, but not like human
beings in the shadow of further torture and death. There are
too few reminders of the ordinary, human, civilian behavior
that one might expect in such a crisis, if only in the form of
the irrelevancies that a Chekhov would introduce. Although
based on literal truth, the drama brings up the philosophically
melodramatic aspect of Sartre's work. He is concerned with
real terrors and horrors—but he makes the worst the essence
of the matter. A strategy for dealing with terror becomes a
whole philosophy of life; the values of the Underground become the norm of the good life, or the only possible life. In his
recent work Sartre seems to be growing more theatrical instead
of more sober.

But in spite of his fear of pity, one might venture a last word
of sympathy. The dread at the heart of existentialism sprang
from dreadful experience that may still seem too remote to
most of us. It is a full sense of tragic realities that are slighted
in more wholesome philosophies: the hopeless predicament,
the intolerable pain, the ultimate solitariness, or simply the
commonplace that man is mortal. What, one might ask, did
John Dewey have to say about death? Who even of his admirers would turn to Dewey in an incurable illness, or on his
deathbed? And short of dread, we might shudder at the conclusion of "The Republic of Silence," written at the conclusion

of the war. "No one failed in his duty," Sartre wrote, "and now we are on the threshold of another Republic. May this Republic about to be set up in broad daylight preserve the austere virtues of that other Republic of Silence and of Night." The outcome in post-war France might dispose us to pardon his excesses. So even might the state of our own Republic of Noise and Neon.

8. TRAGEDY IN AMERICA: O'NEILL

In an interview Eugene O'Neill said: "I'm going on the theory that the United States, instead of being the most successful country in the world, is the greatest failure . . . because it was given everything more than any other country." The occasion was the stir over *The Iceman Cometh*, which was to prove his last major production. Today it is a melancholy experience to reread this legacy of the writer who, by common consent, brought the American stage to maturity and remains its leading playwright.

Any writer "trying to do big work nowadays," he had written, must have behind his immediate subjects this big one: "the death of an old God and the failure of science and materialism to give any satisfying new one for the surviving primitive religious instinct to find a meaning for life in, and to comfort its fears of death with." In *The Iceman Cometh* he was still trying to do "big work," but he had apparently concluded that there was no satisfying faith for modern man; his characters are all failures who can live only on drunken pipe dreams. The play may be more depressing as a work of art. Although it is often effective, especially in its homely, comic realism, as a whole it is painfully long-winded, repetitious, over-explicit, pretentious, and muddled in intention. It emphasizes the tragic aspect of O'Neill's entire career. He was always trying too hard to do big work, and always falling short, sometimes falling on his face. Unlike many American writers, he was not content to repeat a successful formula, constantly experimenting, seeking, trying to grow; but like most, he did not grow very much and never became really mature. The epitaph of the leading American playwright might be: God help him, he meant well.

O'Neill's contemporaries helped him little, in spite of their good will. He was naturally overrated in the excitement over the coming of age of American drama. When his big intentions were not taken at their face value, they were considered more important than his performance. Today, as naturally, he is underrated; hardly a reputable critic would spring to his defense. (Eric Bentley soon gave up in an essay on "Trying to Like O'Neill.") First performed only a decade ago, *The Iceman Cometh* already seems to come from a distant past. And most melancholy is an aspect of the American literary scene suggested by the fate of O'Neill. We tend to forget very quickly the bold, exciting work of the day before yesterday, and to be profoundly ungrateful to the pioneers who made possible our critical sophistication. Our higher critical circles are particularly supercilious toward the literary gods of the twenties and early thirties—such writers as O'Neill, Dreiser, Sandburg, Sinclair Lewis, Sherwood Anderson, and Thomas Wolfe—who contributed to the "second American renaissance." The enthusiasm over this renaissance may now seem naïve; yet it was generous, heartening, and fruitful. We might feel wistful as we listen to the tone of literary discourse today, which is so often irritable or despairing when not fastidiously cool. At least we might be humbler, in the awareness that we may look as foolish to the next generation, and even the new criticism become old-hat.

Without arguing for a moment that O'Neill belongs in the company of Ibsen and Chekhov, I therefore propose to treat him respectfully. He is of some historical importance as a pioneer. His earnest intentions count for something, when we continue to hear that the tragic spirit itself is dead. His better performances are by no means negligible, except to those who would stoop to nothing but the time-tested works worthy of preservation in the great tradition—which has preserved such dismal performances as the plays of Seneca. His best work is good enough to make one unhappy that it is not still better. It has the potentialities of great tragedy: potentialities that neither he nor any other American playwright has succeeded in realizing, and that may not be realized in this generation, but that must be considered before one generalizes about the nature or the future of modern tragedy.

To get done at once with the obvious faults of O'Neill, he was never a master of the light touch. He was handier with the trowel, the bucket, the sledge hammer. He overdid everything, especially when he was trying to be subtle, suggestive, or symbolical. He was weakest when he tried to deal directly with the big subject, as in *Dynamo*. He thought out loud in capital letters, about Man and Life, the Mystery of it all, the Force behind it all. Although he rightly protested against the photographic realism that gives us only "the banality of surfaces," his efforts to be profound, to get at the essential, universal, and permanent, too often led him away from reality, "the living drama of recognizable human beings" that was avowedly his main concern, and that he had a natural talent for rendering. His less ambitious plays, such as *The Emperor Jones* and *The Hairy Ape*, illustrate the kind of poetry of the theater he was capable of: a theater not confined to the banality of contemporary surfaces but contemporary in its idiom, realistic in its particularity. When he sought to be literally poetic he inflated his style so much that his return to reality is likely to seem a ludicrous collapse.

Of O'Neill's "big" plays, the most successful is the most consistently realistic—the trilogy *Mourning Becomes Electra*. In retelling the Greek legend, O'Neill differed from both modern and classical French practice by giving it a realistic setting, in New England at the time of the Civil War. "A hell of a problem," he noted in his Work Diary, "a modern tragic interpretation of classic fate without benefit of gods." The main problem, of motivation, he solved by turning the legend into a psychological drama. He made his Electra (Lavinia) a rival of her mother for the love of her father, her brother, and even Ægisthus (Adam)—and in every case a loser; he endowed his Orestes (Orin) with not only an Œdipus complex but an incestuous love of Electra. In these terms there could logically be no happy ending as in Æschylus and Sophocles. Orestes is destroyed by remorse. Electra is left alone with her Puritan conscience, her hopes all flat. She shuts herself up in the New England mansion with its Greek-temple front—"a grotesque perversion," O'Neill noted, of everything the Greek temple signified.

His whole drama may appear to be a similar perversion of the *Oresteia*. It illustrates both the hazards of realism and the limitations of O'Neill. The colloquial dialogue is sometimes limp ("Honest, Vinnie," and "It's so darned good to be home," and "You mean little" so-and-so). The psychology is labored and sometimes crude; Orin-Orestes in particular suffers from a secondhand Freudianism learned by rote, the half-baked idea that sex is behind everything and repression the root of all evil. Krutch defended O'Neill's psychological interpretation of the legend as the only interpretation that would make it convincing to a modern audience, but realism did not require him to reduce the basic motives to sex, or to drag in the gratuitous incest theme. In any case O'Neill's interpretation tends to defeat his tragic intentions. Orin-Orestes is too neurotic and sickly to stir terror or awe about the tragic fate of man. The whole drama has the lurid air of a case history.

Nevertheless it approaches a grandeur that is not grandiosity. Structurally the firmest of O'Neill's big plays, it has both magnitude and momentum, with a driving rhythm to which even the monotonous prose contributes. In spite of the dubious psychology, it builds up an Æschylean sense of tragic fatality. Except for Orin, the characters are at once lifelike and bigger than life, "good" in something like Aristotle's sense. Lavinia finally grows to heroic stature. O'Neill pointed out that none of the Greek poets had done complete justice to the tragic fate within Electra; Æschylus had simply dropped her, Sophocles left her triumphant, Euripides finished her off with a banal marriage. His own Electra more fully exemplifies the tragic rhythm of purpose, passion, and perception. By the end she realizes that she is doomed to sterility and remorse—but she accepts her fate. She will atone, proudly, without appealing for pity. Mourning does become this Electra.

In other tragedies of O'Neill, such as *All God's Chillun Got Wings, Desire under the Elms, The Great God Brown,* and *Strange Interlude,* this acceptance of a tragic fate is more positive. The defeated may even exult, approach ecstasy through their anguish. His ruling aim, O'Neill wrote, was so far as possible to realize "the transfiguring nobility of tragedy" as it was conceived by the Greeks, but to realize it in modern terms, and in "seemingly the most ignoble, debased lives." He was in fact closer in spirit to Greek tragedy than any other modern dramatist. His high aim may therefore make one more painfully aware of his limitations, both as thinker and as poet. Yet his conceptions were poetic, as suggested by his many admirable titles, and his feeling was not facile or shallow. His tragic drama may gain by comparison with the more sophisticated drama of the Continent.

With most serious American drama the story is much the same. While it usually seems less adult than Continental drama, it also seems less effete and has engendered less arty nonsense. It has remained closer to vital common interests than, for instance, the technically brilliant, influential theater of Jacques Copeau.[9] It has retained a more substantial realism even when seeking to transcend realism, or to dress it up in the latest fashion. But when it is ambitious, a sober patriot can still speak of little but good intentions.

Thus Maxwell Anderson has restated the tragic faith in ring-

[9] Even André Gide was dismayed when Copeau declared that he was never closer to achieving his aim than when he was rehearsing a Japanese Noh drama—"a play," Gide commented, "without any relation to our traditions, our customs, our beliefs." It symbolized the whole effort of Copeau, which enlisted so much talent and energy, and "remained without any direct relation to the epoch."

ing American terms. In his essay "The Essence of Tragedy" he declared that he had at last found this essence in a crucial discovery made by the hero, a "spiritual awakening" that made him a better man. Ultimately it is a "vision of what mankind may or should become." He added—rightly—that it is found in Ibsen and Chekhov as in Æschylus and Shakespeare; and they reawakened in him the American dream:

> They are evidence to me that the theater at its best is a religious affirmation, an age-old restating and reassuring man's belief in his own destiny and his ultimate hope. The theater is much older than the doctrine of evolution, but its one faith, asseverated again and again for every age and every year, is a faith in evolution, in the reaching and the climb of man toward distant goals, glimpsed but never seen, perhaps never achieved, or achieved only to be passed impatiently on the way to a more distant horizon.

Anderson has dramatized this faith in a number of tragedies, notably the popular *Winterset*. Unhappily, *Winterset* indicates the abyss that separates his reach from his grasp. When the embittered hero observes that what men once called love is now blamed on the glands, the young heroine begins his spiritual awakening by offering him an utterly pure love: "And so forever the Freudians are wrong." So Anderson spells out his affirmations in words of one syllable, draped in a poetry that is usually banal when not pretentious. Poetry is in keeping with his aspiration to a higher realism; but he is no poet.

Similar deficiencies mark the drama of Arthur Miller, whose *Death of a Salesman* represents a different kind of tragedy. As the study of a little man succumbing to his environment, rather than a great man destroyed through his greatness, it is characteristically modern. There is no question of grandeur in such a tragedy; the "hero" may excite pity, but nothing like awe. There is a question of dignity and human significance. While the dramatic reviewers were generally enthusiastic about the play as a heart-warming one, or even an "epic drama," the fastidious critics of the quarterlies generally dismissed it as a "very dull business," without illumination or pity, or a string of clichés of "unrelieved vulgarity." It strikes me as a basically humane, honest work. It gives some dignity to the tragedy of Willy by an at once unsparing and sympathetic treatment of his easy good nature, his passion to be well liked, his want of any mind or soul of his own. The pathetic Willy may even symbolize Everyman in the wider sense felt by John Mason Brown: "what he would like to be, what he is, what he is not, and yet what he must live and die with."

But Miller, too, strains for a "big" play. His supra-realistic effects—such as the expressionistic setting, the musical themes for the various characters, and the portentous apparitions of Brother Ben—are too fancy for little Willy, and seem more pretentious because of the flat colloquial dialogue. So do the occasional efforts to sound a deep note. "I search and search and I search, and I can't understand it, Willy," his wife laments over his grave; but throughout the play she has not been searching and has understood Willy well enough. Miller's own understanding of him, however, is unclear. Sometimes it appears that the main cause of his tragedy is capitalism; sometimes it is Babbittry, his own weaknesses; sometimes it is the universal plight of the Little Man. The uncertain intention has led to curiously divergent judgments of simple Willy. In England, Ivor Brown remarked, he was taken as "a poor, flashy, self-deceiving little man," whose passion for popularity was more contemptible than natural; the play was coolly received. In America, Brooks Atkinson described him as "a good man who represents the homely, decent, kindly virtues of a middle-class society"; Broadway audiences wept over him. Marxists might explain the tears shed by New Yorkers over his kind of failure, whom in real life they would despise, as a sentimental evasion of their responsibility for such failures. In any case, the excitement over Willy would seem to be more a social than a literary portent.

Today, about the only other American playwright who gives

reason for excitement is Tennessee Williams. His originality is supported by an exceptional talent for lively, realistic dialogue and character portrayal, as well as sure-fire theater. His notorious sexiness is not the mere secondhand idea of sex —"sex in the head," as D. H. Lawrence put it—that we find in many writers; he can render sex convincingly, in character and action, instead of merely talking about it. But he seems unable to think very clearly about it, or deeply about anything else. In his recent *Cat on a Hot Tin Roof*, for example, he builds up to a powerful climax and then peters out into an illogical happy ending, in which the neurotic hero suddenly returns to normality. Though this may have been a concession to his audience, it follows through one implication of his earlier plays. His tragic theme is the disorder due to sex; the implication is Lawrence's idea that the restoration of sexual order is the key to salvation or peace. This may be reading too much into his plays, but in any case they have no wider or deeper tragic import. If one has no right to deny Williams the subject matter he knows best, one may doubt that he will grow much until he knows considerably more.

All in all, we can scarcely speak of a bright promise in American drama. Talent goes mostly into sophisticated musical comedy, lively melodrama, satire, farce—at best, high-class entertainment. For the slump in serious drama we can only make the obvious excuse: the numbing effects of the war and its aftermath that have been felt in all Western literature. Yet such slumps remain the norm in the history of drama, and do not signal the collapse of all culture. Most ages have lived off the masterpieces of earlier ages. The many revivals of old plays that in recent years have accentuated the dearth of original ones indicate that there is still an audience for serious drama. Shakespeare appears to be as "vital" today as he has been for the last three hundred years. Meanwhile O'Neill at least demonstrated the possibility of a greater American theater. Always honest and earnest, he made no concessions to his audience beyond the theatrical effects that playwrights have exploited ever since Æschylus. Neither was his success clearly due to his limitations. A deeper thinker or more articulate poet might have written in his spirit and found a sufficient audience. Should a genius appear, I see no reason for assuming that he would be condemned to inglorious muteness, or to corruption by Broadway. If he could not make the theater a "great collective, religious phenomenon," speak to or for all America, he might still write great plays. If he could not purge the national soul or deeply influence the national destiny, neither could Shakespeare in Elizabethan England.

CHAPTER VII

CONCLUSION

1. SOME CONTRASTS WITH THE ANCIENT EAST

To form any significant conclusions about the spirit of tragedy in our time, and its future possibilities, one must look beyond the theater to literature in the broadest sense, and finally to our whole culture. For the last hundred years this spirit has found more notable expression in fiction than in drama; today it colors all expressions of thought. It strikes some as the characteristic spirit of the day, in the land of Broadway itself. "Of all peoples in the world," Leslie Fiedler has ventured to say, "we hunger most deeply for tragedy"; and he speculated that perhaps only in America could a tragic literature emerge. Western Europe is given to despair, and to love of its despair, while in the Communist world despair is treason—even pessimism is against the law. America is still hopeful, still has a splendid vision of man's possibilities; and now that it has more sense of its failures, and the inevitability of human failure, it might get a deeper sense of both the splendor of the ideal and the possible dignity of failure. Even *Life* magazine, an optimist might add, told its millions of readers some years ago that what this country needs is the tragic sense of life. As Athens, in becoming a great power in its world, created a tragic literature that was the supreme expression of its national ideals, so might a sobered America.

I should like to end on this high note. If we value the tragic sense of life, however, we must be wary of the national disposition to evade actual indignities by the dream of what "may" be, which steals insensibly into what "will" be. We cannot pretend, either, that a great tragic literature would be our salvation—after all, it did not save Athens. Meanwhile there is reason to doubt that most Americans hunger for tragedy, for those who make fortunes by catering to their tastes think otherwise. There is reason to question the tragic sense even of *Life* magazine. Like *Time,* it is happy to support moral crusades, call for a return to religion and spiritual values; and happier because at the same time it can champion the values of its advertisers, preserve the sanctity of the profit motive, and assure its customers that in our fortunate land we can continue to worship both God and mammon. The tragic spirit is different from the religious spirit; but the antithesis of both is this comfortable, bourgeois, business spirit.

We could get along without a great tragic literature, as almost all societies have managed to do. We are not, in any event, the sole hope of Western civilization. (Fiedler neglected to consider the possibility that a tragic literature might emerge in Latin America, the British Commonwealth, or the Eastern countries now in the Western orbit.) But we might not continue to get along, at least as a free, open society, without more of the tragic sense of life. Immediately it could help to brace us against the dismaying realization that our vaunted progress has not been an escape from history, and that the past is not something dead and done with. Finally it recalls us to the basic commitments of a free society. For the tragic spirit is intimately involved in the distinctive humanistic faith that rose in Greece, and became the living faith of Western civilization in recent centuries. It is a means of toughening this faith—to me an essential means. It illumines both the values and the hazards of this faith, and finally the alternatives to it. I return to the question I raised at the outset: why tragedy has been written only in the West.

Now it is safe to assume that in all societies there have been many men who felt as most of us do: that in spite of our sins we are pretty fine fellows, and don't deserve all the grief that comes our way. All literate societies have produced expressions of something like a tragic sense of life. No doubt they also had some artists who were potentially capable of writing high tragedy. Apparently, however, it is almost impossible for any artist to do great work unless other artists are doing similar work at the same time. When Alfred Kroeber surveyed the major achievements in culture, he found extremely few examples of an isolated genius doing notable work; almost invariably genius appears only when there is a movement, a cluster, a school. In seeking to explain why other societies failed to produce tragedy, we have therefore to generalize about their ruling spirit, taking for granted that there must have been many individual exceptions. And I must count on the reader to add some grains of salt to my generalizations, which will necessarily be very broad as I embark on a kind of Cook's tour of history.

In ancient Egypt the story seems fairly plain. It was a sheltered land of perpetual sunshine, in which every year the Nile brought the life-giving waters on schedule; and from the beginning of its recorded history it was sustained by the divine power, in the person of Pharaoh. The Egyptians had the absurd, sublime faith that everything depended on Pharaoh. Their art reveals that he defeated whole armies of their enemies single-handed—not as a hero, but as a manifest god. If to us his rule looks like despotism, to them it was a supreme favor of the gods; Pharaoh was always on the job, right there on earth. As Henri Frankfort remarked, the ideal on which Egyptian society was founded, and maintained for some three thousand years, represents a harmony between man and the divine that is beyond our boldest dreams. Egyptians might be anxious about their personal destinies, but they were confident about the future of their society, a static order in which no important change was either necessary or possible. Nor were they so morbidly obsessed with thoughts of the grave as they have often been represented, especially by lovers of Greece. The tomb art of the Old Kingdom portrays the early Egyptians as bustling, cheerful extroverts who delighted in nature and the material goods of this life, and made such elaborate preparations for death because it was not an end but a continuation of this life. They were happy in the conviction that you *can* take it with you—all of it, and then some.

Then the Old Kingdom collapsed, in spite of Pharaoh. The Egyptians come to life for us in their bewilderment and shock at the period of anarchy that followed. "To whom can I speak today?" runs the refrain of one poem. Some entertained doubts that might have developed into a tragic sense of life. "Behold," wrote an anonymous skeptic, "no one who goes over there can come back again!" Others began to welcome death as a release from this life, or even hastened the relief by suicide. But as order was restored, Egypt returned to its traditional faith. During the anarchy, when Pharaoh was not clearly on the job, the ancient dying god Osiris had been resurrected for purposes of salvation; with his beautiful sister-wife, Isis, he acted as a savior for the ordinary dead, and became the most popular god of Egypt. The combined power of Pharaoh and Osiris made tragedy unthinkable. Though it was not enough to prevent a great deal of tragic history in the long centuries that followed, the ups and downs led to no more serious doubts about a divine order that was still regarded as static and permanent. Instead, Egypt gradually stiffened into the rigid formalism that has made it a byword for slavish piety. By the end its ruling attitude had become a silent resignation—a hopelessness that may look tragic, but is almost the antithesis of Homer's tragic spirit.

In Mesopotamia the story is more complex. It was a land of cruel summers, with scorching winds and dust storms, in which the Tigris and Euphrates rivers made possible a bountiful life but always a hazardous one; they might bring too little water, or they might bring devastating floods. It was not really a land, having no natural boundaries, and it was always exposed to invasion. The succession of peoples who ruled it—Sumerians, "Babylonians," Assyrians, Chaldeans—never knew the security, fancied or real, of the Egyptians. In retaining the essential forms of Sumerian civilization, they retained a basic anxiety, rooted in an awareness of perpetual flux and uncertainty. The one certainty was that everything depended upon the gods, and that they could not be really depended upon. The gods were bound by no comprehensible order, natural or moral, in a world that the Mesopotamian creation myths indicated had not been created by a supreme authority, but had arisen out of Chaos by heavenly violence and in heavenly confusion. Even the kings, who were divinely elected, could discover the will of the gods only by a perpetual anxious attention to omens and oracles, and they might fail despite the utmost vigilance. The great Ashurbanipal of Assyria poured out his lamentations over the strange evils that had befallen him, the holiest of kings: "How long, O God, wilt thou do that to me?"

Hence the Mesopotamian peoples were given to brooding over their tragic lot. As we have already seen in the Epic of Gilgamesh, they wrestled unhappily with the problem of mortality. The "Lamentation over the Destruction of Ur" expressed the common bewilderment and despair of great cities when their god, for some unfathomable reason, let them be destroyed. The ordinary mortal, naturally, was still more helpless. "I do not know the offense against the god," wrote one unfortunate, "I do not know the transgression against the goddess." All he knew was that he had made some blunder, a mistake rather than a sin; so in his despair he could not know the balm of repentance and forgiveness. The problem of evil grew more acute as the Babylonians developed higher standards of justice, and sought to hold the gods to them. The author of "*Ludlul bel nemeqi*," for example, grappled with the theme of Job. Like Job, the hero is finally reconciled and rewarded, but only after a plain acknowledgment that divine standards are incomprehensible to man:

> What to one's heart seems bad is good before one's gods.
> Who may comprehend the mind of gods in heaven's depth?
> The thoughts of a god are like deep waters, who could fathom them?

And the later "Dialogue of Pessimism," like Ecclesiastes, declares that all is vanity. Love, piety, charity—nothing brings

lasting good to man. The author resolutely sticks to his nega-
tion, which unlike the Book of Ecclesiastes was not dressed
up with a pious moral. He concludes:

> "Slave, agree with me!" "Yes, my lord, yes!"
> "Now then, what is good?
> To break my neck and thy neck,
> To fall into the river—that is good!"

Yet this dismal conclusion helps to explain why the Mesopotamian peoples never developed tragedy. Short of utter
despair, the outcome of all their brooding was complete subservience. Unlike the Greeks, they were incapable of a humanistic faith, in values that man might realize by his own efforts.
Their kind of faith was summed up by their ziggurats: the huge
artificial mounds, crowned by a temple, that inspired the myth
of the Tower of Babel, and that the Hebrews mistook for symbols of presumption. Actually, they were symbols of the utter
dependence of man upon the gods, even an abject humility.
Babylonian theology taught that man had been created only to
be the slave of the gods, and to do their dirty work. The
supreme god, Marduk, himself announced in the Epic of Creation: "Let man be burdened with the toil of the gods, that they
may breathe freely." Man also had to serve his king, the agent
of the gods. To the end, blind obedience remained the ruling
principle in Mesopotamia. The apparent conclusion is that
tragedy can be created only by free men, with minds and wills
of their own.

In general, subservience to the gods and the god-kings was
the characteristic principle of the ancient East. Other societies,
however, raise further issues that throw further light on our
question. Thus the Hebrews were unique in their denial of not
only the gods but the highest goods known to the Near East.
In Mesopotamia, for all the anxiety, there was at least a bond
between man, nature, and divinity; man could appeal to deities
who knew suffering from their own experience. "Help me, for
Thou too . . ." The Hebrews destroyed this ancient bond,

depreciating both man and nature to the greater glory of the
One God. They insisted on His absolute sovereignty, refusing
to ask Him to suffer or to sacrifice Himself. At the same time,
they introduced a new kind of presumption, involving further
paradoxes. They were a chosen people, with whom the Lord
had made a series of covenants. Their Messiah offered more
splendid promises than any ordinary resurrected god, sometimes of their triumph over all other peoples, sometimes of a
universal reign of peace and justice—a heaven on earth. Their
Lord was also a shepherd, so they might "walk through the
valley of the shadow of death" without fear, "for Thou art
with me." Altogether, the Lord was at once more awful and
more intimate than any other god in his intense purposefulness
and incessant concern for his people. The Hebrews were at
once prouder and humbler than any people before them.

So profound a tension might well have given rise to tragedy.
The original story of Job came close to it, and the author of
Ecclesiastes had as tragic a sense of life. Yet these were heretical works. (Ecclesiastes would not have been included among
the sacred writings except for the erroneous belief that Solomon
was its author.) The great prophets of Israel had faced the national tragedy in a different spirit. When they foresaw that the
nation was to be destroyed, they declared that this was right
and good. The people were being punished for their sins, and
their sinfulness would only be confirmed if they rallied behind
their kings and generals; it would be enough if a few were
spared—a "saving remnant" to carry on the Lord's plan. This
was indeed an extraordinary faith. To appreciate it, one must
try to imagine an American prophet today going up and down
the land preaching that America is going to be destroyed by
Russia, that this is just as it should be because of our wickedness, that it would be more wicked to fight for our sinful land—
and imagine how some Christian senators would handle such a
prophet. Then let us add, in fairness to ourselves, that ordinary
Hebrews took a less exalted view of their calamities. They
repeatedly rose to fight for their land; they drew encourage-

ment from other prophetic writings, which foretold in gloating detail the utter destruction of their enemies. But on both counts the national faith was inimical to tragedy. In their loftiest moments the prophets asserted that the national tragedy was not really a tragedy; in their more human moments they assured the people that sooner or later it was bound to have a happy ending. At no time did they challenge the will of Jehovah. If they lamented the lot he had decreed for his people, they doubted his right no more than his might.

The Mohammedan world failed to write tragedy for much the same reason. Islam means literally "surrender to the will of God"; its ideal was a narrower, more rigid version of the Hebraic ideal. Its basic doctrine of predestination involves the usual logical difficulties, for if Allah wills everything it is hard to see how men can do anything else but surrender to his will; it would seem that even their apparent disobedience must be willed by Allah. Nevertheless Moslems clung to this doctrine. In their historical youth and prime they were militant crusaders, with the illogic that seems natural to believers in predestination (such as the Communists today); the torch passed from Arabs to Moors, to Mongols, to Mamelukes, to Turks. As the fire went out, all alike characteristically reverted to a spirit of fatalistic acceptance, ruffled chiefly by occasional outbursts of fanaticism. Although the Arabs and the Persians in particular developed a great poetry, which often had a melancholy tone, the spirit of Islam permitted no serious question of the justice of man's fate, no assertion of human standards.

Ancient India, which produced an elaborate drama, affords a different perspective. Here tragedy was taboo. The wise and holy men of India were generally agreed that the temporal, material, sensory world—what most Westerners call the "real" world—was quite unimportant, if not merely illusory. To them the "real" reality was a timeless, spiritual reality, the World-Soul; the real business of man was to unite his soul with the World-Soul; and the logical means to this mystical union was complete indifference to the temporal world, ideally a complete unconsciousness of it and of the self. Hence tragedy would naturally be regarded as a petty distraction, and any serious concern with it as folly. Throughout the long history of India—a history that Indians never bothered to write, since time was unreal—its spiritual leaders were notoriously indifferent to the miseries of this world, such as the wretched poverty of the masses.[1] This attitude, inhuman as it may seem or may become, is the natural conclusion of mystics in all creeds, including Western ones. As St. John of the Cross said, "Disquietude is always vanity." Plotinus was most explicit regarding the drama of this world:

> Murders, death in all its guises, the reduction and sacking of cities, all must be to us just such a spectacle as the changing scenes of a play; all is but the varied incident of a plot, costume on and off, acted grief and lament. For on earth, in all the succession of life, it is not the Soul within but the Shadow outside of the authentic man that grieves and complains and acts out the plot on this world stage which men have dotted with stages of their own constructing. All this is the doing of man knowing no more than to live the lower and outer life, and never perceiving that, in his weeping and in his graver doings alike, he is but at play.

In China, Lao-tse might have appreciated the spirit of Plotinus. Otherwise the absence of tragedy in Chinese literature seems strange. The historic culture of China was essen-

[1] One would imagine that today, under Western influence, Indians might have a livelier sense of tragedy, but apparently their philosophers still think differently. Several years ago UNESCO arranged a conference of intellectuals from different quarters of the world to discuss "The Concept of Man and the Philosophy of Education in East and West," in the hope of arriving at an agreement on fundamental principles. Although they managed to agree on certain broad principles of good will, such as the undesirability of uncivilized or fanatical minorities, they split sharply over the concept of time and eternity. Most of the Eastern thinkers regarded time as unreal, and so dismissed history as a subject of little importance.

tially humanistic, centered on man and this life rather than on God or Heaven. Its people always had a skeptical, agnostic tendency, exemplified by a typical saying of Confucius. When asked about the worship of the celestial spirits, he replied: "We don't know yet how to serve men, how can we know about serving the spirits?" When asked what about death then, he replied: "We don't know yet about life, how can we know about death?" In their frank devotion to earthly goods, moreover, the Chinese were naturally aware of the costs of these goods. They experienced their full share of tragedy in their national life and in their private lives; it is often reflected in their poetry. And for centuries they had a traditional drama, out of which tragedy might logically have arisen.

To explain why it did not, one might say broadly that the Chinese were a cheerful, pragmatic people who were never given to brooding over the first and last questions. Thus their philosophy was almost entirely ethical and political; they produced little or no metaphysics and theology. More concretely, they were sustained by their traditional worship of the ancestors. Although they had vague ideas about the nature of the afterlife, they knew that when one died his spirit would join those of his ancestors on the family shelf; as he had always paid his respects to the generations before him, and consulted them on all important family decisions, so he would be revered and consulted by the generations after him. From this biological kind of immortality the Chinese evidently got more real comfort than Christians have generally known. They have been notoriously tranquil at the prospect of death—and for the same reason, no doubt, as notoriously callous about killing. But still more pertinent is the Confucian ethics, the accepted ideal of China throughout most of its history. What Confucius sought above all was harmony, and to achieve it he stressed the duties, not the rights, of the individual—duties to the father, the younger brother, the emperor, etc. The tragic spirit is more individualistic and self-assertive. Tragedy has typically featured a hero, proud or passionate—and Confucius did his best to discourage this kind of hero. His ideal was neither the saint nor the hero but the cultivated, urbane, temperate, well-balanced gentleman.

The Noh plays of Japan, lastly, represent a tradition of ceremonial drama, centuries old, that is especially interesting because of its resemblance to Greek drama. (Ernest Fenollosa speculated that it might have been due to Greek influence, carried by Buddhism from India.) It is a ritual drama of masks, enacted on a symbolic stage, structured by lyrical units. It too evolved out of religious rites. Performances, which traditionally were spread over a number of days, celebrated some ceremonial occasion and comprised a series of plays that together made up a "complete action." The usual sequence was a congratulatory piece, concerned with the gods; a battle piece, with the familiar martial themes; a "wig" piece or play for women, on the contrasting theme of love; a "Noh of Spirits," on the transitoriness of this life and the spiritual life to come; a morality play on the duties of man; and finally another congratulatory piece, calling down blessings on all involved. In Ezra Pound's words, the complete performance represents "a complete service of life," symbolizing the eternal recurrences.

Still, it is not a tragic drama. It comes closest in the plays of the Spirits, which the Japanese find intensely dramatic. To the uninitiated the drama is seldom apparent, since there is little conflict; Pound suggests that it amounts to "the tension of the seance," or suspense of awaiting an epiphany. But even so, there is no real uncertainty about the outcome—the Spirits will always appear. If a tragic note is struck by such phrases as "the universal unstillness," in a life that passes like a dream, it strikes us as a decorous unstillness, evoking a quiet sadness; and at the end life passes into the "peaceful kingdom," of the other world. For the Spirits are Buddhist spirits, who are typically not fearsome. Buddha himself was no patron of drama, like Dionysus; he counseled non-attachment to this world, and described art as the broadest path that leads away from salvation. Although the religion that grew up in his name departed as far from his teachings as Christianity has from the teachings of Jesus, it generally moved toward a more genial view of life and the afterlife. In Japan, as in China, Buddhism became essentially a cheerful religion. Like all other faiths, it failed to prevent national tragedy; but it effectually discouraged a tragic sense of life.

2. THE VALUE OF TRAGEDY

The immediate conclusion to be drawn from this rapid survey is that the tragic sense is not the only mature, profound, or dignified sense of life. An essential element of its wisdom, as I see it, is the recognition that no one way of life has a monopoly on truth or dignity, and that its own knowledge includes a knowledge of its ignorance. Reverence for the human spirit should properly induce a respect for its many lofty responses to the challenge of evil, suffering, and death. The way of the Hebrew prophets may be considered loftier than the Greek way. The way of Confucius may be wiser—even more truly Apollonian. The way of the Hindu sages and saints, which to Westerners looks like an escape from reality, may actually be a communion with the ultimate reality; and in any case it induces a serenity and peace of mind that most of us will never know. All these ways, moreover, are a reminder that throughout history the overwhelming majority of men have been unwilling or unable to believe that the universe is soulless and indifferent to man. Today most would still declare that our chief need is not a tragic but a religious sense. In the Western world this means the Christian religion: the most humanistic of the higher religions except Confucianism (which some deny the name of religion), but like almost all the others, a faith that man can transcend tragedy on the plane of eternity.

It is not my business here to dispute this faith. My concern remains the issue forced by modern tragedy. All the voices now crying in the wilderness, exhorting a return to God, themselves testify that a great many thoughtful men are no longer able to accept the traditional faith, and that for a great many more nominal believers it is no longer a vital, sustaining faith. Our knowledge of the universe and man's history, our habits of critical inquiry, and the conditions of life alike in capitalistic and communistic societies have all worked against it. Hence T. S. Eliot has lamented that most modern literature is writter as if Christianity did not exist. Arnold Toynbee describes modern Western civilization as an ex- or post-Christian society.[2] And though he believes that the revival of religion is our only hope for survival, his own *Study of History* indicates that the higher religions all grew out of failure on earth, and have never yet saved a dying civilization. Unless catastrophe destroys all hope for the future, all faith in man's own efforts, one must doubt that Christianity will again become the force that it was in the Middle Ages and the Protestant Reformation.

Meanwhile most men in the West, including Christians, are still committed on principle as well as in practice to the humanistic belief in the value of life on earth, and of human enterprise to improve this life. They cannot accept the traditional Eastern wisdom of passivity, resignation, or renunciation, nor the traditional Christian view that the whole meaning and value of life derive from the life to come. They may agree with Reinhold Niebuhr that free reason, imagination, creativity— man's distinctive gifts and the source of his highest achievements—are also the source of all evil, which is therefore ineradicable; but like him they do not propose to cut the costs by discouraging the exercise of these gifts. In the democracies most are still committed, more specifically, to a belief in the values of freedom and individuality, the right of a man to a mind and a life of his own. And these distinctively Western beliefs, which gave rise to the tragic spirit, make it all the more relevant in a time of crisis.

To me, the tragic sense is the deepest sense of our humanity,

---

[2] Toynbee is also a striking example of the difference between the tragic and the religious spirit. He can view with equanimity the deaths of entire civilizations, in the belief that the sole and sufficient reason for their existence was by their death to bring mankind nearer to the True God.

and therefore spiritual enough. But all men may profit from it, whatever their faith. It is certainly valid as far as it goes, or this life goes. It sizes up the very reasons for religious faith, the awful realities that men must face up to if their faith is to be firm, mature, and responsible. It also makes for sensitiveness to the tragic excesses of all faiths, the inevitable corruptions of all ideals—in the West, more particularly, to the rugged, irresponsible individualism that has battened on the ideal of freedom, and the bigotry and self-righteousness that have flourished in the name of Jesus. It may deepen the sense of community that has been one end of religion. The tragic writer may most nearly realize the ideal mission of the artist stated by Joseph Conrad:

> He speaks to our capacity for delight and wonder, to the sense of mystery surrounding our lives; to our sense of pity, and beauty, and pain; to the latent feeling of fellowship with all creation—and to the subtle but invincible conviction of solidarity that knits together the loneliness of innumerable hearts, to the solidarity in dreams, in joy, in sorrow, in aspirations, in illusions, in hope, in fear, which binds men to each other, which binds together all humanity—the dead to the living and the living to the unborn.

For the many who are unable to believe that man was specially created in the image of God, and guaranteed that his earthly history will be consummated in eternity, herein may be the most available means—beyond animal faith—to spiritual acceptance and order, in a society that has lost its simple faith in progress but nevertheless remains committed to the belief that "something ought to be done" about all our problems, and can be. The tragic spirit can promote a saving irony, in the perception of the naïve or absurd aspects of this belief; a spirit of compassion, through the knowledge of irremediable evils and insoluble dilemmas; and a spirit of reverence, for the idealism that keeps seeking truth, goodness, and beauty even though human ideals are not everlasting. It is proof of the dignity of man, which remains a basic tenet of Western democracy. It is now perhaps the strongest proof because of the very realism, in modern thought and art, that has commonly led to a devaluation of man and nature.

At its best, the realistic spirit is itself a value, and a source of further values. It has meant tough-mindedness, the courage and honesty to admit that we really do not know all that we would like to know, and that most men have passionately claimed to know. In modern science it has meant the admission that our most positive, reliable knowledge of the physical universe is approximate, tentative, hypothetical, and that we cannot know the final, absolute truth about it: a respect for both fact and mystery that gives a pathetic air to the religious thinkers who have leaped to the odd conclusion that this admission of ultimate uncertainty proves the certainty of religious truth. In literature, realism as a technique has often meant superficiality, meagerness, fragmentariness, confusion; but as a controlling attitude it has also toughened the tragic faith. From Ibsen to Sartre, as from Hardy to Malraux, many writers have not only reasserted the dignity of the human spirit but proved its strength by holding fast in uncertainty, or even in the conviction that there is no power not ourselves making for righteousness. Although they cannot readily create heroes with the stature and symbolical significance of the ancient heroes, they may exhibit or exemplify a humbler, more difficult kind of heroism that may be more significant for our living purposes. They no longer leave the worst enemy in the rear.

All this necessarily falls far short of any promise of salvation, and so brings us back to "reality." The spirit of tragedy can never deliver us from tragedy. It cannot take the place of religion. Even in literature it cannot give us the kind of exaltation that some critics now soar to under the spell of Myth. In *The Timeless Theme*, for instance, Colin Still argues that the Living Art of all humanity, like all "authentic" myth and true religion, has "but one essential theme, namely: the Fall of the human Soul and the means of its Redemption." In irony one may remark that he proves his thesis by the easy expedient of dismissing art that lacks this theme as not authentic or living (even though it happens to have lived for a thousand years or so), and that he makes it still easier by asserting that this timeless truth can be grasped only by the Spirit, which most scholars and critics lack. In reverence one should acknowledge that this has in fact been a major theme in Western literature, and that it is the most inspiring theme to many men of good will. In truthfulness one must add that tragedy has had no such uniform, timeless theme, beyond the realities of suffering and death. Modern tragedy is particularly deficient in Spirit; it seldom exhibits or promises Redemption. At most it may help to redeem us from fear or despair, or from the vanity of cheap hopes.

I can conclude on no more exalted note than a verse of Thomas Hardy: "If way to the Better there be, it exacts a full look at the Worst." Come the worst, the survivors of atomic war—if any—will have little stomach for tragedy. Come the better, in something like One World, there will still be sufficient reason for pity and terror, and many more men to experience it with more intensity. The East is now stirring with the willful Western spirit, demanding more of the goods of this world. Tragedy might at last become a universal form, and redeem all the critics who have written so solemnly about its universal and eternal truths. But if so, it will be because the rest of the world has taken a fuller look at the worst, and is no longer resigned to the eternal verities, no longer content to surrender to the will of its gods.

INDEX

Accius, 131
Æschylus, 10, 33, 34, 36, 43, 48,
51, 52, 58, 61–77, 79, 94, 95, 97,
100, 104, 110, 113, 114, 115 n,
116, 118, 121, 130, 136, 141,
235, 298, 305, 314, 316
Agamemnon, 63–4, 65, 66, 67, 68,
70, 71, 114
Ajax, 59, 79–80, 86, 92, 96, 98, 189
Alberti, Leon Battista, 169
Alcestis, 109
Alexander the Great, 239 n
Alfieri, Vittorio, 104, 241
All for Love, 204–5
All God's Chillun Got Wings, 315
All's Well That Ends Well, 185
Ambrose, St., 29
Anaxagoras, 109
Anderson, Maxwell, 315–16
Andromache: of Euripides, 105–6,
107, 112, 113, 114
Andromache: of Racine, 225, 226–
7, 235
Antigone, 52, 80–2, 92, 96, 98, 99
Antiphanes, 51 n
Antony and Cleopatra, 170, 193–4,
204, 230, 254
Apollo, 33, 59, 71, 111, 120, 126
Aristophanes, 58–9, 62, 66, 108,
118, 129–30
Aristotle, 6–10, 16, 18, 19–20, 25,
32, 48, 51 n, 52–3, 62, 72–3, 84,
89, 95, 98, 103, 107, 108, 113,
125, 127, 148, 196, 218, 240, 314
Ashurbanipal, 324
Athaliah, 225, 227, 235–7
Athena, 33, 59, 63, 70–1, 76, 79–
80
Athens, 47, 52, 53, 54, 55, 57, 75–

7, 86, 100, 102, 109–10, 112–13,
128–9, 132, 210, 247, 320
Atkinson, Brooks, 317
Attis, 33, 124, 125
Auden, W. H., 6, 42
Augustine, St., 29

Bacchæ, The, 33–4, 107, 121–5
Bacon, Francis, 162, 165
Bajazet, 226
Balzac, Honoré de, 264, 267
Baroque art, 146, 208, 211, 224
Battenhouse, Roy, 155 n
Baudelaire, Pierre Charles, 224
Bayle, Pierre, 212
Bayreuth, 253, 257–8
Beaumont, Francis, 200
Beethoven, Ludwig van, 70, 252,
256
Bentley, Eric, 304, 312
Berdyaev, Nicolas, 267–8
Berenice, 225, 229–30, 231, 284
Blackmur, R. P., 13
Boas, George, 11
Bodkin, Maude, 29, 298
Boileau, Nicolas, 212, 240
Boris Godunov, 256
Bossuet, Jacques, 212–13
Botticelli, Sandro, 169
Bowra, C. M., 87–8, 90, 92, 96 n
Bradbrook, Muriel C., 151
Bradley, A. C., 170, 174
Brand, 261, 268
Brandes, Georg Morris, 261, 263,
269
Bridges, Robert, 152
Britannicus, 226
Brooks, Cleanth, 13, 200 n
Brown, Ivor, 317

Brown, John Mason, 317
Brunetière, Ferdinand, 212, 217
Bruno, Giordano, 147
Büchner, Georg, 259–60
Buddhism, 279–80, 330–1
Burckhardt, Jacob, 144
Burke, Kenneth, 19, 156
Byron, George Gordon, 104

Calderón de la Barca, Pedro, 149, 167
Calvin, John, 145–6
Capitalism, 145, 199, 317, 332
Capture of Miletus, The, 33, 52
Cassirer, Ernst, 144
Catharsis, theory of, 6–7, 19–20, 32–3, 56
Cato, 241
Cat on a Hot Tin Roof, 318
Cellini, Benvenuto, 144
Chapman, George, 153
Chaucer, Geoffrey, 139
Chekhov, Anton, *283–93*, 294, 300, 310, 316
Cherry Orchard, The, 288, 289, 293
Children of Heracles, The, 113
Chorus: the use of in tragedy, 30, 49, 63–4, 87, 96, 103, 119, 130, 133, 152, 231, 235, 254–5, 295, 296, 305
Christianity: in relation to tragedy, 4, 27–9, 124, 139–43, 160–2, 167–8, 179–80, 187–8, 205–6, 237, 296, 298, 300–1, 331–5
Churchill, Winston, 220
Cid, The, 209, 216–17, 218–19
Cinna, 219
Clark, A. F. B., 210
Clytemnestra, 131–2
Cocktail Party, The, 299–300
Cocteau, Jean, 293 *n*
Coleridge, Samuel Taylor, 23, 171, 173
Comedy, 6, 14–15, 51 *n*, 129–30, 131, 188–9, 202, 288
Conrad, Joseph, 95, 333

Cook, Albert, 15
Copeau, Jacques, 293, 315
Copernicus, Nicolaus, 143, 147, 162
Coriolanus, 170, 178 *n*
Corneille, Pierre, 167, 207, 209, 211, 212, *216–24*, 225, 226, 230, 232, 233, 239, 240, 241, 282, 294, 303
Creditors, The, 278
Croce, Benedetto, 220
Cybele, 33, 124, 125
Cymbeline, 194
Cyrano de Bergerac, 259

Dance of Death, The, 276
Dante Alighieri, 138, 140–1, 161, 167, 263, 290
Danton's Death, 259–60
Darwin, Charles, 276
Death of a Salesman, 316–17
Democracy: the connections of with Greek tragedy, 53, 54–5, 56, 57, 75–7, 100, 128–9; with modern tragedy, 281–3, 332
Demosthenes, 128–9
Dennis, John, 5
Descartes, René, 209, 212
Desire under the Elms, 315
Devotion of the Cross, The, 149 *n*
Dewey, John, 244, 298, 310
Diderot, Denis, 241, 242
Dionysus, 25, 33, 34, 36, 54, 55, 56, 59, 72 *n*, 120, 121–5, 126, 253, 255
Divine Comedy, 74, 140–1, 247, 252
Dixon, Macneile, 15
Dodds, E. R., 56, 99
Doll's House, A, 261, 263, 265
Donne, John, 146, 147, 200, 301
Dostoyevsky, Feodor, 139, 264, 267, 268, 288, 292–3, 301
Drayman Henschel, 281–2
Dream Play, The, 280
Dreiser, Theodore, 282, 312
Dr. Faustus, 150, 159–62, 164, 180

Dryden, John, 203–5, 207, 217, 220, 282
Duchess of Malfi, The, 197–8, 200
Dynamo, 313

Ecclesiastes, Book of, 46, 324–5, 326
Edward II, 159, 163–4
Egypt, 322–3
Einstein, Albert, 249
Electra: of Euripides, 112, 114–15
Electra: of Sophocles, 84–5, 92, 96–7, 98
El Greco, 146
Eliot, T. S., 29, 132 *n,* 150, 153, 166, 167, 175 *n,* 196, 199, 217, 264, 288, *293–301,* 332
Elizabeth, Queen, 169
Elizabethan tragedy, 3, 35, 60, 107, 132, 135, *137–206,* 210, 218, 219 *n,* 261
Ellis-Fermor, Una, 157
Emperor and Galilean, 274
Emperor Jones, The, 313
Enlightenment, the Age of the, 110, 212, 242–3, 249, 252
Ennius, 131
Epicurus, 94, 127
Erasmus, Desiderius, 143, 145, 163
Esther, 235
Euclid, 8
Eumenides, 59, 63, 65, 66, 69–70, 71, 74, 76, 101, 120, 298
Euripides, 10, 33, 51, 52, 58, 59, 63, 64, 66, 67, 72, 79, 83, 86, 94, 95, 100, *103–25,* 130, 131, 133, 212, 227, 315
Everyman, 141, 142, 159, 160

Faguet, Émile, 213 *n*
Family Reunion, 296–8, 300
Father, The, 276, 277
Faust, 162, 252
Fénelon, François, 212–13, 239
Fenollosa, Ernest, 330
Fergusson, Francis, 89–91, 140,

175–8, 224–5, 246, 247, 252, 254, 255, 262, 264, 289–91, 295
Ficino, Marsilio, 144
Fiedler, Leslie, 320, 321
Flaubert, Gustave, 264
Fletcher, John, 200
Flies, The, 303, 304–6, 307 *n,* 308, 310
Fontenelle, Bernard Le Bovier de, 212
France, Anatole, 178–9
Frankfort, Henri, 322
Frazer, James George, 35
Freud, Sigmund, 15 *n,* 29–30, 31, 114, 249–50, 276, 297, 298, 314
Frogs, The, 66, 118
Frye, Northrop, 95
Fuller, B. A. G., 15 *n*

Galileo, 200, 210
Garcia Lorca, Federico, 294
Gerhardi, William, 285, 289
Ghosts, 260–7, 269, 273 *n,* 277
Ghost Sonata, The, 279–80
Gide, André, 315 *n*
Gilgamesh, Epic of, 43–5, 324
Goethe, Johann Wolfgang von, 51, 104, 159, 162–3, 171, 173, 251, 252, 253, 259
Gothic art, 138–9, 142, 143, 169, 189, 202, 251, 269
Gouhier, Henri, 248
Great God Brown, The, 315
Greek tragedy, 3, 18, 32, 34–6, *48–136,* 141, 148, 154, 170, 189, 202, 219 *n,* 222, 252, 253, 258, 259, 264, 272, 286, 291, 294, 295, 296–7, 315
Green Pastures, The, 300

Hadas, Moses, 81, 105, 106
Hairy Ape, The, 313
Hamlet, 12, 18, 25, 138, 167, 171–81, 194, 207, 210, 219 *n,* 247
Harbage, Alfred, 152 *n,* 201–2
Hardy, Thomas, 264, 334, 335

Harris, Mark, 207 *n*
Hauptmann, Gerhardt, 275, *280–3*
Hebbel, Friedrich, 261
Hecuba, 121
Hedda Gabler, 4, 266
Hegel, Georg W. F., 17, 74
Heidegger, Martin, 302 *n*
Hellenistic Age, 61, 126, 129–30, 135, 148
Hemingway, Ernest, 21
Henry V, 177–8 *n*
Heraclitus, 55
Herodotus, 33, 39, 55, 81 *n*, 99
Hesiod, 41, 75
Hinduism, 30, 327–8, 331
Hippolytus: of Euripides, 111, 117–19, 207, 226, 227–8
Hippolytus: of Seneca, 134
Historical criticism: the hazards of, 11–12, 35, 58–61, 71, 81, 150, 155, 238; the necessity of, 12–13, 49, 53, 58, 175 *n*, 263
Hitler, Adolf, 4, 30, 248, 258, 280
Homer, *36–47*, 53, 54, 55, 56, 67, 68, 70, 74, 97, 127, 134, 323
Horace, 219
Hubris, 18, 36, 57, 64 *n*, 72–3, 79, 96
Hugo, Victor, 251

Ibsen, Henrik, 4, 10, 103, 199, 219 *n*, 233, 252, *260–74*, 275, 277, 280, 286, 290, 294, 316, 334
Iceman Cometh, The, 311, 312
Iliad, 37, 38–45, 50
Individualism, 56, 57, 100, 144–5, 159, 168, 268, 333
Infernal Machine, The, 293 *n*, 305
Innocent III, Pope, 139
Ion of Chios, 53 *n*, 78
Ionia, 55, 56, 67, 68, 109
Irene, 241
Ivanov, 285 *n*

Jaeger, Werner, 67–8, 121
James, Henry, 132 *n*, 285

Jansenism, 214, 225, 226–7, 232, 234, 237
Jaspers, Karl, 283, 302 *n*
Jew of Malta, The, 150, 159
Job, Book of, 45–7, 77, 88, 179, 324, 326
John Gabriel Borkman, 271–2
John of the Cross, St., 328
Johnson, Samuel, 5, 165
Jones, Ernest, 174
Jonson, Ben, 201
Joyce, James, 132 *n*, 288
Judaism, 27, 45–7, 325–7
Julius Cæsar, 178 *n*
Jung, Carl Gustav, 29, 30, 31

Kafka, Franz, 132 *n*, 245
Kepler, Johannes, 147, 210
Ker, W. P., 38
Kierkegaard, Søren, 268, 302
King Lear, 171, 185–93, 219 *n*
Kitto, H. D. F., 64, 69, 78, 98, 104–5, 106, 107, 112, 114
Knight, G. Wilson, 170, 182
Kroeber, Alfred, 126 *n*, 322
Krutch, Joseph Wood, 244, 248, 249, 262, 277, 314
Kyd, Thomas, 151–2, 171

La Bruyère, Jean de, 213, 240
La Fontaine, Jean de, 210–11
Lao-tse, 328
La Rochefoucauld, François de, 213
Lattimore, Richmond, 67, 73
La Voisin, 212, 228
Lawrence, D. H., 132 *n*, 318
Leech, Clifford, 189–90
Le Roy, 156
Lessing, Gotthold Ephraim, 8, 241–2
Levin, Harry, 156
Libation Bearers, 65, 66
Life Is a Dream, 149
Lillo, George, 241–2
London Merchant, The, 241, 242

Index

Louis XIV, 208–12, 233, 235, 236, 237–8, 239–40
Lovejoy, A. O., 28
Loyola, Ignatius, 139
Luther, Martin, 214

Macbeth, 9, 21, 193, 219 *n*
Machiavelli, Niccolò, 140, 143, 146, 147
Mack, Maynard, 178
Magna Moralia, 39
Maintenon, Mme de, 235, 239–40
Malraux André, 21, 334
Mann, Thomas, 62, 95, 259, 267
Marathon, 54, 61, 77, 100, 110
Maria Magdalena, 261
Marduk, 325
Marlowe, Christopher, 137, 138, 148, *149–65*, 167, 168, 201, 217–18
Marxism, 75–6, 100, 267, 268, 293, 302 *n*, 307, 317
Masefield, John, 284
Master Builder, The, 270–1, 272
Mauriac, François, 234
McLean, J. H., 105
Measure for Measure, 166, 185
Medea: of Euripides, 9, 21, 115–16, 117, 119, 227
Medea: of Seneca, 133
Melville, Herman, 31
Menander, 130, 131
Meredith, George, 77
Mesopotamian peoples, 43, 323–5
Michael Kramer, 282
Michelangelo, 146, 169
Middle Ages, 28, 137–45, 163, 183–4, 188, 332
Miller, Arthur, 316–17
Milton, John, 104, 167, 205–6, 288
Misanthrope, The, 213
Miss Julia, 276, 294
Miss Sarah Sampson, 241
Mithridates, 225
Modern tragedy, 10, 17, 35, 52, 199, *244–319*, 334–5
Mohammedanism, 327

Molière, 210, 211, 212, 239, 241
Montaigne, Michel de, 143, 146, 147, 163, 169, 173, 211, 213, 214, 215–16
Mornet, Daniel, 209, 212, 213, 231
Moses, 26
Mourning Becomes Electra, 313–15
Murder in the Cathedral, 29, 295–6
Murray, Gilbert, 25, 29, 34–5, 74, 83
Myth, 26, 43, 51–2, 68, 89–90, 110, 128, 129, 142–3, 253, 258–9, 334–5

Natural Son, The, 241
Neo-classical tragedy, 107, 148, 153, *207–43*
Newton, Isaac, 210, 243
Nicole, Pierre, 213, 234
Nicoll, Allardyce, 122
Niebuhr, Reinhold, 301, 332
Nietzsche, Friedrich Wilhelm, 40, 103, 120, 125–6, 128, 135, 217, 218, 253–9, 268, 271, 277
Noah, 300
No Exit, 303–4, 308, 310
Noh drama, 315 *n*, 330
Norwood, Gilbert, 105
N. Towne Betrayal, 142

O'Connor, William Van, 207 *n*
Œdipus at Colonus, 51 *n*, 86, 88, 89, 90, 91–2, 95, 97, 100–2, 120
Œdipus complex, 29–30, 31, 99, 174
Œdipus Rex, 10, 27, 51 *n*, 56, 78, 83–4, 87–91, 93, 94, 95, 98, 99, 100, 119, 160, 210, 262, 293 *n*
Œdipus Rex: of Seneca, 133–4
Olympian gods, 15 *n*, 33, 39, 40–1, 43, 55–6, 59, 94, 117, 125; *see also* Apollo, Athena, Zeus
O'Neill, Eugene, 311–15, 318–19
Oresteia, 65, 67, 69, 70–1, 72, 73–4, 119, 258, 296, 314
Orestes, 112, 119
Orpheus, 124 *n*

Osiris, 323
Othello, 167, 170, 185
Ovid, 129

Pacuvius, 131
Parsifal, 257
Pascal, Blaise, 139, 211–12, 213, 214–16, 223, 232, 243, 301
Passion plays, 28, 141–2
Paul, St., 28
Peer Gynt, 261, 268
Peloponnesian War, 57, 77, 100, 110, 113
Pericles, 57, 78
Pericles, 194
Persians, The, 52, 62, 72
Pessimism: as inherent in the tragic spirit, 17–18; the issues raised by in modern tragedy, 244, 247, 250, 260, 265–7, 288–90, 306–7, 309–10, 311
Phædra, 225, 226, 227–9, 233–4
Philoctetes, 85–6, 92, 95, 98–9, 108
Philosophy: the rise of in relation to Greek tragedy, 4, 55, 56–7, 109, 110, 121, 126–8
Phrynicus, 33, 52
Pickard-Cambridge, A. W., 30
Pillars of Society, 261, 265
Pirandello, Luigi, 294
Pisistratus, 48, 54
Plato, 4–6, 36, 37, 78, 95, 99, 127, 128
Plautus, 131
Plotinus, 328
Plutarch, 33
Polyeucte, 219, 221, 223
Pompey, 131
Posidonius, 127
Pound, Ezra, 132 *n*, 330
Pradon, 238
Prodicus, 109
Prometheus Bound, 62–3, 65, 70, 71, 73, 75, 77, 111, 140
Protagoras, 109
Proust, Marcel, 132 *n*

Rabelais, François, 144, 208
Racine, Jean Baptiste, 10, 104, 207, 209, 211, 212, 217, 221, 224–38, 239, 240, 241, 252, 274, 288
Radhakrishnan, 5, 124
Raglan, Lord, 26–7
Raleigh, Walter, 168, 203
Rats, The, 280–1
Rehearsal, The, 220
Religion: in relation to tragedy, 17–18, 19; the views on of Æschylus, 58, 68–9, 70–5, 77; of Sophocles, 86–95, 97; of Euripides, 111–12, 120; of Marlowe, 160–2; of Shakespeare, 167–8, 179–80, 187–8; *see also* Christianity, Pessimism, Ritual patterns
Renaissance, 137–8, 143–9, 156, 159, 168–70, 195, 199, 202, 208, 211, 218
Restoration drama, 202–5, 206, 209, 220
Revenger's Tragedy, The, 195–6, 207
Richards, I. A., 10–11, 23
Richelieu, Cardinal, 208
Ring of the Nibelungs, 252, 255–6, 258
Ritual patterns: the survival of in tragedy, 25–36, 42, 74, 89–92, 95, 112, 125, 128, 141–2, 159, 175–8, 190–1, 253, 255, 269, 284, 294, 295
Robertson, J. M., 172
Rohde, Erwin, 56
Roman drama, 126, 131–4
Romantic love: the theme of in tragedy, 117, 129, 203, 224, 225, 238–9, 254–5
Romantic Movement, 207, 251–2, 267, 301
Romeo and Juliet, 166, 254
Rosmersholm, 269–70
Rowe, Nicholas, 241
Rowley, William, 151
Russell, Bertrand, 23
Rymer, Thomas, 167

Index

Sainte-Beuve, Charles Augustin, 217, 220, 221, 225, 236
Saint-Evremond, Charles de, 238
Saint-Simon, Comte de, 213, 239
Samson Agonistes, 205–6, 237
Santayana, George, 226, 283
Sartre, Jean-Paul, 217, *302–11*, 334
Schiller, Johann C. F., 38, 243, 251, 252
Schopenhauer, Arthur, 17, 253
Science, 15 n, 55, 147–8, 162, 200, 206, 247, 248–9, 253, 263, 275, 311, 334
Seneca, 107, 126, 132–5, 148, 155, 212, 313
Seven Against Thebes, 62, 65, 72–3
Sévigné, Mme de, 234, 238
Shaftesbury, Lord, 173
Shakespeare, William, 3, 10, 11, 17, 37 n, 95, 138, 146, 148, 149, 151, 152, 153, *165–95*, 198, 201, 202, 204, 206, 216, 218, 224, 230, 241, 247, 251, 252, 256, 259, 264, 291, 301, 316, 319
Shaw, George Bernard, 4, 114, 277
Shelley, Percy Bysshe, 6, 73
Shorey, Paul, 80
Sidney, Philip, 5, 148, 153, 169, 203
Sociological drama, 17, 52, 103, 199, 261–4, 268–9, 281, 282
Socrates, 59, 81, 109, 112, 126–7, 128, 135
Sophocles, 9, 10, 17, 34, 36, 48, 51, 58, 61, 63, 64, 65, 67, 70, 72, *78–102*, 103, 104, 108, 110, 112, 114, 115 n, 116, 121, 130, 131, 135, 160, 224, 247, 303, 314–15
Spanish drama, 148, 149
Spanish Tragedy, The, 151–2, 159
Spenser, Edmund, 169, 203
Spurgeon, Caroline, 174–5, 187
Stalin, Joseph, 293
Stanislavsky, Konstantin, 285 n
Stendhal, 224
Still, Colin, 334–5

Stoicism, 127–8, 134–5, 219
Strachey, Lytton, 210–11, 217, 240
Strange Interlude, 315
Strindberg, August, *275–80*, 294
Suppliants, The, 62, 63, 64–5, 73
Synge, John, 294
Sypher, Wylie, 143–4, 146, 169, 208

Taine, Hippolyte Adolphe, 225
Tamburlaine, 137, 138, 150, 151, 152, 153, 155 n, 156–9, 162, 207, 247
Tate, Nahum, 191 n, 241
Tempest, The, 166, 194–5, 200 n
Terence, 131
Thales, 55
Theater: the Greek, 49–50, 130–1, 154, 247; the Elizabethan, 154–5, 201–2, 206, 245, 247; the modern, 148, 245–6, 318–19
Theodora, Empress, 136
Thérèse Raquin, 275
Thespis, 48
Thomson, George, 75–6, 100, 258
Thomson, J. A. K., 69
Three Sisters, The, 283–4, 286, 292
Thucydides, 113
Tillyard, E. M. W., 138, 175
Timon of Athens, 193
Tintoretto, Il, 146
Tolstoy, Leo, 264, 267, 288
Tourneur, Cyril, 195–7, 199, 201
Toynbee, Arnold, 176, 301, 332
"Tragic flaw": an essential to the tragic hero, 7, 72–3, 81, 83, 85, 87, 168
Tragic hero: the development of the type of, 18, 39–40, 73, 74, 96–7, 140, 155, 159; in modern literature, 245, 262, 270, 275, 277–8, 282–3, 287, 305, 316–17, 334
Tragic irony: the development of in Greece, 15, 18, 36, 69, 78, 95, 112
Tragi-comedy, 10, 11, 103, 288

Tristan and Isolde, 252, 254–5
Troilus and Cressida, 171, 180–5, 193
Trojan Women, The, 112–14, 119
Turgenev, Ivan, 264
Turnell, Martin, 217, 221 *n*, 222, 224–5, 231, 236
Tyche, 127, 130

Unamuno, Miguel de, 301
Uncle Vanya, 285–6, 291
Unities: of time, place, and action, 8, 49, 133, 219, 231

Van Doren, Mark, 194–5
Vicious Circle, see *No Exit*
Victors, The, 303, 308–10
Vinci, Leonardo da, 144
Virgil, 126, 131, 134
Voltaire, 207, 240–1, 242, 256

Wagner, Richard, 252–9, 261, 267
Waldock, A. J. A., 80, 93
Watling, E. F., 67, 97–8
Weavers, The, 281, 282
Webster, John, 153, 197–9, 201
Wedekind, Frank, 274
Weisinger, Herbert, 28, 35
Wellek, René, 13 *n*
Western civilization: the distinc-

tive values of, 162, 321, 332–3, 335
When We Dead Awaken, 272–3, 277
White Devil, The, 197
Whitehead, Alfred North, 68, 210
Whitman, Cedric, 97
Wild Duck, The, 265, 269
Williams, Tennessee, 318
William Tell, 252
Wilson, Dover, 172
Wilson, Edmund, 81, 85, 98–9
Winterset, 316
Winter's Tale, The, 194
Wolfe, Thomas, 164, 312
Women of Trachis, 82–3, 92, 95, 98, 108
Wood Demon, The, 285 *n*
Wotton, Henry, 200
Woyzeck, 259

Xenophanes, 37, 55

Year-Dæmon, 25–6, 34, 36, 48, 90, 141
Yeats, William Butler, 6, 11, 132 *n*, 294

Zeus, 38–9, 40, 46, 56, 70–1, 73, 77, 111
Zola, Émile, 267, 274–5, 281

A NOTE ON THE

T Y P E

IN WHICH THIS BOOK IS SET

THE TEXT of this book is set in Caledonia, a Linotype face that belongs to the family of printing types called "modern face" by printers—a term used to mark the change in style of type-letters that occurred about 1800. Caledonia borders on the general design of Scotch Modern, but is more freely drawn than that letter.

The book was composed, printed, and bound by The Plimpton Press, Norwood, Massachusetts. The typography and binding design are by W. A. Dwiggins.

I lived

was

here

'65

So wa I '75